THEORIZING
DOCUMENTARY

AFI Film Readers
a series edited by
Edward Branigan and Charles Wolfe

Psychoanalysis and Cinema
E. Ann Kaplan, editor

Fabrications: Costume and the Female Body
Jane Gaines and Charlotte Herzog, editors

Sound Theory/Sound Practice
Rick Altman, editor

Film Theory Goes to the Movies
Jim Collins, Hilary Radner, and Ava Preacher Collins, editors

Black American Cinema
Manthia Diawara, editor

The American Film Institute
P.O. Box 27999
2021 North Western Avenue
Los Angeles, CA 90027

THEORIZING DOCUMENTARY

EDITED BY

MICHAEL RENOV

Routledge
Taylor & Francis Group
New York   London

Published in 1993 by

Routledge
29 West 35th Street
New York, NY 10001

Published in Great Britain by

Routledge
11 New Fetter Lane
London EC4P 4EE

This edition published 2012 by Routledge:

Routledge	Routledge
Taylor & Francis Group	Taylor & Francis Group
711 Third Avenue	2 Park Square, Milton Park
New York, NY 10017	Abingdon, Oxon OX14 4RN

Library of Congress Cataloging-in-Publication Data

Thoerizing documentary / edited by Micheal Renov.
    p. cm.—(AFI film readers)
   Includes bibliographical references (p.   ).
   Filmography: p.
   ISBN 0-415-90381-5. — ISBN 0-415-90382-3 (pbk.)
   1. Documentary films—History and criticism.   I. Renov, Micheal,
  1950– . II. Series.
  PN1995.9.D6T45   1993
070.1'8 —dc20   92-33807
                                                                    CIP

British Library Cataloguing-in-Publication Data also available

For Veronica and Maddie

Contents

Acknowledgments   ix

1.   Introduction: The Truth About Non-Fiction
     Michael Renov   1

2.   Toward a Poetics of Documentary
     Michael Renov   12

3.   The Documentary Film as Scientific Inscription
     Brian Winston   37

4.   Document and Documentary: On the Persistence of
     Historical Concepts
     Philip Rosen   58

5.   The Totalizing Quest of Meaning
     Trinh T. Minh-ha   90

6.   Jargons of Authenticity (Three American Moments)
     Paul Arthur   108

7.   Constantly Performing the Documentary: The Seductive
     Promise of *Lightning Over Water*
     Susan Scheibler   135

8.   (Not) Looking for Origins: Postmodernism, Documentary,
     and *America*
     Ana M. López   151

9. Notes on AIDS and Its Combatants: An Appreciation
   Bill Horrigan   164

10. "Getting to Know You . . . ": Knowledge, Power, and
    the Body
    Bill Nichols   174

   Notes   193

   Bibliography   227

   Filmography   247

   Index   253

   List of Contributors   261

Acknowledgments

This book is indebted to all those whose commitment has sustained documentary film culture in the face of the relative indifference of audiences and scholars alike. There is now reason to believe that academic interest has been actively rekindled in nonfiction film, television, and video. It is that renewal of attention to the documentary that has provided the incentive for this volume.

I would like to thank a number of people for their contributions to this book: Bill Germano for his initial interest in the project; Bill Nichols, Chuck Wolfe and Edward Branigan for their acute readings of texts; Harun Farocki for the image which graces the book's cover; Anne Bergman for her administrative support; Elizabeth Cowie and Paul Arthur for sharing their bibliographical data; Harry Benshoff for his zeal in compiling both the bibliography and filmography; and Cathy Friedman for inspiration. The book is dedicated to my daughters, Veronica and Maddie, who are part of the next generation of documentary enthusiasts.

1

Introduction:
The Truth About Non-Fiction

Michael Renov

In the realm of the cinema, all nonnarrative genres—the documentary, the technical film, etc.—have become marginal provinces, border regions so to speak, while the *feature-length film of novelistic
fiction,* which is simply called a "film,"—the usage is significant—has
traced more and more clearly the king's highway of filmic expression.

Christian Metz
"Some Points in the Semiotics of the Cinema"[1]

Once one has distinguished, as does the entire philosophical tradition,
between truth and reality, it immediately follows that the truth "declares itself in a structure of fiction." Lacan insists a great deal on
the opposition truth/reality, which he advances as a paradox. This
opposition, which is as orthodox as can be, facilitates the passage of
the truth through fiction: common sense always will have made the
division between reality and fiction.

Jacques Derrida
"Le Facteur de la Vérité"[2]

The detour signs are up on the king's highway of filmic expression. In
critical circles, royalism has been deposed anyway; the assumption that
dominant cultural forms or theoretical approaches should enjoy the intellectual right of way has been challenged. A new consensus is building.
Attention is being directed toward reality-driven representations from an
ever-wider array of sources: journalistic, literary, anthropological. It may
well be that the marginalization of the documentary film as a subject of
serious inquiry is at an end. After all, the key questions which arise in the
study of nonfiction film and video—the ontological status of the image,
the epistemological stakes of representation, the potentialities of historical

1

discourse on film—are just as pressing for an understanding of fictional representation.

As we are reminded by Ana M. López in her essay in this volume (Chapter 8), one crucial gesture of postcolonial discourse has been its radicalizing of notions of core and periphery, frequently resulting in the discovery of the margin at the center's core. Taking at face value Metz's pronouncement that the documentary is a "marginal province," this collection makes a contribution toward a new valuation of the core and periphery of film and television studies—or, better yet, offers a deconstructive appraisal in which the terms of the hierarchy, fiction/nonfiction, are first reversed then displaced. - *He is going to prove why nonfiction film should deserve*

For, in a number of ways, fictional and nonfictional forms are enmeshed *more praise* in one another—particularly regarding semiotics, *study of symbol* narrativity, and ques- *then* tions of performance. At the level of the sign, it is the differing historical *fiction* status of the referent that distinguishes documentary from its fictional counterpart not the formal relations among signifier, signified, and refer-ent.[3] Is the referent a piece of the world, drawn from the domain of lived experience, or, instead, do the people and objects placed before the camera yield to the demands of a creative vision?[4] Narrativity, sometimes assumed to be the sole province of fictional forms, is an expository option for the documentary film that has at times been forcefully exercised: the suspense-inducing structure of Flaherty's *Nanook of the North;* the day-in-the-life framework of the city symphonies such as *Man With a Movie Camera, Berlin: Symphony of a Great City,* and *A Propos de Nice;* the "crisis structure" of the Drew Associates' films. How do we begin to distinguish the documentary performance-for-the-camera of a musician, actor, or politician (*Don't Look Back, Jane, Primary*) from that of a fictional counterpart (*The Doors, On Golden Pond, The Candidate*)?[5] The ironies and cross-identifications these examples invoke ought to suggest the extent to which fictional and nonfictional categories share key conceptual and discursive characteristics.[6]

Indeed, nonfiction contains any number of "fictive" elements, moments at which a presumably objective representation of the world encounters the necessity of creative intervention. Among these fictive ingredients we may include the construction of character (with Nanook as a first example) emerging through recourse to ideal and imagined categories of hero or genius, the use of poetic language, narration, or musical accompaniment to heighten emotional impact or the creation of suspense via the agency of embedded narratives (e.g., tales told by interview subjects) or various dramatic arcs (here, the "crisis structure" comes to mind). Many more examples could be offered: the use of high or low camera angles (whose effects have been conventionalized in fiction film and television), close-ups which trade emotional resonance for spatial integrity, the use of telephoto or wide-angle lenses which squeeze or distort space, the use of editing to make time contract, expand, or become rhythmic. In every case, elements of style, structure, and expositional strategy draw upon preexistent constructs, or schemas, to establish meanings and effects for audiences. What I am arguing is that documentary shares the status of all discursive forms with regard to its tropic or figurative character and that it employs many of the methods and devices of its fictional counterpart. The label of "nonfiction," while a meaningful categorization, may, in fact, lead us to discount its (necessarily) fictive elements. It would be unwise to assume that only fiction films appeal to the viewer's Imaginary, that psychic domain of idealized forms, fantasy, identification, reversible time, and alternative logics. A view of documentary which assumes too great a sobriety for nonfiction discourse will fail to comprehend the sources of nonfiction's deep-seated appeal.[7]

With regard to the complex relations between fiction and documentary, it might be said that the two domains *inhabit* one another. Philip Rosen examines that co-habitation (described by him as "a generally undiscussed kinship between mainstream cinema and the original documentary tradition") in his essay, "Document and Documentary: On the Persistence of Historical Concepts." Rosen argues that meaning arises through a process of sequentiation which is constitutive of historical discourse; it is also a key ingredient of documentary theory and practice since Grierson. For Rosen, narrativity emerges as a fundamental condition that binds together all three representational practices—history, documentary, and the fiction film.

Ana M. López writes about a Brazilian television mini-series, "America," which offers a view of the United States that eschews the authoritative, constructing its object from "a distinctly in-between position: in between cultures and nations, the political and the poetic, the past and the present, the documentary and the fictional." López's focus on the deployment of specific aesthetic strategies within "America" places the series within the context of postmodernist discourse. Scholars have rarely enlisted such art-based paradigms for their discussions of work derived from the historical world, regardless of the degree of artfulness. Susan Scheibler's discussion of Wim Wenders' *Lightning Over Water* draws on ordinary language philosophy to describe the film's complex weave of constative and performative elements as Wenders tracks the actions and pronouncements of filmmaker Nicholas Ray during his final days. That analysis helps to explain the border status that the film cultivates for itself—between life and death, documentary and fiction, homage and exploitation. The work of Rosen, López, and Scheibler demonstrates that the common bonds between fiction and nonfiction may be illuminated with concepts drawn from historiography, postmodernist theory, and philosophy.

Brian Winston finds that the discourse of science has repeatedly been called upon to legitimate the documentary film and to set a standard for the fiction film. According to Winston, the early and public claims for photography's status as scientific evidence were based on the sense that the photochemically produced image was a fully indexical sign, one that bore the indelible imprint of the real. Photography's social utility followed from its ability to take the measure of things with verifiable fidelity; it could thus be likened to other scientific instruments such as the thermometer or hygrometer.[8] A comparable claim, now more metaphysical than scientific, was made by Andre Bazin more than a century later: "Photography does not create eternity, as art does, it embalms time, rescuing it simply from its proper corruption."[9]

Paul Arthur's "Jargons of Authenticity (Three American Moments)" takes as given a "tangled reciprocity" between documentary practice and the Hollywood narrative, then focuses on the special status of the documentary achieved through its claims to discursive authority. Such claims, triumphantly mounted at particular moments (the late thirties, the late sixties, the late eighties), are, to be sure, historically conditioned and responsive to particular situations. Yet, all of these peak moments of the American documentary film share a defining oppositional relation to Hollywood that shapes the very contours of documentary authenticity. Bill Horrigan's commentary on various AIDS-related documentary practices offers a mix of meditation and historical insight, most specifically toward the ways in which the field of independent media has been challenged and transformed by the AIDS crisis. Horrigan finds in the artists' response to the epidemic a "renewed credibility . . . [for] the importance of people owning and being able to determine the terms of how they are visually represented," with the legacy of feminist film practices figuring strongly. As a curator and critic, Horrigan has helped to organize and make public the richly variable outpouring of AIDS-related work since the mid-1980s; here, he offers a measure of tribute to that work while reflecting upon the discursive and political contingencies that have shaped it.

This focus on historical matters in a book entitled *Theorizing Documentary* should come as no surprise; an historical consciousness is essential for an analysis of the conceptual foundations of documentary film and video.[10] Such an analysis must place the domain of nonfiction texts and practices within a century of cinematic forms as well as their photographic precursors. Indeed, the roots of cinema are co-terminus with documentary's own: Muybridge, Marey, the Lumieres. In the commercial cinema, however, the camera's preservational powers soon were devoted largely to the recording of dramatic performances, then star turns, and their infinite reduplication for the entertainment of mass audiences.[11] This by-now shopworn account of the development of the narrative film's hegemony demands to be reframed, given the increasingly dominant position of nonfiction television in the current marketplace.[12] It is all the more ironic that, even while televised nonfiction forms multiply exponentially, the documentary film continues to struggle for its public identity and financial viability. PBS's summertime series "P.O.V.," one of the few existing outlets for independent work, continues to be the target of conservative reaction; it has been termed "provocative with a liberal tilt," due in no small measure to its broadcast of such work as Marlon Riggs' *Tongues Untied* and ACT-UP's activist video, *Stop the Church*.[13]

Struggles over documentary have taken many forms; I have already alluded to those of the academy (e.g., the critical marginalization qua Metz) and the marketplace. An economically rooted aversion to the documentary form finds expression in some unexpected discursive arenas. To wit: controversy has surrounded the documentary nominations from the Academy of Motion Picture Arts and Sciences in recent years, the claim being that the most popular or ground-breaking documentary films such as *The Thin Blue Line, Roger and Me, Truth or Dare*, and *Paris is Burning* have failed to receive Academy recognition. Some have suggested that a kind of double standard for documentary remains in effect whereby success by any measure, financial or aesthetic, goes unrewarded. One suggested solution, issuing from Miramax Films (distributers of several of the films in question), addresses the very name "documentary." In an open letter to the Academy's executive director, Miramax suggested that the category become "best nonfiction film" so that the "negative connotations" of "documentary" could be jettisoned.[14] This stigma demands to be read symptomatically.

While Brecht's call for "pleasurable learning" would seem to resonate with documentary's etymological roots (the Latin *docere* meaning "to teach"), for many, Brecht's concept remains an oxymoron. In psychoanalytic terms, one component of the spectator's cinematic pleasure involves the play of projection and identification with idealized others who inhabit the filmed world. Can expository forms designed to foreground issues and to propose solutions (with varying degrees of self-consciousness) ever hope to mobilize the forces of desire available through exclusively story forms? The notion of an explicit "documentary desire," a desire-to-know aligned with the drive for an enabling mastery of the lived environs, is one which is explored in my essay, "Toward a Poetics of Documentary." As I am at pains to demonstrate, however, the cognitive requirements to which documentary discourse responds in no way exhausts its functional domain. The expressive capabilities of nonfiction forms, too frequently overlooked, account for an aesthetic dimension which is—on historical as well as conceptual grounds—constitutive.

One of the chief concerns of recent film scholarship has been that of psychoanalysis. Only rarely has nonfiction been the subject of psychoanalytic criticism, due, perhaps, to assumptions of a baseline of rationality and conscious inquiry which govern the making and reception of documentary film in contradistinction to the unconscious (Imaginary) substrate which cuts across and enlivens fictions.[15] I cannot offer here any more than a preliminary indication of documentary's claims to the turf of psychoanalytic criticism.[16] It is important to note, nonetheless, that the pleasures of nonfiction are every bit as complex as those which have been attributed to fictional forms and far less understood. And, historically, it has been psychoanalysis which has addressed itself most decisively to questions of pleasure. Recent work such as that undertaken by Judith Butler has begun to suggest, however, that, with regard to the body and its representations, psychoanalytic approaches have installed a kind of cerebral detour from the corporeal.[17] Documentations of the body, as performative, analytic, or meditative vehicles, have been one sector of nonfiction practice since Muybridge. Bill Nichols' essay in this book (Chapter 10) suggests that recent documentary films have begun to activate new conceptions of the body as the subject of cinematic representation. His attention to the inscription of an embodied, corporeal history in this work points to a lively current of resistance against the Griersonian model "in which the corporeal I who speaks dissolves itself into a disembodied, depersonalized, institutional discourse of power and knowledge."

Of course, it is unwise to generalize any uniform laws of construction for nonfiction film and video and the essays contained in these pages have refrained from doing so. The recourse to history demonstrates that the documentary has availed itself of nearly every constructive device known to fiction (of course, the reverse is equally true) and has employed virtually every register of cinematic syntax in the process.[18] Documentary filmmakers since the days of Flaherty's *Nanook* have frequently chosen to build stories around the heroics of larger-than-life figures plucked from their "real" environs—in short, to narrativize the real. To return to the Derrida quotation with which we began, there is the sense that truth, as understood within the Western philosophical tradition, demands the detour through fictive constructs. The truth of aesthetic forms in the classical mode has been rendered through a kind of "crucible effect" in which reality is subjected to the heat and pressure of the creative imagination— the passage of truth through fiction. According to Derrida, Lacanian psychoanalysis—and the philosophical tradition which it supports—represents truth through two indissociable paradigms: as adequation or as veiling/unveiling. In either case, truth is co-implicated with speech ("present," "full," and "authentic" speech).[19] Derrida, for his part, disengages "truth" from "reality": "What is neither true nor false is reality." For if "truth" entails speech, it also implies a speaking subject. Derrida, in his critique of "truth's" logocentric roots, thus draws attention to its constructed (and propositional) character and in so doing is able to distinguish it from "reality," which, though cognitively constructed, entails no necessary assertion or claim. Reality simply "is." (The distinction between the "true" and the "real" is not foreign to Lacan either; note his description of the Real as "beyond discourse."[20])

I have argued, then, that all discursive forms—documentary included—are, if not fictional, at least *fictive,* this by virtue of their tropic character (their recourse to tropes or rhetorical figures). As Hayden White has so brilliantly described, "every mimesis can be shown to be distorted and can serve, therefore, as an occasion for yet another description of the same phenomenon." This is because "all discourse *constitutes* the objects which it pretends only to describe realistically and to analyze objectively."[21] Every documentary representation depends upon its own detour from the real, through the defiles of the audio-visual signifier (via choices of language, lens, proximity, and sound environment). The itinerary of a truth's passage (with "truth" understood as propositional and provisional) for the documentary is, thus, qualitatively akin to that of fiction.[22] This is only another way of saying that there is nothing inherently less creative about nonfiction representations, both may create a "truth" of the text.

What differs is the extent to which the referent of the documentary sign may be considered as a piece of the world plucked from its everyday context rather than fabricated for the screen. Of course, the very act of plucking and recontextualizing profilmic elements is a kind of violence, particularly when cultural specificity is at issue as it is with ethnographic texts. There the question of the adequacy of a representational system as a stand-in for lived experience arises most forcefully. The question, seemingly epistemological in character, is, in fact, a deeply charged political issue within postcolonial discourse. Trinh T. Minh-ha's contribution to this book (Chapter 5), "The Totalizing Quest of Meaning," takes up the consideration of this matter with some cogency. "Truth is produced, induced, and extended according to the regime in power," she writes, with meaning understood as truth's textual corollary. Trinh argues for the documentary film as an historically privileged domain of truth, a cinematic tradition endowed with the power to capture reality "out there" for us "in here," one whose claims for authority demands to be rigorously questioned on political and philosophical grounds. Trinh's skepticism toward the traditional claims made for documentary's powers to see and to know is echoed throughout this book. These reservations grow out of an awareness of the exploitation of "the real" as currency in an all-devouring image culture.

With regard to the moving image—used for purposes of entertainment, evidence, or sales—indexicality and commodification remain historically linked. In case after case, the value of the image depends upon its ability to inspire belief in its "real" provenance: camcorder footage of disasters, an MTV series about the "Real World" of seven young people sharing a SoHo loft, time-lapsed proof of a cleanser's stain-removing power, a Presidential candidate's encounter with a "live," in-studio audience.[23] Stylistic elements drawn from the documentary past—the grittier and grainier the better—are now routinely added to television commercials selling shoes, motorcycles, or telephone services as an antidote to their implicit fraudulence. If independent documentary filmmaking finds itself all but excluded from the nation's airwaves, its low-tech look (a historical by-product of the work) has been massively appropriated by Madison Avenue—another super-added, special ingredient for a saturated marketplace.

There is another crucial note to sound in this discussion. The violence that followed the 29 April 1992 verdict in the trial of the four police officers accused of beating motorist Rodney G. King suggests an important linkage between visual documentation and value. For despite the very real loss of life and destruction, the furor that has enveloped Los Angeles since the original King arrest in March 1991 has been largely fueled by images and their interpretation: of King's beating; of the shooting of an African American teenager, Latasha Harlins, by a Korean American merchant; of the attack of white truck driver Reginald O. Denny during the postverdict unrest. It is darkly ironic that the original videotape of the King beating—casually shot by a camcorder-wielding bystander, George Holliday, and sold to a Los Angeles television station for $500—has been so repeatedly linked to the events that resulted in $700 million worth of property damage in the big-budget media capital of the world.[24] But the value of the King tape lay elsewhere, far from the sound stages and the star-studded back lots. The trial verdict, arson, and insurrection that rocked Los Angeles and the world issued from rival interpretations of images that were collectively assumed to have an unambiguous historical status. These images were understood to be inviolably "real" even while their meanings came to be vehemently contested. In many quarters, it was assumed that these images "spoke for themselves." We have learned the contrary only through much tragedy.

No longer ought we as a culture to assume that the preservation and subsequent re-presentation of historical events on film or tape can serve to stabilize or ensure meaning. One could imagine that the attorneys who defended the four Los Angeles police officers had perfected their tactics through a careful reading of contemporary film theory, so well did they manage to place the 12 jurors (none of them African American) "in the shoes" of the four defendants. The Holliday footage—viewed by at least a billion people worldwide—was made to support the preferred reading of the defense despite the apparently universal assumption of its status as undeniably "damning" evidence. The meaning of every tortured movement of King's body during the 81 seconds of tape was interpreted by the defense through a variety of analytic techniques (reframing; repetition; reversed, slowed, or arrested movement). These techniques proved capable of "defamiliarizing" the tape's subject matter which, in this case, amounts to dehumanizing the victim. The "human" responses elicited from most viewers (e.g., an identification with the pain of the beating victim) could be wrung out of the "legal" spectator through multiple exposure and through constant recourse to a rationalized and reconstructed version of the event (a process which many a film scholar has experienced in teaching or analyzing an emotionally charged film sequence). In the end, the footage itself, its evidentiary status as "real," could guarantee nothing. Everything hinged on interpretation which was, in turn, dependent on the context established through careful argumentation. One aspect of context—as in all film-viewing situations—existed well outside the visible evidence: the psychological and ideological predispositions of the spectators/jurors.

The framing strategy for the Holliday images depended on appeals to certain preexistent emotions shared by jury members, particularly to fears that mixed the rational and irrational, conscious and unconscious, in equal parts: the growing and altogether rational fear of personal attack in an increasingly violent society commingled with fantasies of larger-than-life black belligerents, crazed with unknown substances, against whom one might understandably lash out again and again. Given such a nightmare scenario, it is not surprising that the jurors succumbed to a kind of shared delirium of the sort described by Julia Kristeva in her essay "Psychoanalysis and the Polis." Kristeva's account begins to explain the ways in which the meanings of so-called objective realities—experienced first hand or through representation—are conditioned by desire or repressed fears. For all of us who believe that documentary images or accounts can simply deliver meanings—intact and in their place—the following passage should issue an unequivocal warning:

> Delirium is a discourse which has supposedly strayed from a presumed reality. The speaking subject is presumed to have known an object, a relationship, an experience that he is henceforth incapable of reconstituting accurately. Why? Because the knowing subject is also a *desiring*

subject, and the paths of desire ensnarl the paths of knowledge. . . .
[W]e normally assume the opposite of delirium to be an objective
reality, objectively perceptible and objectively knowable, as if the
speaking subject were only a simple knowing subject. Yet we must
admit that, given the cleavage of the subject (conscious/unconscious)
and given that the subject is also a subject of desire, perceptual and
knowing apprehension of the original object is only a theoretical, albeit
undoubtedly indispensable, hypothesis.[25]

The desiring subject is also a fearful one. In the hands of skillful attorneys,
the Simi Valley jury was made to share a delirious reading of the King
beating footage that enabled them to find the LAPD defendants not guilty
(while deadlocking on one count against one of the four defendants). If
we are to theorize documentary or even survive in a media environment
which trades so heavily in "real" images, we must certainly be mindful
of the psychoanalytic dimensions.

There are numerous other considerations, pertinent to an inquiry into
the theoretical problems raised by documentary discourse, worthy of
greater attention than can be given them in these few pages. As the
epigraph from Derrida suggests, there is a deeply rooted philosophical
tradition which discourages the privileging of nonfiction forms as objects
of analysis insofar as truth and fiction have been ironically but definitively
aligned. Truth, it has been supposed, depends on fiction, finding its shape
and substance through the agency of human invention. But, as I have
argued, Hayden White's speculations as to the "tropical" character of all
discourse, the extent to which "discourse tends to slip away from our data
towards the structures of consciousness with which we are trying to grasp
them," are deeply pertinent to the documentary instance.[26] No discourse
is ever able to say precisely what it wishes to say insofar as the very saying
is dependent on language forms which are necessarily figurative and
connotatively enmeshed. And furthermore, the "very saying" of what is
to be said is itself premised on another "saying" which is left unsaid.
Language is ultimately a regress which cannot be followed to its end.
As for the statement Derrida attributes to philosophical tradition—"truth
declares itself in a structure of fiction"—it may well be that any presumption of documentary's relative exclusion from the critical ranks is simply
ill-advised. If we substitute "nonfiction" for "truth" in that prescription
but give due emphasis to the efficacy of "structure" within the equation,
we are left with only an apparently paradoxical formulation, albeit one
requiring some qualification. For, it is not that the documentary *con*sists
of the structures of filmic fiction (and is, thus, parasitic of its cinematic
"other") as it is that "fictive" elements *in*sist in documentary as in all film
forms.[27]

The documentary form—the more or less artful reshaping of the historical world—has struggled to find its place within the supposed conflict between truth and beauty.[28] But perhaps, as Trinh T. Minh-ha suggests in her essay, it is toward the "interval" between terms ("a break without which meaning would be fixed and truth congealed") rather than to their identity or dichotomization that our fullest attention should be given. For the reciprocal interrogation of the terms of the inherited hierarchy—fiction/nonfiction—can clarify our understanding of both. And, in the process, documentary's status of dependency can be effectively overturned.

It is, in fact, my belief that this volume constitutes a fruitful reflection upon a whole series of intervals—between truth and beauty, truth and reality, science and art, fiction and nonfiction, constative and performative, self-representation and media coverage, history and theory—in a manner which will significantly advance current thinking about documentary film and video. The king's highway may never be same.

2

Toward a Poetics of Documentary

Michael Renov

Poetics will have to study not the already existing literary forms but, starting from them, a sum of possible forms: what literature *can* be rather than what it *is*.

Tzvetan Todorov
"Poetics and Criticism"[1]

I don't have aesthetic objectives. I have aesthetic *means* at my disposal, which are necessary for me to be able to say what I want to say about the things I see. And the thing I see is something *outside* of myself—always.

Paul Strand
"Look to the Things Around You"[2]

The notion of poetics has been a contested one from the beginning. Indeed, Aristotle's founding treatise, the starting point for all subsequent studies in the West, has long been understood as a defense against Plato's banishment of the poets from his *Republic*. With a rigor and systematicity that has tended to characterize the myriad efforts that followed, Aristotle's *Poetics* set out to show "what poetry is and what it can do"; its opening lines set forth as the field of inquiry "[t]he art of poetic composition in general and its various species, the function and effect of each of them."[3] According to Lubomír Doležel, Occidental poetics has since evolved through several stages: the *logical* (inaugurated by Aristotle's divination of the universal "essences" of poetic art), the *morphological* (the Romantic/organic model issuing from Goethe's analytical focus on "the structure, the formation and the transformations of organic bodies"[4]), and the *semiotic* (from the Prague School through the structuralism of Barthes and

Todorov, the study of literary communication within a general science of signs).[5]

Before any attempt can be made to outline the contours of what might be a poetics of documentary film and video, it is essential to work through some of the conflicting positions which have arisen within the history of poetics, a history that is far from unified. For if the intent of a poetics is, in the words of Paul Valery, to comprehend "everything that bears on the creation or composition of works having language at once as their substance and as their instrument," it would be useful to deploy the analytical rigor of a poetics, now applied to cinematic language, to learn something of the general laws or specific properties of documentary discourse.[6] The attitude of inquiry provided by a poetics is particularly apropos for the documentary insofar as poetics has, as we shall see, occupied an unstable position at the juncture of science and aesthetics, structure and value, truth and beauty. Documentary film is itself the site of much equivocation around similar axes given nonfiction's too-frequently-presumed debt to the signified at the expense of the signifier's play. It is the "film of fact," "nonfiction," the realm of information and exposition rather than diegetic employment or imagination—in short, at a remove from the creative core of the cinematic art. I shall be at pains to contradict these inherited strictures by way of an analysis of documentary's constitutive modalities—its conditions of existence—to more fully articulate a sense of documentary's discursive field and function, aesthetic as well as expository. I will argue that four modalities are constitutive of documentary.

It is an analysis that must be speculative. For if, as Tzvetan Todorov has claimed, poetics is still "in its early stages," even after 2500 years, these initial efforts toward a poetics of the documentary can be little more than first steps. It will be necessary first to trace a preliminary genealogy of poetics to situate its most recent, hybrid manifestations in the social and human sciences, then to attend, in broad strokes, to an elaboration of the discursive modalities of the documentary in film and video.[7]

The Question of Science

Since Aristotle, poeticians have been intent on minimizing the mingling of normative or even interpretive aims with descriptive considerations.[8] The most ambitious projects for a "scientific criticism" have sought to banish interpretation outright, a task not so easily accomplished. Todorov has argued that pure description—the hallmark of science as objective discourse—can only be what Derrida has called a "theoretical fiction": "One of the dreams of positivism in the human sciences is the distinction, even the opposition, between interpretation—subjective, vulnerable, ultimately arbitrary—and description, a certain and definitive activity."[9] It is important to recognize the limits of a method borrowed from the natural sciences applied to aesthetic forms. It is equally essential that a new poetics acknowledges the historical effects of the valorization of science within the humanities.

In Roland Barthes's "The Return of the Poetician," a 1972 paean to the work of Gerard Genette, a description/interpretation dichotomy (and implicit hierarchy) is assumed: "When he [sic] sits down in front of the literary work, the poetician does not ask himself: What does this mean? Where does this come from? What does it connect to? But, more simply and more arduously: *How is this made?*"[10] This heuristic angle to the study of aesthetic forms—the attention to the "simple" and "arduous"—bears a much-remarked upon resemblance to the inductive methods of science.[11] Poetics, frequently understood to be the "science of literature," might, thus, be seen as an intrinsically chiasmatic site of inquiry. Coleridge's organicist formulation of the poem as "that species of composition which is opposed to works of science by proposing for its immediate object pleasure, not truth" would suggest poetics as the science of anti-science.[12] To risk a poetics of documentary is to up the stakes yet again, since it is commonly supposed that the aim and effect of documentary practices must be (to return to the Coleridgean opposition) truth and only secondarily, if at all, pleasure. A documentary poetics would, thus, be the science of a scientistic anti-science! Such involutions of thought may be of little consequence in themselves but they do testify to the particularly vexed character of any systematic investigation of documentary qua aesthetic form. As we shall see, the foundations of a documentary poetics turn on the question of science just as surely as does a history of documentary forms.[13]

Some recent attempts to theorize a poetics have chosen to distance themselves from the debate around science which, in the realm of aesthetics, depends on a clear-cut art/science dichotomy. This is, however, a relatively recent development and should not obscure the epistemological *desire* which has underwritten centuries of rigorous investigation: the longing for aesthetic criticism that approaches the status of science, that "culture-free peek at the universe enabled by a mythical objectivity."[14] We need not look further for evidence of the "science wish" than to the crucial writings of Tzvetan Todorov whose several books in this field include *Introduction to Poetics* (1981) and *The Poetics of Prose* (1977). In the latter work, Todorov characterizes the shared concerns of the several schools whose efforts resulted in a renaissance of studies in poetics in this century—the Russian Formalists, the Prague School, the German morphological school, Anglo-American New Criticism, and the French structuralists.

> These critical schools (whatever the divergences among them) are
> situated on a level qualitatively different from that of any other critical
> tendency, insofar as they do not seek to name the meaning of the text,
> but to describe its constitutive elements. Thereby, the procedure of
> poetics is related to what we may one day call "the science of liter-
> ature."[15]

Todorov's statement, in its longing for a scientific foundation for the study
of literature, speaks a desire for a general theory of aesthetic practices at
issue since Aristotle.

Barthes's "The Return of the Poetician" traces a genealogy for poetics
that culminated in the work of Gerard Genette by way of three patrons—
Aristotle, Valery, and Jakobson. As in the case of Todorov, Barthes's
notion of a return to poetics is predicated on the increasing attention being
accorded semiotic research: "Poetics is therefore at once very old (linked
to the whole rhetorical culture of our civilization) and very new, insofar
as it can today benefit from the important renewal of the sciences of
language."[16] Curiously (or perhaps not, as Barthes's critical value must
surely be linked to his constant "doubling back" upon himself), an earlier
Barthes—in his 1967 essay "From Science to Literature"—could write
that structuralism's highest purpose could be, through positing literature
not as an object of analysis but as an activity of writing, "to abolish the
distinction, born of logic, which makes the work into a language-object
and science into a meta-language, and thereby to risk the illusory privilege
attached by science to the ownership of a slave language."[17] Others working within the tradition of Western poetics have been less inclined to
disavow the investiture of status or intellectual satisfaction afforded by
(para-)scientific inquiry. In the field of film studies, no one has taken up
the mantle of poetics so forcefully as has David Bordwell.

In his brief for a historical poetics of the cinema appearing toward the
end of his *Making Meaning: Inference and Rhetoric in the Interpretation
of Cinema,* Bordwell writes that "poetics aims at *comprehensive* explanation of causes and uses of films . . . [s]uch work . . . puts interpretation
at the service of more *global* investigations of conventions of filmic
structure and function."[18] [emphasis added] For Bordwell, poetics becomes a kind of "metacriticism," capable of explaining not only the
"regulated efforts" which produce texts but also the effects generated by
interpretive practices. "Poetics is thus not another critical 'approach,' like
myth criticism or deconstruction," writes Bordwell. "Nor is it a 'theory'
like psychoanalysis or Marxism. In its broadest compass, it is a conceptual
framework within which particular questions about films' composition
and effects can be posed."[19]

But Bordwell's totalizing claims for poetics' utility and intellectual rigor are equally a rebuff to reigning interpretive approaches; they are certainly wielded as a polemical instrument in his book. Furthermore, Bordwell's concern to import the insights of the "harder" sciences—among them, cognitive psychology—to construct a more systematic and verifiable analytical approach for film scholarship are by now well-known. It is helpful, therefore, to situate Bordwell's or Todorov's claims for poetics within a broader network of ideas, namely, the debates around the discursive status of science.

A. J. Greimas, in an analysis of social scientific discourse, points to a shift engendered by semiotics, from an understanding of science as a *system* to its representation as a *process*, a "scientific doing." As such, science becomes perceptibly linked with poesis at its etymological roots (the Greek "poesis" meaning "active making"). "This doing, which will always be incomplete and will often lead to mistakes, is manifested in the discourses it produces, discourses that are at first sight recognizable only because of their sociolinguistic connotations of 'scientificity.' "[20] Poetics, couched in the active mood of scientific inquiry, can thus be said to address the aesthetic domain with an epistemological urgency usually reserved for the natural sciences: "Semiotics now counts as one of its urgent tasks the study of the discursive organizations of signification."[21]

In an altogether different tone, one that (perhaps unintentionally) calls to mind the recent and important critiques of postcolonial discourse, Helen Vendler has described the particular pleasure afforded by the systematic study of aesthetic texts:

> The pleasure here lies in discovering the laws of being of a work of literature. This pleasure of poetics is not different from the pleasure of the scientist who advances, at first timidly and then with increasing confidence, a hypothesis that makes order out of the rubble of data. The rubble seems to arise and arrange itself into a form as soon as it is looked at from the right angle. . . . If discovering Nepture or the Pacific Ocean has a social function, so does discovering (to the public gaze) the poetry of a new poet; or new aspects to the poetry of an old poet. Texts are part of reality, and are as available to exploration as any terrain.[22]

This will to science, the desire to produce accounts of aesthetic practices whose internal coherence and descriptive adequacy edge them toward the status of science, would seem vulnerable to charges of positivism or ideological naiveté. It is Michel Foucault who has most forcefully alerted us to the "inhibiting effect of global, *totalitarian theories*."[23] Speaking specifically against the functionalist and systematizing theory engendered in the name of Marxism, psychoanalysis or the semiology of literary texts—theory meant to ensure for itself the status of science—Foucault argued that "the attempt to think in terms of a totality has in fact proved a hindrance to research." Foucault's own preference was for the construction of genealogies, defined as "anti-sciences," and for an attention to "local, discontinuous, disqualified, illegitimate knowledges against the claims of a unitary body of theory which would filter, hierarchize and order them in the name of some true knowledge and some arbitrary idea of what constitutes a science and its objects."[24]

But more than championing a particular attitude toward scholarly inquiry—its scale, field of objects, or methods—Foucault raised questions that must surely be addressed to any study, such as that of a poetics, which has historically aspired to "elevate" literary criticism to the status of science. It is precisely the question of power within the domain of critical inquiry, the power radiating from a presumption surrounding certain categories of discursivity, that Foucault raises.[25]

> In more detailed terms, I would say that even before we can know the extent to which something such as Marxism or psychoanalysis can be compared to a scientific practice in its everyday functioning, its rules of construction, its working concepts, that even before we can pose the question of a formal and structural analogy between Marxist or psychoanalytic discourse, it is surely necessary to question ourselves about our aspirations to the kind of power that is presumed to accompany such a science. It is surely the following kinds of question that would need to be posed: What types of knowledge do you want to disqualify in the very instant of your demand: "Is it a science"? Which speaking, discoursing subjects—which subjects of experience and knowledge—do you then want to "diminish" when you say: "I who conduct this discourse am conducting a scientific discourse, and I am a scientist"? Which theoretical–political *avant garde* do you want to enthrone in order to isolate it from all the discontinuous forms of knowledge that circulate about it? When I see you straining to establish the scientificity of Marxism I do not really think that you are demonstrating once and for all that Marxism has a rational structure and that therefore its propositions are the outcome of verifiable procedures; for me you are doing something altogether different, you are investing Marxist discourses and those who uphold them with the effects of a power which the West since Medieval times has attributed to science and has reserved for those engaged in scientific discourse.[26]

Certainly, in the case of the several high-water marks of poetics' study to which Todorov refers in his "Poetics and Criticism," among them New Criticism and structuralism, the attentiveness to the synchronic dimension of the textual object (what Roman Jakobsen has called the "continuous, enduring, static factors" of the text[27]) and to the general principles which govern meaning has been widely attacked as ahistorical, falsely scientistic, blind to the free play of the signifier or the heterogeneity of spectatorial positions.[28] The critique of structuralism's relative inattention to the dynamics of historical transformation was articulated as early as 1966 in Derrida's "Structure, Sign, and Play in the Discourse of the Human Sciences" in which the limits of Claude Levi-Strauss's structuralist approach were outlined:

> More concretely, in the work of Levi-Strauss it must be recognized that the respect for structurality, for the internal originality of the structure, compels a neutralization of time and history. For example, the appearance of a new structure, of an original system, always comes about—and this is the very condition of its structural specificity—by a rupture with its past, its origin, and its cause. One can therefore describe what is peculiar to the structural organization only by not taking into account, in the very moment of this description, its past conditions: by failing to pose the problem of the passage from one structure to another, by putting history into parentheses.[29]

Poetics and Politics

But some recent applications of the poetics model suggest that discursive analyses cognizant of textual structuration, function, and effect can attend with equal cogency to the local and political: for example, James Clifford and George E. Marcus's *Writing Culture: The Poetics and Politics of Ethnography*, Ivan Brady's *Anthropological Poetics*, Nancy K. Miller's *The Poetics of Gender*, and Susan Rubin Suleiman's *Subversive Intent: Gender, Politics, and the Avant-Garde*, particularly her chapter on "The Politics and Poetics of Female Eroticism."[30] James Clifford sees ethnography's poesis as complex, plural, and politically charged. If culture is contested, temporal, and emergent, its adequate representation and explanation can be realized only through "an open-ended series of contingent, power-laden encounters."[31] And yet, the provisional character of the contemporary ethnographer's findings ["garrulous, overdetermined cross-cultural encounter(s) shot through with power relations and personal cross-purposes"[32]] intensifies rather than invalidates the necessity for the kind of discursive self-scrutiny that poetics entails. Suleiman argues that "a genuine theory of the avant-garde must include a poetics of gender, and . . . a genuine poetics of gender is indissociable from a feminist poetics."[33] She argues for a critical practice which, alert though it may be to the deployment of signifying elements (the domain of formal concerns), remains ever vigilant of the (en)gendered relations of power and privilege.

Crucial to both Clifford's and Suleiman's work cited above is the sense that the analysis of cultural/aesthetic practices must take into account the dynamics of the social space that its object occupies. In a very real sense, poetics must also confront the problematics of power. If, as Foucault has argued, the individual is "an effect of power" exercised through subtle mechanisms which "evolve, organize and put into circulation . . . knowledge, or rather apparatuses of knowledge," critical inquiries into the species, functions, and effects of discursive forms must attend to the pressures and limits of social determination—the principles of authority and legitimacy as well as the historical repressions which shape and confine aesthetic forms.[34] It becomes very clear in the examination of the documentary film that the formal characteristics that define the cycles or styles of this filmic form (the actualité, cinépoem, or cinema verité) are historically and ideologically contingent. The film "movements" that have so frequently functioned as the motor force in the development of the documentary (from the Grierson group in Britain to the direct cinema practitioners of Drew Associates to the countercultural radicals of Newsreel) have been, in every case, deeply politicized—as one might expect for such a capital-intensive (and frequently state-sponsored) cultural practice.[35]

This attention to the necessary yoking of the political and aesthetic in the current return to poetics is pushed even farther in another recent study. Smadar Lavie's *The Poetics of Military Occupation: Mzeina Allegories of Bedouin Identity Under Israeli and Egyptian Rule* suggests that the very polarization of poetics and politics may be culturally specific. Lavie's purpose is to show how variations of ritualized storytelling performances, through the richness of their allegorical layering, achieve a kind of indigenous cultural resistance blending poetic and political effects. "While First-World cultures differentiate between the private and public, and between the poetic and the political," she writes, "the Mzeina culture, being under the continual threat of effacement, tells itself in an allegorical way that it exists, metonymizing private experience for the history of the collectivity, and conjoining the local poetics of storytelling with the global political realities of neocolonialism."[36]

What emerges from this overview of recent efforts toward a poetics—of literature, ethnography, and film—is the sense of a shared ambition for the building and testing of general theories of textuality which focus on concrete processes of composition, function, and effect. Whereas the attention to rhetorical device or formal strategy is pronounced, no intrinsic disregard for historical or ideological determinants (including those intrinsic to the critic's own enterprise) can be assumed. Indeed, quite the contrary can be demonstrated. These works, though they aim for an intellectual rigor and a precision of formulation, cannot fairly be pigeonholed as formalist or unself-consciously scientistic. Indeed, as regards the current conjoining of "poetics" and "politics," a logic of supplementarity prevails: Each term functions reciprocally as "an addition that comes to make up for a deficiency" without surrender to an absolute exteriority. ("The supplement is neither a presence nor an absence. No ontology can think its operation."[37]) The recent turn to poetics, then, is marked by a concurrent activation of history ("historical poetics") and of politics ("poetics and politics"). Lavie's challenge to Eurocentric assumptions of a poetics/politics binarism and her analysis of the highly charged syncretist practices she describes reinforce my own sense that rigorous attention to texts can facilitate political understanding.

This extended discussion of poetics is meant to articulate the precise historical context within which a poetics of the documentary may be judged. For any such undertaking necessarily invokes a rich and various tradition of inquiry in the West whose several manifestations in the twentieth century have been instrumental in the shaping of current thought about cultural practices. Given the fundamental aim of poetics—to submit aesthetic forms to rigorous investigation as to their composition, function, and effect—this field of study has become a kind of proving ground for the relations between science and art.[38] While many commentators have lamented the apparent hardening of the "truth & beauty" schism since the Enlightenment and others have analyzed the ideological implications of that presumed split, the work of poeticians continues to redefine these contested boundaries. Most recently, some studies in literature and ethnography have demonstrated that contingencies of a political and historical character have their place within a poetics framework. It is in this context that my own enterprise demands to be understood.

In what follows I shall attempt to outline some fundamental principles governing function and effect for documentary work in film and video within an historical frame through an examination of discursive modality. This effort, though preliminary, will essay the parameters and potentialities of documentary discourse with the ultimate goal the enrichment of the documentary film, that least discussed and explored of cinematic realms. A stunted popular awareness of the breadth and dynamism of the documentary past, the scarcity of distribution outlets for the independent documentarist and the relative critical neglect of nonfiction forms have combined to hamper the growth and development of the documentary.[39]

All of which contributes to the relative impoverishment of a *documentary film culture,* an energized climate of ideas and creative activities fueled by debate and public participation. Such an environment may once have existed in the Soviet Union in the twenties or in this country during the late thirties or early sixties. But, with the consolidation and economic streamlining of commercial television networks (with their preference for "reality programming" over even in-house documentary) and the virtual lockout of the independent from public television series formats such as "Frontline," such an environment exists no more. While recent Congressional action creating an Independent Television Service to support and showcase the work of independent producers resulted from the concerted lobbying efforts of a coalition of independent producers, educators, and concerned citizenry, those gains are being seriously threatened by conservative forces in the Congress. Indeed, the very survival of independently produced, state-supported art in the United States remains in question, a circumstance best illustrated by the continuing drama surrounding the National Endowment of the Arts.[40] If political activism is to remain possible in the early nineties, then it behooves us to remain equally attentive to the sharpening of the conceptual tools required to enhance the development of a viable film culture for the documentary.

The Four Fundamental Tendencies of Documentary

What I wish to consider here in the context of a nascent poetics of the documentary—those principles of construction, function, and effect specific to nonfiction film and video—concerns what I take to be the four fundamental tendencies or rhetorical/aesthetic functions attributable to documentary practice.[41] These categories are not intended to be exclusive or airtight; the friction, overlaps—even mutual determination—discernible among them testify to the richness and historical variability of nonfiction forms in the visual arts. At some moments and in the work of certain practitioners, one or another of these characteristics has frequently been over- or under-favored. I state the four tendencies in the active voice appropriate to their role in a "poesis," an "active making":

1. to record, reveal, or preserve
2. to persuade or promote
3. to analyze or interrogate
4. to express.

I do not intend to suggest that the most meritorious work necessarily strikes an ideal balance among these tendencies or even integrates them in a particular way. Rather I hope to show the constitutive character of each, the creative and rhetorical possibilities engendered by these several modalities. My not-so-hidden agenda is to point to and perhaps valorize certain of the less-frequently explored documentary tendencies in the hopes of furthering the kind of "basic research" in the arts that makes for better culture just as surely as it does better science. This notion of "basic research" is fundamental to a poetics of any sort. In the case of documentary, however, there has been little research of any sort which can shed light on the governing discursive conditions which give rise to what is branded "nonfiction." It is to be hoped that the interrogation of these several documentary modalities can begin to dislodge the sense of historical inevitability attached to whatever (im)balance may obtain within the field of current practices (e.g., the rhetorical function overshadowing the analytical) in order to engage with the wider potential, repressed but available.

The Four Functions as Modalities of Desire

These four functions operate as modalities of desire, impulsions which fuel documentary discourse. As such, the record/reveal/preserve mode might be understood as the mimetic drive common to all of cinema, intensified by the documentary signifier's ontological status—its presumed power to capture "the imponderable movement of the real." Writing in the late 1930s, Hans Richter described the historical demand for filmic preservation with great eloquence: "Our age demands the documented fact. . . . The modern reproductive technology of the cinematograph was uniquely responsive to the need for factual sustenance. . . . The camera created a reservoir of human observation in the simplest possible way."[42] As early as 1901, the cinema was recruited to the service of cultural preservation with Baldwin Spencer's filming of aboriginal ceremonies.[43] Anthropology, in its zeal for the salvaging of "endangered authenticities" [a trope which has drawn fire from many quarters of late—see, in this regard, Trinh T. Minh-ha's essay (Chapter 5)], has seized upon the camera eye as a faithful ally.

One of the crucial texts for a discussion of the desire underpinning the documentary impulse must surely be Andre Bazin's classic "The Ontology of the Photographic Image." As the essay reaches its affective crescendo, any notion of the image's asymptotic relationship to the real is discarded in favor of an account by which the indexical sign becomes identical to the referent. In the following pronouncement, one feels the force of desire (historical? authorial?) as it transforms a discussion about the ontological status of the photographic image into a statement about semiosis itself.

> Only a photographic lens can give us the kind of image of the object that is capable of satisfying the deep need man has to substitute for it something more than a mere approximation, a kind of decal or transfer. The photographic image is the object itself, the object freed from the conditions of time and space that govern it. No matter how fuzzy, distorted, or discolored, no matter how lacking in documentary value the image may be, it shares, by virtue of the very process of its

becoming, the being of the model of which it is the reproduction; it *is* the model.[44]

Bazin's position moves beyond the construction of a scene of absolute self-presence for the documentary sign, suggesting instead an outright immateriality arising from its utter absorption by the historical referent.[45]

There are, to be sure, historical contingencies which temper any claims for "modalities of desire" as eternal or innate. The documentative drive may be transhistorical, but it is far from being untouched by history. While Bazin may have alerted us to such categorical matters as a photographic ontology, he was also attentive to the variable effects which history exercises over audiences and their responses to filmic expression. In his "Cinema and Exploration," Bazin discusses the relative merits of some films which take up the visual reconstruction of scientific expeditions. His preference is for a film such as *Kon Tiki* (Thor Heyerdahl's documentation of a 4500-mile sea voyage) in which only a very little footage—poorly shot, frequently underexposed 16mm blown up to 35mm—provides an authoritative rendering of experience: "For it remains true that this film is not made up only of what we see—its faults are equally witness to its authenticity. The missing documents are the negative imprints of the expedition—its inscription chiselled deep."[46] This predilection for the real at any cost is rendered historical in Bazin's account: "Since World War II we have witnessed a definite return to documentary authenticity. . . . Today the public demands that what it sees shall be believable, a faith that can be tested by the other media of information, namely, radio, books, and the daily press. . . . the prevalence of objective reporting following World War II defined once and for all what it is that we require from such reports."[47] Four decades later—in the wake of countless TV ads which trade on their documentary "look" (shaky camera, grainy black-and-white)—the technically flawed depiction of a purported reality no longer suffices as visual guarantee of authenticity. It is simply understood as yet another artifice. I would thus argue that while the instinct for cultural self-preservation remains constant, the markers of documentary authenticity are historically variable.

As for the category of promotion and persuasion, one might understand the rhetorical function of film as a facilitator of desire in its most rationalist aspect. Given Aristotle's fundamental insight on the necessity of rhetorical proofs to effect change ("Before some audiences not even the possession of the exactest knowledge will make it easy for what we say to produce conviction"[48]), persuasive techniques are a prerequisite for achieving personal or social goals. We may advisedly associate certain historical personages with this tendency of the documentary film (e.g., John Grierson's camera hammering rather than mirroring society). But the promotional impulse—selling products or values, rallying support for social movements, or solidifying subcultural identities—is a crucial documentative instinct to which nonfiction film and video continue to respond.

We might say that the "analyze or interrogate" mode is a response to cognitive requirements, an extension of the psychological activities which, according to Constructivist psychologists, allow humans to organize sensory data, make inferences, and construct schemata.[49] While much attention has been given the role of perceptual and cognitive processes in story comprehension, relatively little has been written on a documentary-based heuristics of cognition or analytics. As Bill Nichols has argued, Frederick Wiseman's films (to name a notable example) deploy "the codes of actions and enigmas that usually pose and subsequently resolve puzzles or mysteries by means of the characters' activities."[50] Moreover, these documentary presentations "imply a theory of the events they describe" by virtue of a sophisticated structuring of the profilmic into an overall ensemble Nichols describes as "mosaic" (each sequence, a semiautonomous, temporally explicit unit in itself, contributing to an overall but non-narrative depiction of the filmed institution). In this instance, the organizational strategy bears with it an epistemological agenda, for such a schema of filmed segments "assumes that social events have multiple causes and must be analyzed as webs of interconnecting influences and patterns."[51] This parameter of documentary discourse is thus tied up with deep-seated cognitive functions as well as a strictly informational imperative; the documentary film addresses issues of seeing and knowing in a manner quite apart from its more frequently discussed fictional counterpart.

The last of the four documentary tendencies encompasses the aesthetic function. It has frequently been presumed that the creation of beautiful forms and documentary's task of historical representation are altogether irreconcilable. Near the beginning of *Of Great Events and Ordinary People* (1979), Raoul Ruiz quotes Grierson to that effect. "Grierson says: 'The trouble with realism is that it deals not in beauty but in truth.' " It then becomes the work of the film to confound that pronouncement, to produce a "pleasure of the text" capable of merging intellectual inquiry and aesthetic value.

The pitting of "truth" against "beauty" is the product of a regrettable (Western) dualism that accounts for the rift between science and art, mind and body. Raymond Williams traces the hardening of the art/science distinction to the 18th century, the moment at which *experience* (i.e., "feeling" and "inner life") began to be defined against *experiment*.[52] Hans Richter's account of cinematic development offers an illustration of the effects of this presumed binarism and its contribution to a kind of documentary anti-aesthetic: "It became clear that a fact did not really remain a 'fact' if it appeared in too beautiful a light. The accent shifted, for a 'beautiful' image could not normally be obtained *except at the expense of its closeness to reality*. Something essential had to be suppressed in order to provide a beautiful appearance."[53] [emphasis added] And yet, despite the limitations of these presumptions, it will become clear that the aesthetic function has maintained an historically specific relationship with the documentary since the Lumières.

It now remains to work through each of the four modalities of the documentary in some detail and through recourse to specific texts in order to trace the contours of a poetics of documentary. What becomes immediately clear is the extent to which individual works slip the traces of any circumscribed taxonomy. Indeed, any poetics of value, despite the explanatory power it might mobilize through an elaboration of conceptually discrete modalities, must be willing to acknowledge transgressiveness as the very *condition* of textual potency. As desire is put into play, documentary discourse may realize historical discursivity *through and against* pleasurable surface, may engage in self-reflection *in the service of* moral suasion. As metacritical paradigms, the four functions of the documentary text may be provisionally discrete; as specific textual operations, they rarely are.

1. To Record, Reveal, or Preserve

This is perhaps the most elemental of documentary functions, familiar since the Lumières' "actualités," traceable to the photographic antecedent. The emphasis here is on the replication of the historical real, the creation of a second-order reality cut to the measure of our desire—to cheat death, stop time, restore loss. Here, ethnography and the home movie meet insofar as both seek what Roland Barthes has termed "that rather terrible thing which is there in every photograph: the return of the dead."[54]

Documentary has most often been motivated by the wish to exploit the camera's revelatory powers, an impulse only rarely coupled with an acknowledgment of the processes through which the real is transfigured. At times, as with Flaherty, the desire to retain the trace of the fleeting or already absent phenomenon has led the nonfiction artist to supplement behavior or event-in-history with its imagined counterpart—the traditional walrus hunt of the Inuit which was restaged for the camera, for example.[55]

An interesting format to consider in this regard is the electronic or filmed diary (e.g., the work of Jonas Mekas, George Kuchar, Lynn Hershman, or Vanalyne Green) which reflects on the lived experience of the artist. In the case of these four artists, the interest lies not so much in recovering time past or in simply chronicling daily life—there is little illusion of a pristine retrieval—as in seizing the opportunity to *rework* experience at the level of sound and image. Whether it is Mekas's street scenes of New York with his world-weary narration voiced-over from many years' remove or Hershman's image overlays which couple self-portraiture with archival footage of concentration camp survivors, these diary efforts exceed the bounds of self-preservation.

The duplication of the world, even of what we know most intimately—ourselves—can never be unproblematic. We know as much from the writings of Michel de Montaigne, 16th-century man of letters, who writes of his attempt to portray not *being* but *passing*. Throughout three volumes of *Essays,* Montaigne remains vigilant to the flux which constitutes us all. He writes near the beginning of his "Of Repentance" (III:2, 610): "The world is but a perennial movement. All things in it are in constant motion—the earth, the rock of the Caucasus, the pyramids of Egypt—both with the common motion and with their own. Stability itself is nothing but a more languid motion." It does not take a poststructuralist to divine the inadequacy of reflection theories of art, those positions which would have us believe that mimesis (even as photographic representation) means producing simulacra which are the equivalent of their historical counterparts. Signifying systems bear with them the weight of their own history and materiality; Freud reminds us that even language, the most insubstantial of signifying systems, has a material existence in the unconscious. When watching the most "verité" of films, we should recall, with Magritte, that this too is not a pipe. Given the truth claim which persists within documentary discourse as a defining condition ("what you see and hear is of the world"), the collapse of sign and historical referent is a matter of particular concern.

Our attempts to "fix" on celluloid what lies before the camera—ourselves or members of other cultures—are fragile if not altogether insincere efforts. Always issues of selection intrude (which angle, take, camera stock will best serve); the results are indeed *mediated,* the result of multiple interventions that necessarily *come between* the cinematic sign (what we see on the screen) and its referent (what existed in the world).[56]

It is not only the ethnographic film that depends so crucially on this fabled ability of the moving image form to preserve the fleeting moment. Think only of the myriad history films so popular in the seventies and eighties that offered revisionist versions of the Wobblies or riveting Rosies. These pieces were predicated on the necessity of offering corrective visions, alternatives to the dominant historical discourse which had scanted the struggles of labor, women, the underclasses, and the marginalized. All too frequently, however, the interest in the visual document—interview footage intercut with archival material—outpaced the historian's obligation to interrogate rather than simply serve up the visible evidence. These were honest, warm, sometimes charismatic people much like ourselves or (even more troubling) as we wished we could be.[57] The kinds of emotional investments and narrative enticements which keep us riveted to our seats during the melodramas of the silver screen were thus mobilized. Problems arose when historical analysis, mindful of contradiction and complexity within and across documents (e.g., competing versions of texts or social phenomena as well as questions raised by translation from one language or vernacular usage to another), was displaced by anecdote and personal memory.

But public history cannot simply be an aggregate of private histories strung together or nimbly intercut. These oral histories remain valuable for their ability to bring to public notice the submerged accounts of people and social movements. But their favoring of preservation over interrogation detracts from their power as vehicles of understanding. Delegating the enunciative function to a series of interview subjects cannot, in the end, bolster a truth claim for historical discourse; the enunciator, the one who "voices" the text, is the film or videomaker functioning as historiographer. Although a thorough discussion of the self-reflexive gesture cannot be undertaken here, it is worth citing Roland Barthes's incisive pronouncements on the discursive status of all documentative utterances:

> At the level of discourse, objectivity, or the absence of any clues to the narrator, turns out to be a particular form of fiction, the result of what might be called the referential illusion, where the historian tries to give the impression that the referent is speaking for itself. This illusion is not confined to historical discourse: novelists galore, in the days of realism, considered themselves "objective" because they had suppressed all traces of the *I* in their text. Nowadays linguistics and psychoanalysis unite to make us much more lucid towards such ascetic modes of utterance: we know that the absence of a sign can be significant too. . . . Historical discourse does not follow reality, it only signifies it; it asserts at every moment: *this happened,* but the meaning conveyed is only that someone is making that assertion.[58]

Art historian John Tagg has written what may be the definitive account of the historically contingent character of documentary representation as evidence (the preservational condition, par excellence) in his introductory essay to *The Burden of Representation: Essays on Photographies and Histories.* Taking as his starting point a critique of Barthes's blissfully personal treatment of the documentary image in *Camera Lucida,* Tagg argues that the indexical character of the photograph can guarantee nothing.

> At every stage, chance effects, purposeful interventions, choices and variations produce meaning, whatever skill is applied and whatever

division of labour the process is subject to. This is not the inflection of a prior (though irretrievable) reality, as Barthes would have us believe, but the production of a new and specific reality. . . . The photograph is not a magical "emanation" but a material product of a material apparatus set to work in specific contexts, by specific forces, for more or less defined purposes. It requires, therefore, not an alchemy but a history. . . . That a photograph can come to stand as *evidence*, for example, rests not on a natural or existential fact, but on a social, semiotic process. . . . It will be a central argument of this book that what Barthes calls "evidential force" is a complex historical outcome and is exercised by photographs only within certain institutional practices and within particular historical relations. . . . The very idea of what constitutes evidence has a history. . . . The problem is historical, not existential.[59]

II. To Persuade or Promote

We would do well at this stage of the argument to review a crucial condition of this study, namely, the paradoxical mutuality of the four documentary functions. For although I am attempting to distinguish among the several modalities of the documentary, the better to understand their effectivity, such an effort must fail if a discrete separability is posed. Over the years, efforts have been made to map the nonfiction firmament through recourse to generic labeling (e.g., "the social documentary"), the determination of documentary types whose exemplars are meant to embody particular attributes (e.g., a social change orientation).

In such instances, one soon runs head-on into the logical paradox of all genre designations best described by Derrida in his "The Law of Genre": "In the code of set theories, if I may use it at least figuratively, I would speak of a sort of participation without belonging—a taking part in without being part of, without having membership in a set." Derrida further challenges the stability of boundaries erected in the name of genre.

And suppose for a moment that it were impossible not to mix genres. What if there were, lodged within the heart of the law itself, a law of impurity or a principle of contamination? And suppose the condition for the possibility of the law were the a priori of a counterlaw, an axiom of impossibility that would confound its sense, order, and reason?[60]

How can we account for a sluice gate of nomination capable of exclusion (the setting of limits) yet infinitely susceptible to expansion? How are we to understand a designation of difference that remains viable only on condition of its potentiality for the violation of its closure (the genre as "dynamic" or transformational)? What is the precise principle of difference that thus obtains? Such, at least, are Derrida's musings on the simultaneous purity and impurity of genre's status. In the present instance, the positing of the efficacy of a nominal isolation of *functional* difference exists concurrently with an equally insistent claim for the mutual interpenetration of regimes at the level of the textual instance. For, of course, one crucial parameter of persuasion in documentary could not occur were it not for the veridical stamp of documentary's indexical sign-status, itself a condition of the record/preserve mode understood as the first documentary function. Nor can we reasonably suppose that the expressive domain is altogether separable from a discussion of persuasive powers. So, in fact, these paradigms of a documentary poetics, though capable of mobilizing explanatory power—at the level of metacriticism—along a vertical axis of historically precise meaning, are never, in fact, encountered vertically. There is no ontological purity at stake.

Persuasion is the dominant trope for nonfiction films in the tradition of John Grierson, the man alleged to have first coined the term "documentary." Polemicist and social activist, Grierson left his mark on the film cultures of Britain, Canada, the United State, indeed the world. For this son of a Calvinist minister, the screen was a pulpit, the film a hammer to be used in shaping the destiny of nations. The promotional urgency which characterized the work of Britain's Empire Marketing Board under Grierson's tutelage in the thirties [e.g., *Night Mail* (1936), *Housing Problems* (1935)] has been equaled both before and since in many state-supported contexts, ranging from Dziga Vertov's exuberant *Man With a Movie Camera* (1929) in the Soviet Union to Cuban Santiago Alvarez's formal as well as political radicalism in such works as *Now!* (1965) and *79 Springtimes of Ho Chi Minh* (1969).

As was the case with the preservational modality, documentary persuasion must be understood as an effect of history within precise discursive conditions. Tagg has written that the effectiveness of much New Deal photography as a tool for mobilizing popular support for governmental policy can only be accounted for within a broadly drawn context of historical forces.

> The very years in which the liberal, statist measures of the New Deal were being enacted and fought for, witnessed a crucial historical "rendezvous" of means, rhetoric and social strategy. Only in this conjuncture could the documentary mode take on its particular force, command identification, and exert a power, not as the evocation of a pristine truth but as a politically mobilized rhetoric of Truth, a strategy of signification, a cultural intervention aimed at resealing social unity and structures of belief at a time of far-reaching crisis and conflict.[61]

While persuasion is most frequently identified with projects exhibiting a singularity of purpose and tone—the stridency of Frank Capra's *Why We Fight* series from the World War II years or Leni Riefenstahl's infamous paean to National Socialism, *Triumph of the Will*—we would do well to consider the greater diversity of the promotional impetus and the complexity of its presentational forms. Do we not, after all, in the instance of Alain Resnais's *Night and Fog*, find ourselves persuaded (moved toward a certain comprehension of the incommensurable) through the starkness of Resnais's iconic choices (a mountain of eyeglasses), the poetic character of Jean Cayrol's writing, or the stateliness of the camera's inexorable tracking across and through time and space? Expressivity—the modulated play of the documentary signifier here isolated as the fourth documentary function—can give rise to persuasion as the concrete instantiation of the signified (rhetorical figures, logical proofs, the structuration of argument at the level of sound and image).

In his *Ideology and the Image,* Bill Nichols recalls for us the Aristotelian triad of proofs operative in the documentary: ethical, emotional, and demonstrative. We can be persuaded by the ethical status of the filmmaker or interview subject, by the tug of heartstrings, or by a barrage of bar graphs. Edward R. Murrow's very presence accounted for much of the social impact of *Harvest of Shame* just as the handicapped veteran interviewed in *Hearts and Minds* moves us more deeply than could all the bona fide experts. The documentary "truth claim" (which says, at the very least: "Believe me, I'm of the world") is the baseline of persuasion for all of nonfiction, from propaganda to rock doc.

One could argue for the relative merits of, say, emotional versus demonstrative proofs—photographs of the suffering versus expert witnesses. Certainly ethical considerations arise within the context of such a discussion; yet I am not concerned here to weigh the value or appropriateness of any particular persuasive approach. More to the point for me is the claim that the persuasive or promotional modality is intrinsic to all documentary forms and demands to be considered in relation to the other rhetorical/aesthetic functions.

III. To Analyze or Interrogate

Analysis, in this context, can be considered as the cerebral reflex of the record/reveal/preserve modality; it is revelation interrogated. Too few documentarists share the critical attitude held by anthropologist Clifford Geertz when he writes: "I have never gotten anywhere near to the bottom of anything I have ever written about. . . . Cultural analysis is intrinsically incomplete. And, worse than that, the more deeply it goes the less complete it is."[62] If this is true for the scholar able to devote years to field work, how much truer might this be for the media artist whose in-depth explorations of topics must be contoured to the requirements of the cultural marketplace and a capital-intensive mode of production?

This documentary impetus transforms the unacknowledged questions that lie beneath all nonfictional forms into potential subject matter: that is, on what basis does the spectator invest belief in the representation, what are the codes which ensure that belief, what material processes are involved in the production of this "spectacle of the real" and to what extent are these processes to be rendered visible or knowable to the spectator?[63] While many of these questions are familiar from the debates around reflexivity and the so-called Brechtian cinema, applicable to fiction and nonfiction alike (the films of Vertov, Godard, and Straub/Huillet have most frequently inspired these debates), their urgency is particularly great for documentary works, which can be said to bear a direct, ontological tie to the real. That is, every documentary claims for itself an anchorage in history; the referent of the nonfiction sign is meant to be a piece of the world (albeit a privileged because a visible and/or audible one) and, thus, was once available to experience in the everyday.

The analytical documentary is likely to acknowledge that mediational structures are formative rather than mere embellishments. In *Man With A Movie Camera*, the flow of images is repeatedly arrested or reframed as the filmic fact is revealed to be a labor-intensive social process which engages cameramen, editors, projectionists, musicians, and audience members. Motion pictures are represented as photographic images in motion, variable as to their projected speed, duration, or screen direction: galloping horses are capable of being halted mid-stride, water can run upstream, smiling children can be transformed into bits of celluloid to be inspected at the editor Svilova's work bench. This is not to say that every documentary must reinvent the wheel or leave in the occasional slate to remind the audience that this is, after all, only a film. What is being suggested here is that presentation is not automatically interrogation and that the latter can be a valuable ingredient for any nonfiction piece. Brecht polemicized that art's real success could be measured by its ability to activate its audience. The flow of communication always ought to be reversible; the teacher ever willing to become the pupil.

Much has been said about empowerment in recent years. The bottom line is that the artwork should encourage inquiry, offer space for judgment, and provide the tools for evaluation and further action—in short, encourage an active response. The film or videotape that considers its own processes rather than seals over every gap of a never-seamless discourse is more likely to engender the healthy skepticism that begets knowledge, offering itself as a model.

Allow me to offer a few exemplary instances of the analytical impulse in the documentary film. In the sound era, the breach between image and its audio counterpart has rarely been acknowledged; synchronized sound, narration, or music is meant to reinforce or fuse with the image rather than question its status. Such is not the case with *Night and Fog* with its airy pizzicatti accompanying the most oppressive imagery of Holocaust atrocities; affective counterpoint underscores the horror. Chris Marker's *Letter From Siberia* (1958) is another departure from the norm. The connotative power of nonlinguistic audial elements (music, vocal inflection) is confirmed by the repetition of an otherwise banal sequence; the sequencing of images and the narration remain unchanged while the accompanying music and tonal values of the narrating voice create differing semantic effects. Every viewer is forced to confront the malleability of meaning and the ideological impact of authorial or stylistic choices that typically go unnoticed. In Jean-Marie Straub and Danielle Huillet's *Introduction to "An Accompaniment for a Cinematographic Scene"* (1972), a musical composition, Arnold Schoenberg's Opus 34, is "illustrated" by the recitation of Schoenberg's correspondence as well as by his drawings, photographs (of the composer and of slain Paris Communards), archival footage of American bombing runs over Vietnam, and the imaging of a newspaper clipping about the release of accused Nazi concentration camp architects. A process of interrogation is thus undertaken through the layering and resonance of heterogeneous elements. Schoenberg's music, the work of a self-professed apolitical artist, becomes the expressive vehicle for an outrage whose moral and intellectual dimensions exceed the parochial bounds of politics proper. Yet the collective coherence of the filmic elements remains to be constructed by a thinking audience. The analytical impulse is not so much enacted by the filmmakers as encouraged for the viewer.

In a culture that valorizes consumption—and the disposable culture responsive to that imperative—it may well be crucial for documentarists to consider the stakes of an intervention: to challenge and activate audiences even in the process of instruction or entertainment. In this regard, analysis remains the documentarist's most crucial support.

IV. To Express

The expressive is the aesthetic function that has consistently been undervalued within the nonfiction domain; it is, nevertheless, amply represented in the history of the documentary enterprise. While the Lumières's actualities may have set the stage for nonfiction film's emphasis on the signified, an historically conditioned taste for dynamic if not pictorialist photographic composition accounts for the diagonal verve of the train station's rendering at la Ciotat. Most sources agree that Robert Flaherty was the documentary film's first poet as well as itinerant ethnographer. Flaherty's expressivity was verbal as well as imagistic in origin; to the compositions in depth of trackless snowscapes in *Nanook of the North* (1922), one must consider as well the flare for poetic language ("the sun a brass ball in the sky"). The cycle of "city symphony" films of the 1920s [*Man With a Movie Camera, Berlin: Symphony of a Great City* (1927), *A Propos de Nice* (1930)] declared their allegiance in varying degrees to the powers of expressivity in the service of historical representation. The artfulness of the work as a function of its purely photographic properties was now allied with the possibilities of editing to create explosive effects—cerebral as well as visceral. The early films of the documentary polemicist Joris Ivens [*The Bridge* (1928), *Rain* (1929)] evidence the attraction felt for the cinema's aesthetic potential, even for those motivated by strong political beliefs.

And yet, the historical fact of a repression of the formal or expressive domain within the documentary tradition is inescapable. Such a circumstance arises, however, more from an institutionalization of the art/science opposition than from an inherent limitation. By way of visible proof and case study, we might consider the photographic work of Paul Strand in whom a dual emphasis, perhaps along the very lines of the "experience/experiment" division posed by Williams, was always distinguishable. Attention was paid to the inexhaustible subject matter of the world around him ("What exists outside the artist is much more important than his imagination. The world outside is inexhaustible."[64]), but equally to its organization by the artist. A palpable tension can thus be said to animate Strand's work in both film and photography, arising from seemingly irreconcilable requirements: for objectivity—an attitude toward his subject matter which his one-time mentor Alfred Stieglitz termed "brutally direct"—and, with an equal level of insistence, for the free play of the subjective self.

The work of Paul Strand reminds us that the documenting eye is necessarily transformational in a thousand ways; Strand's mutations of the visible world simply foreground the singularity of his vision as against the familiarity of his object source. Under scrutiny, the Griersonian definition of documentary—the creative treatment of actuality—appears to be a kind of oxymoron, the site of an irreconcilable union between invention on the one hand and mechanical reproduction on the other. And, as with the figure of the oxymoron in its literary context, this collision can be the occasion of an explosive, often poetic effect. So much can be said, at least, for the work of Paul Strand.

Take, for example, certain of Strand's early photographs from 1915 or 1916 ("Abstraction—Bowls," Connecticut, 1915 and "White Fence," 1916) in which everyday objects or landscapes are naturally lit and composed for the camera in such a way as to urge their reception as wholly constructed artifacts, sculptural or collaged. Strand here enforces a kind of retinal tension between the two-dimensional image surface (forcefully restated by the aggressive frontality of the white picket fence) and the three-dimensionality implied by chiaroscuro or deep-focus photography. There is, at the same moment, a tension of another sort that arises in our apperception of such compositions—that which is occasioned by a clash between a perceived sense of the everyday (objects or vistas that one might encounter casually) and of the wholly formal ensemble (that which has been taken causally, fabricated, for its aesthetic value).

Consider further in this regard Strand's treatment of architectural motifs, tightly framed or nestled in a landscape of competing geometrical and tonal motifs. Is it simply a special case that allows what might be termed the "competent reader" of the photograph to see "Mondrian" with and against the documentary image in one instance ("Basque Facade," Arbonnes in the Pyrennes, 1951) or, in another, a dazzling white arrow pointed heavenward rather than a simple frame structure in a cluster of other dwellings ("White Shed," the Gaspé, 1929)? One of Strand's truly emblematic images, his rendering of Wall Street shot from the steps of the Subtreasury Building, transforms the fact of scale—the monumentality of the Morgan Building and its darkened windows looming over insect-sized humans—into a moral statement. The close-up of the latch of a door in Vermont, made in 1944, performs an inverse operation; distance is replaced by proximity. An unexpected display of scale here alters a realist detail into a textural field intensified by the play between the natural (the swirl of grain) and the man-made (the horizontals and verticals of carpentry). It is, in fact, the photographic artist's discovery of the unanticipated—his ability to unleash the visual epiphany—that wrenches the image free of its purely preservational moorings. As a study of Strand's work and that of other accomplished documentary artists reveals, there need be no exclusionary relations between documentation and artfulness.

It is important to expand the received boundaries of the documentary form to consider work traditionally regarded as of the avant-garde. Films such as Stan Brakhage's "Pittsburgh Trilogy" (three films made in the early seventies—one shot in a morgue, another in a hospital, the third from the back seat of a police car) or Peter Kubelka's *Unsere Afrikareise* share with mainstream documentary a commitment to the representation of the historical real. Significantly, the focus of pieces such as these typically remains the impression of the world on the artist's sensorium and his or her interpretation of that datum (Brakhage's tremulous handheld camera as he witnesses open-heart surgery in *Deus Ex*) or the radical reworking of the documentary material to create sound/image relationships unavailable in nature (Kubelka's "synch event"). For indeed, the realm of filmic nonfiction is a continuum along which can be ranged work of great expressive variability—from that which attends little to the vehicle of expression (the not-so-distant apotheosis of cinema verité—surveillance technology—might serve as the limit case) to that which emphasizes the filtering of the represented object through the eye and mind of the artist. Manny Karchkeimer's *Stations of the Elevated,* for instance, is a film about New York subways and the graffiti that covers them that includes not a single spoken word. It is the composition of images and their orchestration in relation to a dynamic jazz score that accounts for the film's effectiveness.

That a work undertaking some manner of historical documentation renders that representation in a challenging or innovative manner should in no way disqualify it as nonfiction because the question of expressivity is, in all events, a matter of degree. All such renderings require a series of authorial choices, none neutral, some of which may appear more "artful" or purely expressive than others. There can be little doubt that our critical valuations and categories ("artful documentary" or "documentary art") depend on various protocols of reading which are historically conditioned. Moreover, the ability to evoke emotional response or induce pleasure in the spectator by formal means, to generate lyric power through shadings of sound and image in a manner exclusive of verbalization, or to engage with the musical or poetic qualities of language itself must not be seen as mere distractions from the main event. Documentary culture is clearly the worse for such aesthetic straitjacketing. Indeed, the communicative aim is frequently enhanced by attention to the expressive dimension; the artful film or tape can be said to utilize more effectively the potentialities of its chosen medium to convey ideas and feelings. In the end, the aesthetic function can never be wholly divorced from the didactic one insofar as the aim remains "pleasurable learning."

Conclusion

I have, in these remarks, attempted to sketch out the epistemological, rhetorical, and aesthetic terrain within which the documentary enterprise has historically arisen. My purpose has been to clarify and enrich—to clarify certain key issues implicit to our shared pursuits in order to enrich the critical and creative activities that arise out of that commitment. By invoking the model of a poetics for the documentary through the elaboration of four discursive functions—those of preservation, persuasion, analysis, and expressivity—I have hoped to introduce into these considerations a measure of critical stringency capable of encompassing historical and political determinations. By a progressive focus on first one then another of what I take to be the most fundamental functions of documentary discourse, I have attempted to judge their historical contingency, textual efficacy, and mutually defining character. Such a study is necessarily open-ended and demands extension in several directions, not the least of which might be the evaluation of the specific effects of video rather than film practices within each of the functional categories.

As a writer and teacher, I benefit from work which challenges my critical preconceptions and takes the occasional risk. It is my hope that the practitioner can likewise draw upon my research as a basis for an ongoing process of self-examination and boundary-testing. For in the cultural context in which lively debate gives way entirely to survival techniques or business as usual, all pay a price. If a vital, self-sustaining documentary film culture is, indeed, our shared goal, we cannot afford to fail.

3

The Documentary Film as Scientific Inscription

Brian Winston

1

Contemporary positioning of photography as an art does not detract from the camera's status as a scientific instrument. There are two main reasons for this; first, the long history of pictorial representation as mode of scientific evidence, a history which conditions, in part, the research agenda that produces the modern camera; and second (to be dealt with in the next section of this essay), the tendency of modern science to produce data via instruments of inscription whose operations are analogous to the camera.

On July 3, 1839, M. François Arago, the radical representative for the East Pyrenees, rose in the Chamber of Deputies to persuade the French government to purchase Daguerre's patents for the world. In his arguments, he stressed the scientific uses of the apparatus; for instance, to make accurate copies of hieroglyphics and, more generally, for physicists and meteorologists. In short, the camera was to join, as Arago listed them, "the thermometer, barometer, hygrometer," telescope, and microscope as nothing so much as the latest of scientific instruments.[1]

Arago was able to mount this argument because the entire enterprise of modern science, an experimental and, therefore, observational enterprise, had already produced the instruments he mentioned, thus creating a class into which the camera could be inserted. The camera would certainly affect some sorts of artistic production; but as Arago explained it, these were of a kind that had long gone on in the service of science. Hence, his offering the example of the laborious business of hand-copying Egyptian hieroglyphs as a specific case of what photography might best replace.

Images in the service of science are, Elizabeth Eisenstein argues, a result of the spread of the press in Europe. With print, maps, tables, architectural and other patterns, botanical, geographical and anatomical images acquired a new scientific, that is, an evidentiary, force. "[F]ruitful forms of collaboration brought together astronomers and engravers, physicians and painters."[2]

The use of images for scientific purposes can also be found in a distinct painterly tradition uncovered by Peter Galassi. He suggests that the impulse behind works from Dürer's *The Great Piece of Turf* (1504) to de Valenciennes's studies, in the 1780s, of atmospheric conditions is essentially observational in a scientific sense.[3] Even as late as the early nineteenth century, when art and science were assuming their modern oppositional guises, the observational impulse continued to lead some artists to cleave to a certain scientism.[4] In 1836, Constable could still suggest that

> painting is a science, and should be pursued as an inquiry into the laws of nature. Why, then, should not landscape painting be considered as a branch of natural philosophy of which pictures are but the experiments.[5]

Clearly, this is an enunciation of the tradition that grows out of Dürer's clump of grass to include all the great naturalist/illustrators up to the present.

Galassi argues that photography, which required no technological or scientific breakthroughs to be "invented" in the 1830s, lacked an aesthetic basis until then. This basis he locates in the development of a new scientific observational thrust to art which, in Galassi's opinion, brings the various elements together to create photography; although, it can be noted, rhetoric such as Constable's represents at the same historical moment a recovery, or memory, of the Renaissance observational impulse, a tradition Galassi himself outlines. Nevertheless, one would want to add Galassi's insight to more generally understood factors influencing the development of photography, such as the needs of the middle class in the years following the French and Industrial Revolutions for personal and decorative images.[6]

The social pressure to create specific images of individuals resulted in a succession of fashionable techniques from the silhouette through the physionotrace to photography. Despite Arago's rhetoric, it was the portraitists and the miniaturists who were most affected by the introduction of photography, and noisiest in expressing their distaste for the development.

It is, of course, possible to read Arago's speech, which has barely a nod toward photography as a substitute for such painting, as nothing more than a political ploy to placate an outraged army of painters. His insistence on science does, indeed, make this sort of political sense, but it also makes just as much cultural sense, that is, as a plea for science. The "political" solution was that the portraitists figured prominently among the first users of Daguerre's techniques.

The carte de visité democratized the aristocratic miniature. Before photography, it would take the likeness on a coin to trigger the capture of a Louis at Varennes. After photography, the Paris police would use photographs of Communards at the barricades as a basis for arrest. Indeed, photography became an indispensable and widely used criminological tool by the end of the century.[7]

If the democratization of the individual likeness was of primary importance, the provision of other images was not a too-distant second. This demand, arising as did the need for likenesses among the increasingly culturally dominant bourgeoisie, also necessitated a series of technological responses beginning with lithography and continuing with and beyond photography to modern printing and image-reproducing techniques of all kinds. The idea of the photographic reproduction of artworks occurs to a photographic entrepreneur as early as 1860.[8] By the late 1880s, the entire Louvre collection could be ordered in photographic form from a catalog. It is possible to see in this use of photography for artistic reproduction a final affirmation of its scientific heritage. Photography's scientific ability to produce an image mechanically is the earnest of its accuracy as a copy of the original.

Arago wanted the camera to substitute for all artistic endeavors in the service of science and his wish has been largely granted. Indeed, by the 1870s, cameras were producing knowledge of physical phenomena, such as motion, that could not be gained in any other way. (Muybridge's first Palo Alto horse sequences were published in *Scientific American*.[9]) But the old painterly tradition was vibrant enough to persist. Modern scientific artwork can still most readily be seen in natural science texts, the *fons et origo* of the enterprise. Many contemporary versions of these works eschew photography in favor of traditional art. The first Audubon *Field Guide* to use photographs of birds rather than paintings and drawings was not issued until 1977.[10] Paradoxically, it is the contemporary heirs of Audubon who most vividly remind us of one of the camera's primary purposes.

2

Arago's positioning of the photographic apparatus in the scientific realm had another profound cultural effect. In this founding moment in 1839, the climax of 6 months of enthusiasm and fear (on the part of the artistic community), Arago, by stressing science, helped condition the public reception of the new technique. In effect, he officially (as it were) confirmed for the public that seeing is believing, and that the photographic camera never lies; or rather: the camera lies no more than does the thermometer, the microscope, the hygrometer, and so on. All these devices produce analogues of nature. That the camera can be manipulated more easily than, say, the thermometer is less significant than the fact that both instruments produce a representation of reality. It is this process of representation that is shared and reinforces Arago's original vision of the device as being of a piece with other scientific apparatuses.

The instruments cited by Arago were in the service of observation which was, and remains, critical to the experimental method of modern science. Experimental observation was, in Bacon's words,

> the most radical and fundamental towards natural philosophy; such natural philosophy as shall not vanish in the fume of subtle, sublime or delectable speculation, but such as shall be operative to. . . . the benefit of man's life; for . . . it will give a more true and real illumination concerning causes and axioms than is hitherto attained.[11]

Elizabeth Eisenstein cautions us not to read too clean a break with the immediate past into this sort of rhetoric. Observation, as a method, dates back to the Greeks and, for Bacon and his contemporaries, the "great book of nature," itself a medieval conceit, was still to be found more in ancient texts, now newly printed, than in the protolaboratory.[12] She argues not that observation was unknown prior to the printing press but that the dissemination of those observations was particularly prone to scribal degradation. This was because, in the scrolls, "words drifted apart from pictures, and labels became detached from things."[13] Print fixed that.

However, a century and more later, what was to be different for the Baconians was the nature of the observations themselves, exactly because Arago's devices came increasingly into play. Eventually, much of the "book of nature" was to be read in the gauges, meters, and physiographs of the modern laboratory.

To emphasize the degree to which modern science depends on modes of representation of these kinds, let me take sociologist Bruno Latour's "obstinate dissenter," a somewhat deviant person of our own time, who refuses to believe a result reported in a scientific paper.[14] In Latour's exposition, this person eventually penetrates the laboratory of the professor who has produced the result being questioned. The dissenter wants to go behind the text to the actual experiment. " 'You doubt what I wrote?', says the professor. 'Let me show you.' " The obstinate dissenter is led to an array in which a physiograph has been mounted. Out of the device comes a paper on which there is an image just like the ones the dissenter saw reproduced in the original paper.

The obstinate dissenter realizes that, as Latour puts it:

> We are at the junction of two worlds: a paper world that we have just
> left, and one of instruments we are just entering. A hybrid is produced
> at the interface: a raw image, to be used later in an article, that is
> emerging from an instrument.

Latour describes this hybrid as a "fragile film that is in between text and laboratory."

At the heart of the array is a glass chamber in which is suspended the ileum of a guinea pig. When the professor injects substances into the chamber, the ileum responds and the needles of the physiograph dance. Latour writes: "This perturbation, invisible in the chamber, is visible on paper; the chemical, no matter what it is, is given shape on paper"; that is, the shape to which the professor points to stifle the obstinate dissenter's doubts about his results.

Latour equates *scientific instrument* with *inscription device*. For Latour, the work of science is to create setups, arrays which produce inscriptions which can be used in texts and scientific papers. "What is behind a scientific text?" he asks. "Inscriptions. How are those inscriptions obtained? By setting up instruments." And what happens when we are confronted with an instrument? Latour says "we are attending an 'audiovisual' spectacle. There is a visual set of inscriptions produced by the instrument and a verbal commentary uttered by the scientist."[15]

I would like to suggest we have reached a place not unlike that occupied by the viewer of a documentary film.

When documentary filmmakers liken their work to data collection or "voyages of discovery," they implicitly position their audiences as Latourian obstinate dissenters who have penetrated the lab of their filmmaking experiments.[16] All the filmmakers' off-screen denials of objectivity, all off-screen protestations as to their own subjectivity (should they make them), are contained and, indeed, contradicted by the overwhelmingly powerful cultural context of science. As the *Encyclopedie française* puts it: "The photographic plate does not interpret. It records. Its precision and fidelity cannot be questioned."[17] However false this might be in practice, the *Encyclopedie*, without question, accurately sums up the nature of photographic authority, as it is popularly understood. The centrality of this scientific connection to documentary is the most potent (and sole) legitimation for its evidentiary pretentions. Thus, documentarists cannot readily avoid the scientific and evidential because those contexts are "built-in" to the cinematographic apparatus.

There is a powerful argument, grounded in centuries of modern scientific inquiry, for seeing the camera as no more and no less than a device for representing the world of natural phenomena, a device like any other Latourian "instrument." At this level of history and culture, there is no difference between the camera and the, say, thermometer.

3

In the development of the documentary film, the scientific connection was suppressed during the years of Griersonian reconstructional practices. Griersonian Realist filmmakers never actively wanted to reconstruct. It was a technique forced on them, or so they thought, by the sync-sound equipment they used. Inappropriate studio apparatus was seen as being the big impediment to realizing the full observational potential of the form.[18] All it required, in the minds of North American filmmakers at least, was the arrival of more suitable equipment—handholdable cameras and battery-powered tape recorders, enabling instantaneous filming in almost all circumstances. By the mid-fifties, television news had created a large enough market for 16mm sync-sound apparatus for an R&D program to be sustained. By the early sixties, this program had produced the machines of which the Griersonians had long dreamed.[19]

However, the issue was not simply technological. Throughout the period of reconstructional practice, Realist artistic legitimations were given full reign. Now, with the new phase, scientific rationales came to the fore and traditional reconstructed Realist documentary was opposed to observational work—Direct Cinema.

It is, therefore, inevitable that the scientific legitimation for the documentary enterprise came to be most strenuously expressed at the outset of the Direct Cinema phase. Yet observational claims caused the filmmakers many difficulties, especially as the dream of "simply" filming events proved to be as elusive with the new equipment as it had with the old. To cope with external attacks and internal doubts, the Direct Cinema practitioners developed two overlapping and contradictory rhetorics. One luxuriated in the scientific potential of the form, the other (to be dealt with in the next section of this essay) denied it.

With the new equipment in hand, enthusiasm for its observational possibilities knew few bounds. Just as the thermometer gives "real" temperatures, so, in the right Direct Cinema hands, the camera can give "real" life. Richard Leacock claimed:

> Many film makers feel that the aim of the film maker is to have complete control. Then the conception of what happens is limited to the conception of the film maker. We don't want to put this limit on actuality. What's happening, the action, has no limitations, neither does the significance of what's happening. The film maker's problem

is more a problem of how to convey it. How to convey the feeling of being there.[20]

Conveying "the feeling of being there" was simply a technical issue or, rather, a series of technical issues. The drive of the Leacock generation, the second generation of Griersonian documentarists, was for sync portable equipment exactly because they wished to reduce the need for intervention and thereby improve observation. Throughout the sixties, scientism, as it were, triumphs. It is the experimental method and the place of the camera as scientific instrument that provides the context in which the filmmaker/observer emerges—heavily disguised as a fly on the wall.

> With this equipment they [the American Direct Cinema school] can approximate quite closely the flexibility of the human senses. This opens up whole new fields of experience; they can follow their subjects almost anywhere, and because of their unobtrusiveness (they need no artificial lighting) people soon forget the presence of the camera and attain surprising naturalness.[21]

Very quickly, this sort of rhetoric about the new equipment, which implicitly denied the subjectivities of selection and arrangement, took hold: ". . . [t]he effort to capture, with portable sound-film equipment, life as it is lived and not as it is re-invented by the traditional cinema."[22] "The Maysles are more concerned with using their technical skill . . . to record reality without tampering with or imposing on it."[23] "Time and time again, one finds oneself wincing and looking away from the screen because what is coming from it is obviously too real."[24] "It is life observed by the camera rather than, as is the case with most documentaries, life recreated for it."[25] "We find ourselves *there,* with the camera. We are observers, but there is no handy guide."[26] Louis Marcorelles talks about being given by these films "a sensation of life, of being present at a real event."[27]

It is not just critics who adopted this position which trades so simplistically on the scientific connection; filmmakers were also happy to make similar claims. Donn Pennebaker: "It's possible to go to a situation and simply film what you see there, what happens there, what goes on. . . . And what's a film? It's just a window someone peeps through."[28] Robert Drew: "The film maker's personality is in no way directly involved in directing the action."[29] The Maysles were equally emphatic. Al said, "Dave and I are trying to find out what's going on. We capture what takes place."[30]

Not only that—Al Maysles went so far as to eschew editing; and Pat

Jaffe, who with Charlotte Zwerin perfected Direct Cinema editing, herself allowed that:

> When the cameraman is really operating smoothly and moving from one image to another with ease, the footage has the quality and rhythm of a ballet, and whole sequences may be left intact.[31]

When editing occurred, it could be shaped by what had been obtained unconsciously: "Often we discover a new kind of drama that we were not really aware of when we shot it."[32]

Here is Stephen Mamber's "ethic of non-intervention" aborning.[33]

Thus, at the outset, the claims of Direct Cinema were presented as being relatively unproblematic—to be "recording life as it exists at a particular moment before the camera," to produce a cinema, moreover, which would be, to quote a title of a 1961 article of Leacock's, "uncontrolled."[34] In 1963, when Leacock was asked if his aim was to get the people he was filming entirely to forget the camera, he replied: ". . . the story, the situation. . . . is more important than our presence. . . . We don't cheat."[35] The following year, he said of shooting *Happy Mother's Day:* "We never asked anybody to do anything; we were simply observers."[36] As late as the early seventies, Leacock could still claim Direct Cinema as a species of "research data" and inveigh against technicians festooned with equipment.[37] "I'd rather not have a camera at all," he said. "Just be there."[38]

Nonintervention, with its implied promise of unmediated observation, became the prime source of legitimacy for filmmakers as observers. These new observers

> work. . . . believing that the camera finally has only one right—that of recording what happens. They find the events, they don't ask anyone to *do* anything or to say anything.[39]

Such rhetoric does nothing less than release the scientific potential of the apparatus as a tool of observation—"the camera as an impartial and unobtrusive observer capturing the sight and sound of real life."[40] All this was to put documentary on a new footing at this time, one far away from the "ordinary virtues of an art," which Grierson, in the Manifesto, claimed were what distinguished documentaries from other types of nonfiction films. And it was put on this footing with a great deal of fanfare and ballyhoo.

One major consequence, and perhaps the most disturbing aspect of Direct Cinema practice, was that all journalistic/investigative traditions were jettisoned in favor of one "tremendous effort"—which was how Drew described the essential production technique of his method: "The tremendous effort of being in the right place at the right time."[41] This became "the major creative task." This search for "the highly charged atmosphere" did have a number of crucial implications.[42] These were at least as significant as the filming methods (handholding, available light and sound, long takes, crystal control mechanisms) to which much more attention has been paid.

First, "the tremendous effort" approach sustains, more than any other single element in the repertoire of Direct Cinema, the implicit scientific claims of the enterprise—the powerful notion that what the camera saw and the recorder heard was "raw." It reinforces the concept that the filmmakers have not mediated the result. The documentarists are supposedly as new to the actual event as their audiences are to the record of that event on film.

Second, this unreconstructed vision of "reporting" as pure responsiveness led to some very curious results. For instance, a crew was dispatched to cover an Indian election from the point of view of Jawaharlal Nehru and was surprised, but undeterred, to find that the subject was a shoo-in. From the journalistic point of view, there was "no story." In the event, there was also almost no film.[43] It is as if the ethic of nonintervention had expanded to encompass a ban on reading newspapers. All was justified in the name of experimentation, of data collection. What was discovered, whatever it was, was observationally valid.[44] This is not only the posture of science; it is also the clue to the reception of the films.

In these early debates, a certain aggression emerged on the part of the Direct Cinema filmmakers. By 1961, Drew was saying: "In my opinion, documentary films in general, with very few exceptions, are fake."[45] Drew and his associates became "furious" with people who worked in the older way.[46] Al Maysles felt the use of narration and music produced "illustrated lectures" and described much of the documentary work of the National Film Board of Canada as "propaganda."[47]

The insistence on Direct Cinema techniques as the only true path was propounded at a 1963 conference on new documentary, a crucial meeting arranged by the French national broadcasting organization (ORTF) and held in Lyon. The Americans encountered the French and (Mario Ruspoli aside) both discovered themselves to be divided by more than language. The established American feeling that anything less than an automatic approach could not produce documentary film was expressed vigorously:

[b]ecause they could now record actual events and sounds, they believed that anything else, including any sort of rehearsal or post-

synchronization, was immoral and unworthy of a showing at a conference on Cinéma-Vérité. If the material was not spontaneous, they
said, how could it be true?[48]

The basic fact was that, for the first time in the history of the documentary,
such a position of reduced or nonmediation could be articulated.

> And this is a great step forward. If other film makers can follow his
> [Leacock's] lead, it is entirely possible that a whole new documentary
> tradition will arise: a tradition of "meeting the reality of the country"
> in a more intimate, interesting, and humanly important way than any
> Grierson imagined.[49]

One hundred thirty-six years after François Arago claimed the camera
for science, the documentary purists, essentially the American Direct
Cinema proponents, implicitly reasserted that claim on behalf of the
lightweight Auricon and the Eclair. "Great stress was placed on the
objectivity of the film maker." "We . . . attempt to give evidence about
which you can make up your own mind."[50] The notion that such objectivity
could be achieved is grounded in science and the scientific heritage of
photography.

4

Such claims were also immediately attacked. "Among some of the
technicians at Lyon a blinkered approach to the new possibilities was
evident, the result of an inadequate appraisal of the medium," wrote one
English attendee.[51] A little later Jean-Luc Godard, writing in *Cahiers,*
complained:

> Leacock and his team do not take account (and the cinema is nothing
> but the taking of account) that their eye in the act of looking through
> the viewfinder is at once more and less than the registering apparatus
> which serves the eye. . . . Deprived of consciousness, thus, Leacock's
> camera, despite its honesty, loses the two fundamental qualities of a
> camera: intelligence and sensibility.[52]

Godard (who, some five years after these remarks were published, was to
use both Leacock and Pennebaker as camerapersons in an unhappy episode) was still looking, à la Grierson, for "the ordinary virtues of an art"
and arguing, *sotto voce,* the old case for photography as art.[53]

These objections were grounded in a sense that the Griersonian baby
was being thrown out with the bathwater. They were most strenuously
reinforced by another body of opinion that questioned the degree to which

the new style could or could not deliver on its scientific claims. Although not his view, Nöel Carroll best summed it up:

> [N]o sooner was the idea . . . abroad than critics and viewers turned the polemics of direct cinema against direct cinema. A predictable *tu quoque* would note all the ways that direct cinema was inextricably involved with interpreting its materials. Direct cinema opened a can of worms and then got eaten by them.[54]

In the face of such objections, the Direct Cinema practitioners learned to refine their rhetoric, in effect adding a second (and contradictory) strand to it. The techniques of Direct Cinema, especially "[t]he tremendous effort of being there," could encompass the idea of the filmmaker's personality, and in ways that did not compromise the "raw material" claim. An accommodation to a measure of subjectivity could be achieved. This was to be the essential characteristic of this second strand of rhetoric; and, as a result of its deployment, what was said about the films by their makers and by critics would undergo considerable development as the decade progressed.

As early as 1964, Leacock had already developed a way of deflecting the criticism that claims made for Direct Cinema's objectivity were too strong:

> When you make an electrical measurement of a circuit, you do it with a volt-meter. Now the moment you do that, you change the circuit. Every physicist—and I used to be one—knows this. So you design your volt-meter so that very little goes through it. And in a very sensitive situation you need very much less going through it. . . . The physicist is a very objective fellow, *but he is very selective*. He's much more selective than we are. He tells you *precisely* and *only* what he wants you to know. All the rest is irrelevant.[55]

This stance also had the advantage of reendowing the filmmaker with Godardian "intelligence" and "sensibility."

Drew takes a similar, if less sophisticated, line. For him, subjectivity became more or less synonymous with "sensitivity." "Sensitivity" was defined as the quality required to know when an event is "happening." In other words, personality determined when the machines were switched on. That is why Drew can say, "The film maker's personality has much more effect in this form of reporting."[56] Obviously, these admissions and analogies do not compromise Direct Cinema's explicit claim to authenticity exactly because the filmmaker's personality operates only in the context of what is not being filmed, not what is.

By the late sixties, more elaborate rhetorical responses had been built on these early distinctions, essentially allowing for subjectivities to invade the perimeter while preserving the authenticity of the central matter—the uncut footage. Al Maysles:

> We can see two kinds of truth here. One is the raw material, which is the footage, the kind of truth that you get in literature in the diary form—it's immediate, no one has tampered with it. Then there's another kind of truth that comes in extracting and juxtaposing the raw material into a more meaningful and coherent storytelling form, which finally can be said to be more than just raw data.[57]

Note here that the "raw material" is like a "diary." This transformation of science (that is, "raw material" with which "no one has tampered") into subjectivities ("diary") is the key. This sort of sophistry had, using various guises and analogies, come to be the preferred route of escape from the hyperbole of early claims of authenticity.

Al Maysles, it should be remembered, had established himself as the "purest" of the "pure," even refusing to edit his material. When Leacock told his interviewer, Levin, this, Levin dismissed it, saying: "So David [Maysles] does it." Levin went on to tell Leacock that Al Maysles was less fanatical than he had been. "I talked to him again a couple of months ago, and he's not quite so adamant about the purity of cinema verité." This interview was done in August 1970.[58] By this time, Leacock too was less certain than he had been that he was involved in a breakthrough that would "revolutionize the whole industry."[59] However, still seeking the El Dorado of "moments of revelation," he began enthusiastically to explore another techno-fix—sync 8mm.[60]

What Direct Cinema needed by its second decade was an advocate who could protect the central observational premise on the screen in a series of apparently uncompromised, "pure" films while creating an obfuscating blizzard of off-screen rhetoric. Frederick Wiseman, because of the regularity of his output if for no other reason, filled this bill.

However, he too began by being not overly troubled with the observational claims of the style: "It's the idea of using film and film technology to have a look at what's going on in the world."[61] As is clear from the following explanation of why he made his first film, *Titicut Follies*, this was indeed his earliest motivation:

> At Boston University Law School [where Wiseman was teaching in the mid-Sixties] a lot of students go on to become assistant DA's [sic] and DA's [sic] and judges in Massachusetts; yet most people working on the prosecution end of things have little idea of where they are sending people. . . . So that's how I got to know Bridgewater [the mental institution in *Titicut Follies*], and the idea of making the film grew out of that.[62]

Given this intention, the idea that film would provide evidence of events and situations otherwise unavailable as experience, how then is one to explain Wiseman's stance later on in the same interview?

> My films are totally subjective. The objective–subjective argument is from my point of view, at least in film terms, a lot of nonsense. The films are my response to a certain experience.[63]

Elsewhere, Wiseman dismisses the objectivity claim as "a lot of horseshit" or "a real phoney[sic]-baloney argument."[64] This repeated protestation creates a profound contradiction. Specifically in terms of this first film, the question can be asked: Of what value to prospective DAs is a subjective impression of Bridgewater, idiosyncratically created by Wiseman? Either his invasion of Bridgewater is justified as a means of obtaining evidence or his project becomes "mere opinion" and falls by the light of his own announced intention. (Similar questions can be asked of all his subsequent work.)

The confusions between a Direct Cinema intention to acquire evidence of an institutional reality and so vehement a dismissal of the mimetic power of the camera can be easily explained. Wiseman found himself entrapped after making *Titicut Follies* in a series of legal difficulties. These were to condition his whole subsequent approach, both in terms of filmmaking practice and rhetoric.

One of his responses to those problems has been to articulate an ever more sophisticated and increasingly opaque rationale for his work and the "horseshit" issue of objectivity. Here is the matured Wisemanian formulation, if it can be so described, of the objectivity question:

> Which is not to say the films don't have a point of view. But they have a point of view that allows you—or, hopefully, asks you—to think, to figure out what you think about what's happening.[65] I don't know how to make an objective film. I think my films are a fair reflection of the experience of making them. My subjective view is that they are fair films.[66]

With this line of argument—the construction of a questioning viewer behind a smoke screen of legalistic double-talk—our hero springs free of the chains of objectivity and escapes to a postmodernist world of open textuality and critical acclaim. And he takes the entire Direct Cinema movement with him. In the course of the sixties, the whole question of objectivity (and with it the underlying scientific legitimation of the Direct Cinema enterprise) had become shrouded in a miasma of circumlocutions. Wiseman's pronouncements are a new testament, come to fulfill the promise of the old (as it had been haltingly expressed by Leacock, the Maysles, and the others).

But the films are now both self-expression ("a fair reflection of the experience of making them") and objective evidence ("that allows you . . . to figure out . . . what's happening"). There is still a residual claim of objectivity here; and it still relies on an implicit cultural appeal to photography's scientific heritage, that other strand of the Direct Cinema practitioners' rhetoric discussed in the previous section. It is the films themselves that most vividly reinforce this.

Direct Cinema hides its processes as much, if not more, than does Hollywood. The long takes, the lack of commentary, music and sound effects, the absence of cinematic lighting, the understated titles, even the early, persistent use of black-and-white stock—what are these if not earnests of objectivity for an audience schooled in the reception of realist images, earnests vouched for by the subjects' occasional direct gaze at the lens and the occasional jump-cut?[67] The film maker might claim that the work is personal but in technique it is deliberately and systematically "unsigned"—as Pauline Kael put it at the time, the style is "so simple, so basic."[68] Wiseman reportedly pitched topics to his public television patron in equally simple and basic terms: "I want to do a juvenile cout" or "I want to do a study of welfare."[69] For these constituents, if not for Wiseman himself, five centuries of lens culture and the successful efforts of Arago et al. to place the reception of the photography in the realm of science are not to be thrown aside merely by crying "horseshit!"

5

There was another way of avoiding being eaten by the worms, whether of the Godardian sort, nibbling away at the sensibility issue, or the *tu quoque* type, attacking on the mediation front; simply take the position of the other side at Lyon.

The French Cinéma-Vérité practitioners (as they should be called in contradistinction to their Direct Cinema colleagues) took the objectivity problem on directly and tried to solve it by putting themselves into the films. By eschewing the implicit claim of objectivity that nonreflexive material carries within it, Jean Rouch, Edgar Morin, and (at times) Chris Marker sought something more limited but, as they hoped, more incontrovertible—the "truth" of their own observation, guaranteed in some way because we, the audience, could observe them apparently in the act of observing.

(This reminds one of the instructions in a current British police photography manual recovered by John Tagg: "In producing photographs to court, the police photographer must state on oath the time, day and date he took the photographs. . . ."[70])

With a film like Rouch's *Chronique d'Une Été,* Cinéma-Vérité tried to close the gap between a rhetoric of subjective witness and the idea of evidence by avoiding transparent production practices.

> The direct cinema artist aspired to invisibility; the Rouch cinéma vérité artist was often an avowed participant. The direct cinema artist played the role of an uninvolved bystander; the cinéma vérité artist espoused that of provocateur.[71]

The price was that the only appropriate subject for documentaries appeared to be the making of documentaries; but the seeming advantage was that the supposed mimetic power of the camera to collect evidence was, in the more limited arena Cinéma-Vérité created, preserved.

Chronique is, at one level, nothing more than a reversal of normal ethnographic film, with "the strange tribe that lives in Paris" as its subject and even a young African playing the part of the great (white) explorer/ ethnographer.[72] At the time, such a project sat well with Rouch; with the state of French anthropology; and with its major institutions, one of which, the Musée de l'Homme, was the site of the film's climactic sequences. The museum is a monument to Popular Front liberalism and anticolonialism, but it was then coming under attack for the first time for embodying a paternalistic tendency to essentialize tribal culture. Anthropology was experiencing something approaching a crisis occasioned not least by the collapsing legitimacy of field work in general and the ethnographer's monological authority in particular; for example, in France, the classic texts on the Dogon, created by Marcel Griaule, were being subjected to increasing questioning.[73] (One of Griaule's earliest major exploits had been to gather some 3500 African objects now in the Musée de l'Homme. He was also the pioneer of French ethnographic film.[74]) As an anthropologist connected to the museum and numbering Griaule as one of his teachers, Rouch was not untouched by these developments. It was a time to leave Africa and, at home in Paris, deal with some of these questions— the politics of anthropology ("the eldest daughter of colonialism" as Rouch was to call it); the limitations of participant observation ("You distort the answer simply by asking the question"); the usefulness of film as a "note taking tool".[75]

The French had, then, quite different ambitions for, and understandings of, the new apparatus. As anthropologists and sociologists, rather than physicists, journalists, and lawyers, they had perhaps the advantage of a more sophisticated conception of the problems raised by participant observation and other fieldwork issues. It is this awareness in particular that drives *Chronique's* (and Cinéma-Vérité's) reflexivity.

This did not placate the Direct Cinema group. The Americans were as critical of Cinéma-Vérité as they were of more traditional Realist documentaries, claiming, for instance, that *Chronique* was less powerful than their texts because it "seemed to have been manipulated arbitrarily both in shooting and editing."[76] Leacock said the film "bothered me very much."[77] This is, of course, to miss the point that Rouch and Morin were making. They were beyond the simplicities of Direct Cinema where "manipulation" (or rather the supposed lack of it) was the be-all and end-all. On the contrary, Cinéma-Vérité accepted the *tu quoque* charge of mediation with enthusiasm. Moreover, it could not be accused of denying the filmmakers' intelligence and sensibility, either.

However, for all the seductiveness of *Chronique's* reflexive practice, for all the lack of tendentiousness and consistency in the film's rhetorical positioning, for all that one can sympathize with the oppositional political and anthropological impulses behind it—for all this, the film still embraces science and the possibility of the image as evidence.[78]

Despite their on-screen presence, how far are Rouch and Morin with their "research" from Wiseman with his "voyages of discovery"/"spoor collection"? As Morin indicated, *pace* the caveats, they were still after some type of "truth," however problematic.[79] *Chronique,* Morin wrote, "is research. . . . This research concerns real life."[80] This rhetoric had the desired effect. Critics understood this to mean that *Chronique* was an experiment in the realm of the uncertainty principle. Bohr and Heisenberg were both invoked in the *Cahiers* review. The experiment is authenticated because Rouch and Morin knew that

> it is also necessary to isolate the observer from his apparatus of observation. . . . They are honest enough to enter the arena, to put themselves onto the stage (and into the question). . . . They set before us all the conditions of the experiment.[81]

But it is an experiment—science—nonetheless.

On screen, Morin claimed the film

> reintroduces us to life. People approach the film as they do everyday life, that is they aren't guided, because we have not guided the spectator.[82]

That these words are actually said on-camera in an utterly anti-Direct Cinema fashion becomes less important than the fact that they are, exactly, words that could easily have been uttered by a Direct Cinema filmmaker.

The only difference is that Rouch and Morin are, like the police photographer, under oath (because seen) and, thus, less tendentious.

Chronique eschews the transparency of an invisible Direct Cinema filmmaker to offer us another transparency, that of Rouch and Morin in the shot. The scientific status of the image is, therefore, still in play—as was understood by Lucien Goldmann:

> [T]he cinema has no autonomy in relation to equivalence with reality except in so far as it wishes to be seen as a means of aesthetic creation. Which is to say that at the same time as acknowledging the value of experience and testimony represented by Morin and Rouch's film, we are afraid that right from the start it is very close to the limits of this kind of film, and that scientific truth, cinematic realism and aesthetic value are precisely beyond these limits.[83]

At the end of *Chronique,* walking the halls of the Musée de l'Homme, Morin sums up by saying, *"Nous sommes dans le bain"*—"We're implicated."[84] And they are—just as much as any Direct Cinema filmmaker. Direct Cinema (for all its caveats) aspired to be a "fly on the wall." Cinéma-Vérité, as Henry Breitrose notes, wanted to be a "fly in the soup . . . visible for all to notice."[85] Cinéma-Vérité might luxuriate in revealing its processes, allowing for a claim that the work is personal, "signed," and mediated in an open and aboveboard fashion. But the gesture becomes hollow because the spirit of Arago yet hovers over the enterprise, urging us to believe that what we see is evidence, evidence of documentarists making a documentary.

6

The trouble is that neither of the parties at Lyon can 'scape whipping because the intellectual ground had shifted under all these filmmakers. It is the epistemological move to postmodernism that transforms the scientific connection from legitimation into ideological burden. This move prolematizes objectivity for Direct Cinema and renders Cinéma-Vérité's reflexive gestures moot. Another observation of Nöel Carroll's, perhaps inadvertently, best illustrates the enormous extent of this change of terrain. Carroll is dismissive of "arguments against objectivity in nonfiction films" (such as those deployed here).

> unless [he writes] their proponents are prepared to embrace a rather thoroughgoing skepticism about the prospects of objectivity in general. The defense of such a far-ranging skeptical position would, of course, have to be joined on the battlefields of epistemology rather than in the trenches of film theory.[86]

But it is exactly on the broader epistemological battlegrounds that postmodernism was joining the issue. Carroll's trench is easily attacked:

> [T]he world is in a strong sense independent of our possible representations, and may well extend beyond them. This has implications both for what objectivity achieves when it is successful and for the possible limits of what it can achieve.[87]

Others, for whom no strategy presented itself to determine objectivity's "successes," would go further. The skeptics were charging at full tilt:

> [I]t is no longer possible to salvage Western rationality or its totalizing potential from the clutches of context by ahistorical claims to a superior theoretical and methodological armament.[88]

For the result of such thinking, let the attack on Rouch's teacher Griaule cited earlier stand *exempli gratia*. Suffice it to say that such postmodern skepticism embraced even the hardest of sciences. The significance of Latour's reduction of "science in action" to a series of inscription practices (section 2 supra) can also be read as a dispatch from this same epistemological battlefield, a reaction to the hegemonic identification of knowledge with science.[89]

The connection to scientific signification practices suggested by Latour impels us to treat the photographic image as evidence. This requires, in its train, that photography be seen as "realist": "Realism offers a fixity in which the signifier is treated as if it were identical with a pre-existent signified."[90] Whether or not such a relationship can be achieved is, in its turn, subject to serious postmodern doubts. Stuart Hall points out that, once, "the real world was both origin and warrant for the truth of any statement about it."[91] This was particularly true of visual (that is, photographic) texts, but it no longer holds. Hall gives television as an example of how this "origin" and "warrant" doubling is now seen:

> . . . . it would be more appropriate to define the typical discourse of this medium [TV] not as naturalistic but as *naturalized:* not grounded in nature but producing nature as a sort of guarantee of its truth. Visual discourse is peculiarly vulnerable in this way because the systems of visual recognition on which they depend are so widely available in any culture that they appear to involve no intervention of coding, selection or arrangement. They appear to reproduce the actual trace of reality in the images they transmit.[92]

Hall is in no doubt as to how improper these appearances are. He concludes: "This, of course, is an illusion—'the naturalistic illusion.' " The "ontological agnosticism of deconstructive criticism" (in Julianne Burton's phrase) has become a truism.[93]

Documentary more than any other filmic form "produces nature as a guarantee of its truth." Moreover, this "desire for a mimetic relation with nature" is, according to Jurgen Habermas, one of the crucial distinguishing elements of bourgeois art, a perfect example of the ineffability, as Roland Barthes saw it, of bourgeois ideology.[94]

If one takes this skeptical position, then it follows that, reflexivity aside, the more a text appears to produce nature, the more illusionist and ideologically suspect it becomes—the more bourgeois. And, of course, even reflexivity involves the unsupportable reference back to the preexistent signified, for as Michael Renov has said:

> Every documentary issues a "truth claim" of a sort, positing a relationship to history which exceeds the analogical status of its fictional counterpart.[95]

These shifts in epistemology were coming into general play in sync with the development of the Direct Cinema/Cinéma-Vérité schools. It is somewhat ironic, then, that just as documentarists finally got the equipment to illuminate, as they supposed, the real world of externally verifiable data, that world was denied them and they were instead revealed as the constructors of particular ideologically charged texts par excellence.

This is why Wiseman's objection to objectivity, which can, of course, be read as a postmodernist *cri du coeur,* will not so serve his turn. He cannot have his postmodernist cake and eat it. His films are legitimated because of their "direct ontological claim to the real."[96] What has happened is that the claim cannot be sustained and the legitimation cannot be renegotiated in such terms about such texts. Again, this also applies to Rouch's strategies; they too depend on the same suspect "naturalistic illusion."

It is possible, therefore, to claim that the epistemological shift has created a real legitimation crisis for the documentary. But there is more than that. We are also witnessing a development that calls into radical question the entire mimetic status of the photographic image. After 150 years, Arago's basic assumption as to the fidelity and precision of photography is coming under overwhelming *practical* as well as theoretical attack.

Consider the following: A popular British newspaper runs a "Spot the Difference" competition. Readers were asked to identify five differences between two images, scarcely a novel puzzle.[97] However, what is new here is that the two images are not drawings but photographs. An image of the Queen and Prince Philip has been digitally retouched—clothing has been recolored; a pocket book has been removed; the Queen's hat has lost its pompon. Here, digital technology is deployed to *mock* the relationship of the image with the preexistent signified reality of their majesties. And mock it, it can because it is now so easy to manipulate the image and so undetectable. Absolute undetectability is what is really new here.

The technology for digital retouching is becoming a fixture in all newspaper and magazine offices. The pioneering commercial device's brand name is a synonym for the whole process, "Scitex" (cf. "Hoover"). As a verb it is already a term of art, "to scitex," meaning to retouch digitally.

The parallel technology for the moving image exists, marketed as a computer called "Harry." Music video director Ethan Russell spent 6 days with "Harry" altering 42 seconds worth of Hank William's lips on a 1952 kinescope so that he appeared to be singing "Tears in My Beer." On the original, he sang "Hey, Good Looking."[98] Colorization processes are, then, but the beginning. Bette Davis can get to play Scarlett O'Hara after all—and will, if it is to the copyright holder's advantage so to arrange.

It seems to me likely that the implications of this technology will be decades working themselves through the culture. But it is clear that in ways more fundamental than any theorist conceived, the fixity of the relationship between signified and signifier supposed by realism cannot be guaranteed photographically any more. On the battleground of epistemology, the weapon that is Scitex operates with nuclear force. What the chemists bestowed 150 years ago, the computer scientists are now removing.

In the longer term, this leaves the documentary film project in all its guises in parlous state—just as it strikes potentially fatal blows against all evidentiary visual forms, including television news. In the short term, which might well be as long as the next half century given the powerful political investment the culture has in the mimetic force of the image, a number of strategies suggest themselves (albeit not very forcefully) for maintaining some legitimacy for the documentary.

One can take Carroll's part, arguing that it is confusions and misuses of language which have caused us to conflate various senses of "objectivity" with each other and with "truth." Untangling these would allow for a recuperation of the mimetic power of the camera along Bazanian lines. Insofar as this power is generally sustained in the culture, then a documentary form which took advantage of it by "being still responsible to established standards of objectivity" could exist.[99] (This assumes, of course, that there are and will continue to be established standards of objectivity.)

Better, perhaps, to roll with the epistemological blow, abandoning the claim to evidence, excising scientific legitimations and returning to an unambiguous Griersonian privileging of art over science. The price would be a more "analogical" relationship to the preexistent signified. Defining the documentary would require turning back to considerations of how materials could be subjected to "creative treatment" and yet not totally fictionalized. It would, perhaps, still allow for documentary in certain circumstances, say in the developing world, to function as

> a piece of "authentication" inserted into a broader rhetoric that sustains its force on the legitimate referential weight of what is presented on the screen.[100]

This is perhaps the best that can be achieved but it does assume, as with Carroll's position, that a measure of cultural agreement as to the mimetic power of the camera will be sustained—that the image will indeed have some legitimate, if reduced, referential weight.

In all events, it seems to me necessary for the documentary, in some way, to negotiate an escape from the embrace of science. Even if epistemology does not demand this, then the technology does (or will). It is now clear that François Arago did not, after all, give the world a species of thermometer when he argued for the state acquisition of the Daguerre patents. We should never have believed him in the first place.

4

Document and Documentary: On the Persistence of Historical Concepts

Philip Rosen

1. This Is Not a Documentary

As Murphy pointed out to you there, that was unscreened, which means he saw it for the very first time as you saw it, unedited films of, uh, what happened—some of what happened—in the motorcade. If I might explain to you that blurry and confusing scene: obviously what happened, when the shots were fired, the cameraman, who was riding in one of the cars behind the President, very wisely kept his camera running, even as he jumped from the car and ran towards the President's car, and then over towards the people who were shielding themselves, ducking down, trying to avoid what was going on. It was the only way the cameraman could have gotten you a picture of what went on. He very wisely took no time to try to wind the spring on the camera or anything else—just keep it rolling, get as much picture as possible, and get as close as possible to the scene of action. That is what the cameraman did, that is why it looked somewhat unorthodox in terms of what you are used to seeing, and that is why it's such a precious piece of film, because the cameraman *thought*.

Bill Ryan
NBC anchor person during
John Kennedy assassination coverage

At about 1:45 P.M., U.S. eastern time on November 22, 1963, the NBC television network broke into its broadcast day with the bulletin that the President had been shot in Dallas. This began several hours of instantaneous coverage of a classically traumatic event in recent U.S. cultural and political history. It is now possible to watch this coverage as a significant historical document—I use this word advisedly—in the early shaping of that event in public discourse. It is also a document in the history of television news coverage. *Ex post facto,* in comparison to the practices and conventions of U.S. television news in 1992, this 1963 coverage undoubtedly appears primitive. Just on the level of sheer "thematic" content, it is striking to observe the adjustment of the newsmen to the shock of political assassination in the United States. Nowadays, we know that this kind of event would become a widely generalized cultural sign over the next seven years. *We* now always know more than *they* did then. The gap between this "we" and this "they" is, as I will note later, an elementary condition for modern historiography. But my chief concern here is the means of modern historiography and how they encompass documentary film as it has been defined in its founding conceptualizations.

We may begin from the question of what counts as a desirable account of the real in this example, for both historiography and documentary constantly engage with this cultural goal in their practices. On a parallel but distant plane, "primitiveness" also appears in the modes of staging the marathon bulletin. Take the studio mise-en-scène; three white males (Frank Magee, Chet Huntley, and Bill Ryan) sit at a table, appearing cramped against a blank background flat, perhaps hastily put up to obscure other uses of that studio space. They face cameras that accentuate the cramped quality by holding them in medium close-up, with cuts and sometimes pans from one to the other or to photographs that they hold up to the camera. This is a far cry from the spaciousness of our contemporary network newsrooms, which are always at some point (usually openings and closings) shown in a long shot that emphasizes the resources the network has committed to the news department—not just in the number of subsidiary personnel supporting the anchor and reporters, but in its technologies of news recording, gathering, and transmission. A major element of the "primitive" appearance of this assassination coverage is the lack of any of the now conventional signs of massive technological apparati for news gathering.[1]

Yet, consciousness of a technological lack seems to be not just ours, but theirs. It is overtly manifested in the assassination coverage itself. Its pressure point is the unavailability of any first-hand depictions of the events in Dallas. The insufficiency of the television medium is manifest as coverage begins, for the anchorpersons can only read *newspaper* wire service reports and speculate on the situation among themselves. Their commentaries are speculation because they are on camera, "live," in New York as the pertinent events are happening in Dallas, but the problems evinced in the broadcast tell us something about the expectations the medium represents itself as fulfilling. The possibility of liveness is, of course, a distinguishing possibility of broadcast technologies, with television adding moving perspectival images to radio's sound. These media embody a potential for temporal simultaneity between a reality and its electronic encoding and transmission to a spectator in a distant place.[2] It is important to note that this differentiates them from another category of media of mechanical/electronic reproduction such as phonography, photography, and cinema. Both of these categories may be subsumed under the semiotic concept of indexical signification, meaning that both result in representations produced with some degree of participation by the referential object or events themselves. But the second category involves no possibility of liveness. In this case, the availability of the representations of a reality to spectators is subject to noticeable delay because of the time necessary to process, manufacture, and/or distribute the representations. As a result, this latter class of media generally presupposes a temporal disjunction between the referential events producing them and audience apprehension of them, so that their representations become fixed as preservations from a past. To indexical media in which liveness is a possibility, we can oppose these media of indexical traces. (The advent of videotaping of live events for repetition later was a significant and insufficiently discussed overlapping of these two modes, which are often mixed on newscasts.)

This already suggests that documentary cinema, whose reality is necessarily from a past, may embody different, more "historical" expectations than those possible in a newscast. At any rate, news programming is a television mode which typically, if only partially, utilizes liveness, and the emergency bulletin is the epitome of that utilization. Here is a problem for the NBC assassination coverage. In it, the price paid for instantaneity is a technological insufficiency linked to the spatial disjunction between broadcasting site and the referential events being depicted. In an era when portable video/television cameras were not available, there could be no live images from such crucial locations in Dallas as the assassination site and the hospital where Kennedy was treated. The President dies, Lee Harvey Oswald is arrested, and politicians and the populace react, but, far into the story, NBC's reporters are always a little behind. In particular, they seem constantly aware that their broadcast lacks images from the scene.

The technological surplus of television constructions of reality over that of radio—its sibling medium with "live" potential—is clearly the addition of the visual register. On November 22, 1963, NBC newsmen in a New York studio verbally narrate an overt and suspenseful story of the condition of the President "as it happens," with most of the image track being the bodies of narrating anchor persons and the site of narration as the newsroom. One could argue that, as dramatic situation, this story is resolved within 50 minutes by the announcement of the President's death, and the several hours of coverage that follow only narrate anticlimactic consequences (world reaction, a new President, shock and continuity, etc.).

But alongside such narrations, there is a subtextual drama of the medium's struggle to depict itself: Where are the sights not just of the narrating but of the narrated? Can NBC get pictures from Dallas onto the air? This other drama is foregrounded by the fact that the live NBC coverage from the scene in Dallas comes to Frank Magee on camera over the *telephone* from Robert MacNeil, and that there are technical problems in getting MacNeil's telephone transmission audible on air; for a time, direct, simultaneous reports from Dallas (off camera) must be relayed, spoken line by spoken line, by Magee. The camera can only hold on him, listening to the phone and then repeating the news.

But, as part of this subtextual drama, ways are found to insert admittedly insufficient live images other than those of the narration itself: interviews from outside the constricted mise-en-scène of NBC's New York studio, switches to newsmen in Washington, and so forth. However, as if in compensation for the insufficiency of live indexical images from the scene, a series of indexically traced representations is gradually integrated into the coverage. This series begins less than 30 minutes after going on the air, when one of the anchorpersons holds up to the camera a *photograph* taken in Texas of Kennedy in a convertible limousine. Then there is a switch (emphasized by some technical difficulties) to local anchorperson Charles Murphy in a similarly plain desk at the NBC Fort Worth affiliate WBAP. Murphy too can only read—in this case local reports—but at least he is in the geographical area of the story; spatial separation is being broken down. After a switch for comments to David Brinkley in a Washington studio, it is back to WBAP, which finally gets indexical representations from the assassination site: not yet images from the instant and the place of the shooting, but *sound recordings* of interviews with eyewitnesses who recount what they had seen. (The lack of images is oddly accentuated, for as the witnesses are heard, the camera holds on a fidgity Murphy.) Back to New York, where the anchorpersons manifest the problem, with an on-air discussion of the fact that they now have a still photograph of the Kennedys and of how best to show it to the camera. Soon after come the reports of Kennedy's death, which is first read from an Associated Press (i.e., print journalism) teletype report, and only then reported by Murphy and subsequently (on the telephone) Robert MacNeil. Yet, the groping for indexical images from outside the New York studio continues: more still photographs; live shots from Fort Worth and Washington newsrooms conveying newsmens' commentaries as well as interviews with witnesses; and live exterior setups where cameras are readily available—outside the White House, outside the New York studios for reaction interviews with passersby.

This subtextual drama of the medium's aspirations, which progresses through the security of newspaper reports to telephones, photographs, and narration on television from Dallas, all circulates around a kind of black hole, the structuring absence of images from the key scenes of the motivating action. Finally, around 3:00 P.M., the anchors in New York are able to show a photograph (presumably a wirephoto) of bystanders lying flat on the ground at the scene of the assassination. Over this image, MacNeil and Magee provide a verbal narration of the moment of the shooting. At 3:40 P.M., Murphy announces late film is in. But this first motion picture film from Dallas at the time of the assassination turns out to be of an announcement of the shooting at a locale where Kennedy was due to speak. Then at about 4:00 P.M., NBC switches once more to WBAP in Fort Worth and Charles Murphy announces "late and unscreened film," taken from a reporter's car in the Presidential motorcade. Murphy narrates the location of silent traveling shots from the car of cheering crowds on the curbsides, and then comes the moment of the assassination. Neither shooter nor target are visible, of course. Suddenly, the camera seems to vault from the car, in a long take composed of violent, short pans back and forth as the cameraman runs toward the action, finding people taking cover. The result is shaky, blurry, Brakhage-like footage of earth and background buildings that sometimes holds briefly on human figures. A couple of more quick pans and cuts, and the clip runs out after some shots taken from the procession heading toward the hospital and from outside the hospital. Immediately identified by the anchors as important footage, this will be shown again.

At this point, NBC switches back to New York, and Bill Ryan makes the comments I quote to begin this paper. Those comments nicely summarize the stakes of the self-presentation of television coverage. Throughout NBC's narration of the crisis, the overt desire for hard information about the events has been crisscrossed by a (usually) less overt desire for images of the real of the actual scene, a presence of the news apparatus at the moment of the shooting. This moment is already becoming part of a past, for all participants know it will be an event drafted into official History. Yet, when that presence and that moment are indexically represented—when that representation is explicitly said to be valuable because of the presence of the apparatus, the indexicality of the image—the image emerges as insufficient in itself. It must immediately be explained, sense must be made, the very shape of the image requires verbal explication and pinpointing. Ryan's commentary takes up that task, "naturally" and in the interests of clarity, by explaining the effects of such an event on the camera, whose presence is certified and personalized as the skill of an individual. It looks "unorthodox," but it is "precious" thanks to the wisdom of the cameraman. In a kind of climax to the subtextual drama of the medium's aspirations, a micronarrative is constructed around the figure of a skilled filmmaker, the NBC professional who has done his job well and filled in some of the missing images.

Looking back as we must from the age of MTV and a seemingly incessant display of the film and television apparatus, this might seem to be a rather quaint, "pre-postmodern" consciousness, seeking to hold representation in place. Again, there is the felt gap between what we know and they could know; this gap situates us with historians and them as historical agents. But it is instructive to compare this to a documentary film made in 1988, after the event was firmly placed in the past of instituted History, *JFK: A Time Remembered* (Mark Oberhaus, 1988). This film depicts the assassination and the national reaction through a combination of found news footage (images of the past) and the filmmakers' interviews with participants in the events and journalists who covered them (the perspective of the present). *JFK: A Time Remembered* includes that NBC footage of the moment of the assassination, but cuts it up, slightly rearranging its order and interspersing it with both other found footage and interviewees recounting the event. Thus, as the jerky motion of the camera begins, a voice on the sound track says "Suddenly . . .," and we cut to the interview with Larry O'Brien where, he continues, "shots were fired." Additional segments of the NBC long take are also shown, but intercut with other shots of the scene from a less determined time, such as a policeman staring up at the Texas Book Depository. In fact, the blurriest seconds of the NBC camerawork are excised. Thus, on the one hand, the unusual jerkiness of the image is given immediate semantic firmness— suddenness, a break in the ordinary, a shift in History. On the other hand, some of it still counts as excessive, perhaps unreadable, within the purposes of this recollective documentary and so is excised. This suggests something to which I will return, a degree of pastness that exceeds historical sense.

With the notion of film as providing indexical traces of a real past, we approach the arena not only of history, but of documentary, or the convergence of documentary cinema and historiography. No one would argue, I think, that *JFK: A Time Remembered* is not a documentary. In our standard expectations and modes of apprehension, it is recognizable as such, both in its use of footage from the actuality of the events being depicted and because they are arranged in careful sequence and, thus, presented in a form that places and makes sense of that actuality. Such a "well-formed" sequence is justified precisely as History; sense can be made because the event is over. From this perspective, Bill Ryan's commentary is only a halting start at the ongoing project of conversion of a relatively unbridled visual indexicality into sense; the closer the image comes to being reduced to pure presence, the more it threatens to become unreadable and requires explication. In the NBC coverage, the event is just past, barely in the process of becoming History, and a sure, meaning-determining sequence is not yet formed; there has not been time. *JFK: A Time Remembered* has had both production time and cultural time to know its history and so is a proper documentary. The NBC coverage, caught between past and present, is not a "real" documentary.

The measure of this difference is rooted in film history (note how difficult it is to avoid this last word). Classical proponents of the documentary tradition in cinema repeatedly define documentary against what it is not. Thus, when appropriating the term in his "First Principles of Documentary" (1932–1934), John Grierson goes on to distinguish its "lower," less valuable, from its "higher" forms. His preferred category of filmmaking excludes such "films made from natural materials" as travelogues, newsreels, "magazine items," and other short "interests" or "lecture films," as well as scientific and educational films. Beyond such nonfiction film types, "one begins to wander into the world of documentary proper, into the only world in which documentary can hope to achieve the ordinary virtues of an art. Here, we pass from the plain (or fancy) descriptions of natural material, to arrangements, rearrangements, and creative shapings of it." Or, as he put it in a 1937 discussion that connects the preclassical actuality film and the cinema programming of his day, "The newsreel has gone dithering on, mistaking the phenomenon for the thing in itself, and ignoring everything that gave it the trouble of con-science and penetration and thought." Grierson's sometime use of Kantian slogans sketches an epistemology of actuality through film. He rejects neither a concern with the surface of reality nor its aestheticization, but seeks to demonstrate (as he still could say in 1943) that "even so complex a world as ours could be patterned for all to appreciate if only we got away from the servile accumulation of fact and struck for the story which held the facts in living organic relationship together."[3]

Such passages were published during years when the term documentary, often forwarded in contradistinction to the mere filming of "natural mate-rial," was elevated to a major presence in film practices, the discourses surrounding them, and their inscription in film histories. In the English-speaking world, this occurred very much, though not exclusively, in relation to the work and polemicizing of Grierson, his coworkers, and his allies. Here we see the documentary tradition—that spoken of by Grierson as the "higher form" of filming actuality—self-consciously inventing it-self. In this invention, there is rarely, if ever, unvarnished faith in the possibility or, more tellingly, the utility of a complete record of the surface of reality. While some would argue more strongly for the check that "reality" might place on the filmmaking, it was from the beginning a lasting truism of the documentary tradition that patterning, rhetoric, artistry, or something had to be added to the indexical capacity of the medium. This is why Grierson could use concepts of story, drama, and the organic to indicate a prerequisite of genuine, "higher" documentary. Whatever the critic's or practitioner's proclivities with respect to filmmaking, a number of texts and discourses from these years emphasize the importance for documentary of preplanning, of aesthetics, of dramatizing, and even of scripting the reality to be filmed. A consistent formula in the main line of this tradition is that documentary is neither newsreel nor travelogue, but something more profound and certainly something with a more important social mission.[4]

It is precisely the distinction between actuality and meaning, document and documentary, that we see enacted in the recycling of the NBC footage in *JFK: A Time Remembered*. Of course, that footage relates a very privileged kind of historical actuality. But, in one sense, every "normal" film image is supposed to be apprehended as a preservation from the past. It is important to understand that this is so even if what is preserved is an overt fiction; when I comprehend a certain body represented on the screen to be Walter in *His Girl Friday*, at a basic factual level I am seeing the body of the now-deceased individual born Archibald Leitch, which, as the Hollywood institution requires, I know as Cary Grant. Whereas the institution sells images of that body as a unique cluster of appearance, talent, and "personality" "captured" by film, similar points can be made about the entire profilmic field of normalized mainstream cinema. My examples suggest that part of the stake in making documentaries is controlling documents, indexical traces of the presence of a real past, but this is a grounding issue for the cultural history of cinema *in toto*. This is to say, first, that the scope of such questions is not limited to documentary as a specific "mode" or "genre" of cinema. But, furthermore, it also suggests another path of understanding that cultural history. The control of pastness in the register of meanings achieves its most culturally prestigious, disciplined versions in the practice of historiography. The concept of documentary, as a mode of understanding the nature, potential, and functions of cinema and indexical representations, is in intimate ways intricated with the concept of *historical* meaning.

2. What is a Document/ary?

Notions of document and documentary have a genealogy that could be sketched with reference to the concept of historicity. According to the 1933 edition of the *Oxford English Dictionary* (OED), the noun "document" entered the English language by the mid-fifteenth century with two chief derivations from its Latin and Old French roots, now obsolete. One of these interrelated semantic clusters has to do with teaching and/or warning, and the other with evidence or proof. A seemingly subsidiary association arose in the eighteenth century, when the term document developed an association with evidence that is written, such as manuscripts and deeds, but could also encompass such artifacts as tombstones and coins as well as official legal and commercial artifacts such as bills of lading, insurance policies, and so on.

As for the noun "documentary," it seems to have entered the language only in the nineteenth century, when "documentation" was also increasingly common. The OED indicates "documentary" was first used as an adjective straightforwardly indicating reference to documentation, giving examples such as "They were in possession of documentary evidence which would confound the guilty" (Macauley, 1855). But, significantly, this usage now included historiographic extensions such as "Going back beyond annalists to original and documentary authorities" (Pattison, 1861). The 1933 OED does not mention film. However, Griersonianism is fully registered in the 1989 revised edition, which adds a new definition: "Factual, realistic, applied esp. to a film or literary work, etc., based on real events or circumstances, and intended primarily for instruction or record purposes." This is followed by a relatively lengthy group of sample uses, the earliest of which is from John Grierson's 1926 review of *Moana,* and six of which are from the 1930s. This usage expands beyond cinema in the last three examples, dating from 1957 to 1962. These extend the notion of documentary as an effect of factual reality to film makeup, to a book, and finally (in a way Freud might have appreciated) to its putative contrary, as in the seemingly oxymoronic phrase "documentary fiction." The revised OED also adds the new subsidiary term "documentarist," meaning documentary filmmaker, as being in use by the 1950s. All in all, then, Grierson's phraseology appears to have become current almost as soon as he proposed it. This suggests less his own importance than a cultural conjuncture *requiring* some designation of the field he named: an arena of meaning centering on the authority of the real founded in the indexical trace, various forms of which were rapidly disseminated at all levels of industrial and now postindustrial culture.

This cultural conjuncture is undoubtedly connected to the semantic development around concepts of document and documentary stemming from the nineteenth century and lasting into the twentieth, whereby the terms were extended from written evidence and historical artifacts to the factual film and then simply to factuality. This was, in effect, an overall shift in semantic emphasis from education to authentication in an expansion from the written that took in, characterized, and was characterized by the filmic. One could consider that shift as a process of lexical adaptation partly in response to technological changes, or perhaps as a conceptual slide that provides some "historical" basis for a theoretically convenient analogy between writing and film. But it is also the case that such changes were situated in a sociocultural matrix bestowing authority on purported conveyances of a real. The written legal document embodies a real of the intentionality of legal subjects, the original or historical document a real of dated authentication, and (photographic) cinema a real of perceivable concrete past existents in movement. In the evolution of the idea of document, the connection of authenticity and authority goes beyond etymological kinship. The authority of documenting was first drawn from the power implicit in its denotations, that is, warning, admonishing, or teaching; it then became an evidentiary element in an argument or rhetoric; and currently, within a semantic history that seems linked to film, this authority can exceed even its modes of inscription, as a claim that achieves the authority of the real itself.

The period of these semantic expansions in concepts of documentary and document was crucial for the organization of pastness and indexicality as general cultural concerns. Not only did the nineteenth century see the invention of photography, phonography, and cinema (precisely those indexical media on which NBC drew to fill in its lacks while covering the Kennedy assassination). Also, as many have noted, it was a period during which the study of history was professionalized and achieved the sociocultural status of a master Western discipline offering the most prestigious knowledge of a real past. The idea that historiography provided a powerful (even, in some circles, "scientific") kind of knowledge is striking for several reasons. Among these is that one of the now-instituted disciplinary requirements was for an account of the real as coherent sequence; hence, the supposed omnipresence in this historiography of a narrativity of closure, which has recently been so emphasized by Hayden White, who finds it as epistemologically suspect as it is rhetorically powerful. Also, to put it in the most empiricist terms, the past is by definition absent and therefore not susceptible to direct observation, much less experimental manipulation, for both of the latter depend on the presence of an observer and the past is by definition absent to any observer.

As if in response to this difficulty, a central component of the epistemological identity of the new professionalized mastery of the past was a new emphasis on the systematically critical study of traces left by the past in the form of written primary sources—the historical document. Historians often based the validity and specificity of their discipline on rigor of documentation. Thus, by 1875 the honored French historian Fustel de Coulanges could remark that the only way offering success for the present to securely and impartially comprehend the past was "the patient study of literature and documents which each century has left behind." In this recommendation for overcoming the gap between the interests of the present and the reality of the past, Fustel voices the victory of a methodological position usually traced back to the German historiographic school. Its most single influential figure, Leopold von Ranke, was inspired by Barthold Niebuhr's use of philological methods to authenticate sources. The accurate placement of written historical documents was a mark of modern historiography.[5]

The reality of an internally unified sequence was thus to be claimed on the strength of inferences from critically authenticated source documents. A famous formulation of this attitude was Ranke's 1824 introduction to an early work, where he summed up the methods of a historical discourse that might show a past "as it actually happened":

> The basis of the present work, the sources of its material, are memoirs, diaries, letters, diplomatic reports, and original narratives of eyewitnesses; other writings were used only if they were immediately derived from the above mentioned or seemed to equal them because of some original information.

As Ranke's priorities reveal, a fundamental measure of the utility of source documents is their presence at an original scene and their continuous existence since the period in question. That is, the strongest evidence is that whose origins in the past being recounted could be verified.[6]

The OED sketches an extension of the semantics of the document past the limit of written language that eventually seems to register technologies of indexicality. It may reasonably appear, on the other hand, that the modern (post-eighteenth century) discipline of professionalized historiography has most often identified the written document as the crucial, authorizing object grounding historical investigations. However, depending on one's position on the purview of historicity, an expansion of the realm of historical evidence was always a theoretical possibility. Certainly in an age which, for example, saw the development of archeology, evolutionary biology, and psychoanalysis as significant disciplines, it was clear that the methodologically and epistemologically valuable indexical traces surviving from the past are not limited to written ones. By the end of the nineteenth century, partly under the impact of modernity and the growing discursive centrality of the newly identified democratic masses, important historians were envisioning moving beyond written accounts of and by elite power and cultural groups. In 1891, for instance, Frederick Jackson Turner announced the recognition by historians that "all the spheres of man's activity must be considered" to understand the past and declared that all social and cultural practices provided documents in the sense of raw materials for historical arguments: *History is all the remains that have come down to us from the past, studied with all the critical and interpretive power that the present can bring to the past.*

"To the historian," according to Turner, "the materials for his work are in papers, roads, mounds, customs, languages; in monuments, coins, medals, names, titles, inscriptions, charters; in contemporary annals and chronicles; and, finally, in the secondary sources. . . ."[7]

Thus, the extension of the concept of document noted by the OED is registered in the historical profession, in theory if not in common practice. At a certain point, instead of being *sui generis,* the written document is coming to stand synecdochally for all survivals, all traces in continuous existence from a past. This coalesces with a vision of historiography as taking in all sectors and practices of society and culture; hence, Turner's remark that an understanding of local history requires knowledge of global history, and that because political, economic, artistic, and religious history are pertinent to one another, they must all be studied.[8] Implicitly, then, any human activities must be subject to the historian's inspection, hence documentable. So artifacts left to the present from any aspect of past human activity are potential evidence for the historian, connecting past and present.

Taking this to a logical extreme, it might seem that the utopia of modern disciplinary historiography is a complete surveillance, in the sense of the availability of all conceivable historical documents in the broad sense. In this utopia, all traces and all artifacts considered as traces left by the past reality being studied would have to be in continuous existence from the past to the present. Of course, one of the first things apprentice historians learn is to confront this as an impossibility, by shaping investigations according to kinds of documentary evidence that are actually available, by seeking new, previously unused sources, by critiquing the use by others of available sources, and so forth.[9] But even leaving aside the practically necessary incompleteness of the documentary record, there are basic difficulties with this utopia; for example, because the particular occurrences a historian studies remain stubbornly in the past, even the greatest number and range of such documents cannot provide epistemological guarantees—if there are such things—for the historian's final account, but can at best only be the basis of a convincing inference (i.e., a rhetoric) about how the past "actually happened." Most centrally here, this difficulty is not separable from the disciplinary requirement that such an inference should result in a recounting of reality as an internally unified sequence.

In his important study of the logic of modern professionalized historiography, Arthur Danto succinctly explores the conjunction of these two ambitions of complete "documentation" and coherent sequenciation. To conceptualize a historian with perfect documentation of the past, he hypothesizes an imaginery Ideal Chronicler who "knows whatever happens the moment it happens" and instantaneously transcribes "everything that happens across the whole forward rim of the past . . . as it happens, the *way* it happens." Yet, the full, running description of the past that constitutes an Ideal Chronicle would not in itself be historiography as the professional historian conceives it. The historian's account is always produced from a point in time after the sequence is completed; otherwise, the end of the sequence could not be securely identified and, consequently, its integrity would be in doubt. This historiography, therefore, assumes a disjunction in knowledge between actual historical agents and historians, and the possibility of a convincingly secure narrative ending is the site of this disjunction. The historian always locates a beginning and an ending that anchor the sequence as a sequence, but the historical agent would have to know his or her future with absolute certainty to construct a correct integral sequence. Without such certainty, what seems to be an ending might be followed by even more conclusive consequences. For Danto, this explains why there can be no history of the present, but only of the past, why all aspects of history are constructed *ex post facto*. That we, now, always know more than they did, then, is a premise of modern historical knowledge and part of its justification.

A necessary condition for sequenciation of the real, this premise also contaminates the status of survivals from the past, the putative documentary basis for inferrring the reality of the sequence. Danto points out that in practice it seems impossible to regard a preserved survival of the past simply as an index of elements of an ongoing Ideal Chronicle. This is because, as with any historical document in the broad sense, we already have some idea of its possible significances within sets of putatively closed sequences prior to encountering them. At least, this is suggested by Danto's example of Newton's house, which may be preserved to look much as it did in the seventeenth century and so serve as a piece of historical evidence in continuous existence up to the present; however, according to Danto, in the twentieth century we cannot help but see it as an element of an accomplished historical narrative, as "the place where Newton made those great discoveries in the Plague Year of 1665." In short, modern historicity constructs meaningful, unified temporal sequences, and whatever the rhetorical and disciplinary importance of documentary evidence in asserting their factuality, the pertinence of documents is intricated *a priori* with the *ex post facto* significance of the historical sequence.[10]

My intent here is not to plough over hoary ground involving the necessary selectivity of sources, nor the even hoarier ground of distinctions between evidence and interpretation, fact and value, and so forth. It is to highlight something about cinema by comparison to the substructure of modern historicity. The perfect Ideal Chronicle would be the perfect historical source document because (a) it is the unquestionable eyewitness account (allowed by Ranke as a primary source), impartially apprehending everything in the past and leaving a record and (b) like any indexical trace, it derives its current authenticity from the fact that it was present in the past yet survives to the present. "Perhaps the work of the Ideal Chronicler could be given over to a machine," remarks Danto. This machine would be the perfect, omniscient producer of absolutely reliable, complete indexical representations of everything in the past, including, as Danto reminds us, minds. So the prospect seems far off.

But as cultural phantasm, epistemological ideal, or combination of the two, such a machine of universal surveillance may seem to be suggested in some of the discourses around modern indexical media especially since the late nineteenth century. Today, the mise-en-scène of contemporary television news, with CNN as its epitome, seems to signify a technology aiming precisely at this, one which mobilizes all mechanical and electronic capacities yet invented for the purpose of tracking and storing information from all conceivable sectors of human activity. And yet, in its presentness, its ongoing, *unending* succession, news can only guess at, project, speculate about sequence and, therefore, what counts as proper knowledge of the real as History. Hence, perhaps, the currency of the anchorperson adopted from the news reader of radio. Pure presence and pure chronicle, which would imply a historicity without meaning secured by stable sequencing is unacceptable, but Bill Ryan can at least attempt to position even the most extreme, unstable indications of presence to foresee its transformation from pure chronicle to history.

In the discourse of the original documentary film movement, the newsreel is not a documentary; and neither is television news documentary in this sense, much less emergency bulletins. But NBC's 1963 assassination coverage provides an extreme example that indicates tendencies driving even the latter toward documentary. This is a coverage which tries to counter the effects of its own need for simultaneity or "liveness," its own dream of immediate presence at the real. The problem is not just technological insufficiencies with respect to such instantaneity, but the concurrent and contradictory need for meaning. Thus, regularly scheduled television news includes such momentary positionings by announcers, with the anchorperson as the apex of a pyramid of knowledge, and characteristically provides retrospective summaries and accounts, sometimes called "perspective" or "context," for the most recent and contemporary news events. This edges it toward documentary film/video. If shots as indexical traces of past reality may be treated as documents in the broad sense, documentary can be treated as a conversion from the document. This conversion involves a synthesizing knowledge claim, by virtue of a sequence that sublates an undoubtable referential field of pastness into meaning. Documentary as it comes to us from this tradition is not just *ex post facto,* but historical in the modern sense.

3. Documentary Is Not Actuality

There is something odd about a comparison of documentary cinema and historiography that leads to differentiating documentary from less-coherently sequenced constructions of the real; for it does not differentiate documentary from another of its "others," the mainstream narrative film. Instead, it suggests a certain kinship between the two because mainstream cinema also works through the sublation of document into sequence. The "document" here is the shot comprehended as an indexically traced record of a preexistent, profilmic field. Such preexistents include actors' bodies (in certain ways we really do see "Cary Grant"), performances, and studio or location settings. In this kind of cinema, some two hours of such "documents" are sequentially ordered as a less or (most often) more conventionalized narrative form.

This sweeping characterization is open to some objections that I would not completely resist, although full elaboration of consequences is not possible here. A most pertinent one might invoke the play of technical artifice and style in mainstream cinema, asking whether its spectator is not invited to go beyond comprehending the shot solely as document. On the other hand, it is useful to remember that when process shots, special effects, and so forth are foregrounded as in the construction of alternative universes, fantasies, imagined futures, magic, and so on, much of the point is how such manipulations of the image mesh, through composite imagery or editing, with a generalized photographic effect that asserts the prior indisputable existence of elements of profilmic actuality, such as actors' bodies. This was the case even in so techno-hyped a mise-en-scène as that of *Tron*. Or, to take another common usage, when optical "effects" are foregrounded, it is often as "punctuation," as in dissolves or wipes. If these do not place individual shots or scenes in terms of narrative motivation (e.g., dissolve to dream sequence), they demarcate individual scenes as members of a set composing a coherent, whole string of fictional events; that is, they accent and delineate sequential organization. At a fundamental level, then, such intrusions of the technique and artifice are subordinated to the assumption that the mainstream film is composed of shots that are traces of real preexistents whose significance is shaped by an overall sequencing. No matter what variations are possible, this seems interestingly reminiscent of a basic structure of modern historicity.

Within film history, there are some additional rough indications of a generally undiscussed kinship between mainstream cinema and the original documentary tradition. The classical fiction film and the industrialization of entertainment filmmaking developed in tandem roughly between 1909 and 1917. Before this time, the notion of a *non*fiction film as entertainment was not unusual. On the contrary, the so-called actuality film was a leading, though not always dominant, commercial film product up to 1907–1908 when its distribution seems to have radically diminished in the United States. The most commercially successful generic examples were often "topicals" or "visual newspapers" composed of brief, fragmentary sights related to current newsworthy events, but the purview of the actuality was much wider. Pre–1908 film programs might include simple actions from everyday life and one-shot street scenes sometimes traced back to the Lumière's first efforts, exotic "views" of foreign individuals and their practices, landscapes as seen by travellers, even scientific "views" (microbes and so forth). While the fluctuating popularity of such films is now a matter of debate, it is clear that up to 1907–1908 the money-making strategies of popular cinema included claims to make sights of the real available to audiences.

By a decade later, the fictional feature film had been instituted as the leading product of commercial filmmaking and its stylistic and formal practices became the norm for filmmaking in general. In general, the mainstream ethos has strongly tended to denigrate the preclassical era as a primitive time which, whatever its charms, was soon left behind for real "film art." This position was rapidly taken up by influential film historians. Primitiveness and lack of artistry was evidenced by narrational and visual strategies described as simplistic and inflexible, such as setting the camera in front of an unprepared chunk of reality, turning it on for a few minutes, and then presenting the result to audiences. Such accounts teleologically naturalized mainstream practices, and these attitudes have been critiqued in recent scholarship on early cinematic modes of representation.

But furthermore, there seems little doubt that the appeal of many actualities is in the relatively extreme rawness of the real they present, which is ultimately to say that they do not seem overtly planned or reorganized to fit into an intratextual sequence. This is so not just in comparison to later kinds of filmmaking but also in comparison to various accounts of the real available in other contemporary forms such as journalism, narrative prose, and historiography. In the register of the last, actuality shots may indeed appear as relatively pure instances of documents. The move to classical cinema with its concommitant normalization of the fictional feature film as sole leading product appears now to have been one of a set of industrial decisions, enabling regularization of production for a rapidly expanding market. However, it simultaneously constituted an epistemological insistence on integrating the shot into larger narrative structures whereby its meanings could be better controlled and regulated.[11]

In its own originary self-definitions, the documentary tradition shares the denigration of preclassical cinema as primitive with its putative other, mainstream fictional filmmaking. If proponents of documentary banished the newsreels that became a secondary mainstream product from their realm, it is all the more clear that actualities could not be admitted. In the 1930s, Grierson himself associated actuality films with an outgrown childhood—his own as well as the medium's.[12] While the term documentary as applied to cinema did not begin gaining currency until the late 1920s, textbooks have often followed Grierson in dating documentary filmmaking proper a bit earlier; *Nanook of the North,* released just a few years after the economic and cultural success of the fictional feature was assured, is a standard originary monument. The fashioning of such chronologies by textbook writers and the originating documentary polemicists led by Grierson may be critiqued symptomatically. But they do point to a correlation between the institutionalization of the mainstream feature film and the conceptualization of documentary, in which the latter appears as a relatively immediate aftermath of the normalization of the former. Of course, it is not surprising if the documentary ethos appears as a reaction to industrialized entertainment filmmaking, but it is interesting if it simultaneously incorporates some attitudes shared by promoters of the classical feature film.

Evidently the actuality film lacked elements implicitly or explicitly claimed by both the documentary and the mainstream ethos. I am suggesting that basic to these is the value placed on sequenciation. This value lies in the great assistance sequenciation provides for centralizing and restricting meanings derived from the points at which actual contact with the real is asserted—the realm of the document. This is what makes the actuality such an important component in the denigration of the preclassical as constituted in both traditions. Consider that almost all aspects of the visible world lay within the theoretical purview of actuality filmmaking: the smallest or largest event, the most ordinary or extraordinary spatio-temporal fragment was potentially subject to cinematic surveillance and re-presentation as an indexical trace of the real. But although such traces appeared precisely as fragments more or less extracted from the continuum of reality, they may be related to the activity of Danto's Ideal Chronicler. Like the product of this hypothetical agency, actualities in themselves provided fewer means for the filmmaker to attribute significance to the real. This is certainly not to say that there was a complete absence of order, meaning, or even convention in the making and viewing of actualities, nor that, for example, topicals did not represent occurrences that fit into larger, generally understood metanarratives. But, as a matter of degree, such films possessed much less of the textually saturating directionality of meanings based on internal sequenciation and elaboration to which we are so accustomed after seventy-odd years of narrative dominance. Like mainstream narrative, then, the later documentary impulse insists on the elementary structure of modern historicity by rejecting a specter raised by—though not necessarily realized in—the preclassical actuality genre: that of comprehension of the real through a decentralized, potentially free-floating spectatorship.

I say decentralized rather than decentered as a matter of emphasis. For centralization of meaning-production was one of the stakes in the series of transitions away from preclassical practices. Classical narrative form seeks to organize the shots composing it with more or less explicit, often conventionalized principles of sequence that delimit a range of intended meanings, *determinable by the filmmakers within a film text itself*. In preclassical cinema, as Charles Musser has emphasized, meanings could often be structured by *exhibitors*, for example, through lecturers who imposed ideological order on films with their spoken commentaries, or by cutting together shorter actualities to form elementary sequences. Such exhibition practices indicate, first of all, that some sense of the utility of sequence was felt very early, but, second, that in much preclassical practice constructions aiming at such significance were often a result of dispersed, localized rather than centralized activities. The normalization of longer, multishot films and narrative dominance located regularized sequencing and the determination of textual meanings in the production companies. As classical narrative form, common sequencing principles are both culturally widespread and repeatable (important for the industrial organization of entertainment that resulted in the Hollywood mode of production).[13]

While the documentary tradition is not locked into highly conventionalized narrative forms, it does share a commitment to the centralization of meaning through internal sequenciation; hence its own rejection of the preclassical. Thus, just as Danto's Ideal Chronicle is not in itself good disciplinary history, even an omnipresent actuality would not be good documentary filmmaking. The problem posed by actualities for documentary as well as fiction filmmaking is that they are too pure as document; machines of indexical representation, even when used by the most amateurish, can indeed produce a seeming infinity of such documents. The home video camcorder is the latest realization of this socio-technological dream, and it is not surprising if, like its predecessor the home movie camera, it is sometimes invaded by discourses of skill and craft education.

This brings us to a sociological point. A medium which finds its value in relatively unelaborated documents might seem to leave little function for the professional, threatening to individualize sequence and meaning as activities of the spectator. The actuality was a peculiarity, a kind of commercialized, hence professional manifestation of the possibility of representation of the real without necessarily imposing sense from the site of textual production where many of the professionals performed their labors. From this perspective, both Hollywood film and the documentary tradition, in their insistence on craft, skill, sequence—in short on aesthetics and meaning—find a function for a specialized elite in the imposition of significance for the spectator by means of the configuration and organization of documents. We will return to the filmmaking stratum as a professional–intellectual elite. More narrowly, mainstream and documentary film share an underlying logic of the document that helps explain why the normalization of "film art" as narrative cinema was important for the original documentary movement and why documentary has to be more than actuality, travelogue, or newsreel for the Grierson school.

Of course, in the history of the two modes there are also fundamental differences in assumptions about textual form and epistemology. But these stem from differing conceptions of the sequence or of shot-sequence relations rather than from differing definitions of the basic goals for spectatorship of the shot or disputes over the need for sequence. For both of these traditions, as for modern historiography, sequences organize temporality, providing endings that confer retrospective significance on shots. Whereas it need not utilize an overtly narrative form, documentary film must minimally share this assumption with mainstream fictional cinema; hence, the ambivalent relation of documentary to narrative. If there have been tendencies within the documentary tradition to avoid classical narrative form, this has not been true for all its sectors and, more importantly, has rarely committed documentarians to a definitional rejection of narrative *per se*. Given the relation of the ambitions of documentary cinema to modern historicity, this is not surprising; many theorists of history nowadays argue that narrative is the most powerful and perhaps only means for achieving coherent temporal sequenciation. Thus, Grierson and other of its proponents in the 1930s already emphasized documentary as the dramatization of reality, and they often articulated aims on the level of representational forms. Documentary is the "*creative* treatment" of "natural materials" he tells us; it was the need for a *dramatic* apprehension of life that led to the EMB film unit. In this problematic, representational indexicality in itself never results in a strong form of knowledge, and hence is only a precondition for documentary. This is why his higher type of documentary cinema is necessarily an *aesthetic* of the document.

At this level, at least, it may seem such an approach draws industrial entertainment cinema and the documentary tradition too closely together. For it is also clear that certain strands of documentary filmmaking have a long and honorable commitment to alternative and oppositional constructions, with practitioners and supporters conceiving or justifying them on the basis of social and political goals. It is worth remarking that politicized documentarians might have the greatest stake in the inadequacy of the isolated document. Consider again the preclassical actuality. After the more complex, often conventionalized and institutionalized types of sequenciation that were to come in film history, they seem to give the filmmaker radically fewer textual means to direct the spectator's comprehension of the real being transmitted. To continue the comparison, it is as if an historian simply presented the reader with fragmentary source documents from a given period, without overt thesis, narrative, or contextualization. Once, however, the document is placed in a context that makes it part of an assertion of meaning from the real, the reader is defined as the rhetorical aim of that significance. Similarly, for politically committed filmmakers, work in documentary implies that the spectator can be defined as a terrain to be organized, a terrain of struggle over such meanings and hence of social struggles. Of course, there are many different kinds of spectators and filmmaking impulses that can answer to such a description. But this may well be a kind of generalizable definition inherent in most claims to specifically politicized filmmaking.

4. What Does a Documentary Do? From Grierson to Baudrillard

If Griersonian concepts are significant in film history, it is not so much because of his supposed paternity over the term "documentary film" or even his energetic promotion of it as a slogan. Beginning from these, it is useful to say that he was the English-language polemicist who had the perspicacity to articulate a concept that conjoined aesthetic and concrete situational concerns of non-mainstream filmmakers around the indexical characteristics of cinema. Aesthetically, from the point in film history when the Hollywood narrative film became a leading model of economic and mass cultural success, variants of the documentary film have often offered a battle standard for alternative constructions of the medium. These constructions involve a range of documenting and sequencing strategies that claim to be based in the presence of the apparatus at past events; hence, these events are represented as being preserved, to an extremely variable degree, in their actuality. Situationally, documentary film has always offered, in Paul Willemen's words, the possibility of "an artisanal, relatively low-cost cinema working with a mixture of public and private funds, enabling directors to work in a different way and on a different economic scale from that required by Hollywood and its various national–industrial rivals." This helps Willemen explain the interest of at least some Griersonian models for at least some third cinema filmmakers.[14]

But what is the relation for the classical documentary tradition between the situation of documentary cinema *per se* and the overall social functioning of the filmmaker? This is a question which was fundamental for Griersonianism. His answers bear, in surprising ways, on the most recent debates, such as those over Cultural Studies and postmodern theories of signification. The concluding section is, in part, an attempt to begin positioning the persistence of documentary and historicity in contemporary culture.

The crucial sector in the conceptual site staked out by Grierson for cinema was the sociopolitical. It is not coincidental that, as noted earlier, U.S. publications from the 1930s and 1940s forwarding the idea of documentary tend strongly toward politically committed Leftist stances. This should not imply that Grierson himself, with his famous promotion of government sponsorship, was radical. It is well-known that Grierson often insisted that his rationales for the British documentary movement originated not among film aestheticians or theorists, but in the Political Science Department of the University of Chicago. In particular, he recalled discussions of Walter Lippmann's argument that the ideal of successful democracy requires informed, rational decision makers as subject-citizens, but that modern mass society provides insufficient generalized access to the kinds of specific knowledges necessary to produce such beings on a mass scale. As Grierson informally encapsulated it in 1937:

> If I am to be counted as the founder and leader of the movement, its origins certainly lay in sociological rather than aesthetic aims. Many of us after 1918 (and particularly in the United States) were impressed by the pessimism that had settled on Liberal theory. We noted the conclusion of such men as Walter Lippmann, that because the citizen, under modern conditions, could not know everything about everything all the time, democratic citizenship was therefore impossible. We set to thinking how a dramatic apprehension of the modern scene might solve the problem, and we turned to the new wide-reaching instruments of radio and cinema as necessary instruments in both the practice of government and the enjoyment of citizenship. It was no wonder, looking back on it, that we found our first sponsorship outside the trade and in a Government department, for the Empire Marketing Board had, from a governmental point of view, come to realize the same issue. Set to bring the Empire alive in contemporary terms, as a commonwealth of nations and as an international combine of industrial, commercial, and scientific forces, it, too, was finding a need for dramatic methods. For the imaginative mind of Sir Stephen Tallents, head of that department, it was a quick step to the documentary cinema.[15]

This move from the democratic citizen-subject to support of Britain's colonial structures may now seem breathtaking in its un-self-conscious contradictoriness. But in addition to the effectivity of colonialist ideologies, there were specific conjunctural overdeterminations of such contradictions, such as the EMB's giving relatively free aesthetic reign to the documentarians that gathered under Grierson's management. Still, such a passage does reveal certain implications of the vision forwarded by Grierson's early formulations, of a liberal social harmony based on the diffusion of social knowledge. The ultimate issue addressed by Grierson's discourse on the documentary film is nothing less than the fate of individual civic rationality in the face of the differentiated socioeconomic complexity of modern mass life; that is, making modernity work from his version of a liberal, Enlightenment standpoint. The operative difficulty is establishing a mutually effective, overall knowledge among a public that is subject to (and subject of?) divisions—economic, social, regional, and so forth—that are determinants on an unprecedented scale. That is, commonality of knowledge is conceived against such divisions, as a universally harmonizing force. One can see after all how this fundamental Griersonian impulse may lend itself after all to the goal of the EMB to unify the Empire under an ideology of general human (i.e., Western) progress.

In his self-presentation, the epistemological consequences of social division motivate Grierson's turn to another aspect of modern social life, the mass media with film conceived as its most powerful version. In this view, the value of film stems "in the last instance" not just from any purportedly unique representational capabilities—for example, to show the real—but precisely from its mass character. Note first that mass distributability as well as representational characteristics are attached to indexicality. In historiography, an original document stemming from the actual past is unique, "auratic"; the historian must go to it, and most readers of history can, at best, see only facsimiles of it. But in film, a negative image of a shot that documents a fragment of reality can be processed into a relatively countless number of positive images. The release print seen by audiences is a film of a film, a point of great importance for Walter Benjamin, who argues that "to ask for the 'authentic' print of a film makes no sense."[16] But if indexicality is basic to the mass production and distributability of photographic and cinematic representation, this simultaneously means that all positives retain their "aura" of contact with a real past, unlike the facsimile historical document. There is a relay of indexical reproduction, from actual time and space to negative, and from negative to positive prints viewed by the audience. Thus, all positives also have equal representational value or "reality status" as documents for the spectator. In this regime, then, mass distributability is inseparable from the possibility of documentation.

But, as the Lippmann reference indicates, Griersonianism is most basically concerned with the social utility and direction of such massively distributed documentations. This returns us to the idea of a certain artistry, craft, or professionalism as inherent in the very concept of documentary cinema. The crucial utility of film is supposed to begin from its wide distribution potential across socioeconomic and geographical lines that otherwise disrupt flows of mutual knowledge. However, the argument goes, this distributability is socially useful only when it can be appropriated in an innovative way by the right kind of sociocultural agency. This agency is a grouping with which Grierson clearly identifies, namely, a knowledgeable elite motivated by the polis rather than the dollar. Grierson seems to believe that an overriding social and civic virtue can be grasped and manifested by an educated, liberal elite seeking the social good. Implicitly, such an elite must first have access to an encompassing knowledge usually obstructed by specific class and socioeconomic position.

In this respect, Grierson's responsible documentary filmmaker looks much like the "relatively unattached intellectual" as conceived by Karl Mannheim at about the same time Grierson was formalizing his concept of documentary. Bearer of generalized knowledge and, hence, the secret of harmonious social rationality, the intellectual must find social and institutional means to make that knowledge effective. In Grierson, the virtuous filmmaker fulfills a duty to educate, to transmit such knowledge to the modern, divided mass, for whom it is otherwise inaccessible. In the end, the Griersonian conceptualization of documentary film is a theory about the function and duties of elites with respect to the mass of the population, not just as political leaderships but as "educators" who, among other things, are urged to work as productive agents of the media. We have returned to one of the semantic origins of documentary, teaching or warning.[17]

The references to contemporaries such as Benjamin, Lippmann, and Mannheim indicate that, even in his own time, Grierson's social concerns were not unique. Rather, he can be treated as part of a wave of major intellectuals, non-Marxist as well as Marxist, in the first half of the twentieth century who sought to register the emergence of the masses on conceptions of society, culture, and politics. For this wave, issues often turn on the specifying of possible political and cultural relations between intellectuals and masses as separated social strata (often separated by the very capacity to theorize the masses). Just in the West, in addition to Benjamin, Mannheim, and Lippman, such diverse names as Max Weber, Lukács, Adorno, and Gramsci begin to indicate the centrality of this problem and the range of approaches to it. Indicatively, most of these theorists were concerned with conceptualizing history, which since the mid-nineteenth century had designated a privileged mode of knowing and by the early twentieth was a key site of epistemological problematization. But furthermore, the work of many of them remain important touchstones in current debates, though the implications of that continuity around issues of historicity are sometimes obscured by the various theoretical rhetorics of rupture that have culminated in certain notions of the postmodern.

For example, it would be interesting to compare certain of Grierson's views to those of Antonio Gramsci, a thinker roughly contemporary with him who has had formative impact in more recent discussions in Cultural Studies. Gramsci was also concerned with conceiving of intellectual as well as technical elites in relation to modern social divisions. In certain respects, the Griersonian educator fills a slot analogous to that of the intellectual in Gramsci's writings. But in Gramsci's view of modern history, the activities of intellectuals respond to and stand for the interests of specific social groupings struggling to maintain or attain hegemonic status. For Griersonian liberalism, the formulations of his favored types of intellectuals stand, in classic ideological manner, for the ultimate coherence of the social system and the interest of the universal. Documentary cinema appears as a conscious response to modernized mass society, one of whose defining components is, of course, what are now simply called "the media." Grierson fastens on the idea that the appearance of such a society has engendered the reorganization of modes of hierarchizing and distributing knowledge to the extent that key sociopolitical forms, such as "democracy," are endangered unless they find previously unforeseen kinds of reinforcement.

More oppositional conceptions could align the intellectual with more particular sociopolitical groupings. Within cultural theory, a view of social division and contradictions not predicated on the goal of an overall harmony—such as a Gramscian approach promoted by members of the Birmingham wing of the Cultural Studies movement—would involve revision of the trickle-down theory of social knowledge implicit in Grierson, Lippmann, and Mannheim. Within media production, this would enable appropriation of aspects of Griersonianism by filmmakers committed to other kinds of politics. Willemen is correct in pointing out that one major tendency in the historical appropriation of the term documentary film has been by oppositional filmmakers and even resistance groups. And, in general, all of this indicates how the constellation Grierson designated after 1926 with the term documentary film—encompassing not only mechanically indexical signification and constructions of the real, but also mass distributability and the relationships of social strata which produce such representations to social order and the general population—pertains directly to questions central to late twentieth-century debates.[18]

Recent theories of the postmodern may, in fact, seem even more critically pertinent to Griersonian concerns in that they often focus on mass-mediated culture and also emphasize a general breakup of Enlightenment-oriented modes of organizing, producing, and distributing knowledge. In such arguments, the concept of postmodernity announces not just the failure, but the misapprehension at work in the Griersonian project, however modified. Perhaps the most extreme and therefore clarifying of such arguments are those of Baudrillard. I will move toward a conclusion by a somewhat more sustained consideration of where the documentary seems to fit in Baudrillard's account of contemporary culture. This will be to ask about the state of the concepts of document and documentary today; for Baudrillard seems to directly address the central conceptual nodes of the classical documentary tradition in all its Griersonian tenets: the indexical nature of media representation, the consequences of mass distributibility, and the relation of intellectual and masses.

Baudrillard leads a wing of postmodern theory that announces the contemporary dissolution of representation into simulation. Simulation implicates the reading of signs of reality with an inevitable knowledge of both their arbitrariness and the impossibility of experiencing the real outside of the constructedness of the sign-model. With references to Benjamin, Baudrillard seems to attribute this to a quantum increase in the mass distribution of signification generated by mass society, based both in the presence of the new reproductive media initiated in later modernity and the postmodern spread of the universal duplicability of signs through development of worldwide media communications. In a universe of constructed simulations, there is no imposable standard for judging the epistemological adequacy of sign to object, and so Baudrillard declares the end of epistemology based on a subject–object relation mediated through signification; for in a universe of constructed simulation, there is no standard for judging the epistemological adequacy of sign to object.

By the early 1980s, then, Baudrillard had returned to the linkage the mass distributibility of representations of the real to the functioning of elites, a concern which, as we have seen, was well-known in earlier twentieth-century sociocultural theory. But Baudrillard focuses on the self-serving nature of intellectuals' conceptions of contact between themselves and the mass. Intellectuals are said to construct the mass in order to have something to direct information toward, as an addressee that can be moved to the end of promoting the good (liberal or revolutionary) society. Any such version of the mass, whether as the potential site of social harmony or revolution, becomes a fantasmatic social unity and directionality because it now stands revealed as a product of the delusory self-identifications of the intellectuals. This critique can justifiably be applied to the enlightened Griersonian educator who appropriates the distributibility of cinema to reach the masses with his or her own enlightened perspective that surpasses the limitations of social division.

Whatever one's reading of Baudrillard, he is suggestive in treating "the masses" in modernity as an object of desire for the intellectuals, with the latter conceived as a sociocultural stratum that produces formalized social, political, and theoretical conceptions. For Baudrillard, this is most clearly revealed in the postmodern period, when the mass is explicitly manifested as simulation, as in demographic statistical models, but is not referentially representable. Baudrillard sketches a picture of a general population that absorbs and recycles "information" aimed at it and/or about it, but which has no consequent determinable direction and effect except in the models and dreams of intellectuals. Any "truths" of the mass are now manifested only in the modes of enunciating it. Hence, the postmodern end of epistemology is also "the end of the social," according to Baudrillard. Or more precisely, it is the end of the relation between the political and the social as conceived by intellectuals since the Renaissance. Perhaps the best thing one can say of the situation is that the gigantic distribution of mass-mediated signs that characterizes the postmodern finds a directionless mass as brute resistance to the unity of social and political, therefore resistance to the purport of the elites and of intellectuals. As the proliferation of mass-distributed signs normalizes simulation, significations of the real become excessive to the ambitions of the deluded elites and intellectuals seeking to constitute and thereby direct the mass via constructions of the real.[19]

Baudrillard's view of representation is thus intimately connected to his critique of ideas that knowledge, as a possession of intellectuals, can interrogate power and direct history. Signification is now encountered as a "massive" universe of reality effects that can always already be known as such; they are comprehended less like separable representations of the real and more like explicit models that are inextricable from any experience of the real. They never come from or fully find their subjects, for determining origins, goals, or referents can never be fully attached to them, and, therefore, they convince and move no one. Nevertheless, according to Baudrillard, social order requires the real to provide grounds for truth, falsity, rational distinction, and equivalence on which power depends. In an ironic inversion, power must compulsively derive its reality from the model to establish at least some possibility of correspondence with an attendant distinction between the true or the false. As a result, social order, from its need for real outside signification, compulsively propagates simulation, a hyperreal.[20]

What does this view imply for the contemporary status of documentary, whose course has been so intertwined with that of historiography for two centuries? In a universe of simulation, there can be no place for the kinds of relations of intellectuals and politics envisioned even by a Gramsci much less a Grierson, for there can be no history in the modern sense. Modern historicity demands reference to a real outside signification, a spatio-temporal ("historical") specificity; but, in postmodernity, the unending duplicability of the one of the many signs of the real, which enables the mass distribution of that sign, undercuts its claims to a unique representability. By extension, the document, which had been understood since the eighteenth century as auratic and binding, must lose its force. Therefore, it is no surprise if the implication of this position is that the claims of documentary representation are definitively wrong-headed in the age of simulation.

There is a point in *Simulations* where Baudrillard, who often argues by example, embarks on a discussion of *An American Family* (Craig Gilbert, 1973). This film, which was shown on television in 12 parts, was arguably an attempt at an "ultimate" cinema verité documentary. In fact, it might be treated as aspiring to be like an Ideal Chronicle. At any rate, with its use of the lightweight equipment associated with cinema verité, the film was planned as an unprecedented documentary observation of everyday family life over an extended period of time. Instead, the equipment witnessed the breakup of the family, and includes a famous scene where the wife, Pat Loud, tells her husband Bill on camera she wants a divorce.

Baudrillard recalls the ensuing debate over whether the breakup of the Loud's marriage was a result of the seemingly incessant presence of the working crew and camera over several months of their lives. Remarking on the impossibility of arguing that the film is simply a record of a preexisting real, Baudrillard aligns it with the hyperreal because it embodies a referentiality whose truth is unimaginable without its means of sign-production. Thus, the film becomes a stick with which to beat a series of theories that propose the experience of an organizing gaze as exterior to its objects, including psychoanalysis and even Foucault (the panopticon in *Discipline and Punish*). All of these supposedly postulate an implicated and/or empowered subject of vision seeking truth exterior to itself, so all fall to the confusion of the medium with the real it depicts exemplified by the case of *An American Family*. As the sign-referent distinction is supposedly collapsed by cinema verité, so is that between the filmmaker as subject and the Louds as object. Thus, the fate of the documentary in the postmodern world becomes to unveil the irrelevancy of the pretensions of intellectuals. I would add that this also applies to the pretensions of modern historiography to represent the past, which also depends on the work of the historian as a skilled, often professional subject. Not only are subject and object of knowledge conflated, but also cause and effect, hence, meaningful sequence as a property of the referent.

However, before throwing out the pretensions of the classical documentary tradition—and historiography—*tout court,* a closer inspection of this example is in order. Having admitted the utility of Baudrillard's critical attitude for understanding Grierson, I would also argue that Baudrillard rhetorically disavows the close relationship of his problematic with those of somewhat earlier thinkers. (Several of them, such as Gramsci, embody a Leftism he wishes to attack.) The paradox of this extreme postmodern rhetoric of rupture is that it must be mobilized to explain a certain continuity. To put it simply, it would appear that contemporary culture has not fewer but more significations claiming to attach to referentiality. Our concern here is the prominent persistence of documentation in media, beginning from news and informational television programming, and the documentary impulse. Baudrillard's ingenious resolution is to subsume all of this under the sign of the hyperreal, as he does *An American Family*.

Yet, it is striking that the terms in which he discusses the hyperreal of documentary are themselves not new. In fact, they themselves embody a certain theoretical persistence that parallels the cultural persistence of the documentary and the historical. In some ways, the discussions of the film he cites are akin to two centuries' worth of often tortured discussions in the theory of history: To what extent does the writing historian's own subjectivity—conceived as social, cultural, textual, personal, or (most crucially) historical—affect the construction of the past as object? The difference is that, in historiography, issues flow from the subject's absence from a past reality and, in documentary cinema, from its presence. But this is only an inversion; the whole problematic of the film equipment's presence as distorting, shaping, and even exploiting profilmic entities rests on a subject–object opposition which Baudrillard, like much ruptural postmodern theory, believes himself to be collapsing. This is what enables his dismissal of theories of visual representation treating the gaze as external to its object. At best, he is engaged in a deconstructive erasure in which the marks of the erased persist. Nevertheless, this entire move does require the very opposition and separation he is supposedly rejecting. And more specifically, the problem in documentary cinema of the presence of the camera on the profilmic are familiar not only with respect to cinema verité but also in such variants as anthropological filmmaking. In fact, as we have seen, the notion of a shaping consciousness is well-known in the aesthetic of the classical documentary tradition from its beginnings. Baudrillard might well object to the concept of an aesthetic consciousness, but the notion of pure access to the object had never been paramount for documentary filmmaking. It appears that the discussion of *An American Family* he invokes as revelatory occurred because it took up terms that were culturally familiar, not disturbing.

My long digression on Baudrillard and the contemporary situation of the concept of documentary therefore reflects back on several points already made in this chapter, beginning from indexical representation. It is true that, for media of mechanical and electronic reproduction, the question of the presence and effects of the apparatus cannot be disentangled from the indexical quality of a medium. In cinema, indexicality designates the presence of camera and sound-recording machinery at the profilmic event, which, in turn, guarantees that the profilmic really did exist in the past. Now reconsider Baudrillard's account of the general debate over *An*

American Family, which supposedly illustrates the contemporary confusion of traditional epistemological and representational categories. Even in his own account, this debate was never about the reality status of the filmic images and sounds. Instead it was about *causality,* of all things, and a very common-sensical, two-term cause–effect relationship at that: Did the camera cause a divorce that would not have happened except for the filming? That is, was the presence of the cinema apparatus and filmmakers a necessary and sufficient cause for the ensuing divorce? (Note that this can also be rewritten in terms of subject and object: Was the cinema apparatus/crew the subject of the object depicted, or were the Louds their own subject which the image then properly reflects?) Baudrillard has his answers—the filmmaking was the cause/subject, and this is a scandal for representation. But my view is that this answer makes little difference for his case. In fact, *no matter what the answer,* the status of the shot as document of a real that preexists the spectators' viewing remains in force, for, otherwise, the film could be received as a conventional fiction and there would have been nothing to debate.

If so, we are edging back toward familiar territory. Whether or not the truth of the case is decidable, the very terms in which Baudrillard's exemplary debate over a documentary occurs continues to hinge on the truth of the real—that is, representation rather than simulation, a historical referentiality rather than awareness of a constructed model. And in this regard, it is most striking that Baudrillard makes the debate center precisely on an *ending:* "The Louds went their separate ways, etc. Whence that insoluble controversy. . . ."[21] This suggests that sequence is the grounds on which disputes over the presence of the apparatus arise, and where the meaning of a past reality becomes susceptible to discussion. In short, the effects of a confusion of apparatus and profilmic do not necessarily inhibit faith in the preexistence of a real that can be indexed—hence documented—and made meaningful. For this debate turns not on the possibility of an exteriorized gaze at the real (almost always a problematic notion in the documentary film tradition), but rather explaining the sequence of such gazes.

To put it differently, a claim of historical representation does not depend on the existence of an imaginary Ideal Chronicler, but is instead implicated in the inseparability of the chronicling activity and sequenciation. Even if the work of the cinema verité apparatus is to aspire toward being something like an Ideal Chronicler, that work is sublimated into a conclusion around which spectators can organize understandings of a reality preexisting their own viewing. The debate Baudrillard invokes is about explanations and meanings that can appropriately be attributed to a past. It is about history, understood for more than 150 years as the construction of sequence from documents. This is revealed in Baudrillard's own use of this example to invert expectations about causality and the location of subjects of actions, which are typical concerns of historians. Both documentary cinema and its kin, modern historiography, persist, even in Baudrillard's own discourse.

Baudrillard's extension of Benjamin does allow him to refocus the special potential of indexicality with respect to mass distributibility and the relationship of elites and intellectuals to the mass. But this means he is contributing to a discussion that has been ongoing since intellectuals identified modernity and the emergence of the masses. Documentary cinema is one of the twentieth century's conceptual nodes for this constellation. But this is precisely why a cinema verité film such as *An American Family* can be treated as one culminating variant on an older dream as much as a radical novelty. When Baudrillard fastens on the self-definitive stake specialized intellectual and professional strata have in the construction of the real, one can understand his gleeful desire to argue for the increasing irrelevance of that activity. But what he consequently misses is that a film's status as a cultural object rests in great part on what makes it documentary rather than document.

Not only is the unending profusion of indexical significations of the real a constant fact of contemporary life (the Benjaminian point) but so also is the constant scrabbling for sequence in the face of that profusion. This can be observed even in the daily and (on CNN) continuous television news, and even, as we have seen, in catastrophic occurrences such as the Kennedy assassination. Here, we may locate a crucial sociocultural task of professional intellectuals and elites with respect to the real and the masses, one which cannot be willed away with an extremist theory of postmodern, mediatized simulation. The explanatory narrativizing of journalism, the coordinating authority of the broadcast reporter, and especially the anchorperson, testify to the continuing sociocultural importance of this task.

There is another way of putting it, in relation to the documentary cinema tradition. Film historians and theorists have sometimes written as if the main pretense of documentary cinema has been the rather naive one providing unmediated access to an ongoing profilmic event, as if the main line of the documentary cinema tradition consists in a constant attempt to convince the spectator s/he is watching the unfolding of the real, as if actuality could be reproduced through cinema. This has often allowed theorists to apply prevalent critiques of cinematic illusionism.[22] But for the generation of Griersonians who innovated the concept of documentary cinema as well as their successors, even including a number of cinema verité practitioners, this is just not true. We must keep reminding ourselves that the documentary tradition has rarely supposed that the photographic/cinematic "impression of reality" is, in itself, sufficient for knowledge.

Knowledge is supposed to take place on the grounds of the synthetic and generalizing, thus the sequence. Grierson's "higher forms" of documentary do not flow simply from the raw presence of the film apparatus at an event, which is in itself always inadequate. Hence, his appeal to an intellectual elite, for something more must be done than set up chronicling machines. It becomes a social group with the capacity and will to synthesize across differences, in the senses both of fragments of the real in the shot/document and different social sectors reachable by means of the mass distributibility of the cinema.

Documentarians have rarely, if ever, believed in "total cinema," as perfect gaze or Ideal Chronicler; and even if those who have treated it as an ideal goal probably assumed its adequacy no more than the historian. From the beginning, Grierson himself invoked aesthetics, and discourses associated with the classic documentary movements of the 1930s often articulated aims on the level of manipulating representational forms. Such concern with "aesthetics" designates a specific area of concern for sociopolitically informed and concerned media specialists. Indeed, that area could just as well serve the general processes of social order that Baudrillard (often wrongly) believes embarrassed by the profusion of indexical images. They need not be embarrassed because they can occupy it as a place wherein the sequence counters dispersive threats from the massive distributibility of indexicalized "realities." On the other hand, there is no epistemological reason that more divisive knowledges, self-defined as oppositional, could not and often do emanate from that place.

The original negative of a shot of John Kennedy in a motorcade is a document of the preexistence of a certain kind of car, a certain location, a certain event. Positive prints made from this negative became indexical documents of that first document, and by this relay stand as documents for the past event for spectators of *JFK: A Time Remembered*. This same element of indexical sign production—that which gives film its force as document—is the technological basis for the mass distributability of film prized or puzzled over by so many social theorists. Thus, the two poles of reproduction of a preexistent real and distributability are difficult to disentangle from one another. But as such different thinkers as Grierson and Baudrillard recognize, these two poles are intricated with a third factor, the cultural and political functioning of elites. Members of such elites may be conceived as a social stratum, whether intellectual or professional, and as sociopolitically oppositional, complicit, and/or even neutral, as can be seen in social theorists such as Gramsci and Mannheim, to name only two. But the task of such social strata with respect to the poles of media reproduction is not just re-presenting the real in ways that might be culturally guaranteed by an indexical technology, but with constructing and organizing it. In film and television, this is inseparable from general meanings grounding the temporal organizing of shots as sequence.

So when Bill Ryan explained the suddenly deconventionalized jerkiness of the camera in the real at the moment of the Kennedy assassination, he was only doing his job, restoring meaning to an extreme form of document. He began the process of converting document into documentary. In doing so, he asserted his social position as synthesizer of reality against the unmediated, unorganized index. Baudrillard's polemic, considered simply as a description of contemporary culture, misses the pervasiveness, the pull of the documentary, and, implicitly but consistently, avoids the sociocultural persistence of modern historiography in relation to power. Histories are still being written, and the historiographic consciousness continues to appeal to meaning in the real from the document. Postmodernist theory, analysis, and artistic practice are constantly reminding us that there have been significant changes in the balance between document and sequence. But however much the fragmentary and often ephemeral experience of representation in contemporary culture is emphasized, it is not at all clear that a shift in the *norm* of the sequence so radical as to disrupt the fundamental structure of ordering the real on general and synthetic principles has been achieved. The conclusion, then, is not a defense of Griersonianism, but rather its intellectual contextualization and a recognition of the arena it marked out with the term documentary cinema. With a number of important differences, this arena now extends to television and video. Bill Ryan's position, function, and task remain central to conceiving of the documentary mode, its history, and its import. And the profusion of indexical signs may make the documentary mode and the historicity it embodies not less but more pertinent to understanding contemporary culture and politics.

5

The Totalizing Quest of Meaning*

Trinh T. Minh-ha

There is no such thing as documentary—whether the term designates a category of material, a genre, an approach, or a set of techniques. This assertion—as old and as fundamental as the antagonism between names and reality—needs incessantly to be restated despite the very visible existence of a documentary tradition. In film, such a tradition, far from undergoing a crisis today, is likely to fortify itself through its very recurrence of declines and rebirths. The narratives that attempt to unify/purify its practices by positing evolution and continuity from one period to the next are numerous indeed, relying heavily on traditional historicist concepts of periodization.

Nothing is poorer than a truth expressed as it was thought.
Walter Benjamin[1]

In a completely catalogued world, cinema is often reified into a corpus of traditions. Its knowledge can constitute its destruction, unless the game keeps on changing its rules, never convinced of its closures, and always eager to outplay itself in its own principles. On the one hand, truth is produced, induced, and extended according to the regime in power. On the other, truth lies in between all regimes of truth. As the fable goes, What I Tell You Three Times Is True. To question the image of a historicist account of documentary as a continuous unfolding does not necessarily

* A shorter version of this article has been published as "Documentary Is/Not A Name," *October*, No. 52 (Summer 1990): 76–98. This chapter reprinted from Trinh T. Minh-ha, *When the Moon Waxes Red: Representation, Gender, and Cultural Politics* (New York: Routledge, 1991), pp. 29–50.

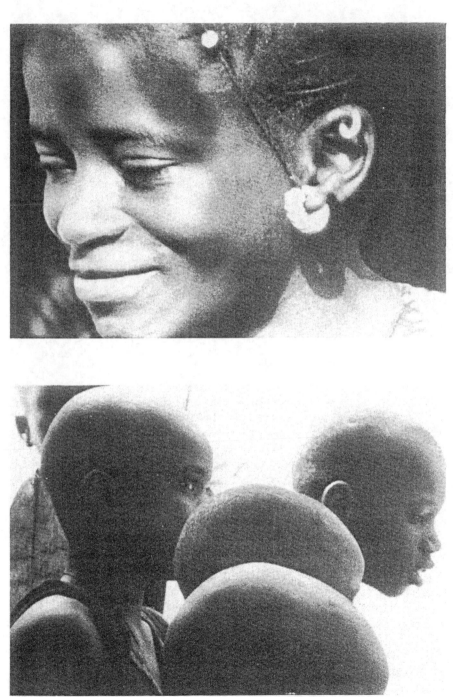

Reassemblage, 1982, by Trinh T. Minh-Ha, 40-min color film.

mean championing discontinuity; and to resist meaning does not necessarily lead to its mere denial. Truth, even when "caught on the run," does not yield itself either in names or in (filmic) frames; and meaning should be prevented from coming to closure at what is said and what is shown. Truth and meaning: the two are likely to be equated with one another. Yet, what is put forth as truth is often nothing more than *a* meaning. And what persists between the meaning of something and its truth is the interval, a break without which meaning would be fixed and truth congealed. This is perhaps why it is so difficult to talk about it, the interval. About the cinema. About. The words will not ring true. Not true, for what is one to do with films which set out to determine truth from falsity while the visibility of this truth lies precisely in the fact that it is false? How is one to cope with a "film theory" that can never theorize "about" film, but only *with* concepts that film raises in relation to concepts of other practices?

> *A man went to a Taoist temple and asked that his fortune be told.* *"First," said the priest, "you must donate incense money, otherwise the divination might not be as accurate as possible. Without such a donation, in fact, none of it will come true!"*
> "The Words Will Not Ring True,"
> *Wit and Humor from Old Cathay*[2]

Concepts are no less practical than images or sound. But the link between the name and what is named is conventional, not phenomenal. Producing film theory (or rather, philosophizing with film), which is not making films, is also a practice—a related but different practice—for theory does have to be (de)constructed as it (de)construes its object of study. Whereas concepts of cinema are not ready-mades and do not preexist in cinema, they are not theory *about* cinema either. The setting up of practice against theory, and vice versa, is at best a tool for reciprocal challenge, but like all binary oppositions, it is caught in the net of positivist thinking whose impetus is to supply answers at all costs, thereby limiting both theory and practice to a process of totalization. *I'm sorry, if we're going to use words we should be accurate in our use of them, It isn't a question of technique, it is a question of the material. If the material is actual, then it is documentary. If the material is invented, then it is not documentary. . . . If you get so muddled up in your use of the term, stop using it. Just talk about films. Anyway, very often when we use these terms, they only give us an opportunity to avoid really discussing the film* (Lindsay Anderson).[3]

In the general effort to analyze film and to produce "theory about film," there is an unavoidable tendency to reduce film theory to an area of specialization and of expertise, one that serves to constitute a *discipline*. There is also advocacy of an Enlightenment and "bourgeois" conception of language, which holds that the means of communication is the word, its object factual, its addressee a human subject (the linear, hierarchical order of things in a world of reification)—whereas, language as the "medium" of communication in its most radical sense, "only communicates itself *in* itself."[4] The referential function of language is thus not negated, but freed from its false identification with the phenomenal world and from its assumed authority as a means of cognition about that world. Theory can be the very place where this negative knowledge about the reliability of theory's own operative principles is made accessible, and where theoretical categories like all classificatory schemes keep on being voided, rather than appropriated, reiterated, safeguarded.

How true is the film theorist's divination? As Sor Juana Ines de la Cruz (a name among many others) would probably defend in her devalued status as a woman in the Church, "true" knowledge has to be separated from its instrumental use.[5] The link between money and fact surfaces in the very instances where it either goes unacknowledged or is adamantly denied. The question of quality in accuracy and truth seems to depend largely on the weight or on the quantity of donation money—incense money, as the priest specifies. Indeed, some of the questions invariably burned in film public debates with the filmmaker are: What's the shooting ratio? What's the budget? How long did it take you to complete the film? The higher the bet, the better the product; the larger the amount of money involved, the more valuable the film, the more believable the truth it holds out. The longer the time spent, the more prized the experience, the more reliable the information. Filmwork is made a *de facto* "low-budget" or "big-budget" product. This is what one constantly hears and has come to say it oneself. "Low-tech," "high-tech," "high-class junk," "low-grade footage." Pressure, money, bigness does it all. . . . The widespread slogan in factual and "alternative" realms may claim "the larger the grain, the better the politics," but what exclusively circulates in mass-media culture is undoubtedly, the money image. Money as money and money as capital are often spoken of as one, not two. The problem of financial constraints is, however, not only a problem of money but also one of control and standardization of images and sounds. Which truth? Whose truth? How true? (Andy Warhol's renowned statement rings very true: "Buying is much more American than thinking.") In the name of public service and of mass communication, the money-making or, rather, money-subjected eye remains glued to the permanent scenario of the effect- and/or production-valued image.

Documentary is said to have come about as a need to inform the people (Dziga Vertov's *Kino-Pravda* or *Camera-Truth*), and subsequently to have affirmed itself as a reaction against the monopoly that the movie as entertainment came to have on the uses of film. Cinema was redefined as an ideal medium for social indoctrination and comment, whose virtues lay in its capacity for "observing and selecting from life itself," for "opening up the screen on the real world," for photographing "the living scene and the living story," for giving cinema "power over a million and one images," as well as for achieving "an intimacy of knowledge and effect impossible to the shimsham mechanics of the studio and the lily-fingered interpretation of the metropolitan actor" (John Grierson).[6] Asserting its independence from the studio and the star system, documentary has its *raison d'être* in a strategic distinction. It puts the social function of film *on the market*. It takes real people and real problems from the real world and *deals with* them. It *sets a value* on intimate observation and *assesses its worth* according to how well it succeeds in capturing reality on the run, "without material interference, without intermediary." Powerful living stories, infinite authentic situations. There are no retakes. The stage is thus no more no less than life itself. *With the documentary approach the film gets back to its fundamentals. . . . By selection, elimination and coordination of natural elements, a film form evolves which is original and not bound by theatrical or literary tradition. . . . The documentary film is an original art form. It has come to grips with facts—on its own original level. It covers the rational side of our lives, from the scientific experiment to the poetic landscape-study, but never moves away from the factual* (Hans Richter).[7]

The real world: so real that the Real becomes the one basic referent— pure, concrete, fixed, visible, all-too-visible. The result is the elaboration of a whole aesthetic of objectivity and the development of comprehensive technologies of truth capable of promoting what is right and what is wrong in the world, and by extension, what is "honest" and what is "manipulative" in documentary. This involves an extensive and relentless pursuit of naturalism across all the elements of cinematic technology. Indispensable to this cinema of the authentic image and spoken word are, for example, the directional microphone (localizing and restricting in its process of selecting sound for purposes of decipherability) and the Nagra portable tape recorder (unrivaled for its maximally faithful ability to document). Lip-synchronous sound is validated as the norm; it is a "must"; not so much in replicating reality (this much has been acknowledged among the fact-makers) as in "showing real people in real locations at real tasks." (Even nonsync sounds that are recorded in-context are considered "less authentic" because the technique of sound synchronization and its institutionalized use have become "nature" within film culture.) Real time is thought to be more "truthful" than filmic time; hence the long take (that is, a take lasting the length of the 400-ft. roll of commercially available film stock) and minimal or no editing (change at the cutting stage is "trickery," as if montage did not happen at the stages of conception and shooting) are declared to be more appropriate if one is to avoid distortions in structuring the material. The camera is the switch onto life. Accordingly, the close-up is condemned for its partiality, whereas the wide angle is claimed to be more objective because it includes more in the frame, hence it can mirror more faithfully the event-in-context. (The more, the larger, the truer—as if wider framing is less a framing than tighter shots.) The lightweight, handheld camera, with its independence of the tripod— the fixed observation post—is extolled for its ability "to go unnoticed," because it must be at once mobile and invisible, integrated into the milieu so as to change as little as possible, but also able to put its intrusion to use and provoke people into uttering the "truth" that they would not otherwise unveil in ordinary situations.

Thousands of bunglers have made the word [documentary] come to mean a deadly, routine form of film-making, the kind an alienated consumer society might appear to deserve—the art of talking a great deal during a film, with a commentary imposed from the outside, in order to say nothing, and to show nothing (Louis Marcorelles).[8] The event itself. Only the event; unaffected, unregulated by the eye recording it and the eye watching it. The perfectly objective social observer may no longer stand as the cherished model among documentary-makers today, but with every broadcast the viewer, Everyman, continues to be taught that He is first and foremost a Spectator. Either one is not responsible for what one sees (because only the event presented to him counts) or the only way one can have some influence on things is to send in a monetary donation. Thus, though the filmmaker's perception may readily be admitted as being unavoidably personal, the objectiveness of the reality of what is seen and represented remains unchallenged." [*Cinéma-vérité:*] *it would be better to call it cinema-sincerity. . . . That is, that you ask the audience to have confidence in the evidence, to say to the audience, This is what I saw. I didn't fake it, this is what happened. . . . I look at what happened with my subjective eye and this is what I believe took place. . . . It's a question of honesty* (Jean Rouch).[9]

What is presented as evidence remains evidence, whether the observing eye qualifies itself as being subjective or objective. At the core of such a rationale dwells, untouched, the Cartesian division between subject and object which perpetuates a dualistic inside-versus-outside, mind-against-matter view of the world. The emphasis is again laid on the power of film to capture reality "out there" for us "in here." The moment of appropriation and of consumption is either simply ignored or carefully rendered invisible according to the rules of good and bad documentary. The art of talking to say nothing goes hand in hand with the will to say and to say only to confine something in a meaning. Truth has to be made vivid, interesting; it has to be "dramatized" if it is to convince the audience of the evidence, whose "confidence" in it allows truth to take shape. *Documentary—the presentation of actual facts in a way that makes them credible and telling to people at the time* (William Stott).[10]

The real? Or the repeated artificial resurrection of the real, an operation whose overpowering success in substituting the visual and verbal signs of the real for the real itself ultimately helps to challenge the real, thereby intensifying the uncertainties engendered by any clear-cut division between the two. In the scale of what is more and what is less real, subject matter is of primary importance ("It is very difficult if not impossible," says a film festival administrator, "to ask jurors of the documentary film category panel not to identify the quality of a film with the subject it treats.") The focus is undeniably on common experience, by which the "social" is defined: an experience that features, as a famed documentary-maker (Pierre Perrault) put it (paternalistically), "man, simple man, who has never expressed himself."[11]

The socially oriented filmmaker is thus the almighty voice-giver (here, in a vocalizing context that is all male), whose position of authority in the production of meaning continues to go unchallenged, skillfully masked as it is by its righteous mission. The relationship between mediator and medium or, the mediating activity, is either ignored—that is, assumed to be transparent, as value free and as insentient as an instrument of reproduction ought to be—or else, it is treated most conveniently: by humanizing the gathering of evidence so as to further the status quo. (Of course, like all human beings I am subjective, but nonetheless, you should have confidence in the evidence!) Good documentaries are those whose subject matter is "correct" and with whose point of view the viewer agrees. What is involved may be a question of honesty (vis-à-vis the material), but it is often also a question of (ideological) adherence, hence of legitimization.

Films made about the common people are furthermore naturally promoted as films made for the same people, and only for them. In the desire to service the needs of the unexpressed, there is, commonly enough, the urge to define them and their needs. More often than not, for example, when filmmakers find themselves in debates in which a film is criticized for its simplistic and reductive treatment of a subject, resulting in a maintenance of the very status quo which it sets out to challenge, their tendency is to dismiss the criticism by claiming that the film is not made for "sophisticated viewers like ourselves, but for a general audience," thereby situating themselves above and apart from the *real* audience, those "out there," the undoubtedly simple-minded folks who need everything they see explained to them. Despite the shift of emphasis—from the world of the upwardly mobile and the very affluent that dominates the media to that of "their poor"—what is maintained intact is the age-old opposition between the creative intelligent supplier and the mediocre unenlightened consumer. The pretext for perpetuating such a division is the belief that social relations are determinate, hence endowed with objectivity. By *"impossibility of the social" I understand . . . the assertion of the ultimate impossibility of all "objectivity" . . . society presents itself, to a great degree, not as an objective, harmonic order, but as an ensemble of divergent forces which do not seem to obey any unified or unifying logic. How can this experience of the failure of objectivity be made compatible with the affirmation of an ultimate objectivity of the real?* (Ernesto Laclau).[12]

The silent common people—those who "have never expressed themselves" unless they are given the opportunity to voice their thoughts by the one who comes to redeem them—are constantly summoned to signify the real world. They are the fundamental referent of the social; hence, it suffices to point the camera at them, to show their (industrialized) poverty, or to contextualize and package their unfamiliar life-styles for the ever-buying and donating general audience "back here," in order to enter the sanctified realm of the morally right, or the social. In other words, when the so-called "social" reigns, how these people(/we) come to visibility in the media, how meaning is given to their(/our) lives, how their(/our) truth is construed or how truth is laid down for them(/us) and despite them(/us), how representation relates to or *is* ideology, how media hegemony continues its relentless course is simply not at issue.

> *There isn't any* cinéma-vérité. *It's necessarily a lie, from the moment the director intervenes—or it isn't cinema at all.* (George Franju)[13]

When the social is hypostatized and enshrined as an ideal of transparency, when it itself becomes commodified in a form of sheer administration (better service, better control), the interval between the real and the image(d) or between the real and the rational shrinks to the point of unreality. Thus, to address the question of production relations as raised earlier is endlessly to reopen the question: How is the real (or the social ideal of good representation) produced? Rather than catering to it, striving to capture and discover its truth as a concealed or lost object, it is therefore important also to keep on asking: How is truth being ruled? *The penalty of realism is that it is about reality and has to bother for ever not about being "beautiful" but about being right* (John Grierson).[14] The fathers of documentary have initially insisted that documentary is not News, but Art (a "new and vital art form" as Grierson once proclaimed). That its essence is not information (as with "the hundreds of tweedle-dum 'industrials' or worker-education films"); not reportage; not newsreels; but something close to "a creative treatment of actuality" (Grierson's renowned definition). *If Joris Ivens has made the most beautiful documentaries that anyone has ever seen, that's because the films are composed, worked out, and they have an air of truth. Sure the documentary part is true, but all around the documentary sections there's an interpretation. And then you can't talk about cinéma-vérité* (Georges Franju).[15]

Documentary may be anti-aesthetic, as some still affirm in the line of the British forerunner, but it is claimed to be no less an art, albeit an art within the limits of factuality. (Interpretation, for example, is not viewed as constituting the very process of documenting and making information accessible; it is thought, instead, to be the margin all around an untouched *given* center, which according to Franju is the "documentary part" or "documentary section.") When, in a world of reification, truth is widely equated with fact, any explicit use of the magic, poetic, or irrational qualities specific to the film medium itself would have to be excluded *a priori* as nonfactual. The question is not so much one of sorting out— illusory as this may be—what is inherently factual and what is not, in a body of *preexisting* filmic techniques, as it is one of abiding by the conventions of naturalism in film. In the reality of formula-films, only validated techniques are *right*, others are *de facto* wrong. The criteria are all based on their degree of invisibility in producing meaning. Thus, shooting at any speed other than the standard 24 frames per second (the speed necessitated for lip-sync sound) is, for example, often condemned as a form of manipulation, implying thereby that manipulativeness has to be discreet—that is, acceptable only when not easily perceptible to the "real audience." Although the whole of filmmaking *is* a question of manipulation—whether "creative" or not—again, those endorsing the law unhesitantly decree which technique is manipulative and which, supposedly, is not; and this judgment is certainly made according to the degree of visibility of each. *A documentary film is shot with three cameras: 1) the camera in the technical sense; 2) the filmmaker's mind; and 3) the generic patterns of the documentary film, which are founded on the expectations of the audience that patronizes it. For this reason one cannot simply say that the documentary film portrays facts. It photographs isolated facts and assembles from them a coherent set of facts according to three divergent schemata. All remaining possible facts and factual contexts are excluded. The naive treatment of documentation therefore provides a unique opportunity to concoct fables. In and of itself, the documentary is no more realistic than the feature film* (Alexander Kluge).[16]

Reality is more fabulous, more maddening, more strangely manipulative than fiction. To understand this is to recognize the naivety of a development of cinematic technology that promotes increasing unmediated "access" to reality. It is to see through the poverty of what Benjamin deplored as "a truth expressed as it was thought" and to understand why progressive fiction films are attracted and constantly pay tribute to documentary techniques. These films put the "documentary effect" to advantage, playing on the viewer's expectation in order to "concoct fables." (Common examples of this effect include: the feeling of participating in a truth-like moment of reality captured despite the filmed subject; the sense of urgency, immediacy, and authenticity in the instability of the handheld camera; the newsreel look of the grainy image; and the oral-testimony-like quality of the direct interview—to mention just a few.)

The documentary can thus easily become a "style": it no longer constitutes a mode of production or an attitude toward life, but proves to be only an element of aesthetics (or anti-aesthetics)—which at best and without acknowledging it, it tends to be in any case when, within its own factual limits, it reduces itself to a mere category, or a set of persuasive techniques. Many of these techniques have become so "natural" to the language of broadcast television today that they "go unnoticed." These are, for example: the "personal testimony" technique (a star appears on screen to advertise his/her use of a certain product); the "plain folks" technique (a politician arranges to eat hot dogs in public); the "band wagon" technique (the use of which conveys the message that "everybody is doing it, why not you?"); or the "card stacking" technique (in which prearrangements for a "survey" shows that a certain brand of product is more popular than any other to the inhabitants of a given area).[17]

You must re-create reality because reality runs away; reality denies reality. You must first interpret it, or re-create it. . . . When I make a documentary, I try to give the realism an artificial aspect. . . . I find that the aesthetic of a document comes from the artificial aspect of the document . . . it has to be more beautiful than realism, and therefore it has to be composed . . . to give it another sense (Franju).[18] A documentary aware of its own artifice is one that remains sensitive to the flow between fact and fiction. It does not work to conceal or exclude what is normalized as "nonfactual," for it understands the mutual dependence of realism and "artificiality" in the process of filmmaking. It recognizes the necessity of composing (on) life in living it or making it. Documentary reduced to a mere vehicle of facts may be used to advocate a cause, but it does not constitute one in itself; hence, the perpetuation of the bipartite system of division in the content-versus-form rationale.

To compose is not always synonymous with ordering-so-as-to-persuade, and to give the filmed document another sense, another meaning, is not necessarily to distort it. If life's paradoxes and complexities are not to be suppressed, the question of degrees and nuances is incessantly crucial. Therefore, meaning can be political only when it does not let itself be easily stabilized and when it does not rely on any single source of authority, but, rather, empties it, or decentralizes it. Thus, even when this source is referred to, it stands as one among many others, at once plural and utterly singular. In its demand to *mean* at any rate, the "documentary" often forgets how it comes about and how aesthetics and politics remain inseparable in its constitution; for, when not equated with mere techniques of beautifying, aesthetics allows one to experience life differently or, as some would say, to give it "another sense," remaining in tune with its drifts and shifts.

> *It must be possible to represent reality as the historical fiction it is. Reality is a paper-tiger. The individual does encounter it, as fate. It is not fate, however, but a creation of the labor of generations of human beings, who all the time wanted and still want something entirely different. In more than one respect, reality is simultaneously real and unreal.* (Alexander Kluge)[19]

From its descriptions to its arrangements and rearrangements, reality on the move may be heightened or impoverished but it is never neutral (that is, objectivist). "Documentary at its purest and most poetic is a form in which the elements that you use are the actual elements"[20] Why, for example, use the qualifying term "artificial" at all? In the process of producing a "document," is there such a thing as an artificial aspect that can be securely separated from the true aspect (except for analytical purpose—that is, for another "artifice" of language)? In other words, is a closer framing of reality more artificial than a wider one? The notion of "making strange" and of reflexivity remains but a mere distancing device as long as the division between "textual artifice" and "social attitude" exerts its power.[21] The "social" continues to go unchallenged, history keeps on being salvaged, while the sovereignty of the socio-historicizing subject is safely maintained. With the status quo of the making/consuming subject preserved, the aim is to correct "errors" (the false) and to construct an alternative view (offered as a this-is-the-true or mine-is-truer version of reality). It is, in other words, to replace one source of unacknowledged authority by another, but not to challenge the very constitution of authority. The new sociohistorical text, thus, rules despotically as another master-centered text because it unwittingly helps to perpetuate the Master's ideological stance.

When the textual and the political neither separate themselves from one another nor simply collapse into a single qualifier, the practice of representation can, similarly, neither be taken for granted nor merely dismissed as being ideologically reactionary. By putting representation under scrutiny, textual theory-practice has more likely helped to upset rooted ideologies by bringing the mechanics of their workings to the fore. It makes possible the vital differentiation between authoritative criticism and uncompromising analyses and inquiries (including those of the analyzing/inquiring activity). Moreover, it contributes to the questioning of reformist "alternative" approaches that never quite depart from the lineage of white- and male-centered humanism. Despite their explicit sociopolitical commitment, these approaches remain unthreatening—that is, "framed," and, thus, neither social nor political enough.

Reality runs away, reality denies reality. Filmmaking is after all a question of "framing" reality in its course. However, it can also be the very place where the referential function of the film image/sound is not simply negated, but reflected on in its own operative principles and questioned in its authoritative identification with the phenomenal world. In attempts at suppressing the mediation of the cinematic apparatus and the fact that language "communicates itself in itself," there always lurks what Benjamin qualified as a "bourgeois" conception of language. *Any revolutionary strategy must challenge the depiction of reality . . . so that a break between ideology and text is effected* (Claire Johnston).[22]

To deny the *reality* of film in claiming (to capture) *reality* is to stay "in ideology"—that is, to indulge in the (deliberate or not) confusion of filmic with phenomenal reality. By condemning self-reflexivity as pure formalism instead of challenging its diverse realizations, this ideology can "go on unnoticed," keeping its operations invisible and serving the goal of universal expansionism. Such aversion for self-reflexivity goes hand in hand with its widespread appropriation as a progressive formalistic device in cinema because both work to reduce its function to a harmlessly decorative one. (For example, it has become commonplace to hear such remarks as "A film is a film" or "This is a film about a film." Film-on-film statements are increasingly challenging to work with as they can easily fall prey to their own formulas and techniques.) Furthermore, reflexivity, at times equated with personal view, is at other times endorsed as scientific rigor.

> *Two men were discussing the joint production of wine. One said to the other: "You shall supply the rice and I the water." The second asked: "If all the rice comes from me, how shall we apportion the finished product?" The first man replied: "I shall be absolutely fair about the whole thing. When the wine is finished, each gets back exactly what he puts in—I'll siphon off the liquid and you can keep the rest."*
>
> "Joint Production,"
> *Wit and Humor from Old Cathay*[23]

One of the areas of documentary that remains most resistant to the reality of film as film is that known as anthropological filmmaking. Filmed ethnographic material, which was thought to "replicate natural perception," has now renounced its authority to replicate only to purport to provide adequate "data" for the "sampling" of culture. The claim to objectivity may no longer stand in many anthropological circles, but its authority is likely to be replaced by the sacrosanct notion of the "scientific." Thus, the recording and gathering of data and of people's testimonies are considered to be the limited aim of "ethnographic film." What makes a film anthropological and what makes it scientific is, tautologically enough, its "scholarly endeavour [to] respectively document and interpret according to anthropological standards."[24] Not merely ethnographic nor documentary, the definition positively specifies, but scholarly and anthropologically. The fundamental scientific obsession is present in every attempt to demarcate anthropology's territories. To be scientifically valid, a film needs the scientific intervention of the anthropologist, for it is only by adhering to the body of conventions set up by the community of anthropologists accredited by their "discipline" that the film can hope to qualify for the classification and be passed as a "scholarly endeavor."

The myth of science impresses us. But do not confuse science with its scholasticism. Science finds no truths, either mathematized or formalized; it discovers unknown facts that can be interpreted in a thousand ways (Paul Veyne).[25] One of the familiar arguments given by anthropologists to validate the prescriptively instrumental use of film and of people is to dismiss all works by filmmakers who are "not professional anthropologists" or "amateur ethnographers" under the pretext that they are not "anthropologically informed," hence they have "no theoretical significance from an anthropological point of view." To advance such a blatantly self-promoting rationale to institute *a deadly routine form of filmmaking* (to quote a sentence of Marcorelles once more) is also—through anthropology's primary task of "collecting data" for knowledge of mankind—to try to skirt what is known as the salvage paradigm and the issues implicated in the "scientific" deployment of Western world ownership.[26] The stronger anthropology's insecurity about its own project, the greater its eagerness to hold up a normative model, and the more seemingly serene its disposition to dwell in its own blind spots.

In the sanctified terrain of anthropology, all of filmmaking is reduced to a question of methodology. It is demonstrated that the reason anthropological films go further than ethnographic films is because they do not, for example, just show activities being performed, but they also *explain* the "anthropological significance" of these activities (significance that, despite the disciplinary qualifier "anthropological," is *de facto* identified with the meaning the natives give them themselves). Now, obviously, in the process of fixing meaning, not every explanation is valid. This is where the role of the expert anthropologist comes in and where methodologies need to be devised, legitimated, and enforced. For, if a nonprofessional explanation is dismissed here, it is not so much because it lacks insight or theoretical grounding, as because it escapes anthropological control; it lacks the seal of approval from the anthropological order. In the name of science, a distinction is made between reliable and nonreliable information. Anthropological and nonanthropological explanations may share the same subject matter, but they differ in the way they produce meaning. The unreliable constructs are the ones that do not obey the rules of anthropological authority, which a concerned expert like Evans-Pritchard skillfully specifies as being nothing else but "a scientific habit of mind."[27] Science defined as the most appropriate approach to the object of investigation serves as a banner for every scientific attempt to promote the West's paternalistic role as subject of knowledge and its historicity of the Same. *The West agrees with us today that the way to Truth passes by numerous paths, other than Aristotelian Thomistic logic or Hegelian dialectic. But social and human sciences themselves must be decolonized* (E. Mveng).[28]

In its scientistic "quest to make meaning," anthropology constantly reactivates the power relations embedded in the Master's confident discourses on Himself and His Other, thereby aiding both the *centri*petal and *centri*fugal movement of their global spread. With the diverse challenges issued today to the very process of producing "scientific" interpretation of culture as well as to that of making anthropological knowledge possible, visually oriented members of its community have come up with an epistemological position in which the notion of reflexivity is typically reduced to a question of technique and method. Equated with a form of self-exposure common in field work, it is discussed at times as *self-reflectivity* and at other times condemned as individualistic idealism sorely in need of being controlled if the individual maker is not to loom larger than the scientific community or the people observed. Thus, "being reflexive is virtually synonymous with being scientific."[29]

The reasons justifying such a statement are many, but one that can be read through it and despite it is: as long as the maker abides by a series of "reflexive" techniques in filmmaking that are devised for the purpose of exposing the "context" of production and as long as the required techniques are method(olog)ically carried out, the maker can be assured that "reflexivity" is elevated to that status of scientific rigor. These reflexive techniques would include the insertion of a verbal or visual narrative about the anthropologist, the methodology adopted, and the condition of production—in other words, all the conventional means of validating an anthropological text through the disciplinary practice of head-and footnoting and the totalistic concept of preproduction presentation. Those who reject such a rationale do so out of a preoccupation with the "community of scientists," whose collective judgment they feel should be the only true form of reflection; for an individual validation of a work can only be suspicious because it "ignores the historical development of science." In these constant attempts at enforcing anthropology as (a) discipline and at recentering the dominant representation of culture (despite all the changes in methodologies), what seems to be oddly suppressed in the notion of reflexivity in filmmaking is its practice as processes to prevent meaning from ending with what is said and what is shown—as inquiries into production relations—thereby to challenge representation itself while emphasizing the reality of the experience of film as well as the important role that reality plays in the lives of the spectators.

> *Unless an image displaces itself from its natural state, it acquires no significance. Displacement causes resonance* (Shanta Gokhale).[30]

> *After his voluntary surrender, Zheng Guang, a pirate operating off the coast of Fujian, was to be given an official post (in return for surrendering). When a superior instructed him to write a poem, Zheng replied with a doggerel: "No matter whether they are civil or military officials they are all the same. The officials assumed their posts before becoming thieves, but I, Zheng Guang, was a thief before becoming an official."*
>
> "The Significance of Officialdom,"
> *Wit and Humor from Old Cathay*[31]

As an aesthetic closure or an old relativizing gambit in the process nonetheless of absolutizing meaning, reflexivity proves critically in/significant when it merely serves to refine and to further the accumulation of knowledge. No going beyond, no elsewhere-within-here seems possible if the reflection on oneself is not at one and the same time the analysis of established forms of the social that define one's limits. Thus, to drive the self into an abyss is neither a moralistic stricture against oneself (for future improvement) nor a task of critique that humanizes the decoding self but never challenges the very notion of self and decoder. Left intact in its positionality and its fundamental urge to decree meaning, the self conceived both as key and as transparent mediator is more often than not likely to turn responsibility into license. The license to *name*, as though meaning presented itself to be deciphered without any ideological mediation. As though specifying a context can only result in the finalizing of what is shown and said. As though naming can stop the process of naming—that very abyss of the relation of self to self.

The bringing of the self into play necessarily exceeds the concern for human errors, for it cannot but involve as well the problem inherent in representation and communication. Radically plural in its scope, reflexivity is, thus, not a mere question of *rect*ifying and *just*ifying (*subject*ivizing.) What is set in motion in its praxis are the self-generating links between different forms of reflexivity. Thus, a subject who points to him/her/itself as subject-in-process, a work that displays its own formal properties or its own constitution as work, is bound to upset one's sense of identity—the familiar distinction between the Same and the Other because the latter is no longer kept in a recognizable relation of dependence, derivation, or appropriation. The process of self-constitution is also that in which the self vacillates and loses its assurance. The paradox of such a process lies in its fundamental instability; an instability that brings forth the disorder inherent to every order. The "core" of representation is the reflexive interval. It is the place in which the play within the textual frame is a play on this very frame, hence on the borderlines of the textual and extratextual, where a positioning within constantly incurs the risk of depositioning, and where the work, never freed from historical and sociopolitical contexts nor entirely subjected to them, can only be itself by constantly risking being no-thing.

A work that reflects back on itself offers itself infinitely as nothing else but work . . . *and* void. Its gaze is at once an impulse that causes the work to fall apart (to return to the initial no-work-ness) and an ultimate gift to its constitution; a gift, by which the work is freed from the tyranny of meaning as well as from the omnipresence of a subject of meaning. To let go of the hold at the very moment when it is at its most effective is to allow the work to live, and to live on independently of the intended links, communicating itself in itself like Benjamin's "the self is a text"—no more no less "a project to be built."[32] *Orpheus' gaze . . . is the impulse of desire which shatters the song's destiny and concern, and in that inspired and unconcerned decision reaches the origin, consecrates the song* (Maurice Blanchot).[33]

Meaning can neither be imposed nor denied. Although every film is in itself a form of ordering and closing, each closure can defy its only closure, opening onto other closures, thereby emphasizing the interval between apertures and creating a space in which meaning remains fascinated by what escapes and exceeds it. The necessity to let go of the notion of intentionality that dominates the question of the "social" as well as that of creativity cannot, therefore, be confused with the ideal of non-intervention, an ideal in relation to which the filmmaker, trying to become as invisible as possible in the process of producing meaning, promotes empathic subjectivity at the expense of critical inquiry even when the intention is to show and to condemn oppression. *It is idealist mystification to believe*

Surname Viet Given Name Nam, 1989, by Trinh T. Minh-Ha, 108-min color and black and white film.

that "*truth*" *can be captured by the camera or that the conditions of a film's production (e.g., a film made collectively by women) can of itself reflect the conditions of its production. This is mere utopianism: new meaning has to* be manufactured *within the text of the film.* . . . *What the camera in fact grasps is the "natural" world of the dominant ideology* (Claire Johnston).[34]

In the quest for totalized meaning and for knowledge-for-knowledge's sake, the worst meaning is meaninglessness. A Caucasian missionary nun based in a remote village of Africa qualifies her task in these simple, confident terms: "We are here to help people give meaning to their lives." Ownership is monotonously circular in its give-and-take demands. It is a monolithic view of the world whose irrationality expresses itself in the imperative of both giving and meaning, and whose irreality manifests itself in the need to require that visual and verbal constructs yield meaning down to their last detail. *The West moistens everything with meaning, like an authoritarian religion which imposes baptism on entire peoples* (Roland Barthes).[35] Yet such illusion is real; it has its own reality, one in which the subject of Knowledge, the subject of Vision, or the subject of Meaning continues to deploy established power relations, assuming Himself to be the basic reserve of reference in the totalistic quest for the referent, the true referent that lies out there in nature, in the dark, waiting patiently to be unveiled and deciphered correctly: To be redeemed. Perhaps then, an imagination that goes toward the texture of reality is one capable of playing upon the illusion in question and the power it exerts. The production of one irreality on the other and the play of nonsense (which is not mere meaninglessness) upon meaning may, therefore, help to relieve the basic referent of its occupation, for the present situation of critical inquiry seems much less one of attacking the illusion of reality as one of displacing and emptying out the establishment of totality.

6

Jargons of Authenticity
(Three American Moments)

Paul Arthur

By now it is, or should be, standard wisdom that documentaries and Hollywood narratives do not issue from separate and pristine worlds but have over the course of their histories maintained a tangled reciprocity—by turns technological, thematic, political—in which each has, in part, defined its purview through cultural myths of what the other is not.[1] Predictably, the results of this interpenetration have historically been neither constant nor symmetrical. Whether approached as cohesive movements, as nexuses of formal practice, ideological weapons, or vehicles of the status quo, American documentaries have never marshalled a serious challenge to the hegemony of fiction film in the representation of social reality. And this is so despite the demonstrable status of nonfiction genres in popular literature and television.

However, two prominent moments of documentary production—New Deal sponsorship in the late thirties and the surge of cinema verité-activated theatrical features in the late sixties—exhibit features crucial to any popular contestation of the regime of studio fiction.[2] The unexpected notoriety around a cluster of nonfiction films released in the last few years provides an occasion to reexamine consistent dynamics in documentary's desultory vision of mainstream intervention and the claims of heightened epistemic authority which undergird that vision.[3] If the territory consigned to documentary historiography has often resembled a frozen tundra, the search for *noncontingent* templates is a project akin to Nanook's igloo: a half-built shelter maintaining the illusion of closure yet exposed to all the elements.

A number of factors tend to converge during documentary's interludes of high visibility. Technological breakthroughs such as sound recording or the lightweight sync-sound rig open production processes to new representational options. Reception garnered by individual films—*The River* (1937), *Monterey Pop* (1967), *Roger and Me* (1989)—stimulate public interest and with it a climate for viable distribution. There is as well the cyclical revival of debate over the moral probity of dominant film practices, their escapism or sensationalism or "irrelevance" to glaring social problems. At the height of the Depression, in the cauldron of late sixties' rebellion, and in the throes of Reagan's disastrous economic policies, journalistic assaults on Hollywood's irresponsibility have directed normally myopic media attention to nonfiction's promise of greater verisimilitude.[4] This translates into the traditional notion that documentary flourishes in the midst of crisis. The crisis scenario, however, must be ballasted by recognition that moments of prominence are also co-extensive with major consolidations in the motion picture industries. Social documentaries of the 1930s developed within and against the growing strength of Hollywood's major studio monopolies. Direct cinema and its theatrical offshoots emerged with the sovereignty of prime-time television, while the recent wave of documentary releases follows the precipitous rise of home video and cable TV and is contemporaneous with an onslaught of "reality-based" programming.[5] In each case, transient cultural leverage has been fueled by, and in turn amplifies, other nonfiction discourses found in literary, art, theatrical, advertising, and other arenas.

This chapter is concerned with several interlocking elements of mainstream documentary as situated at particular historical junctures: the formal embedding of truth claims, guarantees of authenticity, and hierarchies of knowledge; the imaging or textual projection of technology in relation to issues of social power and authority; and the intramural valorization, via allegories of production, of documentary as an alternative and politically progressive cinematic program. My assumption is that regardless of the events or personalities presented, or the ideological forces with which films are aligned—almost exclusively, the undulations of American liberalism—commercial documentaries enact polemical dialogues both with previous nonfiction styles and with reigning codes of dominant cinema. Further, succeeding styles tend to repudiate the methods of earlier periods from the same perspective of realist epistemology attending the nineteenth-century bourgeois novel's "attempt to use language to get beyond language," the absolute desire to discover a truth untainted by institutional forms of rhetoric.[6] Or as Brian Winston suggests of the cinematic conventions inevitably arising from this effort: "The need for structure implicitly contradicts the notion of unstructured reality" and documentary movements are sustained by "ignoring" this contradiction.[7] Each new contender will generate recognizable, perhaps even self-conscious, figures through which to signify the spontaneous, the anticonventional, the refusal of mediating process

Analyzing structures and visual patterns in New Deal and direct cinema documentaries requires that certain established critical axioms be jettisoned; principally, that films of the thirties offer a totally unproblematized declaration of authority—textual as well as social—and that direct cinema, since it expunges any hint of "metaphor and pattern,"[8] is uniquely and universally descriptive (rather than prescriptive). Against this backdrop, recent works can be construed as acknowledging false claims implicit in earlier styles while fashioning determinate conventions under a contemporary rubric of decentered subjectivity and the inadequacy of cinema's cognitive tools.

Pluralism, Technocracy, and Naturalization

Who shall be master, things or men?

The City

Technics can by itself promote authoritarianism as well as liberty, scarcity as well as abundance, the extension as well as the abolition of toil.

Herbert Marcuse[9]

Freighted with unprecedented cultural significance, *The Plow That Broke the Plains* (1936), *The River, The City* (1939), and a few other sponsored documentaries were honed by the imperatives of two historical conditions: widespread mobilization of nonfiction practices as instruments in the expression and propagation of liberal democratic social philosophy; and the increased validity of nonfiction production under terms of economic scarcity. Like its European counterparts, American social documentaries conspired in a public belief that it was advantageous to address pressing needs through a discourse purporting to offer the highest quotient of immediacy, responsiveness, clarity, and verisimilitude. Such epithets were commonly ascribed by politicians and journalists to a variety of remedial government activities from FDR's "Fireside Chats" to the WPA State Guides. Similar virtues were located in the popular reception of radio, weekly news magazines, political theater as "living newspaper," and the first versions of public opinion polls.

The embodiment of approved *political* values as properties of filmic structure and iconography directs an understanding of how this truncated film movement served as an armature of New Deal policy and ideological contestation while advancing a heuristic model of progressive cinema. An initial strategy can be referred to as stylistic fragmentation and multiplicity, a concatenation of discrete segments containing disparate visual and aural cues yet bracketed by a unifying theme and narrational logic. *The City* is the most conspicuous example although *The River* marks a similar preference for mixed materials; for instance, the sandwiching of original footage with maps, archival shots, intertitles, and other graphics presented over a soundtrack combining original music and voice-overs with diegetic voices or sound effects. The division in *The City* into semiautonomous sections has prompted critiques that cite a "crucial weakness [in] placement and tone."[10] In this view, the film loses focus and sacrifices potency due to insufficient structural balance, stylistic unity, or transparency. Its claims to truth, therefore, are vitiated.

The problem with this reproach is it discounts the role of aesthetic alterity in establishing preeminence over competing modes of realism. A brief gloss of *The City*'s ordering principles confirms the impression of disparity as it invites other possible readings. Sections vary in length from 2 minutes to over 15 minutes. Visually, the opening "Colonial" sequence is characterized by static long shots, even lighting, lyrical tracking, and panning movements and circular object motifs. By contrast, the "megalopolis" section features jarring rhythmic montage, extreme camera angles, dislocations of scale, and the absence of eyeline matches. The concluding "Green Belt" section employs narrativized editing of action, a profusion of centered medium shots, and wipes and other soft transitions. In addition, the music track, while developing a consistent set of melodic phrases and

The City (1939).

The City (1939).

motifs, dominates during the "megalopolis" section but retreats to the background in favor of spoken narration for the "Green Belt" segment. The voice-over itself frequently shifts in tone, tense, and mode of address, juxtaposing a hortatory second-person with first- and third-person plural comments.

The polemical thrust of successive tropes is readily apparent. Depersonalization in the metropolis is figured as a disorienting clash of graphic elements, whereas the humanizing appeal of the planned community is reified in familiar Hollywood conventions of spatio-temporal harmony and continuity. The alleviation of urban disorder by social engineering is argued verbally and demonstrated visually. Spoken narration is not the sole or leading repository of the film's "message," as many contend. Visual metaphor and pastiche may prompt abstract ideas not readily conveyed by verbal speech while serving other channels of argumentation. As the reflexive index of a politically ratified method of production, stylistic heterogeneity inscribes a discontinuous, multiple process of creativity onto the film's surface. Shot in different locations by different cameramen, written and edited in successive stages by a loose-knit group—a necessary expedient for documentaries of the period—*The City* invokes, through its structure, a signifier of plural authorship, a trope of individual freedom embedded within a unifying consensus of social directives.

Admittedly, the film's overarching analysis *cum* solution is unfrayed by this symbolic plurality. Yet the lodging of presentational authority in a fore-grounded play of difference metaphorically links the process of produc-tion—and by extension that of viewing—to the social remedies proposed. That is, the rationalized urban planning advocated by the film reconstitutes *gemeinschaft* concepts of individual autonomy in contradistinction to then-rampant conservative attacks on the state's purported authoritarian suppres-sion of individual (municipal, state, regional) liberties.

Additionally, the text's refusal to subsume formal gaps and disparities proffers in its historical context a higher guarantee of verisimilitude. As Alfred Kazin remarked of Christopher Isherwood's contemporaneous *Berlin Stories:*

> If the accumulation of visual scenes seemed only a collection of "mutually repellent particles," as Emerson said of his sentences, was not *that* discontinuity, that havoc of pictorial sensations, just the truth of what the documentary mind saw before it in the thirties?[11]

From this perspective, formal elements appear immiscible because they are ordered by external and unmanipulated properties of daily life. Like instances of literary production such as Dos Passos's *U.S.A.* trilogy or the theatrical wave of "living newspapers," *The City* (and to a lesser degree *The River, And So They Live* [1940]) displays heterogeneity and imbalance as realist tropes, as more concerted obeisance to the textures of lived reality, and, in *The City,* as a demonstration of the unequal parameters of urban growth and decay.

Undoubtedly, cinematic provenance for this mixed presentation derives from the newsreel.[12] Despite the newsreel's alliance with conservative Republican politics, its professed spontaneity helped legitimize an essay-like discursivity, lending *The City* a cloak of provisionality and open-endedness belied by the vehemence of its verbal brief. Yet, if social documentaries tapped the well of authenticity inherent in the newsreel tradition, they also maintained a requisite distance from it through the absorption of avant-garde impulses pioneered by Cavalcanti, Ruttmann, Leger, and especially by Soviet cinema. As Grierson himself was quick to note, emphasis on the "creative treatment" of reality works to blunt the charge of propaganda.[13] Truth and Beauty exist in inverse proportion to one another. The former can be signified through a negation of "classical" codes, while the latter acts to counter assertions of political manipulation.

This tightrope of rhetorical artifice and directness toiled to ensure filmic fidelity as well as relative autonomy.

The precedent of Soviet cinema offered other weapons for an aesthetic arsenal. A matter of frequent debate in thirties documentary circles, Soviet films were admired for their experimental rigor and challenged on grounds of political servitude. Along with montage editing and themes such as the mass hero, American documentaries imported for their own purposes the self-conscious thematization of industrial technology exemplified in the work of Dziga Vertov. Given the tenor of New Deal politics, it is no surprise that films uncritically valorized the role of technology in progressive social change: for instance, *The River* espouses benefits of hydroelectric dams, while *Power and the Land* (1940) lobbies for agricultural modernization. Yet, the bureaucratic machinery required to rationally implant and control mechanical devices posed a more serious representational dilemma. Liberal documentaries were faced with the unenviable task of reconciling the idea of centralized government power to viewers fed on obdurate tenets of individualism, free enterprise, and states rights. Patterns of machine imagery took on a pivotal role in this partisan polemic.

With direct support from government agencies or indirect support from liberal foundations, documentaries were virtually obliged to show the historical advance of capitalist technology and the social relations it enforced as a natural process: organic, not simply dependent on but co-extensive with the utilization of natural resources. There is a central myth rehearsed iconographically and augmented by spoken narration that goes something like this. In an Edenic, preindustrialized past there existed a balance between man and nature, between individual and communal sustenance. Without intended malice (to say nothing of class interest), uncontrolled economic growth upset the balance. Although growth is inherently beneficial, a lack of rationalized limits produces aberrations such as floods, ecological pillage, and uninhabitable cities. The founding harmony can be restored by judicious application of technology in federal programs: Good (i.e., natural) tools placed in the hands of benevolent craftsmen.

Marcuse observes—in an essay written just 2 years after *The City* and indebted to that film's philosophical mentor, Louis Mumford:

> Technology, as a mode of production, as the totality of instruments, devices and contrivances which characterize the machine age is thus at the same time a mode of organizing and perpetuating (or changing) social relationships, a manifestation of prevalent thought and behavior patterns, an instrument for control and domination.[14]

Although Marcuse's critique is directed at the technocratic rationalization of fascist regimes, it is equally pertinent to New Deal advocacy of social

The River (1937).

engineering. He defends the concept of a democratically constituted "public bureaucracy," but perceives the danger in policies underwritten by the "natural law" of, say, Frederick Taylor's "scientific" theories of industrial management. Technology can never be merely a neutral (natural) framework of social organization. Simply stated, Marcuse's position is that machines produce or enforce their own debased axioms of human need in social formations that grant them a paramount role in the alleviation of oppression.

Unable or unwilling, due to constraints of sponsorship or mass appeal, to directly confront the contradictions of a capitalist political economy, documentaries visualize *power* as an abstraction. They routinely conflate idealist properties of advanced technology, human and natural resources, and centralized planning. The linchpin in this metaphoric equation is the fusing of technology—as reified image of federal policy—with elements such as water, forestation, crop growth, and other forms of natural productivity. Bureaucratic solutions are thus figured as technological interventions equipped with the stamp of natural process. It takes a river to harness a river. Further, it was ideologically useful to represent liberal remedies as a return to rather than a divergence from a prelapsarian unity of nature, society, and individual. Real and imagined threats to New Deal philosophy by entrenched conservative interests were rhetorically vanquished or deflected through association of the New Deal with a version of history placing it as the culmination of an authentic, innate process.

Urban overcrowding, like the flooding of the Mississippi or the deracination of the environment, are excesses of ineluctable socioeconomic development. Central government acts to refocus not the social ends but the "techniques." If the river of American historical development overflows its banks and creates human misery, then the well-oiled machine of New Deal policy can step in to resolve privation, restore the course. The narrator at the end of *The City* tells us "a different day begins." This new day, the implementation of federal controls, the promise of a New City, is given symbolic expression in images of children at play. The "rebirth" of *gemeinschaft* society is exemplified by kids sliding down a playground chute, an image then compared with the rush of water over a sluice— creating a small visual epiphany melding machine, childhood, and nature. Cities and forces that govern their growth are confected as organic shapes: A small housing tract and an urban street scene are match cut to the vertical profile of forests; the New York skyline is rhymed in a single composition with a field of weeds.[15]

In *The River,* the Roosevelt administration is described implicitly as a formal mirror of the Mississippi, its branches and tributaries stretching across the nation's continental limits, offering cohesion to the disorderly flow of regional and local conflicts. Similarly, in *Power and the Land,* the collective purchase of electrical power through the Rural Electrification Project is analogized to the communal harvesting of crops. Displacing conflict, competition, capitalism's distorted human license onto images of cooperation, sponsored documentaries enlist montage not as the dialectical forum imagined by Soviet filmmakers but as a device for reconciling otherwise troubling discrepancies of wealth and privilege.[16]

A final plank in the documentary agenda ties images of technology to the apparatus of film production via the argument over control of resources.

The narrator of *The City* challenges: "You decide. Both are real, both are possible." We the citizen-viewers can retain the excesses of the present system of fulfilling human needs or choose what is arguably the next historical stage. There the question "Who shall be master, things or men?" generates the answer: "At last man will take over." What is meant by "man" is open to several readings. Given the polemical stance taken against Hollywood by documentarists of the period,[17] the studio system with its assembly-line manufacture and its profit motive are, by implication, aligned with the uncontrolled forces of private industry and urban growth. Given models such as *The Man With the Movie Camera* (1929) and Leger's *Ballet Mecanique* (1924), the identification between machinery and the mechanics of film production is an inclusive means of celebrating the liberatory potential of advanced technology.

If the charge against American capitalism in thirties' documentaries, meager as it is, concerns a lack of regulation, the failure to employ resources to spread enough benefit to enough people, the same complaint was lodged against Hollywood. The era of a variegated market stocked by small corporate competitors was over; the major studios exerted sovereign control through vertical integration, the star system, and streamlined narrative formulas. If documentaries argued the best method for regulating industrial/natural resources—the efflorescence of private capital or federal controls—the same choice might apply to cinema as industry and social institution. Intent on challenging the domination of fiction film and infused with a heady faith in the cinema apparatus as a progressive instrument for change, engaged artists welcomed government and foundation sponsorship as the promise of an alternative system of production. Funding was inadequate and precarious at best; yet by consciously aligning their fate with New Deal policy, filmmakers acted out of both civic responsibility and self-interest. A majority of creative personnel on these films received their training during the early thirties in radical newsreel and agitprop groups such as the Film and Photo League. They had grown disenchanted with limitations on production and distribution and sought a wider audience and a larger aesthetic vehicle through which to participate in the struggle for social change.[18]

Despite justifiable misgivings over sponsorship, liberal-left documentarists hoped to build a "third term" of film production, one which retained the human-scaled collaborative ethos of their former radical projects while enhancing the ability to affect public opinion. The modest popular success of *The River* and *The City* created a tiny aperture through which a challenge to Hollywood's stranglehold could be envisioned. Promotion of New Deal ideology provided a foundation from which to allegorize the role of documentary in a naturalized landscape of cinema.

Performance, Authority, and Direct Cinema

The period is charged with its stupid issuelessness as with an explosive.

Erich Auerbach[19]

Thirty years removed from the Great Depression, a new generation of documentarists forged a loose-knit coalition whose aesthetic philosophy was primed by resistance to the same common enemy, Hollywood, yet was as vehemently opposed to the methods of *The City* and its cohort. An extensive body of interviews conducted in the late sixties and early seventies forms a collective text that remains the best theoretical account of direct cinema. A set of shared assumptions precipitate around issues of technology, immediacy, and mediation; disputes surface over ethical procedures and, particularly, the chimera of objectivity. There is, however, general agreement that New Deal documentaries and films share a premeditated, even authoritarian, vision of social representation that is no longer tenable. The verbal articulation, in Stephen Mamber's phrase, of an "uncontrolled cinema" is rife with a familiar privileging of phenomenal experience over artifice accompanied, as in realist doctrines of the previous century, by abject denials of fixed tropes or rhetorical structuration. Without invoking the spectre of a cinema verité political unconscious, it is possible to locate in the denial of conventionality a textual crisis of authority, a twinned symptom of fulsome speech and reticence, an ambivalence toward what has been called the "documentary voice."[20]

Much has already been written in reproof of the movement's idealist faith in neutral, noninterventionist recording and editorial reconstruction. In its *ad hoc* polemics, an ethical imperative weds the sync-sound rig to an aesthetic of unscripted, handheld long takes ordered solely by response to profilmic "stimuli." Thomas Waugh correctly scores the "fetishization of the image" and suggests it is driven by a "gospel of inarticulacy."[21] Bill Nichols similarly disdains the "magical template of verisimilitude" fashioned to disguise the work of standard continuities and rhetorical effects.[22] Unquestionably, refinements in lightweight camera and sound equipment increased speed, mobility, and representational purview as it simplified the process of production. However, an almost transcendant faith in equipment defers intentionality as it creates, in the minds of many filmmakers, a virtual metaphysics of presence.

In pragmatic terms, all traditional *a priori* activities, such as research, scripting, rehearsal, and various *posteriori* stages, such as narration, musical scoring, and analytical editing, are either eliminated or collapsed onto the moment of recording. The crucial, if not the only, labor takes place in the confrontation of camera/sound operator and event or social actor. An analogous moment of "focus" occurs as spectators apprehend the image on the screen. Spontaneous, aleatory signification caught in the synapse of recording is unsealed in its phenomenal freshness during the act of reception. As Frederick Wiseman puts it:

> The way I try to make a documentary is that there's no separation between the audience watching the film and the events in the film. It's like the business of getting rid of the proscenium arch in the theater . . .[23]

Behind the curtain of such verbal positioning stands a tableau of glaring contradictions in which the dynamics of "pure observation" are undercut by textual markers guaranteeing the same order of truth enacted in the partisan structures of thirties films. Albeit in a different register, direct cinema inscribes self-validating diegetic figures invested with the movement's own philosophical qualities. There is as well a corresponding reciprocity between filmic rhetoric and the context of liberal ideological discourse, now in decline rather than ascendency. Direct cinema is as much a product of and participant in a popular discourse of social renovation as its predecessor.

The cornerstone of direct cinema's rejection of previous approaches is voice-over narration, engendering the contrary demand to "show" instead of "tell"; a preference for the particular instance over the abstract and, by extension, the holistic (image or human presence) over the fragmentary. By 1960, Robert Drew was promoting a style that would allow filmmakers to "stop talking and let the action within the frame tell the story."[24] Numerous statements follow Drew's lead by connecting the "freedom" (Richard Leacock's term) afforded by the apparatus with the refusal of didacticism or "manipulative" meaning in any form. D. A. Pennebaker takes solace in not having to "label" events,[25] whereas Wiseman wants to avoid the temptation to "formalize" meaning "as a series of rational statements."[26] The implied aversion to language in its ordering, or depleting, of sensory impressions is a pervasive—and quite powerful—facet of the antiauthoritarian program of sixties countercultural and political opposition.[27]

A lesson gleaned from the triumphs and limitations of thirties activism was an abiding mistrust of top-down solutions—at its political extremes a mistrust of social theory *tout court*—expressed in cinema as a complete abandonment of extratextual appeals to authority, the refusal of history as causal explanation, and the disavowal of preconceived agendas and concrete social prescriptions. Albert Maysles provides a striking summary: "I don't see frankly, trying to make a film to create better understanding. Our motivations for making films aren't intellectual ones."[28] Wiseman avers: "I personally have a horror of producing propaganda to fit any kind of ideology other than my own view. . . ."[29] This "horror" is quite palpable, it undergirds the movement's entire aesthetic philosophy. Just as Wiseman "doubts the capacity to motivate people to large-scale social change,"[30] he and his cohort envision the production process as a form of value-free "research" (a term employed by several makers) in which the goal is, as Wiseman again phrases it, "to find out what my own attitude is towards the material that's the subject of my film."[31]

It is possible to extrapolate from these statements the wish to exchange one brand of social science methodology for another. Sponsored documentaries display an obvious debt to reformist sociology, particularly the Chicago School and related theorists such as Mumford. Direct cinema, many of whose adherents came from social science and physical science backgrounds, adopts methodological as well as ethical principles which mirror data-based empirical methods aligned with a corporate liberal fixation on "disinterested" science.[32] Documentary's version of pure observation intersects a sociology of the status quo in which social inequities are simultaneously privatized and made an object of nonapprobatory study. The filmic project becomes, in Wiseman's words, a "natural history" of American life all the more valuable because it "refuses to take sides, cast blame, or offer solutions."[33] The finished works can then be understood as "unanalyzed data," the accretions of a "statistical survey," with filmmakers cast in the role of field workers "with a camera instead of a notebook."[34]

Unlike earlier documentaries in which the presentation of evidence, argument, and scenic displays of collective social transformation govern formal construction, direct cinema insists on decontextualization. Because its "findings" are unfalsifiable, it cedes to itself an imminent freedom from contradiction. Whereas thirties films were construed as overburdened by the general, direct cinema hews to the particular, refraining from classifying individuals as types or social interactions as symptomatic of any larger pattern (although titles such as *Salesman, Showman, High School,* and *Law and Order* suggest otherwise). Judgment is thrust in the lap, or mind, of the individual spectator. Makers and supporters alike subscribe to traditional realist metaphors[35] in claiming a more active, more pluralistic, "democratic" spectatorship arising from the ambiguity of (in theory) unassimilated scenes and/or the lack of mediation through which they are presented. As Nöel Carroll points out, liberal doctrine of the period was transposed cinematically as a space where multiple viewpoints were entertained, a Bazinian principle of perceptual freedom adduced as "an expressive emblem of egalitarianism."[36] In the arena of circulation, a stance of noncontrol neatly attached itself to the demands of the FCC's Fairness Doctrine by which controversial issues were to be presented devoid of "untruthful" partisanship.[37]

One function then of direct cinema's intense specificity is to deny not only the onus of explanation but potential disagreement, relegating knowledge claims to an intersubjective plane, Leacock's "one man's truth." If part of documentary's continual need to guarantee fidelity to the Real entails a sign of openness or plurality, direct cinema attempts to displace the New Deal's formal tropes of heterogeneity onto presumably symmetrical, equivalent acts of recording and reception (the myth of filmmaker as "naive" viewer). Whereas in an earlier period, argumentative mastery or the ability to coherently assemble fragments of reality signaled an objective reckoning of historical process, here nonclosure or simplicity of design are equated with unbiased access or a "multiple consciousness of opposing perspectives."[38]

In league with the movement's confusion of textual "authority" with the "authoritarian," there is a linkage between the privileging of technology as a marker of neutrality and the assertion of individual over technocratic or collective social solutions. Resisting general propositions as a framework through which to understand society, the "personal" is mobilized not, in the jargon of sixties counterculture, as "political" but, to borrow Erich Auerbach's wonderful description of Flaubert, as charged with an explosive issuelessness. Visually as well as philosophically, direct cinema is predisposed toward intimacy, physical proximity, an isolated focus on "personality" struggling for self definition in a web of institutional pressures. This is, in essence, the master narrative at the heart of Robert Drew's celebrated "crisis structure." If one could isolate for thirties films the most characteristic image category, it would probably be groups of people in exterior long shots. In direct cinema's brief commercial foray of the late sixties, the typical configuration is most likely an interior facial close-up.

This formal shift, determined in part by technological advances, social science allegiances, and enveloping humanist discourses, can be retraced at several textual levels. Whereas thirties documentary expressed the quotidian through contrastive editing—as a shared, historically grounded condition—direct cinema constructs everyday life as a temporally distended preserve of idiosyncratic behavior. Refitting a cinematic construct of duration, the long take, to the expression of personhood, immediacy and authenticity are signaled by tropes of uneventfulness within the image, by awkward gaps and silences, the seemingly haphazard trajectories of handheld movements. This visual array conforms to what Roland Barthes locates in literature as "the realistic effect," grounded in the adumbration of "non-signifying detail"; events, gestures, objects seemingly absolved of coded meaning.[39] In direct cinema, social history is transposed into a kind of portraiture; dramatization of social process replaced by dramatization of the camera recording process. The value of concerted action as theme and formal logic gives way to stasis, the individual entrapped by circumstance, as a measure of commitment to the present.

Extrapolated from interviews and films, this schema helps to illuminate direct cinema's central and obsessive attachment to subjects under public scrutiny, to performers in one guise or another, as it clarifies the movement's agenda of self-realization. In the early Drew Associates "Living Camera" productions, network broadcasting dictated a concentration on famous or newsworthy people. Yet it is not simply Kennedy, Nehru, Jane Fonda, Marlon Brando, and the Beatles who are shown navigating among predictable role-playing, humanizing improvisation, and breakdown. It is also racecar driver Eddie Sachs, the salesmen who peddle bibles door-to-door, guards and inmates in *Titicut Follies* (1967), and teachers and administrators in *High School* (1968). Due to self-imposed methodological constraints and the positive program proclaimed for spontaneous observation, direct cinema virtually required preestablished identities or role expectations behind which filmmakers could mask their intervention and against which they could define a heightened authenticity and insight into character.[40]

Significantly, the existential locus of performance provides implicit justification for the camera's presence. Far from exhibiting the flux of spontaneous behavior, what occurs on direct cinema's makeshift stage is already mediated, learned, in greater or lesser degree intended for visual/auditory consumption. Compare the self-conscious, direct-address "routines" of even an inexperienced performer such as the young female English teacher in *High School* to the indirect and cognitively unsettling images of share croppers' cabins in *The River*. For various reasons, the latter sequence required the imposition of fourth-wall theatrical conventions of invisibility, in context a protective shield for social actors and an inadvertent sign of the camera's estrangement. A constant theme of direct cinema is the blurring and remapping of lines between mandated roles and autonomous expressions of personal identity. Designation of celebrity helps maintain the fiction that camera observation is part of a natural landscape of behavior.[41] Whether the camera is addressed directly or buffered by a profilmic audience or interrogator, it is there because of an inherent complicity by which one's "image" or personal identity is a mutual construct of performer and receiver.

It is of little consequence whether a subject is filmed in a public, semipublic, or "intimate" setting. In films such as *Meet Marlon Brando* (1965) and *Don't Look Back* (1966), the narrating posture of image and sound maintains a seemingly discreet neutrality hinged precisely on diegetic figures such as newspaper and magazine reporters who ask the questions and conduct the interviews eschewed by filmmakers on ethico-aesthetic grounds. Thus, an unspoken drive to reveal through verbal language a hidden or more truthful facet of personality is projected onto others. These unwitting go-betweens, in their misguided fealty to rational speech as benchmark of communication (in contrast to direct cinema's faith in the unfettered image) elicit patently unconvincing responses, confirming the probity of an observational style. What can be known of an individual and his or her social surround emanates from the compact of behavioral freedom from artifice struck between camera and subject. Foregrounding of performance can thus paradoxically "defuse it as a threat to its claims for truth."[42] In *Don't Look Back,* Bob Dylan dismisses a reporter's attempt to encode meaning in language: "The truth? The truth is a plain *picture* of a tramp vomiting into the sewer."

Separate films or directorial choices pose diverse enactments of this structuring relationship. In privatized settings such as the working class homes in *Salesman* (1969), the film's ostensible objects—the door-to-door vendors—become surrogates in the interviewing process, drawing out intimate details of clients lives in the course of their sales pitch. The interactions of salesman and client are bracketed, placed in quotes, by recognition of (and endless dialogue about) performance skills: an example of how direct cinema often subcontracts the task of intervention, sometimes commentary and analysis, to central or peripheral players in the profilmic. In *Titicut Follies,* guards are more than willing—when they are not engaged in singing, telling jokes, and reciting anecdotes—to "perform" their mentally deranged charges, eliciting for the camera the most antic, disoriented routines which are set against literal stage acts. Wiseman elaborates parallels between guards and inmates, sane and insane, as he extends a theatrical metaphor in multiple scenes of "public" performance: His "follies" include inmates singing, dancing, delivering long speeches, and playing musical instruments.[43] In Wiseman's and Leacock's films, the gesture of zooming from medium shot to close-up serves as formal correlative of the desire to delve into inner, psychological states while clinging to a facade of unguided attention.

Acute interest in performance leads, finally, to another source of anxiety over the problematic of power and textual authority. Just as social actors are recruited for their ability or failure to direct their own images, the filmmaking process is often allegorized—through the mediation of a performer—as a techno-physical contest and/or an existential quest. An inkling of this self-serving stake in performance appears when filmmakers criticize their previous work or the work of a colleague on grounds of failing to relinquish enough control over meaning—commiting the error of, say, creating a metaphoric relation through editing or visually isolating a potentially symbolic object.[44] At the same time, they freely endorse intricate means by which to suppress the viewer's perception of spatio-temporal discontinuity. From this perspective, if one could command the equipment and physically negotiate the field with absolute fluidity and perceptual acumen, the breach between life and representation might be healed. Recording becomes an arena of personal testing on both sides of the camera. David Maysles speaks of "raw material that doesn't want to be shaped"; Leacock and Pennebaker refer to "challenges" and "confrontations" arising from the recording situation.[45]

Direct cinema's stipulation of transparency and noncontrol as a paradigm of authenticity is at once futile and disingenuous. Even at a technological level, the search for a degree-zero mode of recording is endless. Just as documentarists in the sixties criticized the ponderous production methods of thirties films, Joel DeMott and Jeff Kreines rebuke direct cinema for its reliance on three-person crews:

> Shooting one-person restores the possibility of kinship. The filmmaker doesn't carry on with "his people" in front of "his subjects." The dichotomy those labels reveal, in the filmmaker himself, is gone along with the crew. . . . The filmmaker becomes another human being in the room.[46]

The next step might be remote control or implanted mini-cams, *robo-verité*. Clearly, the bone of contention here is not neutrality but *mastery:* how to realize the ideal performance for image/sound recorders in the theatricalized role of "pure observer." There are in fact plenty of textual models, in particular the grace-under-pressure narrative spun for direct cinema's roster of artists, sports heroes, politicians, and commonplace eccentrics. Among the most concise declarations occurs in *Man Who Dances: Edward Villella* (1970) as the dancer–choreographer states in direct address his "perfect vision of a great performance." It is "easy, smooth . . . linear . . . possessing freshness, honesty . . . quickness, lightness"—in short the very qualities of structure and camera-handling most cherished by direct cinema practitioners.

Nehru (1962), made for television by Drew Associates in advance of the commercial flowering of documentary features, is a remarkable example of recorder–subject interaction as a contest of skill and wit. It constitutes a kind of inventory of possible hurdles and small triumphs registered in the act of filming. According to Stephen Mamber, the film is "an almost open admission of failure,"[47] yet, from another angle, it allows unique access to a powerful subtext in the movement as a whole. Leacock and soundman Greg Shuker admit that the decision to include extensive voice-over commentary, as well as visual references to the recording process, stemmed from the producer's desire to pump up audience interest in footage that ultimately fell short of the convulsive drama suggested in the opening narration: "It was a time of foreboding in India; of war, invasion, signs in the heavens."

As Nehru calmly conducts quotidian affairs of state, the filmmakers fabricate a "crisis" of production. They strike a bargain with the Prime Minister: "He would ignore our presence; we for our part would do nothing to interfere with what was going on . . . ask no questions, simply observe." The progress of the film turns on which party will best serve the bargain. Actually, the subject seems to have little trouble keeping his end, but the filmmakers lurch and stumble, barely able to refrain from probing interview questions they mutter behind the scenes. Shuker gets his equipment caught in a moving jeep transporting Nehru from a frenzied rally and his agile escape from danger is duly recorded and applauded in voice-over. The added commentary reproduces a running phenomenological report on the filming process: "I decide to move my mike in closer"; "Nehru sees something and I pan over to see what it is"; "Now Nehru has noticed us, a slip on his side of the bargain"; "With my camera still moving I'm trying to force my way forward." From an almost Godardian prologue—where the camera equipment is introduced directly to the viewer—to a jitterbug performed by camera and feisty dog at a family dinner, *Nehru* exposes anxiety about not only "seeing" but identifying with, and being *seen by,* the object of the camera's "detached" gaze. The agreement, or more accurately the complicity, inherent in documentary's social intervention is here centered and calibrated in its, often comic, vicissitudes.

Leacock and Shuker discover a diegetic trope for their own professed cinematic philosophy, the Indian concept of *darsham:* an aura of intense but impersonal and unobtrusive witnessing. Nehru is said to embody this state and so, by extension, do the filmmakers. Yet the textual evidence symptomatically suggests a founding ambivalence that is played out in an improvised scenario of presence and absence, where the supposed baggage of a shaping (analytic, polemical, authoritative) ego is tactically withdrawn only to be reinvested in the performative treatment of exemplary personalities. The movement's rhetoric is bonded to its public figures in a mutual validation of agency, the inscription of vocational competence—or, in Wiseman's institutional critiques, malfeasance.

The assertion that direct cinema utilizes its social actors as a relay for or projection of its own cinematic program—encoding specific political and ideological assumptions (including the reification of a patently masculinist performance ethos)—can be placed within sporadic efforts to re-read the movement's contradictions under a rubric of modernist reflexivity.[48] However, in several notable appraisals, failure to acknowledge the hardening of figuration into tropic patterns results in much the same metaphysical morass opened by the filmmakers' own *ad hoc* theorizing. The conventional nature of direct cinema is denied by Gianfranco Bettetini, for instance, when he revalues the documentary sequence shot as fore-grounding processes by which scenes are "manufactured." He compares an inferred constructedness of mobile-camera long takes to Brecht's prescriptions for epic theater, yet adopts a familiar recourse to claims of renewed fidelity to the Real:

> In the sequence-shot, reality is revealed according to parameters that appear to be rather more its own, and less invented, than is the case in narrative situations codified by classical editing.[49]

In his formulation, the sequence shot is an ideal format for a kind of "research" from which the "fortuitous, aleatory and accidental elements . . . find room to expand naturally."[50]

In a similar vein, Jean-Louis Comolli, in an article that confusingly melds related strategies in documentary and the French New Wave, notes how an emphasis on theatrical performance can endow reality with "a new lease of meaning and coherence . . . its truth reinforced by and because of this detour through the 'fictitious.' "[51] He proposes that direct cinema has inherent "political value" because it circumvents a "triple ideological dependency: capital-intensive production, spectacle, and rhetorical convention." It seems to me that this is hardly an improvement on the idealist assertions made by filmmakers on behalf of a heightened authenticity. In effect, this approach disdains documentary's fiction of truth only to install something like the truth of fiction.

Against a backdrop of repeated calls for a more overt, discontinuous, and demystifying set of nonfiction film practices[52] and following more than a decade of political documentaries mixing interviews with archival footage—*The Murder of Fred Hampton* (1971), *Hearts and Minds* (1974), *Union Maids* (1976), *With Babies and Banners* (1977)—some recent mainstream films attempt to revitalize previous practices through a cultural discourse befitting the postmodern moment.[53]

Gilding the Ashes: Toward an Aesthetics of Failure

> My success seemed dependent on the failure of others.
>
> Tony Buba
> *Lightning Over Braddock*

There is currently more popular interest in nonfiction cinema than at any time since the late sixties. This renewal has been spurred by, among other factors, wholesale incorporation of *verité* techniques in TV advertising, the continuing strength of nonfiction genres in the publishing industry, and the onslaught of prime-time dramatic and news series such as "America's Most Wanted" and "Cops" which deploy an array of fictional and direct cinema strategies around tabloid stories. What the recent body of theatrical films—*Sherman's March* (1987), *Lightning Over Braddock* (1988), *Roger and Me* (1989), *Driving Me Crazy* (1990), and *The Thin Blue Line* (1990)—shares with other cultural phenomena is a perhaps unprecedented degree of hybridization. Materials, techniques, and modes of address are borrowed not only from earlier documentary styles but from the American avant-garde and from Hollywood as well. Voice-over narration, found footage, interviews, reenactments, and printed texts mingle in a pastiche that implicitly rejects the boundary distinctions of prior filmic modes. However, unlike related media and literary practices, the new documentary's most salient quality is an explicit centering of the filmmaking process and a heavily ironized inscription of the filmmaker as (unstable) subject, an anti-hero for our times.

As a group the new films do not manifest, or not yet, the coherent polemics, social ambit, or ideological fealties which define New Deal or direct cinema documentaries as part of a movement. In occasional interviews or writings, filmmakers predictably denounce the aesthetic assumptions and impact of earlier styles. Errol Morris says bluntly:

> I believe cinema verité set back documentary filmmaking twenty or thirty years. It sees documentary as a sub-species of journalism. . . . There's no reason why documentaries can't be as personal as fiction filmmaking and bear the imprint of those who made them. Truth isn't guaranteed by style or expression. It isn't guaranteed by anything.[54]

If Morris and company dismiss one type of formal truth claim, their films are organized around a set of strategies in which authority and verisimilitude are rhetorically embedded in a negative register of denial, mockery, and collapse. By inference, the social ideals of bureaucratic control in New Deal films, or spontaneous individual performance in direct cinema, are no longer able to support an edifice of documentary truth.

Indeed, the prospect for completion of a straightforward documentary project of any stripe may be under interrogation. In each case cited above—and in *Demon Lover Diary* (1980), a cogent if little known anticipation of the current style—*failure* to adequately represent the person, event, or social situation stated as the film's explicit task functions as an inverted guarantee of authenticity. The new works are textual parasites, fragments or residues of other works which for one reason or another became impossible to realize.[55] One ramification of postmodern aesthetics, precipitated in part by the anti-metaphysical bent of poststructuralist theory, is that certain types of artistic mastery are culturally suspect. The epistemic ambition to speak from a totalizing framework of knowledge about some fully intelligible reality is anathema. The proscription of unified subjectivity is perhaps especially severe for (politically conscious) white male filmmakers working at the margins of mass culture. Although it is too soon to make any decisive judgment, it is tempting to posit a documentary "aesthetics of failure" that grafts a protean cultural agenda onto traditional problems of authority.[56]

Operating under sanctions of what did *not* happen—an interview with General Motors Chairman Roger Smith; an account of General Sherman's attack on the Confederacy; a collection of filmic portraits of a depressed steel town; a behind-the-scenes promotional trailer for a Broadway musical—filmmakers assume an active presence as diegetic characters and/or voice-over narrators (either spontaneous with the flow of recording or indirect). This presence is marked by a studied self-deprecatory distance and a resultant celebration of formal disjuncture and disorientation. The displacement of textual (non)authority into the profilmic allows as well a return of analytic commentary, discursive sequencing, and associative or metaphoric editing patterns while maintaining some of direct cinema's myth of immediacy. Operating under this libertarian ethos, it is required that filmmakers peel away the off-screen cloak of anonymity and, emerging into the light, make light of their power and dominion.

At once recognizing and missing the point entirely, Gary Crowdus remarks that "*Roger and Me* might have acquired a little more political bite if it had focused a little more on 'Roger' and somewhat less on 'Me.' "[57] In truth, it is precisely Moore's confection of an ineffectual, uncertain journalistic self that lends an Everyman quality to his social analysis. The assertion in all of these films of the recorder's central, albeit amusingly out-of-control, position in the representational process is reminiscent of Jean Rouch's cinema verité self-implication in *Chronicle of a Summer* (1961) and other films. But a willingness to actually take apart and examine the conventions by which authority is inscribed—as opposed to making sport of them—is largely absent.[58] As distinct from Rouch's work, an unrealized or "impossible" project disguises mechanisms of internal validation which are as immunized against contradiction as direct cinema's allegories of performance.

Thirties social documentaries annex cinematic authority in iconographic identification with industrial technology and the power of central government symbolized in this motif, and direct cinema exhibits diegetic figures as mirrors for an ideal of filmic performance. The new films affirm a vested, and ultimately naturalized, stake in the inadequacy of *any* representational system to capture lived reality. *Sherman's March* starts with a brief invocation of common materials out of which historical documentaries are fashioned: maps, still photos, voice-over recitation of facts. It veers quickly into a diaristic account of the filmmaker's journey south and his visits with family and friends. A counterthematic is proposed: "A meditation on the possibility of Romantic love in the South during an era of nuclear weapons proliferation." Although there are occasional metonymic connections among Sherman, romance, and weaponry, what ensues is scarcely a "meditation." In short order, even the ancillary focus becomes a front for the work of self-absorbed disconnection, the external-ized crisis of making a "commitment."

At one point, director Ross McElwee's sister tells him, "You have an instant rapport with people because you have a camera." Indeed, the documentary camera is a derisive, but unmistakably useful, weapon and defensive shield. Most of McElwee's filmed adventures revolve around antiquated, silly projections of masculinity. He frequently compares him-self to Sherman (even donning a Civil War uniform in one shot), yet stresses his inability to conquer any of the targets, female or filmic, in his path. At a Scottish picnic, he watches passively "as men compete in various events of strength and virility." A succession of aspiring perform-ers are interviewed: the women as potential love objects, the men as alter egos or distorted versions of his own doubts and desires. A Burt Reynolds impersonator, and then Reynolds himself, are simultaneously addressed and chided as embodiments of assertive qualities he ambivalently lacks.

McElwee has qualms about the digression from the Sherman project: "I keep thinking I should return to my original plan . . . but I can't stop filming Pat"; "it's all very confusing . . . I can't figure out what to do next." He imagines "a sort of creeping psychosexual despair" that is then echoed in myriad malfunctions. The car breaks down; he forgets to turn on the tape recorder for an important encounter; an amusement park train ride runs into technical difficulties; he cannot frame or adequately follow certain subjects with the camera. Constant self-effacement and irresolution assume the shape of a dramatic device, intended to minimize and deflect the grotesque ambition of finding a love life through cinema verité interac-tion. What the device certifies through negative mastery is finally the sincerity and truth of the filmmaker's observations about himself, women, and social attitudes. In a telling twist of the traditional realist promotion of a "styleless style," *Sherman's March* parades a narrative of introspective abasement as the very sign of unvarnished reflection.

Despite profound differences in approach and aspiration, *Roger and Me* steers an analogous course. Here, the ostensible, unrealized goal is modest and politically pointed: trapping GM's Roger Smith into a spontaneous reckoning of the disastrous human effects of his corporate policies. This scenario is not doomed from the outset. Unlike McElwee, Moore is at pains to demonstrate good faith in meeting his announced goal. There is a gradual awareness, however, that the desired interview would be unilluminating and ambiguous. Lacking the requisite subject–recorder complicity, the filmmaker redirects his failure to engage Smith as proof of his own honorable political sympathies and of corporate America's malfeasance.

Once again ironic citations of misconnection and confusion pile up as the measure of a heightened authenticity. In a humorous prelude devoted to Moore's childhood perceptions of General Motors, he states: "My heroes were people who got out of Flint." He then relates a painful professional experience in San Francisco where, after losing a job as a magazine editor ("California and I were a mismatch"), he returns to Michigan in the same sort of rented truck featured in later scenes of laid-off workers. His new job as filmmaker is consistently identified with the conditions of the (often eccentric) unemployed workers; and it is predicated on their mutual failure to make the system work. Like the ex-worker who breeds rabbits to sell as either meat or pets, the filmmaker demonstrates improvisatory skill by seeming to readjust the shape of his movie as he goes along. That is, unlike *Roger and Me's* corporate nemesis, the film text cannot be constructed like an assembly-line product. Moore's

On location for the making of the documentary film, *Roger and Me*, about the closing of General Motors plants in Flint, Michigan and its effect on the residents of the town are left to right BRUCE SHERMER, JOHN PRUSAK and writer, producer and director MICHAEL MOORE. The film is released by Warner Bros. COPYRIGHT © 1989 WARNER BROS. INC. (ALL RIGHTS RESERVED). FOR USE SOLELY FOR ADVERTISING, PROMOTION, PUBLICITY OR REVIEWS OF THIS SPECIFIC MOTION PICTURE.

social solidarity is grounded in a trope of technical awkwardness, a feigned inadequacy and victimization defined against the ruthless instrumentality of General Motors—and, by extension, Hollywood.

Stalking the aloof chairman, he invents fake identities: "My friends and I decided to pose as a TV crew from Toledo. . . . I wasn't sure what a TV crew from Toledo looked like but apparently the ruse worked." Just then, Moore and his crew are unceremoniously escorted from the building. Found footage from Hollywood movies and industrial advertisements are cobbled together with interviews and observational sequences while popular songs (for example, the Beach Boys' "Wouldn't It Be Nice") impose a flat irony over scenes of economic privation. Prevented from obtaining access to GM headquarters, Moore typically remarks: "I was getting the big blow-off once again." Smith's refusal of contact is dramatized directly and also displaced onto other forms of technical miscarriage. A "Nightline" broadcast from Flint is cancelled when the engineering truck is stolen. Various schemes to rejuvenate the local economy end in collapse. Officials issuing on-screen corporate excuses or cheery prognostications are later fired. When Moore invades the annual GM stockholders' meeting to confront Smith face-to-face, his microphone is turned off. A textual array of breakdowns and exposed limitations presents the filmmaking process as a series of inadequate gestures at empowerment by which fidelity to the Real is simultaneously derided as a goal and instated.

Parallels between documentary process and productive (and nonproductive) labor are even more extensive and politically incisive in *Lightning Over Braddock*. Buttressed by the same autobiographical impulse found in *Sherman's March* and *Roger and Me,* the film interweaves personal history with social history toward a highly subjective account of the depleted fortunes of a Pennsylvania milltown. It opens on a TV interview with Tony Buba, whose previous films on the local economy garnered (for himself and for Braddock) some useful publicity. This gambit leads to a recapitulation in direct speech, voice-over exposition, and film excerpts, of Buba's college life and initiation into documentary filming. Shifting easily between tenses, levels of presentation, and epistemic frameworks, the film issues a kind of metadiscourse that undercuts every spontaneous gesture and sincere mimetic intention.

Present as a muted concern in other films, here the intricate slippage in roles from recorder to social actor to scripted fictional character to commentator provides a structuring logic formalized in an extreme concatenation of materials. There are collisions of video footage and film fragments shot in different gauges; actual and faked interviews and observational sequences; enacted flashbacks and ramshackle Hollywood fantasies such as the local staging of Ghandi's assassination. One can never be sure of the director's interpersonal ties with the featured characters, all unemployed denizens of Braddock. They seem, in turn, autonomous subjects and willing conspirators earning a modest payday before the camera; yet, in sequences with cranky "Sweet Sal" Carulo, a feeling of genuine antagonism creeps in. At an early stage, Buba informs us that the project planned as "Lightning Over Braddock" is under constant revision and that the original scheme of a sweeping portrait of the town must be abandoned.

Toward the end, we are told that grant money ran out before many sequences were finished. The screen goes black (as it does at several points), then forges ahead with new ideas and ambitions—including blowing up (which?) *Lightning* into 35mm for mass distribution and other partially realized projects such as a "steel mill musical." Buba says he is unclear about what he is doing and inserts demands by collaborators that he simply "quit." Later, he renounces his commitment to social documentary altogether and plots to "sell out" to Hollywood, a vocation for which the fictional sequences are to presumably serve as advertisement.

An anarchic pattern of technical struggle, breakdown, and recuperation is directly linked to economic conditions. The film both demonstrates and refuses the "real irony" that "as the layoffs increase, his fortunes rise." Yet power is thwarted by vivid limitations. Buba exploits the inability to use sound for a performance of "Jumping Jack Flash" by a worker scrounging cash as a club entertainer; rights to the song cost $15,000 "three times the per capita income of a Braddock resident." "Hey," he reminds us, "this isn't a Hollywood feature we're making here." The singer's silently moving lips—like the failed business ventures of another figure, Jimmy Ray, and the unfathomable acting career of "Sweet Sal"—binds film and subject in a concordance of nonfulfillment. And here, as elsewhere, it is exactly the open admission of, indeed a central obsession with, inadequacy emblazoned by formal disjunction and underwritten by dramatic displays of nontotalized knowledge—patriarchal mastery in disarray—which performs the labor of signifying authenticity and documentary truth.

In a recent essay, filmmaker–theorist Trinh Minh-ha, following a cogent dissection of documentary myths of verisimilitude, proposes a new nonfiction epistemology based on challenging filmic patterns of authority rather than merely replacing one unacknowledged source of authority with another:

> To compose is not always synonymous with ordering-so-as-to-persuade, and to give the . . . Meaning can therefore be political only when it does not let itself be easily stabilized, and when it does not rely on a single source of authority but, rather empties or decentralizes it.[59]

She advocates a practice in which the subject is constantly "in process," where documentary "displays its own formal properties or its own constitution as work" and where the expression of identity or subjective agency is one in which

> the self vacillates and loses its assurance. The paradox of such a process lies in its fundamental instability; an instability that brings forth the disorder inherent in every order.[60]

Trinh's prescriptions are nuanced and ardently progressive. And she intends her remarks for, and produces her own work within, a cinematic order largely unconstrained by commercial demands for topicality, familiarity, and identification. She would thus appear to have little interest or faith in the transformation of mainstream cinematic genres. Keeping this in mind, it is odd to find her notions—of defeating the "establishment of totality" by creating "a space in which meaning remains fascinated by what escapes and exceeds it"—at least partially tested by recent filmic practice. One explanation for this unexpected convergence lies in the popular translation in multiple fora of poststructuralism's critique of Western metaphysics. For instance, the unavoidable multiplicity of subjecthood and the constructedness of historical truth prop up recent controversies over multicultural education in the United States and the ramifications of the film *JFK* (1991).

It is doubly ironic, then, that the strategies found in these fashionable, mainstream postmodern documentaries remain wedded to the same principles of authenticity, if not the same rhetorical codings, as earlier styles. As I hope is now apparent, *Roger and Me* and its ilk substitute reflexive abnegation for New Deal and direct cinema paradigms of authority. There have been, and will continue to be, versions of the quest for documentary truth which develop different orders of structuration or manage to obviate the most self-contradictory tensions in the opposition of lived reality and tropes of presentation. The three moments of production considered here are yoked in a formal tradition that defines itself according to both Hollywood fictional codes and competing documentary styles. Despite affinities, the individual movements are embedded in and determined by particular historical and cultural assumptions about appropriate expressions of truth, and by corollary discourses that shape available options for representing social reality.

Technology and its imbrication with power is thematized in each instance according to the changing political dynamics of liberalism: in the first, iconographic identification with industrial technology and its ability to rectify social affliction; in the second, an incorporation and masking of the apparatus as an extension of individual cognitive acuity and physical skill; and in recent films, disavowal or technical proficiency as guarantee of non-omniscience and metaphoric link with disenfranchised profilmic subjects. Thus, the role of authorial agency in its manifest relation to technology moves from a stance of partisan intervention to one of neutral, transparent observation to a slippery ambivalence in which the instrument of cinema is a necessarily visible but confoundingly inadequate mediator.

Finally, all three sketch implicit cinematic programs for an exemplary nonfiction treatment of reality. Each construes its values and functions in opposition to Hollywood domination while adhering to certain of that institution's most ingrained effects of knowledge, coherence, and closure. In a sense, what succeeding documentary styles *refuse* of the formulas of narrative fiction bespeak their designated areas of social impact. Sponsored documentaries of the thirties eschew the establishing of strong individualized characters and the attendant possibility of viewer identification while providing familiar cues for dramatic expectation and closure. Direct cinema and, with some readjustment, recent films withhold or actively undermine closure and distend—if not abolish—prospects for dramatic development while offering compensation in the form of diegetic intimacy with sympathetic characters (including the filmmakers themselves). It is highly unlikely that the realist windmills of authority and transparency against which American documentaries have been tilting for 50 years will suddenly disappear or be demolished by postmodern allegories. The quiddity of the form will, for better or worse, continue to pivot on historically specific legitimations of authenticity.

I wish to thank Amy Taubin, Dana Polan, Ivone Margulies, and members of the Columbia University Seminar of Cinema and Interdisciplinary Interpretation for their valuable comments during the preparation of this chapter.

7

Constantly Performing the Documentary: The Seductive Promise of *Lightning Over Water*

Susan Scheibler

In 1979 while at work on the film *Hammett,* Wim Wenders took time off to visit his friend and mentor Nicholas Ray in New York. Wenders's work on *Hammett* was proceeding with difficulty. His visit to Ray, captured in the film *Lightning Over Water,* seems to be as much about his need to overcome a creative block as it is the need to visit a dying friend and father figure. The film, ostensibly a documentary about the life and work of Nicholas Ray, also documents Ray's death even as it performs as documentation of Wenders's own journey into a cinematic relationship.

The multilayered film is punctuated with shots of the editing apparatus. These shots, filmed both in Ray's home and on the Chinese junk carrying Nick's ashes and Wenders's crew, serve to call attention to the apparatus even as they inform, reveal, and puncture the epistemological and ontological promises that underlie the spectatorial expectations of the documentary form.[1]

The signifying system of this particular film slides in and out of the outer filmic frame of Wenders's study of Ray, documenting itself by means of an inner text captured on video. The outer text also slides in and out of its filmic references, shifting between scenes of Wenders's visit to the dying Ray, clips from the body of Ray's own cinematic work, and sequences shot aboard the Chinese junk, filmed after Ray's death and including conversations among the film crew as to the difficulty of finishing a project once the subject is no longer present.

The text of *Lightning Over Water* provides us with an exemplification of the Derridean notion that "every text is a double text" offering an interweaving, a play which "includes the work of meaning or the meaning of work, and includes them not in terms of knowledge but in terms of inscription: meaning is a function of play, is inscribed in a certain place in the configuration of a meaningless text."[2]

The video sequences begin to enact the technology of the documentary form itself, offering a look which seems to align itself with the conventions and codes most often associated with the self-verification of the verité style. These referential conventions promise an authenticity and authorization of their shots and frames as "here it is" real-life footage. The video segments, complete with out-of-focus shots and handheld camera movements, provide the deictic moment associated with what Roland Barthes calls the referential plenitude of photography, the "voilà" that Bill Nichols mentions as the magic of the documentary form.[3]

Yet, while it would seem that the video text is functioning as a documentary of the documentary, a documentation of the film Wenders is shooting, of the film we are watching, these segments also perform the documentary, exposing its absent referent and turning its reflexivity back upon a self other than itself, a turning back upon its subject/object and upon its spectator.

The question of performance, captured by the video camera, involves an element of self-reflexivity, but a reflexivity that lies beyond a disclosure of its own mechanisms. It reflects the gap that emerges between signifier and signified, revealing the abyss that lies at the heart of the cinematic endeavor. The performative element begins to efface the boundaries between what would appear to be the nonfiction document of the life and work of Nicholas Ray and the rehearsal that would seem to define it as a fiction or at least a fictive account of this life and work. The interweaving of discourses introduces issues clustered around the question of what it means to deconstruct both a document and the discourse surrounding that document.

Both the documentary form and the discourse surrounding it appear to be driven by what Henry Staten refers to as "the desire to have the good thing and to have it always, beyond the boundaries of mortality."[4] The desire to represent the unnameable, to name the other, to organize the past and memory into a discourse and to furnish that discourse with referentiality, often seeks to find an articulation through the documentary image. This notion of documentary attempts to legitimize its discourse by means of a claim to a privileged relationship to the real. It imitates historiographical discourse as that which is supposed to have knowledge and allows its desire to be propped on certain epistemological and ontological yearnings. These yearnings, in turn, serve to position the spectator as an omnipotent and omniscient observer, able to traverse the gap between signifier and signified by means of various codes of authenticity and veracity. These codes, in turn, act to guarantee a position of unity and mastery, a suturing over of a lost plenitude and coherence.

For Nicholas Ray, the film *Lightning Over Water* offers an opportunity to seek mastery over death through the performance of subject as film-maker and of object as the one being filmed. As he works on his film, *We Can't Go Home Again,* he attempts to perform a closure for his own life and work. By performing his own life and death in Wenders's film, Ray is trying to see himself whole again, to recapture his own lost imaginary. In turn, by writing and imagining the other film that he will call *Lightning Over Water* (the title bequeathed to Wenders), Ray seeks the cure for death in the cinematic apparatus itself, in the narrative of an originary search marked by a desire to find the perfect ending.

Nick Ray's tragedy is that, as he himself states in his address at Vassar contained within the film, the closer one comes to an ending, the closer one moves to a rewriting that is a beginning. In this way, he expresses not only the metaphysical desire for enclosure, for a stable dimension of existence in which the definition can coincide with the defined, in which there is referentiality and a constancy of identity and knowledge, but also the grief that follows upon the recognition of the impossibility of this desire, a desire as futile as that envisioned in Ray's narrative of the searchers aboard the junk, pursuing a solution to death and mortality.

Ray's tragic desire becomes our own as the film we are watching, coded as a documentary, elicits our own expectations of the nonfiction form. Not only are our expectations aroused but so are those of Wenders himself as he lays claim to the title *Lightning Over Water,* the title Ray had hoped to use for his story of the artist aboard the Chinese junk, traveling toward the drug that would ensure life. By assuming the title, Wenders assumes the search, translating the terms so that it is the apparatus that serves as the much-desired cure for cancer, the object of Ray's narrative. Like Ray, Wenders places his cure aboard the Chinese junk, not in the form of a heavenly narcotic but as the cinematic apparatus signified by the editing equipment on the bow of the boat. Wenders goes a step further by shifting the terms from those of the fiction film to those of the nonfiction, the documentary. By combining the forms and collapsing the narratives, Wenders's film inscribes itself within both the epistemological and onto-logical desires that prop up the drive to documentary.

The term documentary itself reveals an inherent epistemological desire. Its Latin root, *docere,* indicates an ability to teach, to provide mementos of knowledge able to provoke a desire for a place marked by cognition and its relationship to issues of desire and pleasure. Premised as it is on basic expository proposals, the documentary form creates an expectation in a spectator trained to read codes associated with authenticity. Firmly situated within a space of cognitive desire, the spectator "expects to be fulfilled in terms of the real conditions of existence, the pro-filmic event or 'real work' apart from the mediation of the system of textual codes."[5]

Appropriating its photographic genealogy, the documentary form is able to offer itself as a metaphysical guarantee, offering presence and coherence through the possibility of knowledge. This cognitive possibility also allows the documentary form to lay claim to the satisfaction of an ontological desire. The document promises that the limitless text of existence will take on a manageable form and substance, providing the spectator with a position of mastery over a potentially threatening world. *Being* becomes being, observed and thus observable, named and thus nameable by means of the indexical nature of the photographic image which provides the ontological means for the *cogito* (the knowing subject) to create and establish categories by which the world can be known and controlled.

Even as it promises mastery through knowledge, a documentary such as *Lightning Over Water* confronts itself with what it cannot encompass. Interweaving document and performance, fiction and nonfiction, it confronts its own forgetfulness, its place on the edge of the center. As a film generically posed in the style associated with that of a documentary, *Lightning* would appear to promise verification of its status as true or false. Its own position within the spectatorial expectations associated with nonfiction representation encloses it within the never-ending circle of what may be termed a mirror theory of knowledge and truth.

Jameson refers to this state as a "so-called crisis of representation, in which an essentially realistic epistemology . . . conceives of representation as the reproduction, for subjectivity, of an objectivity that lies outside it." He goes on to state that this crisis of representation projects a mirror theory of knowledge "whose fundamental evaluative categories are those of adequacy, accuracy, and truth itself."[6]

In a way, the conventions associated with the documentary form resemble the mirror theory of knowledge for they also seem to invoke a transcendental standpoint outside of a set of representations from which the relation between representations and objects can be inspected. The documentary form often involves a supposition that there are essences which can be accurately represented to a subject in whose mind the object can be reflected. Knowledge becomes the promise of a representation of a transcendental signified to a transcendental subject. The crisis to which Jameson refers is the problem of legitimation precipitated by the interrogation of the status of the object as well as of any possibility of knowing it. It is also the crisis of the documentary or nonfiction film as it must negotiate its spectatorial expectations in the face of its own ontological and epistemological limits. *Lightning Over Water,* enclosed within this desiring system, seeks to find a way out of the bind of documentary's cognitive suppositions, setting itself up as object as surely as it does the work of Nicholas Ray.

In a documentary, the interrogation of the object often takes a form which expresses itself in cognitive terms as a constative event. In his early work, J. L. Austin discusses two aspects of language, referring to one as the constative and to the other as the performative. He defines these in terms of their approaches to the issue of facticity or referentiality; that is, in terms of their relationship or nonrelationship to a claim to authenticity and authority.

The constative can be defined by its dependence on a belief in the possibility of a knowledge that is able to guarantee the actuality and presence, the facticity, of its observations and remarks. The performative, on the other hand, is unconcerned with its relation to facticity, to truth or falsity, performing its enunciative function apart from and outside of issues of verifiability and authenticity.[7]

The constative rests on a promise of consistency and of the resemblence of sign to referent. Calling on the mirror theory of knowledge, it depends on the principle of equivalence which promises that an image equals a representation of its referent, seducing its subject with the promise of the possibility of the referent as a nameable and thus knowable and mastered actuality. What is at stake for the constative is the correspondence between the utterance and its promise of a real referent.

The assumption supporting the possibility of the constative is that language is able to transmit truth, that it can and does provide a means for knowing and mastering reality. The constative stands as a promise that meaning not only will last, but, by so promising, it offers the lure that there is a possibility of a stable and coherent meaning and a stable and coherent subject able to possess that meaning. As Shoshana Felman states in her work on *Don Juan,* the constantive presents a "promise of constancy, a promise that meaning will last, a promise underwritten . . . by the constancy of God himself, by the voice of heaven—a promise that is in the last analysis only the promise of language to refer, to make sense, to ensure a meaning that will be lasting, constant, constative."[8]

An examination of the performative aspect, on the other hand, is an examination of the breaks and ruptures in the constative as well as in the discursive apparatus itself. Performing the constative as excess, the performative reveals the desire for referentiality which adheres to and underlies our concepts of language and culture. The meaning of the constative statement can be seen to slide into and around its own performance, eclipsing its concern with and promise of truth and constancy.

In his essay "Performative Utterances," J. L. Austin defines the notion of performatives as "perfectly straightforward utterances with ordinary verbs in the first person singular present indicative active . . . if a person makes an utterance of this sort we should say that he is doing something rather than merely saying something."[9] Thus, the performative functions "not to inform or to describe but to carry out a performance, to accomplish an act through the very process of its enunciation."[10] The performative takes on meaning only when it is performed. It involves a level of pretense, a masquerade, that demystifies the illusion that the thing at stake is truth or falsity.

It is not enough, however, to pose these two aspects of language. By introducing these terms, one is in danger of presenting a new opposition, a new hierarchy in which the performative displaces the constative and assumes the power of the higher position. In examining a documentary such as *Lightning,* we are confronted with a text that struggles against oppositions and boundaries. This struggle plays itself out in the discursive arena by performatively confronting the constative with its own assumptions of authority, authenticity, veracity, verifiability. The performative, in turn, is displaced by its own constative performance within and around the video segments, a performance which turns on and turns into the conventions which mark it as a documentary.

In her article "The Camera I: Observations on Documentary," Annette Kuhn discusses the codes used by documentary images to offer themselves as truth. These codes serve to connote authenticity, an authenticity I would claim rests on the spectatorial desire for the constative dimension of the text, a resolution of contradiction "between an assertion of truth and a lack of evidence supporting that assertion of truth by a displacement which constitutes a representation as a set of codes which in themselves signal self-evident truth."[11]

These codes of authenticity allow the transparent style found in many documentary films to lay claim to a certain reality effect. The utilization of cinema verité codes promises a sense of directness and immediacy, of events captured as they unfold naturally and in an untampered fashion before the camera. These codes signal a seeming erasure of space between referent and representation, promising an aura of credibility on which the constative moment of the documentary is premised.

As Nichols writes in his essay "The Voice of Documentary," documentary "displays a tension arising from the attempt to make statements about life which are quite general, while necessarily using sounds and images that bear the inescapable trace of their particular historical origins."[12] He goes on to point out that while we understand that these sounds and images function as signs and are not history speaking directly to us, there still occurs a disavowal of the constructed meaning, of the textual voice that is addressing us. Documentary as expository cinema makes a proposal to its spectator in which it promises to "invoke and gratify a desire to know." Expository films make propositions, constative statements, which position the spectator in a relationship of expectancy.

The documentary as constative stands on an expectation of cinematic language as that which is capable of fulfilling its most arrogant promise of representation: the promise to renew the imaginary state of full presence and coherency. In this constative state, the document proposes historical and/or objective fact as its domain. It offers its epistemological and ontological credibility by laying claim to its relationship to photography, a relationship often capitalized on through the use of newsreels, found footage, and photographic stills.

In his collection of essays on the nature of photography, Roland Barthes describes the photograph as that which "always carries its referent with itself." He states that a "specific photograph, in effect, is never distinguished from its referent (from what it represents), or at least it is not immediately or generally distinguished from its referent."[13]

The referent is held to adhere to the photograph, authenticating itself and the image in the process. This "analogical perfection" or "plenitude," to use Barthes' terms, establishes a fullness of relation between appearance and reality, representation and object. The object as photographed and the photograph as object carry within themselves a referentiality that posits a specific ontological relationship premised on the impression that the signifier is able to represent the real in an unmediated fashion, the photograph as constative. ". . . the Photograph is indifferent to all intermediaries: it does not invent; it is authentication itself; the (rare) artifices it permits are not prohibitive; they are, on the contrary, trick pictures: the photograph is laborious only when it fakes."[14]

The authenticity of the photographic image lends to it an ontological authority. The documentary image as constative, by laying claim to its relationship to photography, is able to capitalize on this genealogy as a means of support for an impression of itself as a faithful representation of the real. The documentary's power of authentication seemingly enables it to actualize the real.

For Barthes, "photography's referent is not the same as the referent of other systems of representation."[15] The referents of other representational systems are contingently real. Their referential status is contingent on a relationship to a discursive status created by means of a combination of signs. The photographic referent, on the other hand, is necessarily real. At some time an object was placed before the lens, it has been there. This having-been-there endows the photograph with its inherent referentiality. "What I intentionalize in a photograph is neither Art nor Communication, it is Reference which is the founding order of Photography."[16] Truth and reality appear to meet in the photograph, driven by a compelling belief that the referent which, as Barthes points out, "someone has seen . . . in flesh and blood, or again in person" does adhere to the photograph.[17] This same belief adheres to the documentary image. As Annette Kuhn points out, the "importance of on-the-spot observation and the centrality of the film crew or . . . the camera operator" serves as ". . . the defining characteristics of that body of films (documentary) (or rather, given the terms of the discussion of that filmmaking practice)" which "pivot on the question of the rendering visible . . . the already observable."[18] The having-been-there of the image provides the ground work for the belief that what is seen is what would have been there had not the photographer/ camera crew been present. The tautology of the deictic moment ratifies what it represents as having-been-there, as being exactly what it is.

The sense of immediacy, in turn, guarantees that the referent which adheres to the image is able to certify the existence of what it represents. By pointing out and pointing to the object, observation and description emerge as legitimate enterprises entailed by the photographic image which documents the existence of the real even as it certifies its own authenticity by virtue of its implied "this is it."

Whereas the seeming transparent rendering of phenomenal events creates an aura of authenticity, the revelation of the camera or person behind it quite often serves to reinforce the having-been-there sense of the deictic moment. As Nichols points out, "those rare moments in which the camera or person behind it is acknowledged certify more forcefully that other moments of pure observation capture the social presentation of self we too would have witnessed had we actually been there to see for ourselves."[19] The recognition of the filmmaker/camera/spectator as observer may also contribute to the overall suturing effect of the documentary film. The foregrounding of the apparatus, itself a seemingly performative move in its self-reflexive attitude, may only serve to reinforce the constative aspects of the documentary image. The double move of the codes struggling to efface or deny their own workings as a mode of mediated representation even as they foreground their work to reinforce the deictic moment supplies the documentary with its suturing dimension.

Within cinematic discourse, discussions of suture generally pivot around questions concerning its function within narrative cinema. Central to the concept as applied to narrative or fictional discourse is the presence of a character on whom the spectator's identification and pleasure turns. Kaja Silverman's summary of suture as a cinematic activity reflects this apparent theoretical consensus:

> The viewer's exclusion from the site of cinematic production is covered over by the inscription into the diegesis of a character from whom the film's sound and images seem to flow, a character equipped with authoritative vision, hearing, and speech. Insofar as the spectator identifies with this most fantasmatic of representations, he or she enjoys an unquestioned wholeness and assurance.[20]

This model of suture relies heavily on that proposed by Jean-Pierre Oudart and Daniel Dayan, a scenario that turns primarily on the shot/reverse-shot sequence as the means of suturing over the uncomfortable absence confronting the spectator. Premised on a Lacanian understanding of the subject as caught up in the play of signification, it designates suture as a logic of the signifier, raising the issue of the spectator as subject to assault by the cinematic apparatus. This state of seige defines the tragic nature of cinematic language as that which plays on the perpetual absence and loss confronting the spectator.

In the words of Jacques-Alain Miller, suture

> names the relation of the subject to the chain of its discourse . . . it figures there as an element which is lacking, in the form of a stand-in. For, while there lacking, it is not purely and simply absent. Suture, by extension, (becomes) the general relation of lack to the structure of which it is an element, inasmuch as it implies the taking-the-place-of.[21]

Suture, then, functions to cover over the absence that lies at the heart of the cinematic experience by enclosing the spectator within the apparatic imaginary. The discursive elements of cinema allow it to recuperate the loss of the totality of the image, to replenish a sense of pleasurable wholeness for the subject. In the documentary form, this sense of loss arises when the awareness of the absent referent makes itself known. The ensuing epistemological and ontological distress threatens the spectator's claim to a transcendental status of mastery over a chaotic and disordered universe.

The "I" that must know desires to suture itself into an enunciatory position. Knowledge involves the necessity of leaping the abyss of the subject/object opposition that lies at the heart of one's own subjectivity. This sutured position provides the knowing "I" with a coherent representation from which it may engage in the production of meaning. In the documentary form, this coherency establishes itself within the conventions associated with the constative dimension of verifiability and facticity.

In narrative cinema, the crisis of identification can be covered up through the play of identificatory structures stretched out over the diegesis as a movement between primary and secondary identifications. This dual movement allows the subject to be transported into the realm of the fiction as either a recognizable subject of address or as the omnipotent transcendental subject, able to conquer time and space in the movement of the camera I. The spectator shifts positions between the I/eye of the camera and the I/eye of the character, creating his/her own identity of the enunciated/enunciating I—the "it's me" of the desiring subject.

The movement of the suturing moment which functions in the play of lack and absence constructs its own imagined wholeness which it then passes along to the spectator, offering the cinematic fort/da as a function of its own representation. This play of presence and absence, loss and recovery, passes along the junction of the symbolic and the imaginary, offering a pleasure that is itself both epistemological and ontological.

If the suturing moment functions on the join between the symbolic and the imaginary, caught up in the spectacular moment, then the nonfiction film also offers suture along that join. The imaginary of the documentary, the imagined real, joins with the documentary's symbolic in its concern with language, culture, history, and the other to produce a subject within the promise of the constative. If the fiction film encourages the viewer to establish a relationship with his or her fictional representation, then the nonfiction film encourages the spectator to take up a position of privilege in a relationship of what has been termed the constative dimension. The spectator is invited into this space of authenticity through the ontological and epistemological promise of a constative that relies on its spectacular effects to suture the subject into a presumed imaginary relationship to his or her own relation to the symbolic order, to culture and language.

If, as Michael Renov states, the "purview of non-fiction is the representation and interrogation of the phenomenal world, itself a limitless text,"[22] then the promise of an authentic representation and interrogation becomes as problematic as the text is limitless. The image, read as a transparent rendering of reality, creates for its spectator the imagined condition of an epistemological and ontological plenitude. The desiring subject is promised a profilmic event delivered authentically and fully, a promise which offers to be fulfilled by the constative. The existential bond between sign and referent would seem to allow the limitless text of the phenomenal world to be captured by the cinematic image.

And yet, the task is impossible and the promise is an empty one. Whereas some documentary films may continue to masquerade under the cloak of the full constative, films such as *Lightning* allow the other element of discourse, the performative dimension, to disrupt the apparent mastery of the documentary form as sense-making apparatus. In these films, the performative turns on the moment when the film enunciates its own discourse, exclaims its own utterance even as it exceeds it. The performative text passes judgment on its constative self, demarcating the point at which the divisions between fiction and nonfiction, subject and object, begin to waver.

In the performative, the referential aspect is not viewed as an entity to be captured but as a discourse which expresses its referential knowledge as an act within and through language. As Derrida points out in his article "Signature, Event, Context," the performative differs from the constative in its proposed relation to the referent:

> Differing from the classical assertion, from the constative utterance, the performative's referent . . . is not outside it or in any case preceding it or before it. It does not describe something which exists outside and before language. It produces or transforms a situation, it operates; and if it can be said that a constative utterance also effectuates something and always transforms a situation, it cannot be said that this constitutes its internal structure, its manifest function or destination, as in the case of the performative.[23]

The performative aspect turns the referent inside out, enabling the constative to move away from its center toward the edge, the marginal. This break, this slide in meaning, performs the missing of the real which marks the empty promise of the constative. The desire to anchor the signifier on a transcendental signified is exposed as impossible, revealing the absence of both a transcendental subject and a transcendental object, the mythic element of both epistemological and ontological desire. An attachment to the authenticity of the constative exposes the futility of the attempt to cover over the void which lies at the heart of representation.

In a nonfiction film such as *Lightning,* the constative characteristics of the documentary form are eventually put into conflict by the demands of the performative that lie within and around each constative. At this limit point, the form explodes as the documentary performs the emptiness of its epistemological and ontological claims, not so much because the constative is by virtue of its definition in jeopardy, but because, at the performative moment, the film demonstrates itself as a text which exposes the limits of the cinema in general.

These performative moments which deconstruct documentary erupt when the fictional aspects and the nonfictional collide. At those points, the structure of the document slips between and around the carefully demarcated categories of constative and performative, enabling the text to call attention to its own generic limits. Enunciating marginality, these films are able to call attention to the limits of the documentary form as one promising a privileged relationship to the real and/or the authentic. A film such as *Lightning Over Water* performs its own status on the edges of the cinematic institution, placing itself and its own borders under erasure. While documenting the death of Nicholas Ray, it also documents its own death, its own inability to remain a pure constative, lost in the performance which marks its eclipse.

In any discussion of the performative, language becomes a central concern. The performative, in its demystification of the illusion that the thing at stake is truth or falsity, allows language to become a field of enjoyment, of play and desire. Instead of the constative's striving after a promised constancy, the performative plays with language, unsettling and destabilizing it. While the constative props itself on the promise of and desire for a referent, for a centered presence that is knowable and thus attainable and mastered, the performative ruptures this notion, finding a break, a rift in its movement away from the center toward that which is marked as marginal, inauthentic, the neglected second term of the opposition. Taken together, the constative which performs reveals the emptiness of its promise as constative even as the performative which declares itself reveals the instability of its spectacular status.

To speak of a cinematic moment as performative is to turn a way of speaking into a way of seeing. Performative as performance turns on the spectator, circling around and constituting the subject in a relation to the performance which is documentary. It also turns on the spectator in an act of aggression, rupturing the constative moment, displacing the mastery of knowledge sought in the imperative of the documentary image. The performative exposes the desire for the imagined epistemological and ontological plenitude as what it is—an absent other, an impossible dream, an impossible form. As Gayatri Spivak writes, all texts "carry within themselves the seeds of their own destruction."[24] In *Lightning Over Water,* the seeds of destruction are carried within the tensions between the desire on the part of both Wenders and Ray to make the ends coincide with the means, to offer the promise of the documentary even as they perform their own attempts to master death and cinema.

In the story Ray creates and names *Lightning Over Water,* a painter and his Chinese friend set off in search of a cure for cancer. By casting himself as an artist rather than a filmmaker, Ray, disguised by another name, seeks to name death even as he overcomes it by asserting his own directorial and artistic wholeness. Cinema is used as a means to avoid the closure that is death. Yet the inevitability of death brings with it an awareness of closure, an awareness marked by fear both of the possibility of closure as well as of the fear of its absence.

The role of this story within the film Wenders is shooting, also called *Lightning Over Water,* is to function performatively in the repeated shots of the Chinese junk circling the harbor, carrying aboard it not the two travelers seeking the medicinal cure but Wenders's own film crew seeking another type of cure, a cure for the absent cinematic object. They sit aboard the junk discussing Ray's death and its effect on the unfinished film.

The reference is doubled by the performative shot of the editing equipment on the bow of the junk, film blowing in the wind, wrapping itself around the ginger jar which presumably contains Nick Ray's ashes. And so death becomes the last directorial assertion for both Ray and Wenders. As Derrida states

> To stay alive, to maintain oneself in life, to work, to defer pleasure, to limit the stakes, to have respect for death at the very moment when one looks directly at it—such is the servile condition of mastery and of the entire history it makes possible.[25]

Ray seeks mastery through performance, not only as director/artist, but also through his performance in both the Wenders film and in the clips from the unfinished film, *We Can't Go Home Again*. He expresses his concern about the performance even as he delights in it. Ray's performance at Vassar is topped by his final performance in the hospital room, a performance in which he offers himself as sign, as representation, becoming the mingling of representation that, as Derrida states,

> mingles with what it represents to the point where one speaks as one writes, one thinks as if the represented were nothing more than the shadow or reflection of the representor. A dangerous promiscuity and a nefarious complicity between the reflection and the reflected which lets itself be seduced narcissistically. In this play of representation, the point of origin becomes ungraspable.[26]

Even as he constitutes himself as sign, Ray seeks an emancipation through death, a relationship with death that will, ultimately, constitute his subjectivity. His death guarantees the making of the film, guarantees the satisfaction of a textual closure that will promise the fullness of his life.

For Wenders, the film offers mastery of the death of the other who is the father. He fears and yet is attracted to Ray's death and fears his own seduction by this death. As he describes it, he is afraid of betraying Ray's death and suffering. He promises that, should he find himself in this position, he will need to leave, for he will be mastered by the very thing he is hoping to master yet unable to master it cinematically.

Nicholas Ray figures as father for Wenders, a father already constituted in absence, inscribed in cinematic history as well as in representation through the video and filmic text that Wenders is shooting/performing. Ray's wife Susan confronts Wenders with this paternal legacy when she is asked why Ray has called him to New York. Susan explains that Nick is gathering his family around him, a filial position Wenders denies and rejects in his constative declaration even as he figures Nick Ray as father/cinema/self/other in a performative gesture. As spectator, Wenders watches the performance of the other and of the other's death, seeing Ray's performance of himself as other to himself, an other already constituted in absence, a presence placed and effaced in and by representation, a representation performed and constituted by the cinematic apparatus.

Throughout the film, Wenders refuses to name both Death and the Father. His denial of the father is, in turn, denied as he adopts his paternity within the visual performative of the film itself. The repeated shot of the editing equipment on board the Chinese junk, film blowing in the wind, functions as the performative that comments on, judges, expounds on the meaning of a presence that requires representation. It is cinema concretized in the figure of Ray that Wenders wishes to name as Father, as the other of his own desire and as the structure of death and absence.

Hegel states that

> In question is the death of the other but in such cases the death of the other is always the image of one's own death. No one could enjoy himself thus, if he did not accept one condition: the dead man, who is an other, is assumed to be in agreement.[27]

The film offers Wenders a chance to seek mastery over death by offering mastery over his own subject position as spectator. He looks at himself in Nick, "the reflection, the image, the double which splits what it doubles." The split which becomes a doubling effaces the distinction between subject and object, between Nick Ray and Wim Wenders. As the representation mingles with what it represents, "the description of the object is as contaminated by the patterns of the subject's desire as is the subject constituted by that never-fulfilled desire."[28] As Wenders tells Nick, "My action is defined by yours, by your facing death." This gesture of doubling is itself a performance/performative enunciated in the film by a discussion as to whom the film is really about—Ray or Wenders. At this moment, the film performs its own desire for the center as constituted in the figure of the father, a desire that turns back on itself as it is performed, raising the question of whose desire, whose performance.

As Wenders returns to Nick's apartment to be confronted by Nick's absence, the performative and constative are interwoven in a rupturing move that allows this most moving and seemingly referential moment to play as if rehearsed. Meaning is lost to discourse as the performative wounds the constative, puncturing it and opening it up to expose the emptiness of the epistemological and ontological desire supporting the craving for a documentary and documented image. Knowledge and presence are displaced by the performative. The constative declares its referent to be abandoned by a document that begins to perform in the spaces between signifier and signified. And yet the fact that the sequence occurs on video, a form associated throughout the text with what might be termed the constative dimension, allows it to offer the constative as well as the performative. The sliding between performative and constative, fiction and nonfiction, subject and object, functions as the interval, the space and gap in meaning. The hierarchy is turned inside out and upside down.

Even as the scene of the Chinese junk circling the harbor echoes the scene of the editing equipment in Ray's apartment, so too does the performative echo the constative at the moment of death. The equipment, film, and ginger jar aboard the junk function as an interval performed. The collapse of the performance and document reveal the space at the heart of representation. The title of the film itself doubles, splits, performs in the intervals as a two-edged sign of the status of the text—a document by Wenders/Ray; subject/object effaced, erased, leaving behind a trace of the epistemological and ontological status of a document once promised yet now exposed in its own seduction.

The slippage enters at the spectacular point of the performance as the film comes into us, the spectators. The visual dimension distances us, moves us to the edge of the center as we realize that the film is performing the referent, re-presenting it, not displaying it or presenting it. The performative moment exposes the space between sign and referent. Play inserted into the structure undermines its mastery. The spectator, confronted by the interval, recognizes the performance which is the sliding of signifier to signifier, the impossible task of expressing the limitless text of existence. As constative, it declares its status as performance, as an empty promise of a verifiable and authentic referent.

The documentary form seduces us with the promise of the constative, the promise of a plenitude of meaning embodied in a referent. But meaning is an impossible dream. It cannot be produced within the static closure of binary oppositions. Signification is produced through the open-ended play between the presence of one signifier and the absence of others.

Meaning is never truly present, only performed through a potentially endless process of reference to a chain of absent signifiers. The endless performance of the constative seduces and disrupts its own promise to provide a referentiality that guarantees both epistemological and ontological stability and comfort.

In *Lightning Over Water,* we have the subject "constituting itself in displacement and condensation, in the play that forever distances the other, the object of its desire, from itself."[29] Nick Ray and Wim Wenders stave off death through the film even as they embrace death through film. The paradox of their position becomes a performative that ruptures the film's own structure as document, that serves as its own event. Presence is fragmented into discourse, then further fragmented into both a constative that performs and a performative that declares itself to be a document about death and mastery. Lacking a signature, the cinematic event is determined by the trace of an absent other, performed in a headlong rush into the death of a meaning traversed by the truth of the master and of self-consciousness.

8

(Not) Looking for Origins: Postmodernism, Documentary, and *America*

Ana M. López

America is the original version of modernity. We are the dubbed or
subtitled version.

Jean Baudrillard[1]

I

The nation is a contested site. While many nations—in the Third World,
in Eastern Europe—have, literally, only just begun the process of creating
an "imagined community," the nation-state has simultaneously become
impossible to sustain as a site for coherence or for unitary identification
and representation. If, as theorists as diverse as Benedict Anderson, Tom
Nairn, Eric Hobsbawm, and Homi K. Bhabha have argued, the national
is by definition imagined, unstable, ambivalent, and Janus-faced, understanding a nation today demands a look that can see its narrations, ambivalences, and hybridity; that can see the international within the national. A
privileged location for this look is the space of the margins, frontiers, and
borders that simultaneously define and infiltrate the nation. The center—
the nation—is always different when seen from its margins and finding
the margin at the center's core involves the evocation of an even greater
difference that challenges the transcendental status of the national while
also revealing the very limits of modernity and its neocolonial justifica-
tions. As Bhabha argues in his introduction to *Nation and Narration,* the
transnational dimensions of the nation-state can best be seen when

the margins of the nation displace the center [and] the peoples of the
periphery return to rewrite the history and fiction of the metropolis.[2]

Thus, modifying the title of Bhabha's book, which analyzes the narration of nations, we may ask: What does it mean to document a nation from the margin?

In the case of the five-part Brazilian documentary series *America*, it means, literally, that its analysis of the United States must begin by challenging the national threshold: The series' first episode begins with an extensive precredit sequence in a small town, identified as "deep in the heart of Mexico," that sets the stage against which and through which a "look that shows that the known may be different" will be deployed. In this 1989 TV documentary series, two Brazilians—the well-known writer Nelson Brissac Peixoto and filmmaker João Moreira Salles—"document" an America the likes of which we rarely see from this side of the equator. What is unusual in *America* is not only what the series explicitly attempts to show—an analysis of the North American imaginary focusing on its margins and frontiers—but also how the series positions itself as a documentary vis-à-vis the nation. In fact, *America* rejects all easy categorizations. Unlike cinema-verité, for example, it is not interested in questioning the means of its own production or its representational work. Without any obvious material self-reflexivity, its structure has the complexity of postmodern fiction and its carefully composed and deftly juxtaposed images the plastic impact of contemporary representational art. Also unlike direct cinema (or the bastard form *verité*, identified by Brian Winston as typical of contemporary TV documentaries on both sides of the Atlantic[3]), *America* makes no pretense at objectivity: its resonant poetic voice-over is clearly scripted and its images are composed with painterly care. Furthermore, the interviews with selected personalities (as diverse as Jean Baudrillard, Henry Kissinger, Laurie Anderson, David Rockefeller, and Octavio Paz) that grant authority to the text's various analyses are staged in dramatic mise-en-scène explicitly designed to highlight each individual's traits. Even the interviews with "real" people, albeit anonymous, are staged, insistently directed and idiosyncratic. We also cannot compare *America* to historical or archival documentaries like the recent PBS Civil War series or even the more difficult to categorize *Atomic Cafe*. Although the series makes use of much archival footage and does, in its own way, establish an historical argument about the decay of North American society/culture, it is also singularly unconcerned with historical authenticity, facts, or statistics and demonstrates no desire to reconstruct or witness any specific historical moment other than its own present and the moment of its production and analysis.

After so many disclaimers, what, then, is *America* like? The series is divided into five independent but stylistically and thematically linked episodes identified via aphoristic titles: "Movement," "Mythology," "The

Blues," "Speed," and "Screens." Composed of four or five sections also
identified by brief suggestive phrases used as commercial break calls,
each episode explores the full literal and metaphorical dimensions of its
title. Thus, for example, the second episode dedicated to "Mythology,"
evokes Hollywood, the various American frontiers, steel men and new
cowboys, supermarkets, and, in the section identified as "The History of
a Return," Albany, William Kennedy's *Ironweed,* and the filming of the
recent Hector Babenco movie of the same title. Rather than follow a
chronological or geographical logic, *America* sweeps over the American
landscape and peoples, combining heterogeneous images and phenomena
to produce a series of categories that define another kind of decentered
totality. The associations between the images and phenomena featured are
established by the voice-over narration. However, although authoritative,
the voice-over refuses the logic of rhetorical persuasion and its reliance
on poetic resonance and allusiveness suggests, instead, the openness and
inconclusiveness of fiction.

Part of my argument is that *America* exhibits a hybrid documentary
form combining self-consciousness, awareness, and fascination with the
tenets of postmodernism with the seemingly contradictory desire to present
a social critique. In fact, *America* is not "about" the United States, in the
sense that a *National Geographic* documentary about an African tribe is
about that tribe and ostensibly provides factual information about it. It is,
instead, a documentary about multiple and varied representations of the
United States that reworks those images and rhetorical *topoi*—whether
clichéd or not—through a distinct filter of otherness. *America* explores
the United States as an ambivalent and multifaceted cultural construct
from a distinctly in-between position: in between cultures and nations, the
political and the poetic, the past and the present, the documentary and the
fictional. Thus, the portrait of a nation that emerges not only refuses
standard ideas of a national totality, but also posits the possibility of a
different documentary aesthetic.

Almost by definition, a Brazilian documentary about the United States
has no access to the imperial authority of an ethnographic vision, nor can
it easily exploit the exoticism of the tourist/native dichotomy. But *America*
also rejects the transparency of straightforward ideological critique as well
as the equation of self-reflexivity with critical acuity and distance. By
dismissing questions of fact or "truth value," *America* highlights precisely
the ambivalences of national–ideological constructions that most documentaries on foreign cultures or nations are forced to elide. It posits an
aesthetics of displacement that pushes the documentary to assume a mapping function—linking places in space—as well as a narrative function
that subjugates those links to nonchronological time. As such, the peculiar

history of *America's* production and the nature of its analysis of "America" helps to explain its unexpected appearance on Brazilian television and the significance of its particular vision of the United States for Brazil in 1989.[4]

II

The classification of *America* as a postmodern documentary is unlikely to be challenged by any of its spectators, especially in urban Brazil, where postmodernism is not simply a term bandied about by academics, but an accepted concept regularly discussed by the media (and where Baudrillard and Lyotard are cult heroes whose visits to Brazil were given extensive front-page newspaper coverage). As is typical of "developing" countries, the Brazilian social formation combines, in an uneasy alliance, anachronistic, precapitalist elements with the most advanced capitalist (postcapitalist) forms, and in the last decade, postmodernism has found a secure cultural niche in the arts, media, and advertising in large urban centers (especially in São Paulo). In fact, we can trace the postmodernist sheen of *America* to two fairly well-circulated texts: Jean Baudrillard's *America,* published in Brazil almost immediately after its French release (in 1986, two years before the English-language edition), and Nelson Brissac Peixoto's *Cenários em Ruínas: A Realidade Imaginária Contemporanea [Sets in Ruins: The Contemporary Imaginary Reality],* a collection of stories by one of the co-authors of the documentary.[5] Although the former clearly laid the theoretical groundwork for the documentary's analysis of the American condition, the latter already invoked many of the key images and stylistic devices subsequently used in *America.* More like a series of thematically linked meditations on contemporary fictional *topoi* derived from the cinema than a collection of short stories, *Cenários em Ruínas* couples contemporary subjecthood with internal exile: Always a foreigner in his own country, the unnamed "protagonist" of these essays is caught in a world of media-created pop imagery through which he searches via the plots of novels and films (and the narrativized creative sagas of contemporary film *auteurs* like Wim Wenders and Jim Jarmusch) for his own identity and place.

Despite the circulation of these literary texts, the appearance of what I am calling a postmodern documentary on prime-time Brazilian TV network programming is certainly not a common occurrence. In fact, the appearance of a documentary series of any kind on Brazilian television is already surprising given its constant concern with "entertainment" programming defined as lowest common denominator variety programs, *telenovelas,* and Hollywood serials and movies. Developed under the strict supervision of the military dictatorship that governed Brazil between 1964 and 1985, Brazilian television has been controlled by powerful private media monopolies that under the watchful eye of the military state transformed the medium into a powerful agent for the social and ideological unification of the nation. The Globo network, originally a partner of the Time–Life conglomerate, has been the single most powerful force in Brazilian television since the 1970s (its 50 affiliates attract approximately 70% of the national audience).[6] With access to the best technology, talent, and market research, Globo's *telenovelas* and other variety program formats have become definitive of Brazilian television.

However, the series *America* was not a Globo production. Independently produced by Videofilmes and financed by a number of private corporations,[7] *America* was aired by the Manchete network, a rival to Globo formed in 1983 by the Bloch corporation (with interests primarily in publishing). Following a policy of purchasing some independent productions (instead of relying exclusively on in-house products as does Globo), the Manchete network began to make a small dent in Globo's hold of the national audience in 1989 with the popular period *telenovela, Kananga do Japão,* the exploitative and sensationalistic current events series *Documento Especial (Special Document)* and several documentary series, most notably *African Pop* (a five-part, independently produced series about the worldwide influence and popularity of African music) and *America.* Although Manchete's biggest challenge to Globo's hegemony would be the *telenovela Pantanal,* aired in 1990, its innovative programming in 1989 set the stage for the massive channel turning to come the following year.[8]

III

How can *America* be considered a postmodern documentary? Certainly, the various definitions of postmodernism and arguments about its inevitability and/or effectivity are now quite familiar and hardly need lengthy reiteration. Suffice it, then, to cite, first, Charles Jencks, who talks about postmodernism as a "double coding" or pastiche that combines modernist and traditional techniques nonhierarchically, and Fredric Jameson, who provides, in "Postmodernism, or The Cultural Logic of Late Capitalism," the most complete catalog of the features of postmodernism: a "depthlessness" linked to the cult of the image or simulacrum; a weakening of historicity related to pastiche, historicism, and nostalgia; and the "waning of affect" replaced by *intensités.*[9] Despite the specificity of these descriptions, the term postmodernism has become, as Dana Polan has argued, a "generative apparatus" or "machinal mechanism that encourages a recoding of previous forms and a proliferation of new ones."[10] Furthermore, the political effectivity of postmodernist culture and theory is a hotly contested terrain.[11] However, as Stanley Aronowitz and Henry Giroux argue, postmodernism has problematized popular culture by highlighting the conditions of knowledge embedded in new technologies, by positing the cultural as a field of domination *and* contestation, and by providing a theoretical framework for thinking of otherness as a source of "struggle, collective resistance and historical affirmation."[12] *America's* postmodernism is, thus, a critical one that challenges the standards of the documentary by remapping its frontiers and simultaneously points to changing "configurations of power, knowledge, space, and time that characterize a world that is at once more global and more differentiated" to "effect a shift in power . . . to those . . . struggling to gain a measure of control over their lives."[13]

America is clearly a form of documentary pastiche that exhibits a fascination with and fetishization of the image. Each of its five episodes utilizes a variety of traditional and "modern" documentary strategies, combining them intensely but nonhierarchically. For example, each episode contains at least one sequence designed to function as an echo or reminder of its direct cinema predecessors, where the camera-documentarist enters a private space attempting to capture some kind of objective reality. The first episode, for example, includes a sequence in a California boxing academy, and the third, a "visit" to a blood bank close to the Mexican border. In both cases, the impetus for the images clearly seems to be direct cinema: invading a private space to record/find its truth. However, these sequences are neither given a special truth-value and epistemological significance, nor are they even stylistically pure. They are inserted, without any kind of special markers or commentary, as simply another kind of illustration of the basic theme of each segment. In the first case, what is highlighted is the idea of "movement" which the boxing academy sequence allegorizes in social terms ("making it" up and out of the ghetto) much like the strikingly composed images of highways, cars, and drive-ins which follow it do so physically (and in contrast to the "stillness" of the small Mexican town of the precredit sequence that precedes it). In the second example, the *topos* is the idea of the frontier, with the blood bank sequence (on the American side, but frequented only by destitute Mexicans) closely following a clip of the beginning of *Touch of Evil*. In both cases, the inherent social critique of each moment escapes, sliding away under pressure from its juxtaposition with the purely imagistic. The potentially direct here is contaminated even further by style and the series' fascination with the image. We may have sync sound and a nicely probing handheld camera in each of the sequences, but the spaces are carefully lit and the camera movements measured and graceful rather than obtrusively handheld. Furthermore, what may have been direct footage is, in both cases, edited briskly, denying the images any kind of spatio-temporal assertion of authenticity. The direct invoked here is, ultimately, simply another style to be used and aestheticized according to the logic of the image rather than a privileged mode of knowledge.

Similarly, the use of a poetic, authored voice-over which would seem to harken back to another, more traditional, style of socially relevant montagist documentary (one thinks of Pare Lorentz's *The River* as a model) is also contaminated by its own aesthetic excess and sollipsism. The narration is so poetic, often so abstract, fragmentary, and self-consciously clever that it fails to connect with the images or to locate their place within an overarching argument.

Above all, *America* is a photographer's film. Its images are glossy, carefully composed to maximize their pictorial values, extraordinarily well-lit, and rendered in brilliant colors. And it is the images themselves, as images, that capture our attention most. The words of the voice-over narration often seem to slip away, adding hardly more than a resonant complementary echo or aphoristic verbal image to accompany the visuals. The narration does not provide a model or guide for interpretation as much as it cognitively complements our specular pleasure. That photographs that served as an inspiration for the film *and* the texts of the interviews used by the narration were published as separate, glossy, and quite expensive coffee-table books to coincide with the airing of the series is, therefore, not surprising.[14] *America* is a documentary of multiple surfaces that exploits imagistic intertextuality to further its own specularity: alongside its own images and staged (dramatically filmed) interviews, it uses a plethora of clips, ranging from archival footage of Martin Luther King and the first Americans on the moon to clips from *Que Viva México!, The Searchers, Easy Rider,* and *Ironweed.*

The intertextuality that is established is not only thematic, but also literally superficial—it is the very surfaces of the images rather than the specificity of their cultural meaning that is invoked. In other words, the collision of signs does not lead to a questioning of their status as representations (or even as clichés) but simply exalts them as such. Furthermore, bowing to the constraints of television and the necessity of commercial breaks, the series is also insistently reiterative, repeating images—original or "citations"—from episode to episode (even from section to section) to establish a sense of continuity and its own visual intratextuality. This fetishization of the image—whether visual or verbal—ultimately reduces the historical past invoked to a collection, the equivalent of a vast multimedia photo album with witty captions. And the affect produced is, as Jameson argues about *Diva's* cult of the glossy image, curiously flat while simultaneously aesthetically sublime:

> The silence of affect . . . is doubled with a new gratification in surfaces accompanied by a whole new ground tone in which the pathos of

high modernism [i.e., Munch's *The Scream*] has been inverted into a strange new exhilaration, the high, the *intensité*."[15]

As a postmodern documentary, however, *America* also directly addresses the tension between epistemology and the aesthetic that troubles most theories of documentary. In "The Existence of Italy," Jameson argues that the postmodern or neodocumentary displaces the opposition between art and knowledge onto the image itself.[16] The image's insistence on the "dual presence of the event"—the act of its registration and the instant of history captured—becomes the substance of the documentary in films— like Eduardo Coutinho's *Cabra Marcada Para Morrer* (*Twenty Years Later*, Brazil, 1984) and *Torre Bella* (Thomas Harlan, West Germany, 1977)—in which the process of production is itself violently inscribed into the texts as a visible historical presence that denies representation and asserts praxis. While these films do indeed "loathe" the fictive as Jameson argues, *America*, however, proposes a different answer to Jameson's question: "How to escape from the image by means of the image?"[17] In *America*, the documentary impulse is not an historical force through which the object is seen to be in perpetual change, but a position that allows the text to assert the geographical distance of its vision—a foreign look invested in the plasticity of the images and the poetics of the voice-over-narration—with the freedom of a storyteller that, unlike Walter Benjamin's, is not threatened by information.[18] Perhaps because the fictional has always had a different, more problematic status for Brazilian culture, as Luiz Costa Lima argues in *Sociedade e Discurso Ficcional*,[19] rather than repudiate the fictive, *America* attempts to recapture it as a way to establish a difference that is historical and geographical. In *America*, "information" is neither a goal nor a challenge to the representational, but part of the telling function. Thus, not unlike those postcolonial novels analyzed by Timothy Brennan which combine the informational with the experiential "as voices from the Third World seeking to project themselves into a European setting,"[20] *America* inverts the geographical violence of imperialism by proposing visual and aural images as records of experience, information, and fragments of stories that cannot be completed.

But perhaps what is most "postmodern" about *America* is precisely what a catalog of its postmodern characteristics, especially given that they are such self-consciously adopted ones, fails to elucidate. It is the very nature of the "America" analyzed by *America* that is most postmodern, that determines the necessity of the series' postmodernism, and that allows us to link the specificity of this documentary to the Brazilian context: *America*'s relationship to "America" is curiously replicated in *America*'s own relationship to Brazil.

IV

How is the postmodern voice of the text positioned vis-à-vis the "America" it purports to analyze? (I am using "voice" here as defined by Bill Nichols: "that which conveys to us a sense of the text's social point of view, of how it is speaking to us and how it is organizing the materials it is presenting to us . . . that intangible, moiré-like pattern formed by the unique interaction of all a film's codes."[21]) Claiming neither ethnographic authority nor empirical objectivity, *America,* nevertheless, establishes a necessary distance from its subject that is determined by its position as outsider and as other. Much as its analysis of the margins of America explains the center (the frontiers, immigrants, travelers, detectives, Mexican Americans, Jewish Americans, and African Americans that by their very outsiderness constitute the only possible center of America), the text also remains outside and by doing so acknowledges its inevitable relationship to the inside. As Jean Baudrillard says in his interview in the series, "America is our [everyone's] myth, our unconscious, our utopia." The America of *America* is everywhere, necessarily inside this text as well. Thus, the series' voice-over begins with a self-conscious assertion of location, describing its "look" as foreign and claiming that only that otherness can "reveal that the known may be different." Its analysis of the United States begins, paradoxically, with a look at a small town in the heart of Mexico. Claiming historicity, stillness, and respect for time and memory as Mexican characteristics that distinguish it from its neighbor, it poses Mexico as the closest "other" of the United States, in the words of Octavio Paz in his interview, "as different [from the U.S.] as the wind is from the mountain."

However, *America*'s insistence on its own otherness and multiplicity also represses the position that seems most available to a Brazilian documentary about another nation: its own nationality as a place from which to speak and from which to define its alterity. The repression of the nation as a privileged site from which to look at the United States is already evident in the title of the series, *America.* Which America? North or South? All of it? Including Brazil? The "America" of the text is a stand-in, a simulacrum of an impossible continental totality to which Brazil belongs and from which it is simultaneously excluded.

That this is a Brazilian documentary made by Brazilians for Brazilian television is only acknowledged three times in *America*'s more than 5 hours. In the first episode, while analyzing the ahistorical and antihumanist nature of the American landscape and arguing that Las Vegas represents an inverted image of American values, the voice-over comments: "Americans do in Las Vegas what Brazilians do during carnival: invert daily experience." Obviously invoking Bakhtin-inspired theories of the function of carnival that have been widely circulated in Brazil,[22] the reference to carnival explicitly links a Brazilian phenomenon to the United States. But carnival as a point of reference for Brazil is problematic because what the comment refers to is precisely the contemporary transformation of the Brazilian carnival: its deterritorialization and institutionalization as a tourist industry (like Vegas, in fact) and the waning of the potentially subversive function its social inversions once may have had. As much as Vegas represents a perversion and commodification of the carnivalesque—the institutionalization of a carnivalesque inversion of the work ethic—the Brazilian carnival has also "perverted" its specificity and "Brazilianness" via commodification and tourist exploitation.

More markedly, however, the comment also invokes the important cultural significance of the carnivalesque for Brazil. Far more than just an annual festival of inversions, carnival is an emblem of national identity and, as Robert Stam argues in *Subversive Pleasures,* a master trope that invokes the necessary multiplicity and openness of cultures which are at once "national" and marginal in relation to the centers of power.[23] Defined as cultural "anthropophagy" by the Brazilian modernists of the 1920s and as "tropicalism" by artists in the 1960s–1970s, the carnivalesque response to the liminality of Brazilian culture in the context of neocolonial cultural domination underscored the cannibalistic nature of processes of cultural assimilation via parody, irony, humor, and an aggressive and irreverent intertextuality. However, unlike the cinematic avant-garde of the 1960s–1970s that proclaimed an "aesthetics of garbage" (the sense of a marginal culture doomed to recycle the materials of the dominant one[24]) with films such as Rogerio Sganzerla's *Bandido da Luz Vermelha (Red Light Bandit,* 1968) and Artur Omar's *Triste Tropico* (1974), *America* assumes a different position vis-à-vis the nation and neocolonialism. Unlike the protagonist of *Triste Tropico* (a parodic anthropological fictive documentary) who reverses Levi-Strauss's journey of European self-discovery in Brazil and goes to Europe, like many Brazilian intellectuals, only to discover Brazil, in *America* the traveler has no recourse to an original purity or to a return home. The only points of reference are images that, like carnival, are simulacra of experiences which no longer have an original anywhere. The modernist recourse of devouring the foreign to affirm the national is no longer available, and the search for national identity becomes, therefore, a far more complicated enterprise.

The second reference to Brazil occurs in the second episode and, although explicit, its work is more subtle. While analyzing how U.S. cities cultivate imaginary pasts, especially via images culled from the media (exemplified by a haunting image of San Francisco's Golden Gate Bridge used repeatedly in the credit sequences that is an explicit replica of a similar shot in Hitchcock's *Vertigo*), the text visits a number of small towns named after international metropolises (Paris, Lebanon, Moscow) and lingers in a small town called "Brazil" (in Indiana). The North American Brazil is, of course, a bucolic Midwestern community and the "Brazilian" senior citizen selected for an interview (photographed astride a riding lawn mower) could hardly be said to be representative of the Brazilian national character or identity. Although we do not hear the interviewer's questions, the citizen's comments are obviously responses to a query for difference: in December and January, it is very cold and snowy in Brazil; inflation is a phenomenon identified with big cities and not something the citizens of this Brazil are concerned about. The difference between this imaginary Brazil, a North American simulacrum, and the Brazil watching the documentary in November's sweltering 90 degree weather and with monthly inflation at a then all-time high of 50% is obvious. But what the documentary's insistence on the landscape and tangible existence of this other Brazil emphasizes is the inevitable coexistence of both. Is the Brazil that watches the documentary necessarily more "real" than the simulacrum? As the third reference to Brazil makes clear, hardly.

This final reference appears in the last episode of the series, where Brazil is once again alluded to by the voice-over, in a call for the next section preceding a commercial break: "In the next block, how to be in Paris without ever leaving Copacabana." The segment introduced by this title explores the ubiquity and deterritorialization of modern computer communication technology. In fact, the segment's analysis of the impact of technology on society could be applied to the documentary itself. How to be in America without leaving South America would perhaps be a more appropriate title because this is precisely the effect that the text aspires to produce: the effect of travel, a record of a journey that is simultaneously an assertion of presence (the camera, our foreign eye, was there), and a simulacrum of a necessarily impossible immediacy.

The last three episodes of *America* present a pointed analysis of America's decadence centered on the discussion of the impossibility of developing an historical consciousness because, for America, history—looking back—has meant acknowledging loss and discovering disenchantment (the contemporary impossibility of maintaining the national innocence that once allowed "America" to expand and conquer ubiquitously). Echoing the comments of Octavio Paz in one of the clips from his extensive interview, that "any nation with a history is doomed to decadence," the documentary convincingly argues that America—this America, but also, by extension, the greater America that includes Brazil and is elided from the surface of the text but remains an insistent intertext—necessarily exists in decadence, as a series of shifting and sliding screens (a metaphor of inviolability and transparency that serves as the title of the last episode) constituting an impossible totality that remains central, dominant, and present in its absence or impossibility.

Thus, in the documentary's analysis, the utopia of America—something that was lived as if realized—may now be impossible, not only for the United States, but also for the Brazil that insistently aspires to it. In 1989, a moment when Brazil seemed about to achieve its own utopian dream of democracy postponed by 25 years of military rule, *America* seems to warn that this dream, even before it happens, may be as impossible as any other "American" dream.

<h2 style="text-align:center">V</h2>

This brief analysis has hardly exhausted the complexity of *America,* the allusive richness of its metaphors, surfaces, and playfulness. But I hope to have suggested how this documentary series tackles postmodernity as Fredric Jameson has said in another context, "homeopathically":

> To work at dissolving the pastiche by using all the instruments of pastiche itself, to reconquer some genuine historical sense by using the instruments of what I have called substitutes for history. . . . The only way through a crisis of space is to invent a new space.[25]

Appropriating the methods of postmodernism itself—pastiche, simulacra, images, gloss, and nostalgia—*America* charts a crisis of the American space and its imaginary which also potentially indicates the possibility of mapping a new space from the border and perhaps also *for* the border, the margin, the other everywhere. As Nelson Brissac Peixoto argues in *Cenários em Ruínas,* to survive the "void,"

> those who don't have names nor a place to go, may, nevertheless, begin all over, repossessing these images and banal stories, these fantasy sites now in ruins. The foreigners in their own countries can erect their own sets amidst the ruins.[26]

Speaking from an in-between space to chart the transnational disruptions embedded in the national imaginary of the United States, *America* ends up elsewhere: neither in the Mexican border where it began, nor lost in the exorbitant images of decenteredness that it invokes, but finally addressing the necessary ambivalence of that "Brazilian" national identity it so steadfastly refuses to assume. Itself "Janus-faced," *America* thus addresses all of America, North and South and Brazil itself, with the paradoxical authority of its own neocolonialism. To Baudrillard's assertion that "America is the original version of modernity," *America* offers a postmodern minority discourse that renders inoperable the binarism of original/dubbed, inside/outside, national/foreign, center/periphery. Under erasure by pressure from the margin, the center can only be "documented" as an impossibility that may perhaps be used to renegotiate a different kind of space and time for the history of all forms of cultural difference.

9

Notes on AIDS and Its Combatants: An Appreciation

Bill Horrigan

> Such memory can speak only when indignation and just anger, which impel us to action, have been silenced—and that needs time. We can no more master the past than we can undo it. But we can reconcile ourselves to it. The form for this is the lament, which arises out of recollection. . . . Insofar as any "mastering" of the past is possible, it consists in relating what has happened; but such narration, too, which shapes history, solves no problems and assuages no suffering; it does not master anything once and for all. Rather, as long as the meaning of the events remains alive—and this meaning can persist over very long periods of time—"mastering of the past" can take the form of ever-recurrent narration.
>
> Hannah Arendt
> *"On Humanity in Dark Times: Thoughts About Lessing"*[1]

This is for Darras Robert Pyron (1959–1991): *speculator tectus,* fox's friend

I

What follows—even before that; everything given here; even before that: even *this*—had been written, then abandoned, then destroyed, then written (in Columbus, in LaJolla, in Chicago, in Barcelona), over nine months, a species' gestation period but here a suspension of time pinned to death, not birth. The terror to find speech appropriate to some occasions is majestic. Alexander Kluge, in a case history, makes a commentary from a letter by Alcuin: "Respect for the word involves obligation toward the word . . . hence the recurrent admonition to speak. . . ."[2]

And so.

Here we are in the midst of the AIDS crisis. Yes, you are.
Picture it.

II

The point we have reached in the AIDS crisis is the point of the moment
you are reading this. You are not I.

Forty-five minutes ago, Magic Johnson was heard on National Public
Radio's Weekend Edition program, explaining the importance to him
of participating in tomorrow's (9 February 1992) NBA All-Star Game,
scheduled for live broadcast in 17 countries. His visibility, he said, would
amount to an inspirational boost for all those (sighted) people living with
AIDS, his penultimate sportly spectacle anticipating the full farewell later
this summer in Barcelona at the Olympics.[3]

Eleven days ago, in Barcelona, his intention was not, in fact, unre-
marked. At a venue called the Hot Club, an event billed as a *fiesta actua
con los amigos* was held, sponsored by the *associacio de persones que
vivim amb VIH;* when his image popped up on one of the monitors, it met
with scattered applause. (On the other hand, there was a voice-over, in
Catalan, tongue unknown to me and voicing sentiments unknown to me,
to which perhaps the applause might have been directed.) Today's U.S.
radio commentator (having answered his own question: Is the Basketball
Court a Grave?) seemed less enchanted, and advised in so many words—
actually, ordered flat outright—that Magic Johnson toss in the towel
today and get on with the more important vocation of "inspiring" the
unenlightened, this life-mission lately visited having supplanted his earlier
obligation to perform in sport just as he had been doing, for the delight
of anyone caring to watch. Now it might as well be a page from the Acts
of the Apostles—pleasure's over! time to work! Magic, thunderstruck, is
hearing too many voices.

The question is well-asked: Why this anecdote? Why digression in
advance of the path? While not fully trusting the evasive response that
digression *is* the path (evasive, as it were, in this instance; but not always),
I am here trying to summon and evoke some of what occupies the space
needed to be cleared in order for an inquiring commentary on various
AIDS-related documentary practices to take hold here and flourish. I mean
I am trying to open such a space; and I mean that searching for that space
is frustrated by the specific ubiquity, as well as the specific retractions,
within present social, cultural, and therapeutic discourses of AIDS as a
troubling *fact* of the prevailing global disorder. Speaking seeks its speaker's quarter.

Obviously, it used to be otherwise. When AIDS began circulating in
the news media in the first half of the last decade, as those living remember,

reports were noticeably occasional, and, because of that infrequency, the specter of AIDS was made both more and less disquieting: more, because insofar as you had any reason to care about it, you were armed with only the patchiest bits of data; and less, because the lack of an overall picture abetted your desire to regard it as an eccentric occurrence. At that time, unless you already had a profoundly self-interested investment in knowing about AIDS, it is likely all you knew is what you read in the newspapers. That changed in 1985 when Rock Hudson was announced to be suffering from AIDS-related illnesses; after that, everyone had to know, or to actively mis-know, at least something about AIDS.

But as a literal sensation such that "everyone" was at that moment discussing, Rock Hudson's fate could not, of course, be kept perpetually immediate to all the world's witnesses . . . men still do die, worms still do eat them, and it's still not for love. A point of no return, Hudson's death *locked* AIDS into public consciousness but it cohabits there with hundreds of other more or less urgent (more, mostly) preoccupations of the world citizenry; his death simply normalized AIDS into one more *fin-de-siècle* menace. Unless, that is, it happened to you or to people you knew, which increasingly it did, and then the menace multiplied.

III

Where are we now? Here we are in the midst of the AIDS crisis, trying as before, trying still to understand the terms of its representations, to advance counter or additive representations, to efface those representations favored by the media but disserving the interests of those whose lives the epidemic has diminished. That is a project involving related but separate fronts of activity, and that *fracturing* of fronts—the distraction produced by such fracture, the frustration over having to split energy and attention—typifies the experience of trying with all conviction to "follow" the presence of AIDS-related stories in all media. As with any other "issue," the placement of AIDS on the media's agenda is variable; like child abuse (and its grotesque precondition of "unborn rights"), AIDS is now a permanently "warm" issue able to be ignited into a "hot" issue with the right turn of events (*par excellence:* celebrity victimhood in the Magic Johnson mode), but otherwise relegated to reliable back-burner status.

To that extent, it is now virtually impossible to "follow" AIDS news, as it is at the same time occasional, universal, localized, abstracted, rarified, particular, arcane. For example, lacking medical and/or sociological pedigrees, readers of the International Society for AIDS Education's quarterly journal will find dim illumination; on the other hand, the proliferation across the country of journals and newsletters produced by and for people living with AIDS, filled with pragmatic and community-specific encouragements, has proven to be one of the more remarkable flourishings of self-empowerment the epidemic has made possible. Of course, implied in this perception of fracturing is the increasingly recognized truth that the AIDS "epidemic" is not one phenomenon, not singular, but a multitude of crises and epidemics altering a multitude of communities, identities, practices, and institutions, ranging from areas of epidemiology to the exposure of insurance-industry malpractice to transformations in "dating" rituals to alterations of how social, economic, sexual, ethnic, and work-force identities are both self-defined and policed.

Hence, to talk about AIDS—or to attempt, as this present writing would, to comment on something in relation to AIDS—is to acknowledge AIDS as an agent of infiltration (if not transformation) within the fullness of the social body; hence, to that extent (at least here, at least in me), AIDS as an unquietable constituent of the full field of consciousness from within which any discussion of AIDS-related issues would have to proceed (the field of this consciousness, that is, having been overrun by AIDS, indelibly and already); hence, finally, the conclusive admission that the consciousness presently being set in words (*these words, this voice*) is a colonized one.

The "theoretical legacy" parallel to this subjective one has been expressed nowhere more exactly than by Stuart Hall:

> What is the point of representations, if there is no response to the question of what you say to someone who wants to know if they should take a drug and if that means they'll die two days later or a few months earlier? At that point, I think anybody who is into cultural studies seriously as an intellectual practice must feel, on their pulse, its ephemerality, its insubstantiality, how little it registers, how little we've been able to change anything or get anybody to do anything. If you don't feel that as one tension in the work that you're doing, theory has let you off the hook. . . . How could we say that the question of AIDS is not also a question of who gets represented and who does not? AIDS is the site at which the advance of sexual politics is being rolled back. It's a site at which not only will people die, but desire and pleasure will also die if certain metaphors do not survive, or survive in the wrong way. Unless we operate in this tension, we don't know what cultural studies can do, can't, can never do; but also, what it has to do, what it alone has a privileged capacity to do. It has to analyze certain things about the constitutive and political nature of representation itself, about its complexities, about the effects of language, about textuality as a site of life and death.[4]

IV

The charge of this writing centers on relationships between awareness of AIDS-related issues and documentary film/video productions and practices. Considerable attention has been paid to this intersection within the independent media community, on both the level of specific works being produced (1985 seeming to be the year in which notable work began appearing) and on the level of critical/curatorial commentary being generated in support of informed representational tendencies (late 1986 being the time of William Olander's "Homo Video" show at New York's New Museum, which included pioneering public service announcements by the Gay Men's Health Crisis, Los Angeles' AIDS Project, Stuart Marshall's seminal *Bright Eyes*, Gregg Bordowitz's . . . *some aspects of a shared lifestyle*, John Greyson's *Moscow Does Not Believe in Queers*, Peter Adair/Rob Epstein's *The AIDS Show*, and the "How To Seduce a Preppy" episode from Rick X's *The Closet Case Show*).

Soon thereafter, in this country, the journal *October* devoted the entirety of an issue to "AIDS: Cultural Analysis, Cultural Activism" (ed. Douglas Crimp, Winter 1987), in which many articles referenced the documentary practices being mobilized in relation to the crisis; and the American Film Institute's 1987 Video Festival in Los Angeles presented 8 hours of AIDS-related work as part of a program entitled "Only Human," assembled by B. Ruby Rich and myself. In Spring 1988, Deep Dish TV produced and delivered to over 300 public access stations nationally a 1-hour-long compilation entitled "Angry Initiatives, Defiant Strategies." The late, irreplaceable Lyn Blumenthal of the Video Data Bank proposed, in 1987, the idea of compiling a series, for purchase only, of artist/community-produced and educational AIDS-related works, and this became a reality in 1989 when John Greyson and I worked with Kate Horsefield and Gail Sax to produce the 25 tape, 3 cassette collection, *Video Against AIDS,* which has since had considerable currency in this country and in Canada, through the participation of V-Tape in Toronto.

Since these relatively early interventions, AIDS-related documentary practices have continued to be exercised and refined, and now simply to catalog the extent of such production represents a massive undertaking.[5] Still, certain generalities do emerge.

One of these became clear in 1990 when the Gallery Association of New York State asked me to organize a series of AIDS-related short films (as distinct from videotapes) for a 2-hour touring program titled "AIDS: An Issue of Representation." This, in the end, became a challenge because the overwhelming majority of compelling work being produced was bypassing the film medium in favor of video, a circumstance remarked upon by B. Ruby Rich:

> The potential of video as a medium to carry on and further a mandate once solely assumed by film—i.e., the elaboration of formal strategies and means of production that could further the evolution of the medium

as well as advance, if not action, then at least dialogue, on social problems and political organization, has been made clear most explicitly by the response to the AIDS crisis of the late-1980s.

In this instance video artists have responded to a particular social crisis through the immediate deployment of equipment, invention of aesthetic approach, and creation of new and effective distribution networks. There has been no hierarchy of form, no exclusionary kinship system of artists, no correct-line bastion of orthodoxy. Work has built on other work; video has been a player within a social movement and at the same time has taken this movement's concerns as the material for making art. Elegy, testimony, meditation, investigation, and intervention have each defined a number of works. Aesthetic strategies that had been elaborated for their own sake by video artists in the past now find a concrete application to a particular cause. Artists in general have avoided the ad hoc campaign-based functionalism that so often undermined the art/politics collaborations of the past, opting instead for an aesthetics of invention.[6]

That said, it is also true that the field of AIDS-related media production, happily unregulated in its disavowal of univocality, has become configurable according to virtual genres, which John Greyson has identified, as in the following menu:[7]

1. Cable-access shows addressing such topics as discrimination experienced by PLWAs (persons living with AIDS) and lesbian efforts against AIDS

2. Documents of performances and plays addressing AIDS

3. Documentary (memorial) portraits of PLWAs, most of whom had died by the time the tapes were completed

4. Experimental works by artists deconstructing mass media hysteria, lies, and omissions

5. Educational tapes on transmission of and protection against the HIV virus, designed for specific community audiences (women, blacks, Latinos, youth, prisoners), often commissioned by AIDS groups

6. Documentaries portraying the vast range of AIDS service organizations and support groups that have sprung up around the country

7. Safer-sex tapes that adapt the conventions of porn to teach their bisexual, straight, and gay audiences the eroticization of safer sex

8. Activist tapes, which document the demonstrations and protests of an increasingly militant AIDS activist moment

9. A growing handful of tapes for PLWAs, outlining issues of alternate treatments for HIV infections and AIDS-related diseases.

To this listing, Greyson has responsibly appended the qualifying observations that not only is each of these genres susceptible to formation by the proximity of its companion classes but that the mainstream media's coverage of AIDS, to which most of the works in this list in some sense "react," does

> shift and shimmy much faster than any media critique can allow.
> . . . However relatively horrendous mainstream media representations continue to be, they are always moving, attempting to keep pace with the shifts (both reactionary and progressive) in dominant and oppositional discourses of AIDS, be they scientific, bureaucratic, governmental, or grassroots. Any theory of the mass media that sees such AIDS representations as monolithic misses the daily contradictions and slippages. . . . Like current wisdom concerning treatments for HIV infection and the opportunistic diseases that can accompany AIDS, we must recognize that this representational war will only be won when we select and combine, appropriate to each case and context, a variety of "cures."[8]

Greyson's article from which the above remarks have been taken, "Strategic Compromise: AIDS and Alternative Video Practices," remains the most recommended source for an explication of how and which representational decisions and figurative/syntactic devices work in the service of a beneficial (in all senses) AIDS discourse, his text having the further virtue of insisting that the documentary-driven impulses shared by the works under review have arrayed before them, in dutiful documentary fashion, nothing less than the plenitude of the real, embraced precisely in its nuances, contradictions, evasions, and recondite sexual, political, economic and, as it were, spiritual contingencies.[9]

It has been heard, casually, that the magnitude of the AIDS crises is responsible for fundamentally transforming documentary practices. Not in my view a demonstrably valid claim (since we will never know what the world, or the field of independent production, would have otherwise been like had AIDS not intervened), it is, on the other hand, a fair claim to note that the responses of activists, artists, and affected communities have provided the field of independent media with an aspiration and a challenge such as has brought renewed credibility (or maybe it's just renewed attention) to the importance of people owning and being able to determine the terms of how they are visually represented (the legacy of ground-breaking feminist film practices here being clearly evident). This is not some variation on essentialist demand (i.e., the view that only a person infected with HIV can or should speak/write/represent that status), but is, instead, a recognition that the needs of the living are only served when the complexities of all such lives are rendered as such—*as* complex, subjective, particularized—and for reasons beneficial to them. As Greyson notes, the mainstream media's construction of AIDS, despite being not static, continues, nevertheless, to respond to AIDS too often in terms of the priorities and policies put in place by governmental directives and expediency. For example, the overwhelming emphasis in public service announcements on notions of prevention and precaution are certainly of a piece with the Republican decade's preference for the rights of the unborn over the needs of the living. (It is also surely no accident that the Hollywood community has been much more responsive to pediatric and fetal AIDS-related issues than to, say, IV-drug-related populations or to the decimation of communities of color.)

Typically absent from mainstream media's attention to AIDS is what is journalistically understood as feature coverage: reporting and explanation of issues, individuals, and occasions not linked to breaking "hard" news, thus relatively free of all the overdeterminations of partisanship and sensation attached by nature to that which has been qualified for presentation precisely *as* "news."[10] Whereas much of the independent documentary work by AIDS producers has had to assume the responsibility of providing "news" (e.g., explaining the issues involved in activist demonstrations when faced with the network news' reduction of the event to a 6-second blip; relaying information on alternative or "radical" treatment options in the face of FDA drug strictures, profiteering drug companies, and a too-often craven and collusive medical establishment), the field has also had to be relied on to provide the more broadly therapeutic function of having people directly touched by HIV being able to share representations of themselves and the communities of affinity they inhabit.

This arguably is a break, or perhaps just a divergence, from the issue-oriented documentary practices in this country during the decades immediately preceding the AIDS crises; at any rate, the proliferation of documentary production (ranging from the homemade and public access, to works commissioned and sanctioned by specific school and religious groups, to works intended for those in the scientific, medical, and public policy sectors, to safer-sex instructional shorts intended to be viewed in the context of a bar or appended to a porn tape) suggests in the diversity of its formal tactics and in the varying dispositions of attitude and voice that the notion of AIDS as a cleanly charted terrain on which one might operate with certainty and full assurance has to be retired as a damaging fantasy.

AIDS challenges documentary practices—calls for their refinement, perhaps, or exposes some unspoken assumptions regulating the relationship between who is viewer and who is viewed—in the sense that it has made comparable demands with respect to the myriad workings of the social order in general, that "social order in general" being the discursive construct here lightly advanced just as a way of reinforcing an insistence on the provenance of AIDS as being one of vast and profound dispersion.[11]

V

Dispersion.

An earlier variation on these notes had been marked by a comment a prolific AIDS documentary producer had made to me, in the course of a conversation about the virtues and the limits of nonfictional work in this struggle. I had been wondering if various producers of our mutual acquaintance—individuals theretofore self-designated as "artists" whose particular aesthetic and cultural alliances would probably, in other (pre-AIDS) circumstances, have reduced the likelihood of their ever having turned to documentary formats—now had abandoned the wish to produce pieces in no way necessarily referencing the realities of AIDS. Somewhat to my surprise, this individual responded by violently averring that activist production "was failing," that producing educational tapes "was thankless," and that the results, thus far, of most AIDS-related documentary interventions "was negligible—whose life has been saved?"

This response, once uttered, was tacitly understood to have been spoken in the language and in the categorical terms of personal depletion, burn out, the forestalling of despair. But in an odd way, this dismissal—this dismissal of a practice made by an individual committed then as much as now to the viable urgency of that practice—echoed the philistine dismissal more commonly addressed to fictional or "artistic" practices than to properly documentary or fact-based ones: namely, that art is of dubious value because it is incapable of, not interested in, providing any mode of "proof" or "solution."

Hovering throughout this conversation was a speculation I could not manage to dispel (while at the same time understanding its fundamental irrelevance), wondering in effect what kinds of work all these AIDS producers would have created had AIDS not determined what, in an ethical sense, they were to end up devoting themselves to. This speculation was in turn haunted, for me, by a recent reading of Roman Jakobson's 1931 essay on Mayakovsky, and especially by the text's resonating title: "On a Generation that Squandered Its Poets." This extraordinarily moving lament, occasioned by the death of Mayakovsky and written while Jakobson was in Berlin, reflects less on "the fact that Russia's great poets have ceased to be, but rather that not long ago she had so many of them."[12] I still am not clear as to how this essay continues to reverberate, for me, when pondering the "sacrifice" many AIDS producers have made in terms of placing the imperatives of the crisis above all else; Jakobson's example, after all, centers on a generation of young poets who, in their ecstatic embrace of ideas of a revolutionary future, lacked all conviction in the potency of the present, only to discover (fatally, in the event) that "as for the future, it doesn't belong to us either,"[13] and this, as circumstance, hardly offers exemplary anticipation of the historical moment in which AIDS work is now being produced. Or perhaps it is just that, despite the fit being far from exact between Jakobson's text and the specific contradictions of this moment, a certain struck noble tone occurs at least to this observer to be the note worth striking under the circumstances.

If such a thing exists as the "documentary community" (and I suppose it does, if the continued existence of the Flaherty Seminars is any indication), presumably some of the established workers in its ranks have contributed energy into AIDS-related work. But what is more conspicuous is how a community of AIDS-related documentary producers, ones whose motivating allegiance is to fighting the epidemic coursing among them, has evolved and flourishes parallel to that larger community. This strikes me as ennobling, and of those practitioners not alone; and to the extent that Jakobson's text pays homage to a generation of individuals whose devotion to doing what they should do to save the world by creating the world, then perhaps some of the terms for an adequate appreciation of all those working independently in AIDS-related media might begin to emerge. You think the crises are bleak now? They are, but can you imagine how bleaker it would have been had network television and daily journalism had to have been relied on as sole providers of solace and truth? Many of us who cannot imagine such a climate fail in the imagining because in that event we would already have been dead.

10

"Getting to Know You . . .": Knowledge, Power, and the Body

Bill Nichols

"Documentary" suggests fullness and completion, knowledge and fact, explanations of the social world and its motivating mechanisms. More recently, though, documentary has come to suggest incompleteness and uncertainty, recollection and impression, images of personal worlds and their subjective construction. Documentary has its troubles and opportunities, which these changes reflect. Both trouble and opportunity have to do with the politics of epistemology and representation. How do we come to know others and the worlds they inhabit? If knowledge arises, in large part, from subjective, embodied experience, to what extent can it be represented by impersonal and disembodied language? What strategies are available to us for the representation of people, their experience, and the encounters we wish to have of them?

These questions revolve around issues of specificity, particularly issues of power, knowledge, and the physical body. Specificity invokes a realm of embodied knowledge and situated activity. It implies an opposition to the still prevalent documentary tradition favoring disembodied knowledge and itinerant activity. The material, situated position of the body of the social actor is recruited, sublimated, repressed, or discarded by narrative and mythopoetic agencies. History—embodied, corporeal history—is at odds with narrative and myth.

In a paper presented at a conference on "Film and Representations of Culture," Leslie Devereaux makes this point emphatically in reference to scientific knowledge, even in its ethnographic variant:

> The conventions of scientific writing work against the portrayal of experience in favor of elicited systems of thought, and observed regularities of public behavior, usually reported as behavior, that is, with

the emphasis on action rather than interaction, and on prescription rather than on contingency, which amounts to grave distortion of human actuality. In this rhetorical form it becomes hard not to render people homogenous and rule following, no matter the disavowals we utter about this. Our scientized standards of evidence privilege speech over feeling and bodily sensation, which are assimilated to the personal. The personal, the putatively private, is an indistinct category of suspicious character.[1]

Some documentaries have begun to insist on the representation of experience and, therefore, the body itself as witness. It is not simply the knowledge possessed by witnesses and experts that needs to be conveyed through their speech, but also unspoken knowledge that needs to be conveyed by the body itself. The commentary in Trinh T. Minh-ha's *Surname Viet Given Name Nam* conveys this point (ironically, in voice-over) when it says "Witnesses go on living, to bear witness to the unbearable." The interviews that structure this film, though, both confirm and challenge the idea of the body as witness to lived experience. Trinh resorts to classic devices of fictional mise-en-scène to heighten the subjective sense of the interviewee's body bearing witness, including the use of nonprofessional Vietnamese actors to play the parts of native Vietnamese women. Vietnamese women in the United States are called on to represent the bodies, and words, of women living in Vietnam. The expressivity of the body is central to this representation, but it is a form of representation that breaks with documentary conventions of authenticity by resorting to a performance.[2]

It is no coincidence that the attempt to give witness to personal, subjective experience rather than categorical knowledge coincides with an increased reliance on the techniques of fiction in documentary. The goal of this reliance is usually more to achieve a sense of historically situated subjectivity than to transform the historical person into a narrative character or mythic persona. At the same time, however, these techniques themselves can also spell trouble for both generic conventions and audience expectations regarding the historical authenticity of the documentary film.[3]

Representation is not merely a process for conveying knowledge or experience but is itself at the heart of the dilemma. To present a realistic likeness of something is to efface the agency of representation so that the likeness comes to the fore. To stand for someone or something else is to assert the agency of representation so that an issue or concern comes to the fore. These are two simultaneous acts of documentary representation: one leads quite readily toward classic forms of realism, the other toward classic forms of rhetoric. The rhetoric is often more obvious than the realism. The self-evident act of rhetorical representation can encourage a tendency to distrust images as political, ideological representation, whereas the invisibility of realism may prompt an overvaluation of images as factual, historical representation.

A third term can be added to the process of representation: Not only is there the rendering of likenesses and the act of standing for another person or group, as in parliamentary representation, there is also the process of making a case, as in a legal representation of the facts. The issues of specificity focus the tensions within this three-part definition of representation. Images are always of concrete, material things recorded at specific moments in time, but these images can be made to point toward more general truths or issues. To what extent can the particular serve as illustration for the general? Not only *what* general principle but *whose* general principle does the particular illustrate? To what extent are generalizations misunderstandings of the nature of the particular, the concrete, the everyday and what does this mean for historically located individuals? The body is a particularly acute reminder of specificity and the body of the filmmaker even more so. Where do filmmakers stand and how do they represent their stance? To what extent should they question their right to represent the perceptions and concerns of others? Do they represent their own knowledge as situated or omniscient? What are the consequences of these choices?

Our knowledge of historical reality is under siege. Imperfect utopias and diverse affinities propose themselves as alternatives to the master narratives of Aristotelian reason, Christian salvation, capitalist progress, and Marxist revolution. How do we tell what happened in the past if we do not have the familiar framework of the logic of problem solving, the theology of damnation and redemption, the economics of progress, or the politics of revolution to guide us? How do we represent—meaning to depict, to speak for, and to argue about—what is no longer present under these conditions? And, as a corollary, how do we represent individuals who may not represent the truth as much as subjective experience and different interpretations of it?

One well-known answer that is still dominant but open to question is to use archival film footage and the testimony of experts or witnesses. For filmmakers, this choice escapes the present-tense limitations of an observational mode of representation and allows for more overt forms of authorial or rhetorical intervention. Relying on archival footage also removes the need for reenactments with their embarrassing failures of authenticity. Reenactments risk implying greater truth-value for the *re-created* event than it deserves when it is merely an imitation or copy of what has already happened once and for all. Reenactment was once an accepted convention of documentary representation, but observational styles all but destroyed its credibility. Compared to the vivid impression of reality conveyed by early cinema verité, reenactments seemed encrusted with the traditions of studio filmmaking.

But the matter of authenticity is not so easily settled. In what ways is a reenactment less authentic than a recounting? In a typical recounting, we hear what someone says about an event that has long since happened while we see "authentic" archival images of the event itself. Does this strategy not confer greater truth-value on the spoken word than it deserves? Is the spoken word not a reenactment in its own right, an interpretation aided by hindsight and motivated by an implicit point of view shaped over time? Testimony and commentary give priority less to what happened then in any pure sense than to what we now think happened and what this might mean for us. The working of hindsight is vividly demonstrated in Connie Field's *The Life and Times of Rosie the Riveter* (1980) in which the women witnesses recount their wartime experience in terms of their contemporary understanding of feminist issues. Similarly, the personal histories recounted in *Word Is Out* (1977) draw upon the women's movement's stress on the personal as political and a post-Stonewall aura of frank openness to reconstruct lives whose history might well have been recounted quite differently at an earlier historical moment. In Ken Burns's *The Civil War* (1990), the commentary by present-day experts stresses the significance of this war in the light of the subsequent 130 years of American history, particularly in terms of race relations and the continuing struggle of African Americans for equality.

By avoiding reenactments, the use of interviews to recount events together with archival footage (fact or fiction) avoids the problem of a "body too many," where actors double for historical figures. Actors can never *be* the person they imitate in reenactments. Instead, historical documentaries that rely on archival footage are faced with a "body too few," lacking both actors and the historical figure: The historical person is either deceased or no longer the person s/he used to be. The challenge becomes to restore specificity to an historical figure or event. Representing the subjectivity, perspective, style, and perceptions of people is no simple matter of offering likenesses, of providing "stand-ins" who propose to relay these qualities to us, or of making a case about what an experience was like for someone else. Archival footage is only a partial, though valuable, solution to these issues of representation.

Archival footage also presents epistemological problems that are seldom confronted. A conventional notion of authenticity is commonly invoked that implies "These images are historical (old), therefore they are authentic (true)." This functions as the equivalent of a default value with historical material: Unless we are given reason to think otherwise, we will accept them as authentic signs of their times. We know the past by (re-)seeing it. Some films, such as Connie Field's *Rosie the Riveter* or Marion Riggs's *Ethnic Notions* (1987), contest this assumption by recontextualizing archival footage (in these cases, government "information" films about the role of women in the workplace during World War II and historical examples of racist imagery, respectively). Others, like Trinh's *Surname Viet Given Name Nam* (1989), rework archival footage by optical printing to bring out what had been subordinated or repressed meanings. (In *Surname Viet,* this involves footage of women prisoners who purportedly avoided the North Vietnamese enemy that is re-presented in slow-motion without its original American voice-over: the footage becomes far more ambiguous and suggestive of a fluid, dance-like grace and dignity that its original use as "news footage" suppressed.) By recontextualizing archival footage, rather than using it as confirmation for verbal commentary, some filmmakers have begun to challenge the epistemological assumptions normally embedded in historical documentaries.

The reliance on testimony and commentary by witnesses and experts that usually parallel archival footage also raises problems of belief or credibility. Our willingness to agree with what is said relies to a surprisingly large extent on rhetorical suasion and documentary convention. The filmmaker relays his or her tacit confidence in what is said to the viewer. (This is another "default" function in documentary: "Trust those who speak to the camera unless given reason to do otherwise.") Iconic authentication (filling the background of the shot with evidence of the speaker's status—bookshelves, laboratories, authenticating locations in general) heightens credibility. But as Peter Adair demonstrates in *Some of These Stories Are True* (1982), what social actors say may as easily be fiction as historically authentic. [We do not know until we see the credits which of the three stories have been scripted, much as we cannot separate fact from fiction in *No Lies* (1973), *David Holzman's Diary* (1968), or *Daughter Rite* (1978) until we see the credits, and grant them a veracity greater than the representations to which they refer.]

The Thin Blue Line (1987) adopts a fairly sophisticated strategy regarding the authenticity of both witnesses and reenactments. *The Thin Blue Line,* like Jill Godmilow's *Far From Poland* (1984) and Donald Brittain's *Hal Banks: Canada's Sweetheart* (circa 1985), uses reenactments less to authenticate the past than to stress the variability of its interpretation. *The Thin Blue Line* eschews archival footage, either factual or fictitious. Instead, it uses reenactments of events surrounding the murder of a Dallas policeman and the subsequent arrest and conviction of the wrong man (Randall Adams). *The Thin Blue Line* finds alternatives to archival footage partly because no documentary footage of the crime itself existed, partly because even if it did exist, it would not reveal what Errol Morris wants most to reveal: On one hand, the subjective processes by which we each construct a history that corresponds to present needs and, on the other, the subjective, nightmarish experience of being considered guilty of a crime one did not commit.

The Thin Blue Line detaches itself from the prevailing reliance of documentary on authentic images. Instead of "actual" proof—"real" images of the murder weapon or the crime itself, for example—Morris resorts to typical or stereotypical images of a crime and its prosecution. "Murder weapon," "police interrogation," "signed confession," these stock items of the crime film appear in evocative more than "authentic" forms. We see either stylized reenactments or illustrations of the kind found in dictionaries. Morris offers these iconic representations rather than authentic footage of the actual objects and events. Such generalized images remind us of the degree to which our perception of the real is constructed for us by codes and conventions. By moving from the register of "authentic" to that of "generally typical," Morris creates a minor dissonance that upsets our usual assumptions about the historical authenticity of what we see. It is but a small step to realize that the conventions of documentary themselves guarantee the authenticity of that to which they refer.

The Thin Blue Line also evokes a past self, the historical figure of the man, Randall Adams, as he was imagined or seen by others. Morris represents for us the figure or image, the stereotype of "criminal," not by distorting what Adams says or does, but by representing what others imagine he said and did. He allows us to see how "criminality" is constructed by an historically, materially motivated subjectivity. The film stresses this subjective quality partly by representing the key figures more suggestively than conclusively. We see actors who resemble Randall Adams and David Harris reenacting what may have happened, but we do not see them clearly enough to be able to identify them as stand-ins. Dim lighting, silhouettes, and long shots serve to heighten the subjective quality of the reenactments; like the witnesses, we "fill in" the contours provided to us with presumed identities and inferred actions.

For each person who describes what happened at the scene of the crime, there is a different reenactment. (A vivid, if exaggerated, moment in this process occurs when one of the more dubious witnesses describes her lifelong fascination with detective work: Morris counterpoints her description with footage from a Boston Blackie film, suggesting the clichéd, black-and-white nature of her view of crime.) No one reenactment provides the O'Henry twist we may anticipate, in which the surprising truth of the matter is finally revealed. Morris demonstrates that a documentary need not guarantee that a reenactment present the official version of "what really happened." Instead, Morris shows how policemen and prosecutors, those accused and those accusing others, construct the past they need, burdening it with all the specificity of detail and motivational logic that customarily serves as a guarantor of judicial certainty.

Reenactment in *The Thin Blue Line* offers a sense of how memory and desire are historically situated and subjectively motivated, even in the thick of an impersonal process of legal justice. Morris' multiple "flashbacks" to the police interrogation of Randall Adams and to the scene of the crime urge us to see the subjective dimension that permeates historical representation. Morris questions the reliability of evidence while still asserting that there is a reality to which memory and representation allude.

In a similar spirit, Trinh's *Surname Viet Given Name Nam* does not reenact events or the past directly. Instead, it reconstructs the interviews that gave witness to them. These stylized interviews (formally composed with slightly stilted, monotonal speech) emphasize the mediating function of the interview itself and the processes of translation involved in moving from one language, one culture, and one socioeconomic system to another while still attesting to the experiential fact of different realities. Both Trinh's and Morris's films contest a hegemonic organization of reality that rationalizes or accounts for differences of interpretation within a single controlling frame. Although this point seems to emerge in a more academic or reflexive fashion in *Surname Viet,* both films make clear that they are not simply involved in a game of formal reflexivity or historical relativity. Randall Adams is now a free man, thanks in part to the evidence provided by *The Thin Blue Line*. The women who play the Vietnamese interviewees in *Surname Viet* make clear that they, too, despite their new lives in the United States, continue to suffer from the four virtues and three submissions that have implanted themselves in the bodies of Vietnamese women for centuries. Representation operates neither univocally nor transparently, but it continues to function as a mediation between one person's reality and that of another.

Issues of specificity, subjectivity, and knowledge are not limited to the historical documentary. They also arise in the movement, common to documentary, from the specific to the general, from the concrete instance to the lesson learned, from the material event to mythic meaning and moral significance. This movement goes by many names: exposition, explanation, storytelling, and many more. In each case, questions arise: What generalizations are appropriate? What categories can serve to facilitate understanding and the acceptance of difference rather than diminish our receptivity to the unique in the name of the typical, reducing difference to the measure of otherness, superiority, and dominance?[4]

One way to get specific is to ask about the actual person who undertakes this movement, the filmmaker. We cannot discuss the particular for long without addressing the peculiarity of the often absent filmmaker who urges us to draw larger lessons from the specific ones he or she learned and filmed. This is an old convention in documentary. It feels "natural" for events to refer to larger issues. They fall into place along the plot lines of our master narratives. We assume they hold greater importance than the person or presence of the filmmaker who provides them for us. But this begs the central question. This is somewhat easier to see if we put another assumption into question. What if the person filming is not "one of us" but someone whose location or position is already marked as different? This becomes particularly noticeable when the filmmaker is an exile, a Third World exile, for example, who then puts on display for us the first world "sanctuary" s/he inhabits. The self-evident quality of situations and events, and the filmmaker's place within them, become disturbed; they fall subject to unexpected reinterpretations that undercut the naturalness they might well otherwise have had.

One excellent example is Marilu Mallet's *Journal Inachevé* (*Unfinished Diary*, 1983). The film, by a Chilean exile living in Montréal, addresses the politics of location directly. It stresses the centrality of the local over the global, the specific over the general, the concrete over the abstract. The experience of place and subjectivity is tactile, everyday, corporeal. *Unfinished Diary* is not an exercise in imagination, an expansion of self by constructing an Other, like the Orient, Third World, or even Canada, that can then provide the welcoming features of an old, familiar friend. It is not engaged in the game of representing a foreign culture whose mystery the process of translation into familiar concepts and categories dispels by means of commonsense.

Mallet's stress on the incidental and specific moments in her own daily life, coupled with her memories of Chile and longing to have a place of her own, render *Unfinished Diary* the opposite of the travelogue or its "respectable," that is, more institutionally disciplined, sibling, the ethnography. Movement and travel no longer serve as a symbol for the expansion of one's moral framework, the discovery of cultural relativity, the heroics of salvage anthropology, the rituals of self-improvement in the *bildungsroman* tradition, or as training in the civil responsibilities of empire (or the multinational, corporate environment of today). Movement and travel no longer legitimate the subject's right to speak through/with *disembodied* discourses, *disembodied* but *master* narratives and mythologies in which the corporeal I who speaks dissolves itself into a disembodied, depersonalized, institutional discourse of power and knowledge. This is the Griersonian–Lorentzian legacy in documentary that Mallet rejects.

For Mallet, as for the dispossessed exiles and members of a diaspora, movement and travel become an experience of displacement and dislocation, of social and cultural estrangement, of survival, and of self-preservation. Mallet explores and proposes strategies of resistance practiced through an *embodied,* corporeal discourse of self-representation. This is vividly represented in two adjoining scenes. The first is of Mallet, her child, and her husband at the time, Michael Rubbo, at home with other Chilean exiles who entertain them with clever reparteé spoken to guitar accompaniment.[5] The second is of Mallet and Rubbo in their kitchen discussing the previous scene, Mallet's film, and their relationship. It represents a parting of the ways. Rubbo describes how he would have filmed the scene, capturing the reality of their son's inability to understand the reparteé because it is in Spanish. (Mallet, Chilean by birth, speaks in French, and Rubbo, Australian by birth, in English in this scene about speech, communication, and meaning.) Mallet refuses to accept his sense of reality; she is after something different. This is left undefined, but, to me, it centers on the representation of the embodied and precarious subjectivity of the authoring subject who cannot speak with the certainty of a Descartian rationalist. For Mallet, the musical reparteé itself as a form of personal expressivity and social protest whose rhythm and affective texture can be represented in film has higher priority than pointing out that their son did not understand the Spanish words. This would lapse back toward conventions of semantic understanding which her stress on affective, situated knowledge call into question because their son may well have understood qualities of the music apart from the meaning of the lyrics.

The kitchen scene itself also defines their differences in outlook. Rubbo wants to look in on unfamiliar realities: Mallet wants to speak of her own experience. Rubbo declares them incompatible as a couple. Mallet does not disagree, but whereas Rubbo announces it as a discovered fact, Mallet responds to it as a painful hurt with which she must still come to terms. The scene is not from a Michael Rubbo film, as Mallet puts it at one point, where we might expect to learn about contemporary marital difficulties from the perspective of and with the voiced observations of investigative cineast Michael Rubbo [as we learn about cosmetic surgery in Rubbo's *Daisy: The Story of a Facelift* (1983)]. Instead, the scene *represents* (in the multiple scenes of the word) the marital difficulty it might otherwise report. Not shot from Mallet's point of view in a literal sense, the absence of any external, mediating commentary or perspective together with the degree to which the filmmaker is herself implicated in the emotional intensity of the scene makes it almost impossible to regard it as an example of anything other than itself. As a result, it represents the specificity of exile and dislocation that refuses to become a theory of or commentary on itself.[6] Like all representations of experience, theories and world views are implicit in what we see, but what we see is not offered as an example or illustration of any theory. Quite the contrary. It is a difference that makes an enormous difference.

The politics of location points to the importance of testimonial literature and first-person filmmaking generally. Testimonials are first person, oral more than literary, personal more than theoretical. It is a form of representation that explores the personal as political at the level of textual organization as well as at the level of lived experience. It contrasts with the traditional essay where the authorial "I" speaks to and on behalf of a presumed collectivity. The "I" of testimonials embodies social affinities but is also acutely aware of social difference, marginality, and its own place among the so-called Others of hegemonic discourse. [Rigoberta Menchu's *I, Rigoberta Menchu: An Indian Woman in Guatamala* (London: Verso, 1984) and Cherrie Moraga's *Loving in the War Years* (Boston: South End Press, 1983) are excellent examples of written testimonials that parallel many of the preoccupations of Mallet's *Unfinished Diary*.] Mallet's style for locating herself, her displacement of the "history lesson" from its privileged position as justification for or conclusion to her account, her refusal to make herself into the figure of the tour guide that most first-person commentary in documentary evokes—pointedly identifying for us the larger truths and bigger issues exemplified by her particular experience—all propose a radically distinct model for documentary representation.

Her scenes cannot be described as examples, models, or evidence in the service of an argument without betraying the very strategy she adopts. They are scenes not from *a* marriage but *her* marriage, not from a life but her life. Their significance resides in their particularity not in their typicality. To take them as examples or evidence is to slide toward a Geertzian problematic where representation becomes the province of Us discussing Them in ways that no longer matter very much to Them.[7]

Raoul Ruiz, a Chilean exile working mostly in France, also addresses the politics of location in his *De Grands Evénements et des gens ordinaire* (*Of Great Events and Ordinary People,* 1979). About a national election as seen in his own Parisian arrondissement, *Of Great Events and Ordinary People* is also a meditation on documentary form, and the odd way in which documentary images appear to yield an impression of reality when their juxtaposition is so often disdainful of any specific time and place. Classic, Griersonian documentary and television journalism are seldom great respecters of the specificity of time and place. Images are wrenched and torn from all manner of locations as example, model, and evidence. Ruiz demonstrates the effect with a series of disparate still-life images strung together. In the context Ruiz provides, they serve only as evidence of the strangeness of roping images together rather than to authenticate qualities inherent in the historical world. If anything, Ruiz demonstrates how this tendency to illustrate with disparate images is a quality of cinematic construction rather than the historical world.

Ruiz's strategy carries us through a series of observations that are not yoked together with the glue of semantic coherence, given in disembodied commentary that conforms to the conventions of our prevailing narratives. His observations refuse to add up or present the big picture. When he does suggest a larger frame, it is less via a linear argument than via an evocative, surreal juxtaposition that stresses the incommensurate, irreconcilable quality of sound and image, here and now, there and then, Chile and France, native/exile, First World/Third World by shifting to found footage of Third World scenes.

Compared to the sharp documentary clarity of his own footage, the found footage is grainy, poorly color balanced, and very contrasty. It has the feel of heavily reworked and recirculated imagery. A French election is one thing, a Chilean exile in Paris another, the images of the Third World that circulate within the first still another. No synthesis is attempted, only recognition of the violence hegemonic unity and anthropological description, thick or thin, requires. It is a requirement Ruiz refuses. As the film's coda puts it in an ironic voice-over statement that accompanies these disparate images of Third World culture (the very type of images Ruiz has warned us against as Our kind of imaginary representation of the world out there):

In this way the future documentary will endlessly repeat these three truths:

So long as poverty exists, we shall still be rich.

So long as sadness exists, we shall still be happy.

So long as prisons exists, we shall still be free.

The interrelationship of the comforts of physical separation and the distress of social compartmentalization, of elections here and oppression there, of clarity in one series of images and graininess in another confront us directly in this bold, and defamiliarizing, juxtaposition.

A politics of location inevitably poses questions about the body.[8] We may think of the body as the most local and most specific aspect of ourselves. It can also be a quite troublesome element when we wish to generalize beyond ourselves and transcend our corporeal bounds. We can regard the body in documentary from three perspectives, each representing a different dimension of our conception of self: (1) the body of the social actor who is agent and subject of historical actions and events, situations and experiences; (2) as the body of a narrative character who is the focus of actions and enigmas, helpers and donors all propelling the narrative toward closure; and (3) as a mythic, ahistorical persona, type, icon, or fetish which serves as the object of both desire and identification.

Tensions exist among these choices. For example, between the histori-cally conditional body of a social actor and the ahistorical icon or fetish of a mythic persona, the vicissitudes of time clash with the claims of immortality. The tension is all the stronger when it exists in relation to one and the same body such as we find with an Adolf Hitler, Joan of Arc, Michael Jackson, or Marilyn Monroe. Monroe was simultaneously an historical person, subject to the same vicissitudes as any other person; a narrative character in stories not of her own making (the tragic figure of innocence destroyed by commerce, the victim of male fantasy) and a mythic persona or fetish (comedienne extraordinary, American sex goddess).

Brenda Longfellow's *Our Marilyn* (1988) speaks in the first-person voice of another exile from the institutional domain of representation: the voice of a woman who, over the course of the film, reflects on her own identity and its social construction. The confessional voice-over commentary remains unattached to a visible body of its own. Perhaps it stands for the filmmaker; maybe it is representative of many Canadian women. In either case, it is a voice reflecting on questions of body image more than the fact of physical presence *per se*. The quest for a body image to give psychic incarnation to the speaker's (still absent) presence motivates the commentary.[9] *Our Marilyn* is about the narrator's search for a specific female identity to the extent that it is based on a body other than her own. This other body is imaginary but also divided—divided in this case by national identity and alternative subjectivities.

Is "our" Marilyn, Marilyn Bell, a long-distance Canadian swimmer who was the first woman to swim across Lake Ontario, to be the mirror of "myself:" or is "their" Marilyn, Marilyn Monroe, to represent the *me* that must come into being in the space between such alternatives? The historical body takes form along the armatures of historical, mythic, and narrative options made available to it. *Our Marilyn* asks how to represent, in cinematic form, the female body—not as idealized nude or object of desire: not as temptress or provider but as a body *in* action. The desired Marilyn represents a state of physical being and action, not a frozen icon or image, not a character in someone else's narrative, but a *vehicle* for the presentation of self.

Our Marilyn asks how we may represent women's subjective experience of corporeal being. How can the female body be the subject of a film, centered in the frame, and still not be the object of male erotic pleasure? To what extent can physical endurance and psychic exhaustion such as that experienced by Marilyn Bell during her almost day-long swim be represented without the concomitant fetishization/eroticization of physical effort found in conventional fictions—think of the films of Ethel Merman, Delores Del Rio in general, or, more recent works like *Personal Best*

(1982) and *Flashdance* (1983)? Can the viewer be constructed, as Teresa de Lauretis proposes, as female regardless of the viewer's actual gender?[10]

Our Marilyn suggests ways in which that question can be answered affirmatively through the experimental techniques it deploys (optical printing, sound effects, slow motion, and the prolongation of the act of marathon swimming) to immerse us literally and metaphorically in the sensations of the female body in action, in motion. An extended portion of the film is given over to what is usually neglected in the coverage of marathon-like events: the middle, that infinite moment of sustained but repetitive effort and the hallucinatory state of mind it induces that constitutes the basic substance of physical endurance. We see and hear what Marilyn Bell might have seen as she churns on through the cold lake waters toward a destination that remains far beyond sight. It approximates, ironically, an out-of-body experience in which physical motion establishes one rhythm while the mind explores spaces and sensations of its own devising. This remarkably prolonged representation supports neither narrative suspense nor mythic idealization. Like Errol Morris's reenactments of the murder at the center of *The Thin Blue Line,* Longfellow's reenactment of Bell's epic swim instills an all-too-readily lost subjective dimension to historical fact. This is not a projected image of male desire but a more direct evocation of female subjectivity arising from an act of the physical body and historical person.

Differences circulate within the realm of social experience and risk aligning themselves along the fault lines of the social imaginary—them/us, masculine/feminine, Canadian/American, either/or. *Our Marilyn* leaves differences "at sea," circulating around questions of crucial importance. The film refuses to generalize or conclude, to abstract from the particular to the universal. Physical effort, swimming in this case, is affiliated less with a narrative of self-discovery or conquest than with disembodiment or dislocation. Marilyn Bell's achievement occupies a largely forgotten space in the cultural history for which Marilyn Monroe is an apotheosis. Bell, like Mallet and Ruiz, struggled to define a space of her own. The voice-over commentator of *Our Marilyn* continues that struggle, using icons and traces of the historical deposited in the social imaginary.

In a similar experimental–documentary vein, Marlon Riggs explores the suppressed space of black gay male experience in *Tongues Untied* (1989). Rigg's work evades categorization. Neither documentary nor experimental within established conventions, even those of reflexive documentaries, *Tongues Untied* functions as a poetic evocation and rhetorical exhortation that refuses to describe or decry when it can demonstrate feelings, attitudes, and assumptions that a less fully embodied and situated perspective could not reach. Like Mallet, Riggs puts his own body, and life, at risk. Our first sight of Riggs is as a nude figure, moving slowly through the frame in a dim, abstract space as though searching for something not yet present. There can be no mistake that the body itself, its physicality and color, are utterly central to the testimonial tone and poetic charge of the tape.

Riggs takes a different route from the cooler, more questioning poetry of Trinh Minh-ha or the more ironic juxtapositions of Raoul Ruiz. *Tongues Untied* is aflame with passion. It demonstrates the centrality of survival and dignity; race, sexual orientation, and self-esteem; coded forms of expression (rap and snap), and open forms of loving. And it does so in relation to the physical bodies of Marion Riggs, Essex Hemphill, and several others. Riggs jumps from one scene and one demonstration to another—from a choreographed dance by a group of black men across a playground basketball court to a searing monologue on racism delivered straight to the camera—evoking feelings and rhythms, textures and tonalities that belong to the visceral, political experience of everyday life.

Like all of the other film and videomakers discussed here, Riggs favors an experiential, evocative voice that calls into question the conventions of historical representation. The recurrence of the word "evocation" needs some clarification at this point. Evocation differs from representation at least in degree if not kind. These experiments with specificity and a politics of location described here parallel the call for a "post-modern ethnography" by Stephen Tyler. His description, "(evocation) defamiliarizes commonsense reality in a bracketed context of performance, evokes a fantasy whole abducted from fragments, and then returns participants to the world of common sense—transformed, renewed and sacralized," approximates what *Tongues Untied* achieves.[11]

Like *Our Marilyn, Tongues Untied* avoids giving us the usual sociological evidence about the problems of identity and self-esteem. Like Mallet in *Unfinished Diary*, Riggs situates himself on screen, on the spot, quite literally when a series of newspaper photographs of black men who have contracted AIDS ends with a photograph of himself. Like Ruiz and Trinh, he raises questions about identity, place, and the experience of exile—even in the heart of one's "own" culture—and of invisibility—even in the midst of a gay subculture. Like Morris and Trinh, he offers highly stylized, abstracted images that make no claim to historical authenticity. They evoke the moods and tones of typical encounters; they invoke the stereotypes and icons of typical attitudes. They, like Trinh's newsreel footage and Morris's reenactments, remain subject to contestation and revision. Riggs has shaped a work of extraordinary intensity that rejects any claim to disembodied knowledge. Instead, it dwells on the pain, pride, doubt and knowledge that cannot be separated from the body in which they reside.

The tape's structure is that of a series of fragments or vignettes. Unlike his more conventional, voice-of-God documentary on racial stereotypes in the media, *Ethnic Notions* (1987), *Tongues Untied* does not adopt the classic expository model of problem/solution. Like Ruiz's *Of Great Events and Ordinary People,* the film tends to accumulate impressions and evidence but without subordinating them to a controlling argument. Just as Ruiz concludes with a juxtaposition of first and third world images and values that suggest attitudes lying behind the process of a French election without determining it, Riggs concludes on a note that is less an explanation or a solution than a challenge. Riggs's last voice-over commentary is, "Black men loving black men is *the* revolutionary act." This challenge hits the viewer viscerally. Whether the viewer is the one intended and spoken to by Riggs (black, urban, gay males) or not, the effect of the tape's structure is to position any viewer to receive this statement from precisely this point of address. When de Lauretis proposes that a feminist film aesthetic might construct viewers who occupy a feminine subjectivity, regardless of their own gender, she offers a proposition that can be profitably extended to other subjectivities. Riggs himself puts the point in practical, nontheoretical terms that capture perfectly the importance of specificity to the reconstruction of knowledge as embodied experience:

> Now I realize you can speak in a very small, focused, particular way. . . . I don't mean a trivial way, but in a particular sense that is very community identified, personal, and yet reach people who are not necessarily part of your immediate culture.[12]

These films and videotapes—*The Thin Blue Line, Surname Viet Given Name Nam, Of Great Events and Ordinary People, Unfinished Diary, Our Marilyn,* and *Tongues Untied*—bring the power of the universal, of the mythical and fetishistic, down to the level of immediate experience and individual subjectivity. How does a text restore that order of magnitude which characterizes lived experience when it can only represent through evocations what lies beyond its own bounds? One set of answers, it seems, avoids invoking the power of disembodied knowledge and abstract conceptualization in favor of the enabling power stemming from situated knowledge and the subjectivities of corporeal experience.

Afterword: On Rodney King

What better epitaph could we place on the tombstone of a scholarship that has lost sight of the historical world than

> Above all, it is the reference principle of images which must be doubted, this strategy by means of which they always appear to refer to a real work, to real objects, and to reproduce something which is

logically and chronologically anterior to themselves. None of this is true.

Jean Baudrillard
The Evil Demon of Images[13]

No *question* of magnitude surrounds the footage of Rodney King's beating by the LAPD. The viewer experiences a tension between the representation and the represented that viscerally exceeds the moment and the frame. A gap opens that demands redress. A moral and political imperative compels such a demand and will not tolerate indifference. The beating was the speech of an institution (the LAPD) that announces on every car its credo, "To Serve and Protect." The trial was the speech of an institution (the judiciary) that guarantees equality for all. The violent aftermath was the speech of those beyond these discourses of the Law. It was the speech of the unseen and the unheard, proclaiming indignation, anger, and even hatred in a language incomprehensible to those at the other end of the freeway, inside the lacunae of shopping malls, airports, and cultural centers, in front of televisions and monitors, insulated from the historical world as fully as Baudrillard himself appears to be.

Bad boys, bad boys; whatcha gonna do; watcha gonna do when they come for you?

theme song
"Cops"

A riot is the language of the unheard.

Martin Luther King

The Rodney King footage sweeps Baudrillard's doubt aside. This "mere" footage—without stylistic flourish, bereft of edited constructs of time, space, metaphor, or psychology—affirms the fate of the black, male body at the hands of the police. Not a documentary in the sense of a finished text—although it was never seen in any other context than that of televisual flow, network newscasting, editorial comment, and collective evocation—this mere footage seems as definitive in its meaning as surveillance camera records, satellite images, or, in a grotesque inversion of values, home movies.

The definitive quality of such images stems from the propensity of documentary film, and footage, to serve as a fiction (un)like any other. One key difference lies in the assumptions and expectations brought into play by viewers within a documentary context. (This context may rest on belief more than certainty—full and complete authentication—but it is no less powerful for it.) The sight of brutal violence, or its extreme manifestation, brutal death, engages us quite differently in documentary. This is not a simulation. There is no getting up, dusting off, and going on as if nothing had happened. The imprint of history registers on the flesh. (The corpse or wounded body is what simulation models—like the media coverage of the Gulf War—prove determined to avoid.) The camera brings this historical imprint before us and we assume that there is indeed a referent, the body of Rodney King in this case, forever altered by what it is we witness.

The body stands at risk. Prophylactic measures must be taken. In the eyes of the LAPD and those who might see *Grand Canyon* (Kasdan, 1991) as the soothing antidote to the nightmare fantasy of straying from the freeway and actually entering the world of Rodney King, unfortunately, the body at risk belongs to those who form a thin blue line of defense against the threat posed by Rodney Kings. Assumptions and expectations move in a very different direction. The defense lawyers for the four LAPD officers charged in the beating turned Rodney King from victim to dangerous provocateur and converted police response from raw brutality to panicky self-defense. Their skill testifies to the malleability of footage that may document what happened on one level but not guarantee its meaning on another. The historical imprint may attest to authenticity, but meaning remains the result of interpretations applied and accepted.

Images can indeed provide a form of authentication regarding something anterior to themselves (excluding the "evil demons" of digital sampling and computer-generated images), but the surrounding frames, contexts, narrative structures, televisual forms, viewer assumptions, and expectations vie with one another. They constitute, in aggregate, a social arena devoted to interpretative struggle. Though "won" by the defense within the courtroom, the verdict's appeal began immediately in the city's streets. All the events that constitute the aftermath of the trial form another locus of struggle. Whether these events will be heard, understood accurately, and addressed effectively remains to be seen.

Moments like the beating of Rodney King, the explosion of the space shuttle Challenger, the obliteration of installations by "smart bombs," or the police beating of black youth at Howard Beach bring us face to face with the fragility and mortality of the body. Such moments often demonstrate the uneven distribution of such mortality in terms of the unequal likelihood of being the target of violence for males/females, people of color/whites, young/old, upper or middle class/poor or underclass. Such moments cut through the narrative frames and explanatory nets cast around them. They effect a dual perception that confronts an enormous gap between representation and referent, affirming the pain and loss suffered by the social actor, the historical subject, while acknowledging the inadequacy of response channeled toward and through the representation itself, despite the enormity of its impact. This very enormity, excess of the most compelling kind, demands struggle within a larger interpretative arena, outside the frame, beyond the screen, in that anterior world whose future delineation remains up for grabs.

Notes

1. Introduction: The Truth About Non-Fiction

1. Christian Metz, "Some Points in the Semiotics of the Cinema," *Film Language: A Semiotics of the Cinema,* trans. Michael Taylor (New York: Oxford University Press, 1974), 94.

2. Jacques Derrida, "Le Facteur de la Vérité," *The Post Card: From Socrates to Freud and Beyond* (Chicago: The University of Chicago Press, 1987), 467–468. In this essay, Derrida launches a rigorous critique against Jacques Lacan and his psychoanalytic theories along lines which had been sketched out previously [see ff. 44 in *Positions,* trans. Alan Bass (Chicago: University of Chicago Press, 1981), 107–113]. Derrida is critical of what he judges to be a fundamental logocentrism in Lacan's thought, with special attention given the Lacanian notion of "full speech": a (metaphysical) designation for "a reordering of past contingencies" achieved through analysis and in language, a construct in which "truth" and "presence" are understood to be co-implicated. In "Le Facteur de la Vérité," Derrida thus distances himself from Lacan and from the philosophical orthodoxy which aligns "truth" with "fiction," no matter how paradoxically. I invoke the essay by way of establishing the complex and contested terrain of ideas upon which any discussion of "truth" and "non-fiction" must necessarily depend rather than as an endorsement of the Lacanian prescription.

3. The nonfiction referent's "historical status" is arrived at through a complex set of relations among perceiver, material, signifier, signified, and referent rather than awarded a priori. This status is neither fixed nor absolute and can be remanded on the basis of subsequent knowledge.

4. In his essay contained in this volume, Philip Rosen (Chapter 4) places documentary forms within a category he calls "indexical signification" ("representations produced with some degree of participation by the referential object or events themselves"), but distinguishes among them on the basis of their temporal potentialities. Thus, broadcast technologies—radio and television—can be said to occupy a significantly different position from those derived from the technologies of mechanical reproduction— phonography, photography, and cinema—with regard to their preservational,

hence historiographical, utility. During the past two decades, the widespread use of electronic news-gathering technologies which make broadcast and storage simultaneously available challenges this distinction.

5. Bill Nichols contrasts fiction-based performance from the "virtual performance" of documentary in his essay, "Getting To Know You" (Chapter 10, note 2). In the latter instance, social actors play themselves albeit in a manner that may be influenced by dramatic conventions. The question is complicated in the myriad films in which social actors are also professional performers; the celebrity subject has been the stock-in-trade of one important strand of the post-direct-cinema documentary tradition (e.g., *Showman, Meet Marlon Brando, Don't Look Back, Truth or Dare*). In such cases, the question of performance—virtual or real—can itself take center stage.

6. Bill Nichols provides a thorough and lucid account of the relations between documentaries and fictions in "Telling Stories with Evidence and Arguments," a chapter of his *Representing Reality: Issues and Concepts in Documentary* [(Bloomington: Indiana University Press, 1991), 107–133]. While averring that the two forms are equally constructed, Nichols distinguishes between the *story* basis of fictions and the *argument* or "rhetorical fiction" undergirding documentaries. One useful shorthand distinction Nichols draws between fiction and nonfiction is between their respective orientations towards *a* world as opposed to *the* world. (113).

7. It is in this regard that I take measured opposition to a focal point of Bill Nichols' important new study of documentary, *Representing Reality*. Nichols begins the book by aligning documentary film with "other nonfictional systems that together make up what we may call the discourses of sobriety," by which he means science, economics, politics, foreign policy, education, religion, and welfare (3). He is right to point to the ways in which these domains, which claim a direct relation to the real, exert power over individuals and societies. The note he sounds here emerges as the core concern of the book—an attentiveness to matters of "domination and conscience, power and knowledge, desire and will" (4). It is my sense that, of this list, desire remains the outcast, so that unconscious, delirious, fantastic, or ecstatic elements are underserved. Sobriety brings with it a favoring of consciousness, of intentional or programmatic aims, effects best examined in the light of day. My own theoretical concerns return me to documentary's delirious as well as to its sober self. My predilections are rooted in more than theoretical abstractions, however, as they lead directly to aesthetic investigations of the sort that occupy me in "Toward a Poetics of Documentary" (Chapter 2 of this volume).

8. The television coverage of two earthquakes in southern California (28 June 1992) brought home to me the continuing relevance of the camera-as-scientific-instrument school of thought. Throughout much of KNBC's Sunday morning coverage of the temblors and their effects, a small inset image labelled "LIVE" remained visible at the lower right hand of the screen, compliments of the "Channel 4 Seismo-cam." The video window displayed a seismograph, its needle registering the most minute fluctuations of seismic activity, all in real time. While the station's coverage moved from one remote location to another, from the Caltech experts to the hapless victims and back again, the Seismo-cam kept the viewer wordlessly informed of every lull and tremor in the pattern of aftershocks. In this case, the documentative image functioned as a public amplification of the scientific instrument; the mediated seismograph provided vital information instantaneously to millions. The "Channel 4 Seismo-cam" expands the range of indexical functions for the televised image. Just as the Weather Channel provides a running index of meteorological statistics (time,

temperature, barometric reading, wind velocity), the Seismo-cam offers the visible proof of (potentially lethal) bodily sensation.

9. Andre Bazin, "The Ontology of the Photographic Image," *What Is Cinema?*, trans. Hugh Gray (Berkeley: University of California, 1967), 14.

10. In this regard, I echo Tom Gunning's pronouncement from his introduction to *D. W. Griffith and the Origins of American Narrative Film:* "I strongly believe that history and theory must proceed in tandem in film study, with the methods of one supplementing the undertakings of the other" (4). The recent publication of three books which reorient our historical understanding of the cinema while extending the theoretical debates around narrativity, spectatorship, and Marxist cultural theory respectively offer ample testimony to this salutary convergence: Gunning's *D. W. Griffith and the Origins of American Narrative Film* (Urbana: University of Illinois Press, 1991); Miriam Hansen's *Babel & Babylon: Spectatorship in American Silent Film* (Cambridge: Harvard University Press, 1991); and Jane M. Gaines's *Contested Culture: The Image, The Voice, and the Law* (Chapel Hill: The University of North Carolina Press, 1991).

11. Such a shorthand account of the rise to power of the feature-length fiction film at the expense of the documentary plays as a near-parody of traditional film history. Recent reinvestigations of early film history have replaced myth with nuanced historical accounts of the evolution of cinematic language, institutions, and spectatorship. Tom Gunning, for example, has argued convincingly that the early cinema was not primarily a narrative form. His notion of the preeminence of a "cinema of attractions" which, prior to 1908, focused more on the display of curiosities than on the development of stories and characters leaves open the way for more detailed study of the functions and effects of early documentary forms. See, in this regard, his "The Cinema of Attraction: Early Film, Its Spectator and the Avant-Garde," *Wide Angle* 8, nos. 3, 4 (1986), 63–70.

12. The proliferation of nonfiction television forms is a subject that requires far more attention than can be given here. Suffice it to say that, in a moment of escalating production costs, independents and major networks alike have begun to subscribe to the belief that "truth" is more profitable than fiction: "America's Funniest Home Videos" and its clones; reality-based programs ("Cops," "America's Most Wanted," et al.); breakfast news format (with the "Today Show" now annexing weekend mornings) and morning-till-night talk shows and tabloids (from Geraldo to Arsenio and on to David Viscot); C-SPAN, for gavel-to-gavel junkies; and the news magazines. "Dateline NBC" is that network's sixteenth effort to succeed in the prime-time news magazine format that has become a cash cow for its rivals. "60 Minutes" is CBS's biggest money-maker ever, earning as much as $70 million a year [Michele Willens, "Sweet Sixteen?," *Los Angeles Times* Calendar, 22 March 1992, 7]. In a newly competitive media environment in which 24-hour specialized cable channels are the norm, the three major networks are entering the round-the-clock news business with a vengeance. Talk, if not exactly cheap, is still cheaper than traditional entertainment formats.

13. Sharon Bernstein, "Show's Founder Steps Out of the 'P.O.V.' Hot Seat," *Los Angeles Times,* 6 July 1992, F11.

14. Robert Epstein, "Academy's Latest Film Stir-Fry," *Los Angeles Times,* 12 March 1992, F9.

15. In this regard, see note 6 in which Bill Nichols makes documentary film converge with other "discourses of sobriety." This identification presumes a rationalist founda-

tion for documentary rather than one which issues from an encounter of the creative imagination with the historical world.

16. The psychoanalytic trope which most approximates for the documentary the fiction-based role of projection/identification may well be voyeurism of an unvarnished sort. The lure of Madonna's *Truth or Dare*, for example, is the promise that we may catch a glimpse of the star performer with defenses down and, thus, recover a voyeurism which outstrips exhibitionism. The fact that, in that film, exhibitionism wins out over voyeurism can be attributed to Madonna's dual function as the film's voyeurized centerpiece as well as its executive producer. The emergence of the executive producer as the authoritative credit skews the film more toward television than cinema—music television, that is. At one important level—one that might help to explain the film's financial success—*Truth or Dare* as documentary exposition plays as little more than a stylish wrap-around for Madonna's music videos. Many a documentary critic has commented on the necessary "tension" that must exist between a cinema verité filmmaker and his or her subject. It is this edginess that incites the viewer's interest in the hopes that some unexpected insights will be produced, unmasking the performing subject. In *Truth or Dare*, that struggle for control over the film's revelatory powers never, in fact, materializes. It is replaced by a display of the artist/producer's considerable "daring," but a daring that is always to be understood as the willingness of the one who authorizes the images to reveal something shocking.

17. One pioneering effort in the union of psychoanalytic theory and documentary criticism occurs in the final chapter of William Guynn's *A Cinema of Nonfiction* (Rutherford: Associated University Presses, 1990) entitled "The Nonfiction Film and Its Spectator" (215–231). Clearly referring to Metz's famous "Fiction Film and Its Spectator" essay, Guynn traces documentary's modifications to the economic and topographical terms of the filmic state and to the cinematic apparatus. He points to the capacity of nonfiction to produce filmic displeasure through its disclosure of "real" and, therefore, ungovernable tragedy (e.g., the Holocaust). Moreover, according to Guynn, documentary spectatorship demands a higher degree of vigilance, thus invoking the defense mechanisms of the ego: "The cinematic apparatus by its very configuration tenders a promise of libidinal pleasure that the spectator here is led to refuse: the documentary film is an object inappropriate to desire" (223). While Guynn's discussion represents a breakthrough for the way in which it introduces documentary into psychoanalytic debates, his construction of desire is, in my view, a rather orthodox one; the notion of documentary desire deserves to be interrogated, thoroughly and in its own terms.

18. Consider, for example, the adoption of the conditional mood in the work of Chris Marker (*Letters from Siberia, Sans Soleil*) or Peter Watkins (*Battle of Culloden, The War Game*) in which the depiction of potential rather than experientially available worlds is faithfully (or whimsically) rendered; or the ways in which some video artists have chosen to overlay present-tense, autobiographical images with archival footage to suggest the historically determined character of the self (e.g., Lynn Hershman's layering of self-portraiture and Holocaust footage in her *Electronic Diary*). The point here is that there is no necessary limitation to the visual or auditory conceits available to documentary film and video any more than there is for fiction.

19. A great deal of the early scholarship in semiotic film theory treated the question of the status of film as language, the extent to which the cinematic object could be substituted for the traditional linguistic one. The previous debates addressed important but relatively "local" distinctions such as that between "language" and "language

system" and, thus, depended on cinema's satisfaction of specific defining characteristics developed within post-Saussurean structural linguistics. In Derrida and White's usages, "speech," "mimesis," and "speaking subject" (like "trope" and "figuration") are more global constructs which appertain to all discursive activities.

20. Derrida, "Le Facteur de la Vérité" (463, 467–471). For a brief discussion of the Lacanian variant of the "real," see Alan Sheridan's "Translator's note" in Jacques Lacan, *Ecrits: A Selection,* trans. Alan Sheridan (New York: W. W. Norton & Company, 1977). "The 'real' emerges as a third term, linked to the symbolic and the imaginary: it stands for what is neither symbolic nor imaginary, and remains foreclosed from the analytic experience, which is an experience of speech . . . 'the real is that which always returns to the same place'. . . . Hence the formula: 'the real is the impossible' . . . the ineliminable residue of all articulation, the foreclosed element, which may be approached, but never grasped: the umbilical cord of the symbolic" (ix–x).

21. Hayden White, "Introduction: Tropology, Discourse, and the Modes of Human Consciousness," *Tropics of Discourse: Essays in Cultural Criticism* (Baltimore: The Johns Hopkins University Press, 1978), 3,2.

22. In my own discussion, I have chosen to retain Derrida's usage, "the *passage* of the truth through fiction," for its resonance with the Freudian notion of "bahnung" which has been variously translated as "fraying," "facilitation," and "breaching." In all versions, "bahnung" names a conception central to Freud's metapsychology: the breaking down of "contact-barriers" between neurones through which sensory impressions become memory. The term is crucial to Derrida's argument in his seminal "Freud and the Scene of Writing" [*Writing and Difference,* trans. Alan Bass (Chicago: University of Chicago Press, 1978), 196–231]; "passage" in the above phrase thus retains the Derridean sense of a differential or trace structure, a construct available to analysis.

23. The cited examples of the mutually reinforcing linkage between indexicality and commodification are all historically specific. Amateur video footage of an undulating San Francisco Bay Bridge provided the strongest public images of the 1989 earthquake. In the summer of 1992, MTV's "The Real World" introduced an "American Family"-style verité approach to the youth demographic with a mini-series documenting a three-month life-style experiment (a strategically mixed collection of young people—all hipply artistic—share their lives and feelings with the cameras and each other). Television advertisers have been using "authentic," time-lapsed documentations of a product's potency since the medium began selling its wares. And, in the newest Presidential campaign strategy, televised, one-on-one exchanges between candidates and citizen audiences have achieved prominence. The most notable of these was yet another MTV offering in which Democratic hopeful Bill Clinton sparred with a roomful of 18–24-year-olds, closing with a Q & A "lightning round": favorite painter—El Greco; astrological sign—Leo; Clarence Thomas or Anita Hill—Anita Hill. In every case, the historical linkage between indexicality and commodification provides the unspoken support for the mass reproduction of scenes derived from the real.

24. While countless commentaries on the Rodney King trial and its aftermath appeared almost instantaneously, in-depth analyses focusing on the circulation and use of the Holliday videotape footage have yet to be produced, this despite general agreement as to its special status. *Newsweek's* Jonathan Alter has said of the footage that it "immediately became one of the half-dozen most widely watched TV clips in the

entire history of the medium, right up there with Ruby shooting Oswald and the Challenger explosion" ["TV and the 'Firebell'," *Newsweek*, 11 May 1992, 43].

25. Julia Kristeva, "Psychoanalysis and the Polis," *The Kristeva Reader*, ed. Toril Moi (New York: Columbia University Press, 1986), 307.

26. Hayden White, "Introduction: Tropology, Discourse and the Modes of Human Consciousness," *Tropics of Discourse: Essays in Cultural Criticism* (Baltimore: The Johns Hopkins University Press, 1978), 1.

27. I have argued that documentary style, structure, and expositional strategy are as tropic and figurative in their character as their fictional counterparts. The "fictive" elements to which I have previously alluded include: character "construction"; poetic language; emotionalizing narration or musical accompaniment; "embedded" narratives; dramatic arcs; the exaggeration of camera angles, camera distance, or editing rhythms.

28. The pronounced polarization of truth and beauty, characteristic of Western aesthetics since the Enlightenment, will be examined more fully in my contribution to this volume, "Toward a Poetics of Documentary (Chapter 2)."

2. Toward a Poetics of Documentary

An earlier version of this essay was delivered as the keynote address to the Twelfth Annual Ohio University Conference in November 1990. I am grateful to Bill Nichols, Chuck Wolfe, and Edward Branigan for their careful reading and for suggestions which have greatly benefited this text.

1. Tzvetan Todorov, *The Poetics of Prose*, trans. Richard Howard (Ithaca: Cornell University Press, 1977), 33.

2. Quoted in Calvin Tomkins, "Look to the Things Around You," *The New Yorker*, 16 September 1974, 90.

3. Aristotle, *Poetics*, trans. Gerald F. Else (Ann Arbor: The University of Michigan Press, 1967), 4, 15.

4. Lubomír Doležel, *Occidental Poetics: Tradition and Progress* (Lincoln: University of Nebraska Press, 1990), 56.

5. Despite the historical limitations of Doležel's account of the evolution of Occidental poetics—he ends in 1945, prior to the postwar effloration of inquiry in France—the book offers a useful periodization of poetics in the West and a sense of the rich ancestry of contemporary manifestations.

6. Valery's definition is cited in Tzvetan Todorov's *Introduction to Poetics*, trans. Richard Howard (Minneapolis: University of Minnesota Press, 1981), 7.

7. I will insist on including video in the discussion of documentary film even while noting that the two media forms are irreducibly distinct. It is my sense that the four modalities of documentary discourse traced here obtain for both film and video but manifest themselves differently and within distinguishable historical contexts. One brief example must suffice by way of illustration. It might be said that video has emerged as a discursive field with a particular relationship to preservation, the first documentary function. Videotape was developed in 1956 as a storage system for an electronic signal and has been deeply enmeshed with surveillance technologies ever since. For unlike the Lumières' cinematic apparatus which, from the first, could double as a camera and a projector, television—a medium of transmission dating to the 1930s and earlier—required another technology to effectuate the preservation of

the sounds and images it produced. Video is, among other things, television's preservational other. On purely historical grounds, it would simply be a mistake to conceptualize the preservational dimension of documentary video as identical to that of its filmic counterpart. The case could be made in similar ways for each of the four modalities of documentary discursivity for video. Such a working through is much deserved but must await another occasion.

8. See Earl Miner's *Comparative Poetics: An Intercultural Essay on Theories of Literature* (Princeton, NJ: Princeton University Press, 1990), particularly his introductory chapter, "Comparative Poetics" (12–33).

9. Todorov, *Introduction to Poetics* 4–5. Todorov does not entirely discount the possibility that there could be a substantive separation of interpretation and science (hence, poetics) because the latter is neither entirely descriptive nor interpretive but instead works for "the establishment of general laws of which this particular text is the product" (6). Todorov does not so much critique science (as the scholar's dream discourse) as indemnify it against its potential detractors. That critique will be Foucault's.

10. Roland Barthes, "The Return of the Poetician," *The Rustle of Language*, trans. Richard Howard (Berkeley: University of California Press, 1989), 172.

11. Barthes' position in the question of the separability of interpretation and description is, as ever, complex. In his 1977 "Inaugural Lecture" at the College de France, Barthes argued that, in regard to the presumed opposition between the sciences and letters, "it is possible that this opposition will appear one day to be a historical myth" [*A Barthes Reader*, ed. Susan Sontag (New York: Hill and Wang, 1982), 464]. The statement is equivocal: It could mean that, in the manner of Todorov, there is no description without interpretation (thus, all science is, to a degree, "artful") or simply that literary studies is capable of being undertaken with the rigor of science (thus, some aesthetic inquiry is the epistemological equal of science). The statement could also be understood as a statement about Barthes's own intellectual history, his journey from the painstaking semiological treatises of the 1960s to the essayistic writings of the late 1970s. The art/science split has certainly been the subject of much debate (see, for example, the classic exposition of the problem in C. P. Snow's *Two Cultures* or Raymond Williams' entry on science in *Keywords*). Of all branches of aesthetic inquiry, poetics confronts the question most vigorously.

12. From Coleridge's *Biographia Literaria* (1817), as cited in Doležel (87).

13. See, in this regard, Brian Winston's essay (Chapter 3 of this volume).

14. Ivan Brady, "Harmony and Argument: Bringing Forth the Artful Science" in Ivan Brady, ed. *Anthropological Poetics* (Savage, MD: Rowman & Littlefield Publishers, Inc., 1991), 19.

15. Todorov, *The Poetics of Prose*, 236. As is the case with Barthes, Todorov cannot fairly be pigeonholed, in this instance as an apologist for an airtight science of literature. In his *Introduction to Poetics*, he writes that "the relation between poetics and interpretation is one of complementarity par excellence. . . . A massive imbalance in favor of interpretation characterizes the history of literary studies: it is this disequilibrium that we must oppose, and not the principle of interpretation" (7, 12). It is just this judiciousness toward the poetics/interpretation encounter that seems to be missing in David Bordwell's more polemical account of contemporary film scholarship in his *Making Meaning*.

16. Roland Barthes, "The Return of the Poetician," *The Rustle of Language*, trans. Richard Howard (Berkeley: University of California Press, 1989), 172.

17. Roland Barthes, "From Science to Literature," *The Rustle of Language*, trans. Richard Howard (Berkeley: University of California Press, 1989), 7.

18. David Bordwell, *Making Meaning: Inference and Rhetoric in the Interpretation of Cinema* (Cambridge, MA: Harvard University Press, 1989), 270–271.

19. *Ibid.*, 273.

20. A. J. Greimas, *The Social Sciences: A Semiotic View* (Minneapolis: University of Minnesota Press, 1990), 11.

21. *Ibid.*, 11–12.

22. Helen Vendler, *The Music of What Happens: Poems, Poets, Critics* (Cambridge: Harvard University Press, 1988), cited in Ivan Brady, ed., *Anthropological Poetics*, frontispiece.

23. Michel Foucault, "Two Lectures" *Power/Knowledge: Selected Interviews and Other Writings, 1972–1977*, Colin Gordon, ed. (New York: Pantheon Books, 1980), 80.

24. *Ibid.*, 81, 83.

25. While Foucault's injunction against the unspoken coefficient of power attached to discursive forms deemed "science" represents an important intervention, it is only fair to add that Foucauldian genealogies mobilize a considerable power of their own. Foucault's point is most useful when understood historically, as a comment upon the epistemic force realized (in the West and since the Enlightenment) through the very appellation of science.

26. *Ibid.*, 84–85.

27. Roman Jakobson, "Linguistics and Poetics," *The Structuralists From Marx to Levi-Strauss*, eds. Richard T. De George and Fernande M. De George (Garden City: Anchor Books, 1972), 88.

28. It is not inconsequential that the moment of Anglo-American film theory's intellectual formation (one now hears the label "seventies film theory") coincided with the passage from high structuralism to something "post" in France. The transfer of ideas from France to Britain and then to the United States created a lag of sorts so that American film students were learning Christian Metz's "le grand syntagmatique"—zealously structuralist in concept and execution—even while Metz himself was reinventing film theory in Lacanian terms (a system of thought not immune from Foucault's admonition against global, totalitarian theories). The growing influence of cultural studies on aesthetic analysis—and the displacement of general theories by localized ones (e.g., models of cultural resistance)—has placed us at an ever-greater remove from the systematic (if utopian) inquiry of the structuralist project. The drama of intellectual reinvention of the 1970s can be charted in the writings of a key ideologue of the era, Roland Barthes, over little more than a decade. In 1964, he wrote (in "The Structuralist Activity") of the way that structuralism manifested "a new category of the object, which is neither the real nor the rational, but the *functional,* thereby joining a whole scientific complex which is being developed around information theory and research" (153) (reprinted in Richard and Fernande De George, eds., *The Structuralists From Marx to Levi-Strauss*). By 1975, Barthes could muse ironically over his fascination with science. Of his taste for algorithms, he could say: "Such diagrams, he knows, even fail to have the interest of locating his discourse under the aegis of scientific reasoning: whom could they deceive?" [Roland Barthes, *Roland Barthes by Roland Barthes* (New York: Hill and Wang, 1977), 100.] Given the devaluation of structuralism's programmatic aims, a taste for poetics did not appear, until rather recently, to have survived into the present

era. But this resurgent genus of aesthetic inquiry is, one could say, poetics with a "difference."

29. Jacques Derrida, "Structure, Sign, and Play in the Discourse of the Human Sciences," *The Structuralist Controversy: The Languages of Criticism & the Sciences of Man,* Richard Macksey and Eugenio Donato, eds. (Baltimore: The Johns Hopkins Press, 1970), 263.

30. The books cited: James Clifford and George E. Marcus, eds. *Writing Culture: The Poetics and Politics of Ethnography* (Berkeley: University of California Press, 1986); Ivan Brady, ed. *Anthropological Poetics* (Savage, MD: Rowman & Littlefield Publishers, Inc., 1991); Nancy K. Miller, ed. *The Poetics of Gender* (New York: Columbia University Press, 1986). Susan Rubin Suleiman, *Subversive Intent: Gender, Politics, and the Avant-Garde* (Cambridge: Harvard University Press, 1990). It is worth noting, in the matter of the resurgence of interest in poetics as well as the broadened contemporary understanding of the range of topics comprehended, that *The Poetics of Gender* was composed of papers presented at the *eighth* in a series of annual colloquia initiated by Michael Riffaterre at Columbia University's Maison Francaise. The sessions on gender followed others on poetry, the text, intertextuality, the reader, the author, the body, and ideology.

31. James Clifford and George E. Marcus, eds., *Writing Culture: The Poetics and Politics of Ethnography* (Berkeley: University of California Press, 1986), 8. See, in particular, Clifford's "Introduction: Partial Truths," 1–26.

32. James Clifford, *The Predicament of Culture* (Cambridge, MA: Harvard University Press, 1988), 25.

33. Susan Rubin Suleiman, *Subversive Intent: Gender, Politics, and the Avant-Garde* (Cambridge, MA: Harvard University Press, 1990), 84.

34. Foucault, *Power/Knowledge,* 98, 102.

35. The linkage of the direct cinema practitioners with the Griersonians or Newsreel might strike some readers as odd in this discussion of political determinations. After all, the Drew Associates (Leacock, Pennebaker, the Maysles) seem, at first glance, to have been far more concerned with the potentialities of the new technology (principally synch sound via lightweight rigs) than with politics. To preserve such a distinction would be to miss the point at many levels. To take only one line of argument in this regard: Direct cinema's stance of narrationless neutrality was the ideal aesthetic for American television culture as it began to emerge from the 1950s and the "end of ideology." For an extended amount of the ideological contingencies of the direct cinema movement, see Brian Winston's essay (Chapter 3).

36. Smadar Lavie, *The Poetics of Military Occupation: Mzeina Allegories of Bedouin Identity Under Israeli and Egyptian Rule* (Berkeley: University of California Press, 1990), 337–338.

37. Jacques Derrida, *Of Grammatology,* trans. Gayatri Chakravorty Spivak (Baltimore: The Johns Hopkins University Press, 1974), lxxi, 314.

38. In my discussion of the contemporary relations between art and science, I have stressed the scientificity of aesthetic inquiry (the realm of poetics) at the expense of addressing science's historical concern for beauty. By way of redress, I offer a series of quotations excerpted from Ivars Peterson's popular survey of contemporary mathematics, *Islands of Truth: A Mathematical Mystery Cruise* [(New York: W. H. Freeman and Company, 1990), 288]. In a section entitled "Figures of Beauty," Peterson offers the following selection of quotations from leading 20th-century

mathematicians as evidence of the pleasures to be found at the highest levels of mathematical inquiry, a montage which, taken cumulatively, suggests that accounts of the allegedly ineradicable, post-Enlightenment split between art and science have been grossly overstated:

> Mathematics, rightly viewed, possesses not only truth, but supreme beauty—a beauty cold and austere, like that of sculpture, without appeal to any part of our weaker nature, without the trappings of paintings or music, yet sublimely pure, and capable of stern perfection such as only the greatest art can show.
>
> Bertrand Russell

> Much research for new proofs of theorems already correctly established is undertaken simply because the existing proofs have no aesthetic appeal.
>
> Morris Kline

> It is true aesthetic feeling which all mathematicians recognize. . . . The useful combinations are precisely the most beautiful.
>
> Henri Poincaré

> My work has always tried to unite the true with the beautiful, but when I choose one over the other, I usually choose the beautiful.
>
> Hermann Weyl

> Beauty is the first test: There is no permanent place in the world for ugly mathematics.
>
> G. H. Hardy

39. It is gratifying to note that the critical tide is now beginning to turn; judging by the number and quality of recent conference presentations and books recently completed or underway, considerably more attention now seems to be accorded nonfiction work. But in relative terms, theoretical considerations of the documentary lag far behind.

40. Much has been written about the uncertain status of the peer panel review process for NEA grants in the spring and summer of 1992. Under the leadership of a Bush appointee, Anne-Imelda Radice, the National Endowment of the Arts has rescinded a handful of grants for art works whose subject matter was deemed erotic.

41. Long after fashioning this fourfold typology for documentary discursivity (which has evolved in my teaching over a decade), I noted the possible relationship to Hayden White's discussion of the four "master tropes" (metaphor, metonymy, synecdoche, irony) which reappear in critical thought from Freud to Piaget to E. P. Thompson. White attributes to Vico the notion that this diataxis of discourse "not only mirrored the processes of consciousness but in fact underlay and informed all efforts of human beings to endow their world with meaning" [Hayden White, *Tropics of Discourse: Essays in Cultural Criticism* (Baltimore: The Johns Hopkins University Press, 1978), 5].

42. Hans Richter, *The Struggle for the Film*, trans. Ben Brewster (New York: St. Martin's Press, 1986), 42–44.

43. Karl G. Heider, *Ethnographic Film* (Austin: University of Texas Press, 1976), 19.

44. Andre Bazin, "The Ontology of the Photographic Image," *What Is Cinema?*, trans. Hugh Gray (Berkeley: University of California Press, 1967), 14.

45. Some years later, Derrida reminded us that all writing places memory and forgetfulness in tension. The creation of a documentary image may be a memorializing gesture but it equally implies an acknowledgment of the radical alterity of the sign,

defined as the place where "the completely other is announced as such—without any simplicity, any identity, any resemblance or continuity—in that which is not it" [Jacques Derrida, *Of Grammatology,* trans. Gayatri Chakravorty Spivak (Baltimore: The Johns Hopkins University Press, 1974), 47]. Writing is "at once mnemotechnique and the power of forgetting" (Derrida, *Of Grammatology,* 24]. From this perspective, one might say that the documentative desire responds both to the pleasure principle and its beyond.

46. Andre Bazin, *What Is Cinema?,* trans. Hugh Gray (Berkeley: University of California Press, 1967), 162.

47. *Ibid.,* 155, 158.

48. Aristotle, *Rhetoric,* trans. W. Rhys Roberts (New York: Random House, 1954), 22.

49. For a brief account of the cognitivist paradigm and its relation to matters of filmic narration, see David Bordwell, *Narration in the Fiction Film* (Madison, WI: University of Wisconsin Press, 1985), 29–47. See, generally, Bordwell's "A Case for Cognitivism" in a special issue of *Iris* devoted to "Cinema and Cognitive Psychology," Vol. 5, No. 2 (1989), 11–40.

50. Bill Nichols, *Ideology and the Image: Social Representation in the Cinema and Other Media* (Bloomington: Indiana University Press, 1981), 210.

51. *Ibid.,* 211–212.

52. Raymond Williams, *Keywords: A Vocabulary of Culture and Society* (London: Flamingo, 1976), 278.

53. Richter, *The Struggle for the Film,* 46.

54. Roland Barthes, *Camera Lucida,* trans. Richard Howard (New York: Hill and Wang, 1981), 9.

55. The threshold of audience acceptance for documentary reconstruction or reenactment remains volatile; it is dependent both on historical moment and subject matter. "Pre-enactments" (visions of what *could be,* presented in a documentary format) have proven to be most controversial when the future vision they offer is apocalyptic. Both Peter Watkins' *The War Game* (1966) and Ed Zwick's *Special Bulletin* (1983)—two films about nuclear disaster—proved plausible enough for contemporary audiences to foster political battles (the BBC refused to screen Watkins's film as planned) or public dismay (the media coverage following the *Special Bulletin* broadcast offered testimony to the panic caused despite the disclaimers which accompanied the broadcast). The controversies which swirl around the question of documentary reconstruction/reenactment—"post-enactments"—seem inescapable insofar as they address a core issue for all documentary—veracity. Most attacks against *The Thin Blue Line* or *Roger and Me,* for example, have been based upon the presumption that authorial liberties taken toward the presentation of the "facts" have vitiated the films' possible claims to authenticity. (Question: Can documentary truth ever afford to be stylized?) The popular attachment to truth in cinema suggests that the erosion of referentials associated with the postmodern is being resisted in some quarters with great intensity.

56. See Michael Renov "Re-Thinking Documentary: Toward a Taxonomy of Mediation," *Wide Angle,* Vol. 8, Nos. 3 and 4, 1986, 71–77.

57. For a detailed discussion of the psychosocial dynamic engaged through an idealization of the "other" in documentary film practices, see my "Imaging the Other: Representations of Vietnam in Sixties Political Documentary," *From Hanoi to*

Hollywood: The Vietnam War in American Film, Linda Dittmar and Gene Michand, eds. (New Brunswick, N.J.: Rutgers University Press, 1990), 255–268.

58. Roland Barthes, "Historical Discourse," *Introduction to Structuralism,* ed. Michael Lane (New York: Basic Books, Inc., 1970), 149, 154.

59. John Tagg, *The Burden of Representation: Essays on Photographies and Histories* (Amherst: The University of Massachusetts Press, 1988), 3–5.

60. Jacques Derrida, "The Law of Genre," *Glyph* 7 (Spring 1980), 204.

61. Tagg, *The Burden of Representation,* 13.

62. Clifford Geertz, "Thick Description: Toward an Interpretive Theory of Culture," *The Interpretation of Cultures* (New York: Basic Books, 1973), 29.

63. My discussion of the analyze/interrogate modality would suggest that documentary interrogation necessarily entails reflexivity. This is certainly not the case as any return to the historical roots of the analytical impulse of documentary cinema will testify. Whether one considers the earliest Muybridge experiments in animal locomotion, Vertov's belief in the perfectibility of the kino eye, or the interrogation of visible action in Timothy Asch's *The Ax Fight* which essays social-scientific explanation over simple description, it is clear that the *interrogation* (here distinguished from the *observation*) of social reality via camera and recorder has been one of the documentarist's chief concerns. My own preference is to focus on instances of the analytical function which include an additional metacritical level of interrogation insofar as they, in taking their own discursive operations as a crucial component of analysis, provide an ideal model for study. This is not to suggest that the analytical impulse in documentary is excluded from all but the most reflexive instances. Rather, it is my sense that the reflexive text constitutes a kind of limit case or crisis of documentary analytics which can illustrate the functional grouping most vividly.

64. Quoted in Calvin Tomkins, "Look to the Things Around You," *The New Yorker,* 16 September 1974, 45.

3. The Documentary Film as Scientific Inscription

1. Quoted in Joseph Maria Eder, *History of Photography,* trans. Edward Epstean (New York: Dover, 1972), 238ff.

2. Elizabeth Eisenstein, *The Printing Revolution in Early Modern Europe* (Cambridge: Cambridge University Press, 1983), 26.

3. Peter Galassi, *Before Photography* (New York: Museum of Modern Art, 1981); p. 25, Fig. 17; p. 27, Fig. 21–22, plate 1.

4. Raymond Williams, *Keywords* (New York: Oxford University Press, 1976), 233ff.

5. Galassi, *Before Photography,* 25.

6. (a) John Tagg, *The Burden of Representation* (Amherst: University of Massachusetts Press, 1988), 37. (b) Gisele Freund, *Photography and Society* (Boston: David R. Rodine, 1982), 35, 57.

7. (a) Freund, *Photography and Society,* 88. (b) Tagg, *The Burden of Representation,* 74ff.

8. Freund, *Photography and Society,* 96.

9. 10/8/1878, quoted in Robert Hass, *Muybridge: Man In Motion* (Berkeley: University of California Press, 1976), 116. See also: Eder, *History of Photography,* 501ff.

10. *Audubon Field Guide to the Birds of North America: Eastern Region:* ibid, *Western Region,* 1977, passim.

11. Francis Bacon, *The Advancement of Learning,* quoted in Marie Boas, *The Scientific Renaissance 1450–1630* (London: Fontana, 1970), 236.

12. Eisenstein, *The Printing Revolution in Early Modern Europe,* 191ff.

13. Eisenstein, 199.

14. Bruno Latour, *Science in Action* (Cambridge, MA: Harvard University Press, 1987), 64ff.

15. *Ibid.,* 71.

16. Thomas Atkins, "The Films of Frederick Wiseman: American Institutions," *Sight and Sound,* Vol. 43, No. 4 (1974), 233. Elsewhere Wiseman has spoken of his work in terms of natural history, specifically, "spoor collection." See Alan Rosenthal, *The New Documentary In Action* (Berkeley: University of California Press, 1971), 70; or Donald McWilliams, "Frederick Wiseman," *Film Quarterly,* Vol. 24, No. 1 (1970), 22.

17. Quoted in Pierre Bourdieu, *Photography,* trans. Shaun Whiteside, (Stanford: Stanford University Press, 1990), 73.

18. (a) Patricia Jaffe, "Editing Cinema Verite," *Film Comment,* Vol. 3, No. 3 (1965), 44. (b) Richard Leacock, "La Camera Passe-Partout," trans. Louis Marcorelles, *Cahiers du Cinema,* No. 94 (April, 1959), 37ff.

19. By 1953, Sudwestfunk-Fernsehen, the TV station in Baden-Baden, had adapted all three cameras in the American "Auricon" range (built by Walter Bach) by taking out the optical system and inserting a "Klangfilm" magnetic recorder instead. The adapted cameras used mag. stripe film. The station had projectors, kinescope, and editing rooms all equipped to work with mag. stripe [Ann-Ruth Martin, "Magnetic Sound on TV Newsfilms in Germany," *Journal of the SMPTE* 65 (June 1956), 336.] At the end of 1955, Bach himself announced, "particularly for TV newsreel work," the "Filmagnetic" following this German lead [Advertisement, "Presenting Auricon Filmagnec," *Journal of the SMPTE* 64 (December 1955), 705; Walter Bach, et al., "Magnetic 16mm Single-System Sound-on-Film-Recording Camera Equipment," *Journal of the SMPTE* 65 (November 1956), 603.] In the technical literature, both texts and advertisements, the camera is shown mounted on a standard wooden tripod with large head. The operator is wearing headphones and twiddling with the camera's small external sound amplifier which he (inevitably) has on a shoulder strap. Thus, for documentary purposes the "Auricon" was still deficient. It was an unergonomic box and too heavy, at 26 lbs, to be carried with any ease. At a minimum, the body needed to be recast in a lighter metal. The American Direct Cinema pioneers began to do this themselves, but Bach, responding, produced a "Special Model CM 77" of the "Pro–600" with a lightweight body but otherwise not redesigned, "especially for documentary filming" [Anon, "A new lightweight version of the Pro–600", *Journal of the SMPTE* 69 (September 1960), 701].

A more sophisticated approach was taken by André Coutant who adapted, in 1958, a small cinematographic device, which he had developed for the French missile program, into a self-blimped camera designed to be carried—the "Eclair." It was introduced into the United States commercially in 1963 as the "Eclair NPR," where it was brilliantly represented and was a "resounding success" [Edmund DiGiulio, "Development in Motion Picture Camera Design and Technology—A Ten-Year Update," *Journal of the SMPTE* 85 (July 1976), 485]. Unlike Bach, Coutant made no attempt to build a sound system into the "Eclair". The camera required a separate audio recorder to be run in sync with it—a double (as opposed to single) system.

Portable tape machines for motion picture work were by then available, the first having been marketed in 1949 [William Stancil, "A Self-Contained Recorder for Motion Picture Sound," *Journal of the SMPTE* 70 (August 1961), 597]. The French "Perfectone," the first battery-driven hi-fidelity lightweight recorder was introduced to the United States in March 1959. Although not specifically designed for movie work, it was demonstrated with a "Camette" blimped camera [Anon, "The Perfectone Model EP6A Portable Magnetic Recorder," *Journal of the SMPTE* 68 (March 1959), 198ff.] However, the "Perfectone" was not to dominate the field. The "Nagra" was introduced to the American market in December 1960 [Anon, "Nagra Tape Recorder," *American Cinematographer* (December, 1960), 762]. It became the industry standard not least because its designer, Kudelski, specifically manufactured a model for the 16mm film market—the "Nagra III B" introduced in 1962 [Anon, "The Nagra III B," *Journal of the SMPTE* 71 (November 1962), 902].

20. Gideon Bachmann, "The Frontiers of Realist Cinema," *Film Culture*, Nos. 19–23 (Summer 1961), 16. Also see *Film Culture*, Nos. 24–29 (Spring 1962), 9. The quotes also appear in Louis Marcorelles, "L'Expérience Leacock," *Cahiers Du Cinéma*, No. 140 (February 1963), 12 [transl. in *Cahiers du Cinéma: 1960–1968*, ed. Jim Hillier and trans. David Wilson (Cambridge, MA: Harvard University Press, 1986), 265].

21. Peter Graham, "Cinéma-Vérité in France," *Film Quarterly* (Summer 1964), 34.

22. James Blue, "Discussion with the Maysles," *Film Comment* Vol. 2, No. 4 (1964), 22.

23. Maxine Maleff, "The Maysles Brothers and 'Direct Cinema,' " *Film Comment*, Vol. 2, No. 2 (1964), 20.

24. Ron Blumer, "King's *A Married Couple*," *The Documentary Tradition*, ed. Lewis Jacobs (New York: Hopkinson and Blake, 1971), 571.

25. Charles Taylor, "Focus on Al Maysles," in Jacobs, *The Documentary Tradition*, 401.

26. Patrick Sullivan, " 'What's All The Cryin' About?' The Films of Frederick Wiseman," *The Massachusetts Review*, Vol. 13, No. 3 (1979), 453.

27. Louis Marcorelles, "L'Expérience Leacock," 16 (trans. in Hillier, 268).

28. G. Roy Levin, *Documentary Explorations* (New York: Anchor, 1971), 235, 254.

29. Bachmann, "The Frontiers of Realistic Cinema," 14.

30. Haleff, "The Maysles Brothers and 'Direct Cinema,' " 23.

31. Jaffe, "Editing Cinema Verite," 46.

32. Mark Shivas, "Interviews: Richard Leacock," *Movie*, Vol. 8 (April 1963), 17.

33. Stephen Mamber, *Cinema Verite in America* (Cambridge, MA: MIT Press, 1974), 145.

34. (a) Jaffe, "Editing Cinema Verite, 43. (b) Richard Leacock, "For An Uncontrolled Cinema," *Film Culture*, Vol. 19 (Summer 1961), 23.

35. André Labathe and Louis Marcorelles, "Entretien avec Robert Drew et Richard Leacock," *Cahiers du Cinéma*, Vol. 24 (February 1963), 26.

36. Mamber, *Cinema Verite in America*, 197.

37. Mamber, *Cinema Verite in America*, 208.

38. Mamber, *Cinema Verite in America,* 201.

39. Mark Shivas, "New Approach," *Movie,* Vol. 8 (April 1963), 14 (italics in original).

40. Taylor, "Focus on Al Maysles," 403.

41. Bachmann, "The Frontiers of Realistic Cinema," 15.

42. Daniel Klughertz, "Documentary—Where's the Wonder?" in Jacobs, *The Documentary Tradition,* 456.

43. Shivas, "Richard Leacock," *Movie,* Vol. 8, p. 17.

44. I would add that a third consequence of the abdication of the research function was ethical. The downgrading of established professional preparations was particularly vexed given that the "charged atmosphere" these filmmakers sought was all too often to be found around social deviants or victims. The films were to be, almost entirely, "victim documentaries." The danger of subject exploitation, implicit in the intrusive use to which the technology was put, was exacerbated by this sort of "shoot first" ethos. Not only that; there was little inclination to "ask questions later" either. In professional discourse, technical issues almost entirely replaced all other topics. For instance, major discussion was devoted to perfecting unobtrusive sync marking systems, for the old clapper board obviously had no place in the world of noninterventionist film. My recollection, reaffirmed by Henry Breitrose's contemporary comments, is that discussion of the moral problems raised by "following subjects almost anywhere" were drowned in the noise of the debate about the machines. "One often wonders whether the films are made by men using machines . . . or by machines alone" [Henry Breitrose, "On the Search for the Real Nitty Gritty: Problems and Possibilities in Cinema Verite," *Film Quarterly* (Summer 1964), 37].

45. *Bachman,* "The Frontiers of Realistic Cinema," 17.

46. Ian Cameron, "William Klein," *Movie,* Vol. 8 (April 1963), 20.

47. Haleff, "The Maysles Brothers and 'Direct Cinéma," 22, 23.

48. Shivas, "New Approach," 13.

49. Ernest Callenbach, "Going Out To The Subject II," *Film Quarterly,* Vol. 14, No. 3 (1961), 40.

50. (a) Klugherz, "Documentary—Where's the Wonder?," 456. (b) Shivas, "Richard Leacock," 18.

51. Shivas, "New Approach," 13.

52. Jean-Luc Godard, "Richard Leacock," *Cahiers du Cinéma,* Nos. 150–151 (December 1963/January 1964), 140 (transl. and abstracted) Peter Graham, "Cinéma-Vérité in France," *Film Quarterly* (Summer, 1964), 31.

53. Levin, *Documentary Explorations,* 204, 245–248. Al Maysles also worked for Godard but rather more successfully. In January 1965, he shot "Montparnasse-Levallois," Godard's segment of *Paris Vu Par. . . .* See Taylor, "Focus on Maysles," 405.

54. Nöel Carroll, "From Real to Reel: Entangled in the Nonfiction Film," *Philosophical Exchange* (Brockport, NY: State University of New York, Brockport, 1983), 6ff.

55. James Blue, "One Man's Truth: An Interview with Richard Leacock," *Film Comment* Vol. 3, No. 2 (1965), 16 (italics in original).

56. Bachman, "The Frontiers of Realistic Cinema," 15.

57. Levin, *Documentary Explorations,* 277.

58. Levin, *Documentary Explorations*, 204.

59. Shivas, "Richard Leacock," 17.

60. Levin, *Documentary Explorations*, 203.

61. Levin, *Documentary Explorations*, 315.

62. Rosenthal, *The New Documentary In Action*, 67.

63. Rosenthal, *The New Documentary In Action*, 70.

64. (a) Levin, *Documentary Explorations*, 321. (b) McWilliams, "Frederick Wiseman," 22.

65. Ira Halberstadt, "An Interview with Fred Wiseman," *Nonfiction Film Theory and Criticism*, ed. Richard Barsam (New York, Dutton, 1975), 301.

66. Levin, *Documentary Explorations*, 322.

67. Emerging scholarship on the first decades of Direct Cinema suggests that the reception of the films might have been, in effect, conditioned more by the filmmakers' rhetoric than by claims of objectivity. For audiences to have believed such claims implies naiveté and arguing, on the contrary, for audience sophistication in this regard is attractive; but in this case it is difficult. Attempts to rethink the reception of Direct Cinema are on very shaky ground if the changing rhetorical positions taken during the first decade are insufficiently examined and if too much reliance is placed on the sophistries of the second rhetorical strand (as I have categorized it). Claims that audiences 30 years ago must have seen the construction and mediation of the earliest Direct Cinema films fail to acknowledge both the deep-seated position of the photographic apparatus as scientific and the particular excitement and enthusiasm engendered by the technological advances in 16mm equipment. Such revisions therefore, need to be treated with caution.

68. Quoted in Sullivan, " 'What's All the Cryin' About?' The Films of Frederick Wiseman," 467.

69. Thomas A. Benson and Carolyn Anderson, *Reality Fictions: The Films of Frederick Wiseman* (Carbondale: Southern Illinois University Press, 1989), 310.

70. Tagg, *The Burden of Representation*, 97.

71. Erik Barnouw, *Documentary: A History of the Non-Fiction Film* (New York: Oxford, 1974), 255.

72. Edgar Morin, "Chronicle of a Film," *Studies in Visual Communications*, 13.

73. James Clifford, *The Predicament of Culture: Twentieth-Century Ethnography, Literature and Art* (Cambridge, MA: Harvard University Press, 1988), 24, 52, 58ff, 76ff.

74. (a) Clifford, *The Predicament of Culture*, 55ff. (b) Jean Rouch, "The Cinema of the Future?" *Studies in Visual Communication*, Vol. 11, No. 1 (1985), 33.

75. (a) *Le Monde*, Pairs, 16 June 1971, quoted in *Anthropology—Reality—Cinema: The Films of Jean Rouch*, ed. Mick Eaton (London: BFI, 1979), 26. (b) Dan Georgakas, Udayan Gupta and Judy Janda, "The Politics of Visual Anthropology", *Cinéaste*, Vol. 8, No. 4 (1978), 22. (c) Quoted in Eaton, *Anthropology—Reality—Cinema*, 32.

76. Ellen Freyer, "*Chronicle of a Summer*—Ten Years After," in Jacobs, *The Documentary Tradition*, 438.

77. Levin, *Documentary Explorations*, 216.

78. I have always found it easier to sympathize with Rouch's positions than with the

Direct Cinema group's. He is insightful, provocative, and original. For example: "It is ineffectual to continuously assert your own opinions. . . . I plan to make a cine-portrait of Margaret Mead. For me, she is what we call in anthropology a 'totemic ancestor,' so we're already in the imaginary. . . . The objectivity of the lens is . . . an incredible stimulant for the observed as well as the observer [Dan Yakir, "*Cine-Transe*, The Vision of Jean Rouch," *Film Quarterly*, Vol. 31, No. 3 (1978), 3, 6, 7]. "Every time a film is shot, privacy is violated" [Jean Rouch, "The Camera and Man," in Eaton, *Anthropology—Reality—Cinema*, 55]. "It's impossible to make a film with the people concerned in your film if you stop contact with them when the film is finished" (Interview with Louis Marcorelles, quoted in Eaton, *Anthropology—Reality—Cinema*, 4) "Now, this extremely strange game we were playing, may also be extremely dangerous" [James Blue, "Jean Rouch in Conversation with James Blue," *Film Comment*, Vol. 4, Nos. 2, 3 (1967), 85]. Rouch deploys an irony which stands in seductive contrast to Direct Cinema tendentiousness. Nevertheless . . .

79. Morin, "Chronicle of a Film," 28.

80. Morin, "Chronicle of a Film," 6.

81. Fereydoun Hoveyda, "Cinéma Vérité ou réalisme fantastiqué," *Cahiers du Cinéma*, Vol. 125 (November 1961), (trans. in Hillier, *Cahiers du Cinéma*, 249).

82. " 'Chronicle of a Summer': The Film", (transcript), *Studies in Visual Communication*, Vol. II, No. 1 (Winter 1985), 69.

83. Lucien Goldmann, "Thoughts on *Chronique d'un été*," *Le Cinéma et la Vérité*, *Artsept*, (ed. Raymond Bellour) 1963 (trans. John Higgins), *Anthropology—Reality—Cinema*, 66.

84. " 'Chronicle of a Summer': The Film", 70. The American subtitle mistranslates "*Nous sommes dans le bain*" as "We're in for trouble"; the English, "I think we are in trouble." This last caused me to mistitle a paper I prepared for the 1978 Edinburgh Television Festival which was reprinted as "Documentary: I Think We Are In Trouble" in *Sight and Sound*, Vol. 48, No. 1 (1978), 2ff.

85. Henry Breitrose, "The Structure and Functions of Documentary Film", *CILECT Review*, Vol. 2, No. 1 (1986), 47.

86. Carroll, *Philosophical Exchange*, 8.

87. Thomas Nagel, *The View From Nowhere* (New York: Oxford University Press, 1986), 91.

88. Lorraine Nencel and Peter Pels, "Critique and Reflexivity in Anthropology," *Critique of Anthropology*, Vol. 9, No. 3, 83.

89. Jurgen Habermas, *Knowledge and Human Interest*, trans. Jeremy Shapiro (London: Heinemann, 1972), 4.

90. Tagg, *The Burden of Representation*, 97.

91. Stuart Hall, "The rediscovery of 'ideology': return of the repressed in media studies," *Culture, Society and the Media*, Michael Gurevitch, Tony Bennett, James Curran and Janet Woollacott, eds. (London: Routledge, 1982), 75 (italics in original).

92. *Ibid.*, 75.

93. Julianne Burton, ed., *The Social Documentary in Latin America* (Pittsburgh, PA: University of Pittsburgh Press, 1990), 361.

94. (a) Jurgen Habermas, *Legitimation Crisis*, trans. Thomas McCarthy (Boston, Beacon

Press, 1975), 78. (b) Roland Barthes, *Mythologies*, trans. Annette Lavers (London, Paladin, 1972), 142.

95. Michael Renov, "Rethinking Documentary: Toward a Taxonomy of Mediation," *Wide Angle*, Vol. 18, No. 3/4 (1986), 71.

96. *Ibid.*, 71.

97. *Sunday Mirror Magazine*, 23 June 1991, 56.

98. Personal communication; see also, Brian Winston, "In The Eye of the Beholder", *Harvard Information Technology Quarterly* (Spring 1990), 30ff.

99. Carroll, *Philosophical Exchange*, 31.

100. Ismail Xavier, "*Iracema:* Transcending Cinema Verite," in Burton, *The Social Documentary in Latin America*, 363.

4. Document and Documentary: On the Persistence of Historical Concepts

1. Actually, 1963 is a year that stands as a threshold in the development of the mise-en-scène of the U.S. network newsroom as a nerve center collecting and colligating knowledge of national and international scope. It was only in 1961 that U.S. television network news departments began establishing bureaus outside of New York, Chicago and Los Angeles. In the fall season of 1963, CBS expanded its nightly network news program from 15 to 30 minutes, and NBC followed almost immediately. The status of this event is indicated by the fact that the first expanded evening of news on both networks featured exclusive interviews with President Kennedy.

2. Strictly speaking, of course, this simultaneity is not quite achieved; from the perspective of the spectator, sociocultural and economic relationships, and ideology, however, I would argue that the possibility of temporal simultaneity is embedded in the self-presentation and functioning of such media.

3. John Grierson, *Grierson on Documentary*, rev. ed., ed. Forsythe Hardy (New York: Praeger, 1966), 145–46, 201, 290.

4. For the influence in this approach in U.S. publications, see, for example, Joris Ivens, "Collaboration in Documentary," *Films*, Vol. 1, No. 2 (1940), e.g., p. 30 for the discussion of personal style, conception, and script as faced with actuality, and p. 35 on reenactment in documentary. Compare several articles reprinted in *The Documentary Tradition: From Nanook to Woodstock*, ed. Lewis Jacobs (New York: Hopkinson and Blake, 1971), including Leo T. Hurwitz' 1934 anticapitalist, anti-Hollywood manifesto "The Revolutionary Film—Next Step," which opposes the "synthetic documentary film" to the newsreel (p. 91), but for whom "drama" remains a key term; Evelyn Gerstein, "English Documentary Films" (1936), which again begins by opposing documentary to the newsreel and goes on to make further distinctions in favor of the documentary's knowledge value; Ben Bellit, "The Camera Reconnoiters" (1937), which opposes Frontier films to travelogues on the one hand and Hollywood on the other, quoting Paul Strand to indicate that documentary goes beyond newsreels and travelogues in finding the "basic dramatic meanings implicit in the documents" (p. 143), and Herbert Kline, "Films Without Make-Believe" (1942). The opposition of documentary versus newsreel and travelogue shows up again in Philip Dunne, "The Documentary and Hollywood" (1946), reprinted in *Nonfiction Film Theory and Criticism*, ed. Richard Meran Barsam (New York: Dutton, 1976).

5. Two seminal essays in this context are "The Discourse of History" and especially "The Reality Effect," both reprinted in Roland Barthes, *The Rustle of Language,* trans. Richard Howard (Berkeley: University of California Press, 1989). Compare Hayden White, *Metahistory: The Historical Imagination in Nineteenth-Century Europe* (Baltimore: Johns Hopkins University Press, 1973), and "The Value of Narrativity in the Representation of Reality," "The Question of Narrative in Contemporary Historical Theory," and "The Politics of Historical Interpretation: Discipline and De-Sublimation," all reprinted in Hayden White, *The Content of the Form: Narrative Discourse and Historical Representation* (Baltimore: Johns Hopkins University Press, 1987). On the relation of media of indexical representation to conceptions of the real as historical and to historiography, see Stephen Bann, *The Clothing of Clio: A Study of the Representation of History in Nineteenth-Century Britain and France* (New York: Cambridge University Press, 1984). The quotation is from Fustel de Coulanges, "Introduction," *The History of the Political Institutions of Ancient France,*" translated in *Varieties of History, from Voltaire to the Present,* ed. Fritz Stern (New York: Vintage, 1972), 188.

6. Leopold von Ranke, "Preface: *Histories of the Latin and German Nations from 1494–1514,*" *Varieties of History,* 57, 56. (See Note 7). I have slightly modified the translation of the notorious phrase *wie es eigentlich gewesen,* which has been inflected in several ways by both English and French translations. For a pertinent summary view of the emergence of modern historical temporality in Germany on which I draw for my general comments about historicity, see the first essay "Modernity and the Planes of Historicity," Reinhart Koselleck, *Futures Past: On the Semantics of Historical Time,* trans. Keith Tribe (Cambridge, MA: MIT Press, 1985).

   It is probably fair to say that most of the recent theoretical work done on modern historiography has interrogated the assumption of meaningful sequence rather than documentary sources. Perhaps the best known example is Hayden White, in both *Metahistory* and the essays in *The Content of the Form.* For an interesting conception of documentary film that invokes some of White's work on historical sequentiation and the construction of reality in relation to cinematic indexicality, see Bill Nichols, "History, Myth and Narrative in Documentary," *Film Quarterly,* Vol. 41, No. 1 (1987), 9–20. Nichols ingeniously separates timelessness and identification out from narrative, which he associates in an almost Ricouer-like way with configuring temporal flux and historicity; however, it is worth noting that this is not an approach one would usually associate with White. Influenced by Northrop Frye as well as structuralist and poststructuralist narratology, White generally conceives of narrative form in a restricted number of archetypal, temporally overarching categories. A major element of White's critique of modern historiography is that a given category of narrative will tend to impose similar patterns and hence meanings on very different historical references.

7. Frederick Jackson Turner, "The Significance of History," reprinted in *Varieties of History, from Voltaire to the Present,* ed. Fritz Stern (New York: Vintage, 1973), 201.

8. *Ibid.,* 201, 203–204.

9. If anyone doubts the weight carried by these procedures and practices around the historical document in the historical profession, they might review the recent David Abraham controversy. In this affair, a Leftist junior faculty member working on the conditions for the emergence of German National Socialism was attacked by well-established senior members of the historical profession for distorting and/or mistak-

enly recounting documentary evidence, even though in the end these supposed distortions do not seem to have had significant import for his overall arguments. Its demonstration of the power of generally unquestioned standards of documentation is all the more striking in that the controversy seems ultimately to have been political—political in the ordinary sense but also involving the politics of the profession. As a starting point, see "The David Abraham Case: Ten Comments from Historians," *Radical History Review*, No. 32 (March 1985), 75–86.

10. Arthur C. Danto, *Narration and Knowledge (including the integral text of Analytic Philosophy of History)* (New York: Columbia University Press, 1985), revision of *Analytic Philosophy of History* (1968), 148–53, 157–58. For reasons of space and my own exposition, which includes consideration of nonlinguistic representations of the past, I am taking these elements somewhat out of their context, which is Danto's explication of his concept of the narrative sentence. I should note, however, that Danto's analysis also allows for cases in which endings change among successive generations of historians, because as time goes on additional events occur and different sequenciations become reasonable.

11. An excellent selection of the recent historiography of the preclassical is *Early Cinema: Space, Frame, Narrative*, ed. Thomas Elsaesser with Adam Barker (London: British Film Institute, 1990). In addition, on preclassical film types, see Robert C. Allen, "Contra the Chaser Theory," reprinted in *Film Before Griffith*, ed. John L. Fell (Berkeley: University of California Press, 1983), 109–112. On the disappearance of actualities, see Allen, *Vaudeville and Film 1895–1913: A Study in Media Interaction* (diss. 1977, reprinted New York: Arno, 1980), 212–220; compare David Levy, "Edison Sales Policy and the Continuous Action Film 1904–06" *Film Before Griffith*, 222. But see also the methodological critique of Allen by Charles Musser, "Another Look at the Chaser Theory," *Studies in Visual Communication*, Vol. 4, No. 4 (1984), followed by the exchange between Allen and Musser (45ff). For an argument that there is narrative structure in actualities, see Marshall Deutlebaum, "Structural Patterning in the Lumière Films," in *Film Before Griffith*.

12. *Grierson on Documentary*, 199–201.

13. On the Hollywood mode of production, see David Bordwell, Janet Staiger, and Kristin Thompson, *The Classical Hollywood Cinema: Film Style and Mode of Production to 1960* (New York: Columbia University Press, 1985). On the transitions leading to classicism, see both it and various articles reprinted in *Early Cinema*, starting with the several by Charles Musser ("The Travel Genre in 1903–04; Moving Towards Fictional Narrative" and "The Nickelodeon Era Begins: Establishing the Framework for Hollywood's Mode of Representation") and Tom Gunning ("Non-Continuity, Continuity, Discontinuity: A Theory of Genres in Early Films" and "Weaving a Narrative: Style and Economic Background in Griffith's Biograph Films"). See also Musser, "Another Look at the 'Chaser Theory.' " Seminal claims about spectatorship in early cinema are made in Gunning, "The Cinema of Attractions: Early Film, Its Spectator and the Avant-Garde" in *Early Cinema*. Among many elaborations on the move toward classicism as a tightening of spectatorship that followed from this article, see Miriam Hansen, "Adventures of Goldilocks: Spectatorship, Consumerism and Public Life," *Camera Obscura*, No. 22 (January 1990), 49–71. Another discussion is Philip Rosen, "Disjunction and Ideology in a Preclassical Film: *A Policeman's Tour of the World*," *Wide Angle*, Vol. 12, No. 3 (July 1990), 20–36.

14. Paul Willemen, "The Third Cinema Question: Notes and Reflections," *Questions of Third Cinema*, ed. Jim Pines and Paul Willemen (London: BFI, 1989), 5. Willemen

also aligns Italian neorealism with the Griersonian documentary movement as offering a parallel model to third cinema.

15. "The Course of Realism" in *Grierson on Documentary*, 207. See also "Propaganda and Education," 288–90. Compare the following: "For the troubles of the press, like the troubles of representative government, be it territorial or functional, like the troubles of industry, be it capitalist, cooperative or communist, go back to a common source: to the failure of self-governing people to transcend their casual experience and their prejudice by inventing, creating and organizing a machinery of knowledge. . . . This is the primary defect of popular government, a defect inherent in its traditions, and all its other defects can, I believe, be traced to this one" Walter Lippmann, *Public Opinion* (New York: Macmillan, 1960 [1922]), 364–65; see chapter 25 for an argument that the remedy is the interpolation of a cadre of professionalized experts between government and the citizen.

16. Walter Benjamin, "The Work of Art in the Age of Mechanical Reproduction," *Illuminations*, trans. Harry Zohn (New York: Schocken, 1969), 224.

17. Compare Karl Mannheim, *Ideology and Utopia: An Introduction to the Sociology of Knowledge*, trans. Louis Wirth and Edward Shils (New York: Harcourt, Brace, 1936), e.g., pp. 154–161.

18. For Gramsci on the social processes involving intellectual and technical elites, see "The Intellectuals" in Antonio Gramsci, *Selections from the Prison Notebooks*, ed. and trans. Quintin Hoare and Geoffrey Nowell-Smith (New York: International Publishers, 1971), 5–25, and the remarks on the dialectic of intellectuals and masses in the section entitled "The Study of Philosophy" (333–343). Examples of recent influential appropriations of Gramsci by different kinds of cultural theorists are Stuart Hall, "Gramsci's Relevance for the Study of Race and Ethnicity" and "The Problem of Ideology—Marxism without Guarantees," both in *Journal of Communication Inquiry*, vol. 10, No. 2 (1986); and (sometimes more implicitly) Gayatri Chakravorty Spivak, "Can the Subaltern Speak," *Marxism and the Interpretation of Culture*, ed. Cary Nelson and Lawrence Grossberg (Urbana: University of Illinois Press, 1988) and "Subaltern Studies: Deconstructing Historiography" reprinted in Spivak, *In Other Worlds: Essays in Cultural Politics* (New York: Routledge, 1987). A collection on the history of politically committed Leftist documentary cinema is Thomas Waugh, ed. *"Show Us Life": Toward a History and Aesthetic of the Committed Documentary* (Metuchen, NJ: Scarecrow, 1984).

19. Jean Baudrillard, *In the Shadow of the Silent Majorities . . . Or the End of the Social*, trans. Paul Foss (New York: Semiotext (e), 1983).

20. Jean Baudrillard, *Simulations*, trans. Paul Foss, Paul Patton, and Philip Beitchman (New York: Semiotext (e), 1983). See, e.g., pp. 39–46.

21. Baudrillard, *Simulations*, 49. On *An American Family* and what it is supposed to illustrate, see pp. 49–58.

22. For a sophisticated rather than naive example written at the high point of such critiques, see the opposition between spectacle and documentary in Steve Neale's still useful consideration of spectacle, documentary, and the film image, *"Triumph of the Will*: Notes on Documentary and Spectacle," *Screen*, Vol. 20, No. 1 (1979), 85: "[Spectacle] addresses the imbrication of looking and the visible not [as in documentary] as the *prior condition to the construction of a form of knowledge* about a particular subject or issue, but rather as that which hovers constantly across the gap between the eye and the object presented to it in the process of the scopic drive. Documentary *disavows this gap altogether*, subordinating both instances to that set

of essentially empiricist codes of exposition required to promote its knowledge effect [emphasis added]." Note the quick slippage from the careful wording in the first italicized passage to the absoluteness of the second. I am suggesting such a wide-spread attitude elides too much within the history of documentary, but even theoretically there are problems. (What, within psychoanalysis, is it to disavow something "altogether"? Classically, this is treated as impossible, and disavowal involves some minimal degree of oscillation between knowledge and belief.)

5. The Totalizing Quest of Meaning

1. Walter Benjamin, *One-Way Street and Other Writings* (London: Verso, 1979), 95.

2. J. Kowallis, trans. *Wit and Humor from Old Cathay* (Beijing: Panda Books, 1986), 164.

3. Quoted in G. Roy Levin, *Documentary Explorations: Fifteen Interviews with Film-Makers* (Garden City, NY: Doubleday & Company, 1971), 66.

4. Benjamin, *One-Way Street,* 109, 111.

5. See Jean Franco's rereading of her work in *Plotting Women: Gender and Representation in Mexico* (New York: Columbia University Press, 1989), 23–54.

6. John Grierson, *Grierson On Documentary,* ed. Forsyth Hardy (1966; reprinted, New York: Praeger, 1971), 146–47.

7. Hans Richter McCann, "Film as an Original Art Form," *Film: A Montage of Theories,* ed. R. Dyer Mac Cann (New York: E. P. Dutton, 1966), 183.

8. Louis Marcorelles, *Living Cinema: New Directions in Contemporary Film-making,* trans. I. Quigly (New York: Praeger, 1973), 37.

9. John Rouch, in Levin, *Documentary Explorations,* 135.

10. William Stott, *Documentary Expression and Thirties America* (1973; reprinted, New York: Oxford University Press, 1976), 73.

11. Quoted in *Living Cinema,* 26.

12. Ernesto Laclau, "Building a New Left: An Interview with Ernesto Laclau," *Strategies,* No. 1 (Fall 1988), 15.

13. Georges Franju, in Levin, *Documentary Explorations,* 119.

14. Grierson, *Grierson on Documentary,* 249.

15. Georges Franju, in Levin, *Documentary Explorations,* 119.

16. Alexander Kluge, *Alexander Kluge: A Retrospective* (The Goethe Institutes of North America, 1988), 4.

17. John Mercer, *An Introduction to Cinematography* (Champaign, IL: Stipes Publishing Co., 1968), 159.

18. Georges Franju, in Levin, *Documentary Explorations,* 121, 128.

19. Kluge, *Alexander Kluge: A Retrospective,* 6.

20. Lindsay Anderson, *Alexander Kluge: A Retrospective,* 66.

21. This distinction motivates Dana Polan's argument in "A Brechtian Cinema? Towards a Politics of Self-Reflexive Film," ed. B. Nichols, *Movies and Methods,* Vol. 2 (Los Angeles: University of California Press, 1985), 661–672.

22. Claire Johnston, "Women's Cinema as Counter-Cinema," ed. B. Nichols, *Movies and Methods,* Vol. 1 (Los Angeles: University of California Press, 1976), 215.

23. Kowallis, *Wit and Humor*, 98.

24. Henk Ketelaar, "Methodology in Anthropological Filmmaking: A Filmmaking Anthropologist's Poltergeist?" *Methodology in Anthropological Filmmaking*, eds. N. Bogaart and H. Ketelaar (Gottingen: Herodot, 1983), 182.

25. Paul Veyne, *Did the Greeks Believe in Their Myths? An Essay on the Constitutive Imagination*, trans. P. Wissing (Chicago: University of Chicago Press, 1988), 115.

26. See James Clifford, "Of Other Peoples: Beyond the 'Salvage Paradigm,'" *Discussions in Contemporary Culture*, ed. Hal Foster (Seattle: Bay Press, 1987), 121–130.

27. See *Theories of Primitive Religion* (Oxford: Clarendon Press, 1980).

28. E. Mveng, "Récents développements de la théologie africaine," *Bulletin of African Theology*, Vol. 5, No. 9. Quoted in V. Y. Mudimbe, *The Invention of Africa: Gnosis, Philosophy and The Order of Knowledge* (Bloomington: Indiana University Press, 1988), 37.

29. Jay Ruby, "Exposing Yourself: Reflexivity, Anthropology and Film," *Semiotica*, Vol. 30, Nos. 1–2 (1980), 165.

30. Shanta Gakhale, in *The New Generation. 1960–1980*, ed. Uma de Cunha (New Delhi: The Directorate of Film Festivals, 1981), 114.

31. Kowallis, *Wit and Humor*, 39.

32. Benjamin, *One-Way Street*, 14.

33. Maurice Blanchot, *The Gaze of Orpheus and Other Literary Essays*, ed. P. Adams Sitney, trans. L. Davis (Barrytown, NY: Station Hill Press, 1981), 104.

34. Claire Johnston, "Women's Cinema as Counter-Cinema," 214.

35. Roland Barthes, *Empire of Signs*, trans. R. Howard (New York: Hill & Wang, 1982), 70.

6. Jargons of Authenticity (Three American Moments)

1. The imbrication of documentary and fiction modes is a formidable topic but, contrary to indications, it is not central to my concerns. Nonetheless, what I have in mind ranges from fiction film's recourse to extratextual authority (e.g., the opening of *Psycho*), direct incorporation of nonfiction footage (as in *Reds*) to the miming of formal strategies such as direct cinema's handheld sequence shots (*Medium Cool*); on the other side of the ledger, documentaries from Flaherty on adapt coherence effects of continuity editing. Parker Tyler, in a 1949 essay, lays a critical foundation for further discussion [in *The Documentary Tradition*, ed. Lewis Jacobs (New York: Hopkinson and Blake, 1971), 251–266]. I note a tendency among recent commentators to discuss nonfiction's signs of transparency as mirroring those of the classical Hollywood. See, for example: Jeanne Hall, "Realism as Style in Cinema Verite: A Critical Analysis of *Primary*," *Cinema Journal* Vol. 30, No. 4 (1991), 29; Bill Nichols, "The Voice of Documentary," *Movies and Methods Vol. II*, ed. Bill Nichols (Berkeley: University of California, 1985), 260; E. Ann Kaplan, "Theories and Strategies of the Feminist Documentary," *Millennium Film Journal*, 12 (1982–83), 81. Nöel Carroll assails the blurring of fiction/documentary distinctions in "From Real to Reel: Entangled in Nonfiction Film," *Philosophic Exchange* 14 (1983), 5–15.

2. It should be clear that by "challenge" I mean the rather nebulous arena of cultural perception, not box-office. The quite different economic desiderata of TV, however, make parity a plausible condition. As to the scope of impact, direct cinema, at the

apex of its commercial success in 1967–1968, circulated more than a dozen features with varying degrees of mass appeal, including *Don't Look Back, Monterey Pop, Warrendale, The Endless Summer, Portrait of Jason, A Face of War, Rush to Judgement, Years of Lightning,* and *Day of Drums.*

3. An objection can be raised that my easy periodization performed suppresses the reality of continual diachronic shifts and that an account of such shifts is especially crucial to the historicization of nonstudio modes. A similar objection is that isolation of American films masks a complex interdetermination with European documentary (to say nothing of Neo-Realist and New Wave movements). In response, my aim is to establish continuities among movements often addressed as antipodal. And that while recognizing the mesh of transnational and transgeneric exchanges, it is useful to see how *primary* allegiances in social documentaries are welded to discourses of national self-interest.

4. The case for heightened effectivity in nonfiction cultural production during the thirties is discussed at length in William Stott, *Documentary Representation and Thirties America* (New York: Oxford University, 1973) 65–141. John Hallowell, in *Fact and Fiction* (Chapel Hill: University of North Carolina, 1977), sketches a confluence of social anxieties and cultural demands as contributory to the revaluation of nonfiction and rise of New Journalism during the sixties. That period's manifold critique of Hollywood and the centrality of TV's war reporting were two obvious conditions of possibility for commercial documentary.

5. *TV Guide* (November 9, 1991; p. 3) reported that the fall 1991 roster of prime-time series included *18* news and nonfiction hybrids, a fivefold increase from 1989. Relations between theatrical documentaries and their enveloping industrial contexts is a forceful, if gnarled, topic somewhat tangential to this essay.

6. George Levine, *The Realist Imagination* (Chicago: University of Chicago Press, 1981), 12.

7. Brian Winston, "Documentary: I Think We are in Trouble," *New Challenges For Documentary,* ed. Alan Rosenthal (Berkeley: University of California Press, 1988), 21.

8. Richard M. Barsam, "American Direct Cinema: The *Re*-presentation of Reality," *Persistence of Vision,* Nos. 3/4 (Summer 1986), 132.

9. Herbert Marcuse, "Some Social Implications of Modern Technology," *The Essential Frankfort School Reader,* ed. Andrew Arato and Eike Gebhardt (New York: Continuum, 1985), 139.

10. William Alexander, *Film on the Left* (Princeton, NJ: Princeton University Press, 1981), 254. In the same section, Alexander cites identical charges by contemporaneous writers such as Richard Griffith and James Arthur.

11. Cited in Stott, *Documentary Representation and Thirties America,* 77.

12. It should be recalled that at the height of their popularity newsreels were not only a staple of film exhibition, there were theaters devoted entirely to the showing of nonfiction short subjects.

13. Among several versions of Grierson's cagey equivocation, see Forsyth Hardy, ed., *Grierson on Documentary* (New York: Praeger, 1971), 237–248.

14. Marcuse, "Some Social Implications of Modern Technology," 138.

15. Similar iconographic patterns of naturalization are found in British films of the same period such as *Night Mail* (1936), *Housing Problems* (1935), and *The Line to*

the Tschierva Hut (1937) in which, for instance, a locomotive is compared both metonymically and through editing to clouds, mountain tops, flights of birds, etc.

16. This notion of montage as reconciliation is taken from William Guynn's excellent essay, "Politics of British Documentary," *Jump Cut* 8 (March–April 1975), 27. A similar tendency to use Soviet-style montage as an instrument of conceptual blurring is displayed in Riefenstahl's *The Triumph of the Will* (1934).

17. There are numerous examples from every point on the political compass. Grierson's influential stance can be found in Hardy, *Grierson on Documentary*, 146–147.

18. For an overview of the development of radical documentary groups in the early thirties, see Alexander, *Film on the Left*, 3–113.

19. Erich Auerbach, *Mimesis*, trans. Willard Trask (Princeton, NJ: Princeton University Press, 1953), 491.

20. Bill Nichols, "The Voice of Documentary," 261.

21. Thomas Waugh, "Beyond *Verité:* Emile de Antonio and the New Documentary of the Seventies," *Movies and Methods Vol. II*, 242, 235, respectively.

22. Nichols, "The Voice of Documentary," p. 261. See also Hall, "Realism as Style in Cinema Verite," for a rehearsal of related objections.

23. Thomas R. Atkins, *Frederick Wiseman* (New York: Monarch Books, 1976), 44.

24. Cited in Robert C. Allen and Douglas Gomery, *Film History: Theory and Practice* (New York: Knopf, 1985), 224.

25. G. Roy Levin, *Documentary Explorations* (Garden City, NY: Doubleday, 1971), 235.

26. Atkins, *Frederick Wiseman*, 43.

27. Anthropologist Victor Turner offers lively discussion of the counterculture's case against verbal language in *Dramas, Fields, and Metaphors* (Ithaca, NY: Cornell University Press, 1974), 262–266. In terms of both film practice and theory, Stan Brakhage exemplifies the American avant-garde's parallel revolt against socially regulated, hence morally and artistically bankrupt, language.

28. Levin, *Documentary Explorations*, 280.

29. Atkins, *Frederick Wiseman*, 56.

30. *Ibid.*, 56.

31. Levin, *Documentary Explorations*, 315.

32. Allen and Gomery make a similar point in *Film History*, pp. 233–234. For a critique of the empiricism sweeping the American academy in the late fifties and early sixties, see Frankfort Institute for Social Research, *Aspects of Sociology*, trans. John Viertel (Boston: Beacon Press, 1956).

33. Atkins, *Frederick Wiseman*, 29.

34. Stephen Mamber, *Cinema Verite in America* (Cambridge, MA: MIT Press, 1974), 221, 152, 3, respectively.

35. Early pronouncements on the ethical superiority of the nineteenth-century realist novel by Taine, Saint-Beuve, George Eliot, and others mobilize nearly identical aesthetic–political metaphors. See George J. Becker's *Documents of Modern Literary Realism* (Princeton, NJ: Princeton University Press, 1963).

36. Carroll, "From Real to Reel," 23.

37. Allen and Gomery, *Film History*, 231.

38. Atkins, *Frederick Wiseman*, p. 4. In *Telling the Truth* (Ithaca, NY: Cornell University Press, 1986), Barbara Foley describes the changing historical character of literary mimesis and rehearses orthodox arguments for the separation of factual and fictional literature on the basis on nonclosure versus closure, "correspondence" rather than "coherence," and so on (74–84).

39. Roland Barthes, "The Realistic Effect," trans. Gerald Mead, *Film Reader* 3 (1978), 133–135.

40. Two types of resistance to the lure of celebrity are evident in direct cinema: Wiseman's diffused focus on institutional roles as opposed to individual identity; and the poignant noncompliance in the recorder–actor agreement in *Happy Mothers Day* (1963).

41. Mamber, in *Cinema Verite in America*, recognizes the importance of public personality to direct cinema but draws a rather different set of conclusions; see pp. 90 and 183.

42. Michael Renov, "Re-Thinking Documentary," *Wide Angle* Vol. 8, No. 3/4 (1986), 73.

43. Wiseman traces his horror at the Bridgewater mental hospital to field trips taken with his law students. It should be pointed out that 1967 was a ripe year for the trope of mental illness as political theater/performance with, to cite two examples, Peter Brook's wildly popular staging of Peter Weiss' *Marat/Sade* and psychiatrist R.D. Laing's bestselling book *The Politics of Experience* (NY: Ballantine, 1967), on madness as a liberatory response to modern life.

44. For examples of this occasionally humorous internecine critique, see Levin, *Documentary Explorations*, 219, 285.

45. *Ibid.*, 277, 182–183, 198, respectively.

46. Cited in David Schwartz, "Documentary Meets the Avant-Garde," *Independent America: New Film 1978–1988* (Astoria, NY: American Museum of the Moving Image, 1988), 28.

47. Mamber, *Cinema Verite in America*, 85.

48. Two alternative, and I think largely compatible, readings of direct cinema's textual legitimation are provided by Hall, "Realism as Style in Cinema Verite" (pp. 38–39) and Allen and Gomery, *Film History* (235). Both concern the manner in which TV documentaries of the early sixties embed direct demonstrations or hints of their own superiority over competing cinematic or journalistic types of representation.

49. Gianfranco Bettetini, *Realism and the Cinema*, ed. Christopher Williams (London: Routledge and Kegan Paul, 1980), 222–223.

50. *Ibid.*

51. Jean-Louis Comolli, *Realism and the Cinema*, 226.

52. For a selection of demands for the revision of documentary along materially reflexive lines, see Kaplan, "Theories and Strategies of the Feminist Documentary," (p. 80), Renov, "Re-Thinking Documentary" (p. 75), Nichols, "The Voice of Documentary" (p. 263), and Jay Ruby, "The Image Mirrored," *New Challenges for Documentary*, ed. Alan Rosenthal (Berkeley: University of California Press, 1988), 64–77.

53. The mention here of an intervening group of films posing an alternative to direct cinema may seem a bit misleading, raising a further problem of periodization. Unquestionably, documentaries of the past few years owe a considerable debt to the methodological "break" of the seventies discussed in Waugh, "Beyond *Verite*," and

in Nichols, "The Voice of Documentary" (pp. 268–271). Nonetheless, my feeling is that recent work is no more comfortable with the rhetorical certainties of seventies films than they are with those of direct cinema. More to the point, the group of films I cite avoid the self-valorizing tactics whose historical pattern I chart.

54. Cited in Carl Plantinga, "The Mirror Framed: A Case for Expression in Documentary," *Wide Angle,* Vol. 13, No. 2 (1991), 51. In a related show of defiance, Michael Moore claims that his intention in *Roger and Me* was never to make a "straight documentary" and has little sympathy with classical conventions: Harlan Jacobson, "Michael and Me," *Film Comment,* Vol. 25, No. 6 (November 1989), 24.

55. *The Thin Blue Line* is slightly different; the set of images for which it is a self-conscious substitute is not another film but the actual murder it kaleidoscopically reenacts.

56. It is unclear to me whether the tropes ascribed to recent films have broader application. That said, I intrepidly adduce a brief art review by Kim Levin in *The Village Voice* (February 4, 1992; p. 71): "Curator Ralph Rugoff explores the new aesthetic of the hopelessly pathetic in this display of deliberately shabby, awkward, flawed, idiotic or otherwise impaired art objects. Sad, funny, inept, and absolutely right for right now. . . ." Among the artists included in the show were Mike Kelley, Jeffrey Vallance, Cady Noland, and Jim Shaw.

57. Gary Crowdus, "Reflections on *Roger and Me:* Michael Moore and his Critics," *Cineaste,* Vol. 17, No. 4 (1990), 30.

58. I want to stress a divergence between the recent documentary style and the venerable history of what might be called anti-documentaries, from Bunuel to Straub/Huillet to Welles and Ruiz. The brittle irony found in the new American revival does little to subvert the "naturalness" of documentary's *dispositif.*

59. Trinh T. Minh-ha, "Documentary Is/Not a Name," *October,* Vol. 52 (Spring 1990), 89.

60. *Ibid.,* 95. She argues against superficial modernist gestures of reflexivity, exposure of the apparatus or anti-illusionist markers of materiality, endorsed somewhat ambiguously by Jay Ruby in "The Image Mirrored" and other essays.

7. Constantly Performing the Documentary: The Seductive Promise of *Lightning Over Water*

1. It is not my intention to collapse the epistemological and ontological concerns into one or to reduce either one to the other. Each term deserves its full and complete treatment; however, that project does not lie within the scope of this paper. Since I am discussing the documentary promise in terms of both, I generally refer to them as an equation of sorts.

2. Jacques Derrida, "Freud and the Scene of Writing," *Writing and Difference* (Chicago: The University of Chicago Press, 1978), 260.

3. Bill Nichols, *Ideology and the Image* (Bloomington: Indiana University Press, 1981), 240.

4. Henry Staten, *Wittgenstein and Derrida* (Lincoln: University of Nebraska Press, 1984), 152.

5. Nichols, *Ideology and the Image,* 206.

6. Frederic Jameson, "Foreward," in Francois Lyotard, *The Postmodern Condition: A Report on Knowledge* (Minneapolis: University of Minnesota Press, 1984), viii.

7. While Austin did set forth the terms performative and constative in his early theory, he abandoned these categories in favor of an examination of the force of the utterance. In his later work, he recast his interest in the opposition between the performative element and that of the constative in terms of the illocutionary force or meaning of a statement. I am using his terms performative and constative as a means of discussing what I consider the epistemological and ontological thrust of discourse and as a means of explicating other levels of reflexivity in a documentary text.

8. Shoshana Felman, *The Literary Speech Act: Don Juan with J. L. Austin, or Seduction in Two Languages* (Ithaca: Cornell University Press, 1983), 35.

9. J. L. Austin, "Performing Utterances," *Philosophical Papers* (Oxford: Clarendon Press, 1979), 233ff.

10. *Ibid.*

11. Annette Kuhn, "The Camera I: Observations on Documentary," *Screen*, Vol. 19, No. 2 (1978), 76.

12. Bill Nichols, "The Voice of Documentary," *Film Quarterly*, Vol. 36, No. 3 (1983), 17ff.

13. Roland Barthes, *Camera Lucida: Reflections on Photography* (New York: Hill and Wang, 1981), 5.

14. *Ibid.*, 87. For a discussion of John Tagg's critique of Barthes' position, see Michael Renov's contribution in this volume (Chapter 2).

15. *Ibid.*, 76.

16. *Ibid.*, 77.

17. *Ibid.*, 79.

18. Kuhn, "The Camera I," 73.

19. Nichols, "The Voice of Documentary," 20.

20. Kaja Silverman, *The Acoustic Mirror: The Female Voice in Psychoanalysis and Cinema* (Bloomington: Indiana University Press, 1988), 13.

21. Jacques-Alain Miller, "Suture (elements of the logic of the signifier)," *Screen*, Vol. 43, No. 4 (1977/78), 25.

22. Michael Renov, "History and/as Autobiography: The Essayistic in Film and Video," *Frame/work*, Vol. 2, No. 3 (1989), 10–11.

23. Jacques Derrida, "Signature, Event, Context," *Margins of Philosophy* (Chicago: University of Chicago Press, 1982), 321.

24. Gayatri Chakravorty Spivak, "Translator's Preface," Jacques Derrida, *Of Grammatology* (Baltimore, MD: Johns Hopkins University Press, 1974), liii.

25. Jacques Derrida, "From Restricted to General Economy: A Hegelianism Without Reserve," *Writing and Difference* (Chicago: University of Chicago Press, 1978), 255.

26. Jacques Derrida, "Linguistics and Grammatology," *Of Grammatology* (Baltimore, MD: The Johns Hopkins University Press, 1976), 36.

27. Cited in Derrida, "From Restricted to General Economy," 258.

28. Spivak, "Translator's Preface," lix.

29. Jacques Lacan, *Ecrits* (New York: W. W. Norton and Co., 1977), 672.

8. (Not) Looking for Origins: Postmodernism, Documentary, and *America*

1. Jean Baudrillard, *America,* trans. Chris Turner (London: Verso, 1989), 76.

2. Homi K. Bhabha, "Introduction," *Nation and Narration* (New York: Routledge, 1990), 6.

3. Brian Winston, "Direct Cinema: The Third Decade," *Sight and Sound,* Vol. 52 (Autumn 1983), reprinted in Alan Rosenthal, ed., *New Challenges for Documentary* (Los Angeles: University of California Press, 1988), 518–519.

4. The year 1989 was a year of drastic changes for Brazilian society. Racked by hyperinflation which by November had reached a high of 50% per month, the nation devoted itself to the preparations for its first presidential election in 25 years. Despite the nonintervention of the military establishment, a new constitution, and a democratically elected congress, the country seemed to be simultaneously at a standstill, waiting for a new leader, and to be spinning out of control. The media, especially television, was playing its usual role in capitalist developing societies, serving up its usual fare of entertainment programming, news reporting, and political advertising (two 1-hour blocks per day — one in the morning, one during prime time—on radio and television, apportioned free-of-charge to the more than 25 different political parties according to the size of their constituencies).

5. Jean Baudrillard, *America* (Rio de Janeiro: Rocco, 1986) and Nelson Brissac Peixoto, *Cenários em Ruínas: A Realidade Imaginária Contemporanea* (São Paulo: Editora Brasiliense, 1987).

6. For information about the history of the development of Brazilian television, see Alcir Henrique da Costa, Inimá Ferreira Simoes, and Maria Rita Kehl, *Um País no Ar: Historia da TV Brasileira em 3 Canais* (São Paulo: Brasiliense, 1986); Fernando Barbosa Lima, Gabriel Priollo, and Arlindo Machado, *Televisão e Vídeo* (Rio de Janeiro: Zahar, 1985); and Michéle and Armand Mattelart, *O Carnaval das Imagens: A Ficção na TV,* trans. Suzana Calazans, (São Paulo: Brasiliense, 1989).

7. Joao Moreira Salles, the son of a former ambassador to the United States who is also the owner of one of the largest Brazilian banks, obtained financing for the production from a number of companies (most notably CrediCard and the Companhia Brasileira de Metalurgia e Mineração) under legislation known as the "lei Sarney" which gave tax breaks in exchange for corporate cultural financing. (This legislation was abolished in 1990, shortly after the airing of *America,* when newly elected president Fernando Collor de Mello introduced an economic plan that eliminated all state support for cultural activities.)

8. *Pantanal* was Manchete's first serious challenge to Globo's hold on the prime-time audience. Set in the swampy Pantanal region (rather than in an urban center or a bucolic past), the *telenovela*'s slower rhythms, earthiness, ecological sensibilities, *and* explicit nudity and sexuality consistently attracted more viewers than the Globo *telenovela* it was aired against (*A Rainha da Sucata* [*The Queen of Scraps*]). With its hegemony seriously challenged, Globo underwent a series of almost hysterical programming changes designed to recapture its audience. However, now accustomed to changing channels (and given the growing popularity of TV sets equipped with remote control units that facilitate channel switching), Brazilian audiences have remained comparatively fickle since then.

9. Charles Jencks, *What is Postmodernism?* (New York: Academy Editions, 1986);

Fredric Jameson, "Postmodernism, or The Cultural Logic of Late Capitalism," *New Left Review*, Vol. 146 (July–August 1984), 53–92.

10. Dana Polan, "Postmodernism and Cultural Analysis Today," *Postmodernism and its Discontents: Theories, Practices*, E. Ann Kaplan, ed. (New York: Verso, 1988), 49.

11. The term itself has been subject to various ideological appropriations and is marked by a wide variety of interpretations. For useful discussions of the various postmodern positions, see: Jonathan Arac, ed., *Postmodernism and Culture* (Minneapolis: University of Minnesota Press, 1986); Stanley Aronowitz and Henry Giroux, *Postmodern Education: Politics, Culture and Social Criticism* (Minneapolis: University of Minnesota Press, 1991); Hal Foster, ed., *The Anti-Aesthetic: Essays on Postmodern Culture* (Port Townsend, WA: Bay Press, 1983); Andreas Huyssen, *After the Great Divide* (Bloomington: Indiana University Press, 1986); Andrew Ross, ed., *Universal Abandon? The Politics of Postmodernism* (Minneapolis: University of Minnesota Press, 1988).

12. Aronowitz and Giroux, *Postmodern Education*, 71.

13. *Ibid.*, 115.

14. *America: Depoimentos* and *America: Imagens* (Rio de Janeiro: VideoFilmes/Companhia das Letras, 1989).

15. Fredric Jameson, "*Diva* and French Socialism," *Signatures of the Visible* (New York: Routledge, 1990), 60–61.

16. Fredric Jameson, "The Existence of Italy," *Signatures of the Visible*, 155–229.

17. *Ibid.*, 162.

18. Walter Benjamin, "The Storyteller," *Illuminations* (New York: Schoeken, 1969), 83–109.

19. Luiz Costa Lima, *Sociedade e Discurso Ficcional* (Rio de Janeiro: Editora Guanabara, 1986).

20. Timothy Brennan, "The National Longing for Form," in *Nation and Narration*, 56.

21. Bill Nichols, "The Voice of Documentary," *Film Quarterly*, Vol. 36 (Spring 1983), reprinted in Rosenthal, ed., *New Challenges for Documentary*, 50.

22. See, for example, Roberto da Matta, *Carnavais, Malandros e Herois* (Rio de Janeiro: Zahar, 1978).

23. Robert Stam, *Subversive Pleasures: Bakhtin, Cultural Criticism, and Film* (Baltimore, MD: Johns Hopkins University Press, 1989), 122–156.

24. Ismail Xavier, "Allegories of Underdevelopment: From the 'Aesthetics of Hunger' to the 'Aesthetics of Garbage,' " Ph.D. dissertation, New York University, 1982.

25. Anders Stephanson, "Regarding Postmodernism: A Conversation with Fredric Jameson," *Social Text* 17 (Fall 1987), 42.

26. Brissac Peixoto, *Cenários em Ruínas*, 8.

9. Notes on AIDS and Its Combatants: An Appreciation

1. Hannah Arendt, "On Humanity in Dark Times: Thoughts About Lessing," *Men in Dark Times* (New York: Harcourt, Brace, and World, 1968), 21.

2. Alexander Kluge, "E. Schincke," *Case Histories* (Holmes and Meier, 1991), 74.

3. Magic Johnson was named Most Valuable Player in the All-Star Game, 9 February 1992.

4. Stuart Hall, "Cultural Studies and Its Theoretical Legacies," *Cultural Studies,* eds. Lawrence Grossberg, Cary Nelson, and Paula Treichler (NY: Routledge, 1992), 284–285.

5. New York's Media Network attempts to keep abreast of AIDS-related media production. For information: Media Network, 121 Fulton Street, New York, NY 10038/ (212) 619–3455.

6. B. Ruby Rich, "Don't Look Back: Film and Video from Then to Now," *Breakthroughs: Avant-Garde Artists in Europe and America, 1950–1990,* ed. John Howell (NY: Rizzoli/Wexner Center for the Arts, 1991), 170.

7. John Greyson, "Strategic Compromises: AIDS and Alternative Video Practices," *Reimaging America,* eds. Mark O'Brien and Craig Little (Philadelphia: New Society Publishers, 1990), 61.

8. *Ibid.,* 62.

9. Some of these issues were publicly addressed in discussions at the How Do I Look? conference held in New York City in 1989, as documented in *How Do I Look?: Queer Film and Video,* eds. Bad Object Choices (Seattle: Bay Press, 1991), especially the discussions following presentations by Cindy Patton ("Safe Sex and the Pornographic Vernacular," 31–63), Richard Fung ("Looking for My Penis," 145–168), and Kobena Mercer ("Skin Head Thing," 169–222).

10. In the realm of giving credit where credit is due, it should be registered here that MTV, whatever else one might think of it, has continued to use its news programs and issue-oriented specials to provide humane, unsensational AIDS coverage, particularly in terms of profiling people living with AIDS.

11. Inevitably, as historical trauma, and without presuming to claim on either experiential or political levels a relation of exact resemblance, AIDS summons comparisons to the Holocaust. Simply in terms of the present putative subject of independent documentary production, however, the comparison is interestingly off-balanced: virtually all documentary productions attempting to come to terms with the Holocaust exist in its wake, hence are acts of memory, retribution, reconstruction, in contrast to AIDS-related work, which exists exactly in the midst of what it seeks to combat. One wonders if it will want to be relived via media evocation decades after a cure has been found.

12. Roman Jakobson, "On a Generation that Squandered Its Poets," *Twentieth Century Russian Literary Criticism,* ed. Victor Erlich (New Haven, CT: Yale University Press, 1975), 164.

13. *Ibid.,* 166.

Thanks, variously, to John Greyson, Janet Jenkins, Bruce Jenkins, Steve Fagin, Helen DeMichiel, Julia Scher, W. B. Cook, Melodie Calvert, Geoffrey Stier, Lawrence Downes, Gregg Bordowitz, Judith Mayne, and B. Ruby Rich, none of whom necessarily shares all the judgments given above.

10. "Getting to Know You": Knowledge, Power, and the Body

1. Leslie Devereaux, "Some Thoughts on Presenting Experience," delivered at "Film and Representations of Culture," Humanities Research Centre, Australian National University, Canberra, September 28, 1989, 5.

2. Performance, in the conventional sense of the skilled act of representing another person's thoughts and actions (be that person fictitious or among the historically living), can be contrasted with "virtual performance," which is the style of self-presentation favored in documentary. In this mode, social actors, people, play themselves. They act as they normally would, and do so in a manner that conveys many of the expressive qualities we have come to associate with a conventional performance. Though unrehearsed and unscripted, their virtual performance has expressive resonance and emotional power. It may correspond to how they normally conduct themselves in everyday life, but it also corresponds to the conventions of realistic acting, particularly of the Stanislavsky sort, with which we are accustomed.

3. I explore the tangled relationships between fiction and documentary, including their different uses of narrative, at considerable length in *Representing Reality: Issues and Concepts in Documentary* (Bloomington: Indiana University Press, 1991).

4. Edward Said puts the issue this way: "Can one divide human reality, as indeed human reality seems to be genuinely divided, into clearly different cultures, histories, traditions, societies, even races, and survive the consequences humanly?" [*Orientalism,* (New York: Vintage, 1979) 45]. The other side of the questions, of course, is, given the reality of such divisions, whether those placed in subordinate categories can afford to ignore the existence or effect of these divisions. The desire to eliminate hierarchy and the categories that sustain it remains idealist when it fails to account for the relations of dominance and control, hegemony and power that currently prevail.

5. Michael Rubbo's own film work, mostly for the National Film Board of Canada, is widely known. Some of his films include: *Mrs. Ryan's Drama Class* (1969), *Sad Song of Yellow Skin* (1970), *Wet Earth and Warm People* (1971), *Waiting for Fidel* (1974), *Solzhenitsyn's Children . . . Are Making a Lot of Noise in Paris* (1978), and *Daisy: The Story of a Facelift* (1983).

6. Mallet's film contrasts significantly with Ross McElwee's *Sherman's March* (1985). McElwee remains within the travel/ethnography tradition in which the personal journey presents the possibility of self-discovery rather than the threat of loss and even annihilation. We have little sense of that multiplicity of subjectivities that figures so heavily in the consciousness and experience of exile in McElwee's diaristic adventure. On the contrary, the self he represents is the unified subject of classic Western narrative, embarked on the equally classic quest, albeit in a slightly ironic vein, for a suitable female mate. McElwee, like travel writers for the last several centuries, defines himself in juxtaposition to the world he moves through rather than in relation to a world that surrounds and constrains him.

7. In "Thick Description: Towards an Interpretative Theory of Culture," Clifford Geertz [The Interpretation of Cultures (NY: Basic Books, 1973), 3–30] offers a nuanced, exemplarily empathetic account of the need to interpret the actions of others in meaningful terms. His distinctions among a blink, a wink and a parody of a wink, and among the perspectives and values of a Berber tribe, a Jewish trader, and a French colonial officer in Morocco remind us how important it is to understand the meanings others intend or achieve. Anthropology takes up the challenge of *representing* the actions of others meaningfully. Representation is, therefore, a dominant characteristic of anthropology, as it is of documentary. Mastering the tools of anthropological representation is a crucial challenge for the student of this discipline. "Anthropology" is one word for institutionalized techniques designed for the representation of others. ("Documentary" is another.) But this conception of anthropology, Geertz's conception, creates, but does not acknowledge, representa-

tion as trouble for the Other. Who speaks to whom about what? We speak to us about them. This is the trouble. Others are represented (passive tense) without the possibility of self-representation. This goes unrecognized because anthropological training gives the anthropologist the power to represent others meaningfully—for other anthropologists. We might reformulate Geertz's theoretical proposal in other words: To the extent that the art of anthropological thickness *uses* the Other as an example in a discourse where s/he lacks representation of his/her own, anthropology is a dangerous art, recruiting, from the start, representation into the terms of hierarchy rather than difference. Even more eloquent is Trinh T. Minh-ha's comment, "A conversation of 'us' about 'them' is a conversation in which 'them' is silenced. . . . Anthropology is finally better defined as gossip. . . ." in *Women, Native, Other: Writing Postcoloniality and Feminism* (Bloomington: Indiana University Press, 1989), 67, 68.

8. I have explored this question in two previous, related essays, "Questions of Magnitude," in John Corner, ed., *The Documentary and Mass Media* (London: Edward Arnold Publishers, 1986), Vol. 107–122, and "History, Myth and Narrative in Documentary," *Film Quarterly*, Vol. 41, No. 1 (1987), 9–20. I also address it at length in *Representing Reality: Issues and Concepts in Documentary* (Bloomington: Indiana University Press, 1991).

9. The films discussed here differ notably in how they represent the position of the filmmaker. Mallet's film and Marion Riggs's *Tongues Untied* both make the physical presence of the filmmaker central. They put themselves on the spot, in the frame. Trinh Minh-ha, Raul Ruiz, and Brenda Longfellow remain behind the scene, their presence is represented by authorial devices of voice-over commentary, visual and aural style, and film structure. (Ruiz does appear in one scene as himself, attempting to secure an interview with the mayor whom we never see.) This absence, though, does not open up the space that is usually reserved for omniscient, disembodied knowledge. The voice-overs that we hear and other structuring devices make it clear that the emphasis remains on situated knowledge and the situation of the filmmaker him- or herself. Differences in textual strategies render *Our Marilyn* a more visceral, affective work than Ruiz's or Trinh's. Intellectual or poetic sensibilities, respectively, move *Great Events* and *Surname Viet* toward a more contemplative consideration of self, body, and representation. The filmmaker him- or herself has something at stake in their own physical representation in *Unfinished Diary* and *Tongues Untied* that we do not feel as acutely in the other three works even though they, too, address similar questions of location and bodily representation. It is not a matter of correct and incorrect choices but of a difference that makes a difference in the overall effect of the work.

10. Teresa de Lauretis, "Guerrilla in the Midst: Women's Cinema in the 80s," *Screen*, Vol. 31, No. 1 (1990), 6–25.

11. Stephen Tyler, "Post-Modern Ethnography: From Document of the Occult to Occult Document," James Clifford and George E. Marcus, eds., *Writing Culture: The Poetics and Politics of Ethnography* (Berkeley: University of California Press, 1986), 126. Tyler's essay is a sustained critique of the politics of representation and the scientific rhetoric of *mimesis*. His account tends toward the mystical and laments a lack of concrete exemplification ("There is no instance of a post-modern ethnography," 136). His lament may well have been softened had he considered film texts rather than only written ones. The capacities for evocation in film are not necessarily superior, but the conceptual and motivational framework for the filmmakers discussed here has already escaped the ethnographic "bind," which Tyler wishes to

move beyond, by never having been caught within it. These works may not exemplify what Tyler calls for but they may well serve as an instigation toward its realization within the domain of ethnography itself.

12. Robert Anbian, *"Tongues Untied* Lets Loose Angry, Loving Words: An Interview with Marlon Riggs," *Release Print,* Vol. 13, No. 2 (1990), 6.

13. Jean Baudrillard, *The Evil Demon of Images* (Sydney: Power Publications, 1988), 13.

Bibliography

Compiled by Harry M. Benshoff

Anyone who teaches or writes about documentary film and video is painfully aware of the scarcity of resource guides. The popular film encyclopedias containing the usual facts and figures have tended to exclude nonfiction altogether. On the other hand, the past 20 years have witnessed a steady accretion of critical writing on documentary in journals ranging from the very scholarly to the journalistic, to which number can be added the "classic" work of generations past. The following listing is a thorough but not all-inclusive bibliographical guide to the books, articles, and (substantive) interviews which comprise the body of documentary scholarship in the English language. Included are writings on documentary film and video irrespective of the exhibition venue—theatrical, nontheatrical or television—to the general exclusion of work on that many-headed creature, nonfiction television. In the case of anthologies containing three or more listable essays, we have chosen to list the entire book rather than the individual articles.

[Editor]

Achtenberg, Ben. "Helen van Dongen: An Interview," *Film Quarterly*, Vol. 30, No. 2 (Winter 1976–77), 46–57.

Agel, Henri. *Robert Flaherty*. (Paris: Cinema d'Aujourd Hui, Editions Seghers, 1965).

Aitken, Ian. *Film and Reform: John Grierson and the Documentary Film Movement* (London: Routledge, 1990).

Alexander, Donald. *The Documentary Film* (London: British Film Institute, 1945).

Alexander, William. 1975. "Frontier Films, 1936–1941: The Aesthetics of Impact," *Cinema Journal*, Vol. 15, No. 1, 16–27.

———. 1981. *Film on the Left: American Documentary Film from 1931 to 1942* (Princeton, NJ: Princeton University Press).

Algate, Tony. "1930s Newsreels: Censorship and Controversy," *Sight and Sound*, Vol. 46 No. 3 (Summer 1977), 154.

Allen, Jeanne. "Self-Reflexivity in Documentary," *Ciné-Tracts*, Vol. 1, No. 2 (1977), 37–43.

Allen, Robert C. and Douglas Gomery. *Film History: Theory and Practice* (New York: Knopf, 1985).

Alpert, Jon and Keiko Tsuno. "Conversations with Jon Alpert and Keiko Tsuno," *Videography*, Vol. 5, No. 9 (1980), 54–69.

Anderson, Lindsay. "Only Connect: Some Aspects of the Work of Humphrey Jennings," *Sight and Sound*, Vol. 25, No. 4 (1954), 181–186.

Arlen, Michael J. *Living Room War* (New York: Viking Press, 1969).

Armes, Roy. "Georges Franju," *French Cinema Since 1946, Volume Two* (New York: A.S. Barnes and Co., 1966), 21–30.

Armstrong, Dan. "Wiseman's *Model* and the Documentary Project: Toward a Radical Film Practice," *Film Quarterly*, Vol. 37, No. 2 (1983–84), 2–9.

Arthur, Paul. 1976. "Visual Structure and Ideology in *Triumph of the Will*," *The New Light*, No. 12.

———. 1980. "Some Notes Around a Film by David Lamelas," *LAICA Journal*, No. 28, 71–81.

Arts Inquiry, The. *The Factual Film* (London: Oxford University Press, 1947).

Atkins, Thomas R. "America's Institutions—The Films of Frederick Wiseman," *Sight and Sound*, Vol. 43, No. 4 (1974), 232–235.

Atkins, Thomas R., ed. *Frederick Wiseman* (New York: Simon and Schuster, 1976; New York: Monarch, 1976).

Aufderheide, Patricia. 1987. "Left, Right, and Center: El Salvador on Film, *Afterimage*, Vol. 15, (December), 10–14.

———. 1989. "The Saga of Tony Buba," *American Film*, Vol. 14 (June), 11–12.

Bachman, Gideon. "The Frontiers of Realist Cinema: The Work of Ricky Leacock," *Film Culture*, No. 22/23 (1961), 12–23.

Baechlin, Peter and Maurice Muller-Strauss. *Newsreels Across the World* (Paris: United Nations Educational, Scientific, and Cultural Organization, 1952).

Banks, Marcus. "The Seductive Veracity of Ethnographic Film," *Society for Visual Anthropology Review*, Vol. 6, No. 1 (1990), 16–21.

Barkhausen, Hans. "Footnote to the History of Riefenstahl's *Olympia*," *Film Quarterly*, Vol. 28, No. 1 (1974), 8–11.

Barnouw, Eric. 1972. "Robert Flaherty," *Film Culture*, 53–55 (Spring).

———. 1974. *Documentary: A History of the Non-Fiction Film* (New York: Oxford University Press).

Barr, Charles, ed. *All Our Yesterdays: 90 Years of British Cinema* (London: British Film Institute). 1986.

Barr, William R. "Brakhage: Artistic Development in Two Childbirth Films," *Film Quarterly*, Vol. 29, No. 3 (1976), 30–34.

Barron, Arthur. "The Identification of Reality," *Film Quarterly*, Vol. 27, No. 4 (1975), 26.

Barsam, Richard M. 1973. "Leni Riefenstahl: Artifice and Truth in a World Apart," *Film Comment*, Vol. 9, No. 6, 32–38.

———. 1973. *Nonfiction Film: A Critical History* (New York: Dutton).

———. 1975. *Filmguide to* Triumph of the Will (Bloomington: Indiana University Press).

———. 1986 "American Direct Cinema: The Re-Presentation of Reality," *Persistence of Vision,* Vol. 3, No. 4, 131–157.

———. 1976. *Nonfiction Film: Theory and Criticism* (New York: E. P. Dutton & Co., 1976.

———. 1988. *The Vision of Robert Flaherty: The Artist as Myth and Filmmaker* (Bloomington: Indiana University Press).

Barthes, Roland. 1970. "Historical Discourse," *Structuralism, a Reader,* ed. Michael Lane (London: Jonathan Cape), 145–155.

———. 1978. "The Realistic Effect," trans. Gerald Mead, *Film Reader,* No. 3, 131–35.

Bauche, Freddy. "Georges Franju," *Premier Plan,* No. 1 (September 1959), 1–24.

Bazelon, Donald T. "Backgrounds to *Point of Order,*" *Film Comment,* Vol. 2, No. 1 (1964), 33–35.

Bazin, André. *What is Cinema?,* Volume 1. trans. Hugh Gray (Los Angeles: University of California Press, 1967).

Becker, George J., ed. *Documents of Modern Literary Realism* (Princeton: Princeton University Press, 1963).

Ben-Horin, Daniel. "The Sterility Scandal: *Song of the Canary,*" *Mother Jones* Vol. 4, No. 4 (May 1979), 51–63.

Bennett, Deborah J. "George Cashel Stoney: An Interview," *Journal of the University Film Association,* Vol. 25, No. 4 (1973), 65–68, 83–84.

Benson, Thomas W. and Carolyn Anderson. *Reality Fictions: The Films of Frederick Wiseman,* (Carbondale: Southern Illinois University Press, 1989).

Berg-Pan, Renata. *Leni Riefenstahl* (Boston: Twayne, 1980).

Beveridge, James. *John Grierson: Film Master* (New York: Macmillan Publishing Co., Inc., 1978).

Bickley, David. 1977. "Joris Ivens: Filming in China," *Filmmaker's Newsletter,* Vol. 10, No. 4 (1977), 22–26.

———. 1981. "Connie Field," *Sightlines,* Vol. 14, No. 4 (1981), 23–25.

Biskind, Peter. "*Harlan County USA:* The Miner's Struggle," *Jump Cut,* No. 14 (1977), 3–4.

Blue, James. 1965. "One Man's Truth: An Interview with Richard Leacock," *Film Comment,* Vol. 3, No. 2, 15–22.

———. 1965. "Thoughts of *Cinéma Vérité* and a Discussion with the Maysles Brothers," *Film Comment,* Vol. 2, No. 4.

———. 1967. "Direct Cinema," *Film Comment,* Vol. 4, No. 2/3, 80–81.

Bluem, A. William. *Documentary in American Television* (New York: Hastings House, Publishers, 1965).

Boddy, William and Jonathan Buchsbaum. "Cinema in Revolt: Newsreel," *Millenium,* No. 4/5 (1979), 43–52.

Bohn, Thomas William. *An Historical and Descriptive Analysis of the "Why We Fight" Series* (New York: Arno Press, 1977).

Boker, Carlos. *Joris Ivens, Filmmaker: Facing Reality* (Ann Arbor, MI: UMI Research Press, 1981).

Bond, Ralph. "Cinema in the Thirties: Documentary Film and the Labour Movement," *Culture and Crisis in the Thirties*, ed. Jon Clark et al. (Lawrence and Wishart, 1979).

Bordwell, David. "Dziga Vertov—An Introduction," *Film Comment*, Vol. 8, No. 1 (1972), 38–45.

Bowles, Stephen E. "And Time Marched On: The Creator of the *March of Time*," *Journal of University Film Association*, Vol. 29, No. 1 (Winter 1977), 7–13.

Boyle, Deirdre. "Guerrilla Television," *Transmission*, ed. Peter D'Agostino (New York: Tanam Press, 1985), 203–214.

Buchanan, Andrew. "The Documentary: A Film About Ourselves," *Going to the Cinema* (Phoenix House, 1947).

Buchanan, Donald William. *Documentary and Educational Films in Canada, 1935–1950: A Survey of Problems and Achievements* (Ottawa: Canadian Film Institute, 1952).

Burch, Noel. 1959. "Four Recent French Documentaries," *Film Quarterly*, Vol. 13. No. 1, 56–61.

———. 1978. "*Hogarth, England Home and Beauty*—Two Recent British Films and the Documentary Ideology," *Screen*, Vol. 19, No. 2.

———. 1979. "Film's Institutional Mode of Representation and the Soviet Response," *October*, No. 11, 77–96.

Burton, Julianne. 1986. *Cinema and Social Change in Latin America: Conversations with Filmmakers* (Austin: University of Texas Press).

———. 1990. *The Social Documentary in Latin America* (Pittsburgh, PA: University of Pittsburgh Press).

Calder-Marshall, Arthur. *The Innocent Eye: The Life of Robert Flaherty* (London: W. H. Allen, 1963).

Callenbach, Ernest. 1959. "The Understood Antagonist and Other Observations," *Film Quarterly*, Vol. 12, No. 4, 16–23.

———. 1961. "Going Out to the Subject," *Film Quarterly*, Vol. 14, No. 3, 38–40.

Campbell, Russell. *Cinema Strikes Back: Radical Filmmaking in the United States 1930–1942* (Ann Arbor, MI: UMI Research, 1982).

Campbell Russell, J. Safford, S. Brody, and W. Alexander. "Radical Cinema in the 30s: Film and Photo League," *Jump Cut*, No. 14 (1977), 23–33.

Carroll, Nöel. "From Real to Reel: Entangled in Nonfiction Film," *Philosophical Exchange*, No. 14 (Winter 1983), 5–45.

Carynnyk, Marco. "The Vertov Papers," *Film Comment*, Vol. 8, No. 1 (1972), 46–51.

Challenge for Change Newsletters, Fall 1968–Winter 1972, National Film Board of Canada.

Chanan, Michael. *The Cuban Image* (London: BFI Publishing, 1985).

Ciment, Michel. "Joy to the World! An Interview with Marcel Ophuls," *American Film*, Vol. 13 (September 1988), 38–43.

Clifford, James. *The Predicament of Culture* (Cambridge, MA: Harvard University Press, 1988).

Clifford, James and George E. Marcus, eds. *Writing Culture: The Poetics and Politics of Ethnography* (Los Angeles: University of California Press, 1986).

Cohen, Hart. "*The Ax Fight:* Mapping Anthropology on Film," *Ciné-Tracts*, Vol. 2, No. 2 (1979), 62–73.

Collier, John. *Visual Anthropology: Photography as a Research Method* (New York: Holt, Rinehart and Winston, 1967).

Colls, Robert and Philip Dodd. "Representing the Nation: British Documentary Film, 1930–1945," *Screen*, Vol. 26, No. 1 (1985).

Cooper, Merrian C. *Grass* (New York: Putnam 1925).

Corner, John, ed. *Documentary and the Mass Media* (London: Edward Arnold, 1986).

Crawford, Peter Ian and David Turton, eds. *Film as Ethnography* (New York: Manchester Univ. Press, 1992).

Crawford, Stanley. "From Visionary Gleams to *Cinéma Vérité*," *Film*, No. 40 (Summer 1964) 34–38.

Crofts, Stephen and Olivia Rose. "An Essay Towards *Man with a Movie Camera*," *Screen*, Vol. 18, No. 1 (Spring 1977), 9–58.

Crowdus, Gary. "Reflections on *Roger and Me:* Michael Moore and his Critics," *Cineaste*, Vol. 17, No. 4 (1990), 30–32.

Cunningham, Stuart. " 'Direct' and 'Concrete' Cinema: A Working Paper," *On Film*, No. 11 (Summer 1983), 34–38.

Curran, James and Vincent Porter, eds. *British Cinema History* (Weidenfeld and Nicholson, 1983).

Czezot-Gawrak, Zbigniew. "Notes on a General Theory of the Film Document," *Cultures*, Vol. 11, No. 2 (1974).

Davenport, Sue. "*The Life and Times of Rosie the Riveter*: Invisible Working Women," *Jump Cut*, No. 28 (April 1983), 42–43.

Davidson, David. 1980. "Borne out of Darkness: The Documentaries of Werner Herzog," *Film Criticism*, Vol. 5, No. 1, 10–25.

————. 1980. "Direct Cinema and Modernism: The Long Journey to *Grey Gardens*," Personal Paper, 1–7–80.

Dayan, Daniel, Elihu Katz, and Paul Kerns. "Armchair Pilgrimages: The Trips of John Paul II and Their Television Public: An Anthropological View," *On Film*, No. 13 (Fall 1984), 25–34.

De Antonio, Emile. 1964. "The Point of View in *Point of Order*," *Film Comment*, Vol. 2, No. 1, 35–36.

————. 1971. "Radical Scavenging: An Interview," *Film Quarterly*, Vol. 25, No. 1, 3–15.

————. 1973. "Interview," *Artforum*, Vol. 11, No. 7 (March), 79–83.

————. 1973. "Interview," *Arts In Society*, Vol. 10, No. 2, 209–219.

————. 1982. "In the King of Prussia," *Film Quarterly*, Vol. 36, No. 1, 28–32.

————. 1982. "History is the Theme of All My Films: An Interview," *Cineaste*, Vol. 12, No. 2, 20–28.

De Brigard, Emilie. *Anthropological Cinema* (New York: Museum of Modern Art, 1974).

Delahaye, Michel. "Leni Riefenstahl," *Interviews with Film Directors*. ed. Andrew Sarris (Indianapolis, IN: Bobbs-Merrill, 1967), 48–55.

Delmar, Rosalind. *Joris Ivens: 50 Years of Filmmaking* (London: BFI, 1979).

Dempsey, Michael. "Quatsi Means Life: The Films of Godfrey Reggio," *Film Quarterly*, Vol. 42 (Spring 1989), 2–12.

Durgnat, Raymond. *Franju* (London: Studio Vista, 1967).

Eaton, Mick, ed. 1976. "Film Culture: Anthropology and Film," *Screen*, Vol. 17, No. 3, 113–118.

———. 1979. *Anthropology/Cinema/Reality: The Films of Jean Rouch* (London: BFI).

Edmunds, Robert. *About Documentary: Anthropology on Film* (Dayton, OH: Pflaum Pub., 1974).

Elder, Bruce. "Modes of Representation in the Cinema: Towards a New Aesthetic Model," *Ciné-Tracts*, No. 2 (Spring 1979), 55–61.

Ellis, Jack C. 1986. *John Grierson: A Guide to References and Resources* (Boston: G. K. Hall & Co).

———. 1989. *The Documentary Idea* (Englewood Cliffs, NJ: Prentice Hall).

Ellsworth, Liz. *Frederick Wiseman: A Guide to References and Resources* (Boston: G. K. Hall & Co., 1979).

Ellul, Jacques. *Propaganda: The Formation of Men's Attitudes* (New York: Vintage, 1973).

Enzensberger, Masha. "Dziga Vertov," *Screen Reader 1* (London: Society for Education in Film and Television, 1977), 394–411.

Epstein, Edward Jay. *News From Nowhere* (New York: Vintage, 1973).

Erens, Patricia. *"The Times of Harvey Milk:* An Interview with Robert Epstein," *Cineaste*, Vol. 14, No. 3 (1986), 26–27.

Evans, Gary. *John Grierson and the National Film Board: The Politics of Wartime Propaganda* (Toronto: University of Toronto Press, 1984).

Fabian, Johannes. *Time and the Other: How Anthropology Makes Its Other* (New York: Columbia University Press, 1983).

Factual Film, The (an Arts Inquiry Report) (London: Oxford University Press, 1947).

Feldman, Seth. 1973/74. "Cinema Weekly and Cinema Truth: Dziga Vertov and the Leninist Proportion," *Sight and Sound*, Vol. 43, No. 1, 38–44.

———. 1977. *Evolution of Style in the Early Works of Dziga Vertov* (New York: Arno Press).

———. 1979. *Dziga Vertov: A Guide to References and Resources* (Boston: G. K. Hall & Co.)

Fereydoun, Hoveyda, "Cinema Verite, or Fantastic Realism," *Cahiers du Cinéma in English*, Vol. 2 (RKP, 1986).

Fielding, Raymond. 1957. "Time Flickers Out: Notes on the Passing of *March of Time*," *Quarterly of Film, Radio, and Television*, No. 4 (Summer), 354–361.

———. 1959. "Mirror of Discontent: The *March of Time* and its Politically Controversial Film Issues," *Western Political Quarterly* (March 1959), 145–152.

———. 1978. *The March of Time, 1935–1951* (New York: Oxford University Press).

Film and the Historian (London: British University's Film Council, 1968).

Film Archive of China and the Editorial Department of New World Press. *Joris Ivens and China* (Beijing: New World Press, 1983).

Film Comment ("Special Issue on Leni Riefenstahl"), Vol. 3, No. 1 (1965).

Film Comment ("Special Issue on Documentary Film"), Vol. 9, No. 6 (1973).

Film Comment. ("Special Section on Arthur Barron"), Vol. 6, No. 1 (1970), 6–25.

Film Comment. ("Special Section on Emile De Antonio"), Vol. 4, No. 2/3 (1967), 2–53.

Film Comment. ("Special Section on Visual Anthropology"), Vol. 7, No. 1 (1971), 33–51.

Film Culture ("Special Section on Leni Riefenstahl"), No. 56/57 (Spring 1973).

Film Library Quarterly. (Special Issue on "Humphrey Jennings: Artist of the British Documentary"), Vol. 8, No. 3/4 (1975).

Film Quarterly. ("Special Issue on Humphrey Jennings"), Vol. 15, No. 2 (1961–62).

Firstenberg, Jean Picker. "The State of Documentary," *American Film,* Vol. 11 (September 1986), 77.

——. "Documentary Audiences: Signs of Growth," *American Film,* Vol. 12 (October 1986), 69.

Fischer, Lucy. "*Enthusiasm:* From Kino-Eye to Radio-Eye," *Film Quarterly,* Vol. 31, No. 2 (1977–78), 25–36.

Fisher, Andrea. *Let Us Now Praise Famous Women: Women Photographers for the U.S. Government, 1935–1944* (New York: Pandora Press, 1987).

Flaherty, Francis H. *The Odessey of a Filmmaker* (Chicago: University of Illinois Press, 1960).

Flaherty Oral History Collection. Interviews by Bruce Harding for International Film Seminars, 1973–74. Special Collections, Columbia University, New York. Unpublished.

Flaherty Papers. Letters, Diaries, etc. of Robert and Frances Flaherty. Special Collections, Columbia University, New York. Unpublished.

Flaherty, Robert. *My Eskimo Friend* (Garden City, NY: Doubleday, 1924).

Foley, Barbara. *Telling the Truth* (Ithaca, NY: Cornell University Press, 1986).

Fusco, Coco. *Young British and Black: The Work of Sankofa and Black Audio Film Collective* (Buffalo, NY: Hallwalls/Contemporary Arts Center, 1988).

Gallagher, Tag. "Ford's War Documentaries," *Film Comment,* Vol. 11, No. 5 (1975), 40–46.

Galley, D. W. "Patterns in Wartime Documentaries," *Film Quarterly,* Vol. 10 (Winter 1955), 125–135.

Gardener, Robert. "Chronicles of the Human Experience: *Dead Birds,*" *Film Library Quarterly,* Vol. 2, No. 4 (1969).

Gavron, Laurence. "Jean Rouch 'Revisited'," *On Film,* No. 8 (Spring 1978), 26–31.

Geller, Evelyn. "Paul Strand as a Documentary Filmmaker," *Film Library Quarterly,* Vol. 6, No. 2 (1973), 28–30.

Georgakas, Dan, Udayan Gupta, and Judy Janda. "The Politics of Visual Anthropology: An Interview with Jean Rouch," *Cineaste,* Vol. 8, No. 4 (1978), 16–24.

Giercke, Christoph. "Dziga Vertov," *Afterimage,* No. 1 (April 1970) (pages not numbered).

Giles, Dennis. "The Name *Documentary:* A Preface to Genre Study," *Film Reader*, No. 3 (1978).

Goetz, William. "The Canadian Wartime Documentaries *Canada Carries On* and *World of Action*," *Cinema Journal*, Vol. 16, No. 2 (1977), 59–80.

Gomez, Joseph A. *Peter Watkins* (Boston: Twayne Publishers, 1979).

Gordon, Linda. *"Union Maids:* Working Class Heroes," *Jump Cut*, No. 14 (1977), 34–35.

Goretta, Claude. "Aspects of French Documentary," *Sight and Sound*, Vol. 17, No. 4 (1956–57), 156–158.

Graham, John. "There are No Simple Solutions: Frederick Wiseman on Viewing Film," *The Film Journal*, Vol. 1, No. 1 (1971), 44–47.

Graham, Peter. *"Cinéma Vérité* in France," *Film Quarterly* Vol. 17, No. 4 (Summer 1964), 30–36.

Grant, Barry Keith. *Voyage of Discovery: The Cinema of Frederick Wiseman* (Urbana: University of Illinois Press, 1992).

Gray, Hugh. "Robert Flaherty and the Naturalistic Documentary," *Hollywood Quarterly*, No. 5 (1950–51), 41–48.

Grenier, Cynthia. 1957. "Franju," *Sight and Sound*, Vol. 26, No. 4, 186–190.

———. 1958. "Joris Ivens: Socialist Realist and Lyric Poet," *Sight and Sound*, Vol. 27, No. 4, 204–207.

Grierson, John. 1948. "Prospect for Documentary: What is Wrong and Why?" *Sight and Sound*, Vol. 17, No. 66, 55–59.

———. 1966. *Grierson on Documentary*, ed. Forsyth Hardy (London: Faber and Faber).

Griffith, Richard. 1953. *The Worlds of Robert Flaherty* (New York: Duell, Sloan, and Pearce).

———. 1960. "Flaherty and Tabu," *Film Culture*, No. 20, 12–13.

Gunston, David. "Leni Riefenstahl," *Film Quarterly*, Vol. 14, No. 1, 4–19.

Guynn, William. 1975. "Politics of the British Documentary," *Jump Cut*, No. 6, 10–12, 27.

———. 1990. *A Cinema of Nonfiction* (Rutherford, NJ: Associated University Presses).

Hagebolling, Heide. *Pablo Picasso in Documentary Films* (New York: P. Lang, 1988).

Hall, Jeanne. "Realism as Style in *Cinéma-Vérité:* A Critical Analysis of *Primary*," *Cinema Journal*, Vol. 30, No. 4 (1991), 24–50.

Hall, Stuart. 1972. "The Social Eye of the Picture Post," *Working Papers in Cultural Studies*, No. 2 (Spring), 71.

———. 1972. "The Determinations of News Photographs," *Working Papers in Cultural Studies*, No. 3 (Autumn), 53.

Hall, Stuart, Ian Connell and Lidia Curti. "The 'Unity' of Current Affairs Television." *Popular Television and Film*, ed. Tony Bennett (London: BFI, 1981), 88–117.

Hammond, Charles Montgomery, Jr. *The Image Decade: Television Documentary 1965–1975* (New York: Hastings House, Publishers, 1981).

Harcourt, Peter. 1964/65. "The Innocent Eye," *Sight and Sound*, Vol. 34, No. 1, 19–23.

———. 1973. "Alain Resnais," *Film Comment*, Vol. 9, No. 6, 47–51.

Hardy, Forsyth. 1947. "The British Documentary Film," *Twenty Years of British Film 1925–1945*, ed. Michael Balcon et al. (London: The Falcon Press Limited, 1947).

———. 1979. *John Grierson: A Documentary Biography* (London: Faber and Faber Ltd).

Harris, Lyle Ashton. "Cultural Healing: An Interview with Marlon Riggs," *Afterimage* Vol. 18, No. 8 (March 1991), 8–11.

Heider, Karl G. *Ethnographic Film* (Austin: University of Texas Press, 1976).

Hinton, David B. *Three Films of Leni Riefenstahl* (Metuchen, NJ: Scarecrow Press, 1978).

Hitchens, Gordon. "Joris Ivens Interviewed," *Film Culture*, Vol. 53–55 (Spring 1972), 6–11.

Hockings, Paul, ed. *Principles of Visual Anthropology* (The Hague: Mouton, 1975).

Hodgkinson, Anthony W. and Rodney E. Sheratsky. 1975. "Humphrey Jennings and 'Mass Observation:' A Conversation with Tom Harrison," *Journal of the University Film Association* (Fall), 31–35.

———. 1982. *Humphrey Jennings: More Than a Maker of Films* (Hanover, NH: University Press of New England, 1982).

Hogenkamp, Bert. 1976. "Film and the Worker's Group in Great Britain," *Sight and Sound*, Vol. 45, No. 2, 68–76.

———. 1986. *Deadly Parallels: Film and the Left in Britain 1929–39* (London: Lawrence and Wishart Publishers, 1986).

Holloway, Ronald. "Social Documentary in Yugoslavia," *Film Society Review*, Vol. 6, No. 7 (1971), 42–98.

Hollowell, John. *Fact and Fiction* (Chapel Hill: University of North Carolina, 1977).

Holm, Bill and George Irving Quimby. *Edward S. Curtis in the Land of the War Canoes: A Pioneer Photographer in the Pacific Northwest* (Seattle, University of Washington Press, 1980).

Hoover, Dwight W. *Middletown: The Making of a Documentary Film Series* (Chur, Switzerland: Harwood Academic Publishers, 1992).

Hurwitz, Leo. "One Man's Voyage: Ideas and Films in the 1930s," *Cinema Journal*, Vol. 15, No. 1 (1975), 1–15.

Infield, Glenn B. *Leni Riefenstahl: The Fallen Film Goddess* (New York: Crowell, 1976).

Inscriptions. (Special Issue on "Traveling Theories, Traveling Theorists"), No. 5 (1989).

Issari, M. Ali and Doris A. Paul. *What is Cinéma Vérité?* (Metuchen, NJ: The Scarecrow Press, 1979).

Ivens, Joris. 1940. "Collaboration in Documentary," *Films*, Vol. 1, No. 2, 30–42.

———. 1956. "Borinage—A Documentary Experience," *Film Culture*, Vol. 2, No. 7, 6–11.

———. 1969. *The Camera and I* (New York: International Publishers, 1969).

———. (Unpublished). *Ivens Papers*. Letters and Other Documents of Joris Ivens. Nederlands Filmmuseum, Amsterdam. Unpublished.

Jacobs, Lewis, ed. 1958. "Free Cinema I," *Film Culture*, No. 17, 9–11.

———. 1971. *The Documentary Tradition: From Nanook to Woodstock* (New York: Hopkinson and Blake).

Jacobson, Harlan. "Michael and Me," *Film Comment*, Vol. 25, No. 6 (1989), 16–26.

Jaffe, Patricia. "Editing Cinema Verite," *Film Comment* (Summer 1965), 43–47.

Jennings, Mary-Lou, ed. *Humphrey Jennings: Filmmaker/Painter/Poet* (London: BFI, 1982).

John Greirson Project, The (McGill University). *John Grierson and the NFB* (Toronto: ECW Press, 1984).

Johnson, W. "Shooting at Wars . . . Three Views," *Film Quarterly*, Vol. 21, No. 2 (1967–68), 27–36.

Jones, David Barker. *The National Film Board of Canada: The Development of its Documentary Achievement* (Ann Arbor, MI: UMI Research Press, 1976).

Journal of the University Film Association. (Special Issue on "The Documentary Impulse: Current Issues"), Vol. 29, No. 4 (1977).

Jump Cut. (Special Section on "Radical Cinema in the 30s: Film and Photo League"), No. 14 (March 1977), 23–33.

Kaplan, E. Ann. "Theories and Strategies of the Feminist Documentary," *Millenium Film Journal*, No. 12 (Fall–Winter 1982–83), 44–67.

Karchheimer, Manny. "Is There Life After *Cinéma Vérité?*" *Film Library Quarterly*, Vol. 13, No. 1 (1980), 23–25.

Kartemquin Collective. "Filming for the City: An Interview with the Kartemquin Collective," *Cineaste*, Vol. 7, No. 1 (1975), 26–30.

Kinder, Marsha and Beverle Houston. "Night and Fog," *Close Up: A Critical Perspective on Film* (New York: Harcourt, Brace, and Jovanovich, 1972), 122–126.

King, Noel. "Recent 'Political Documentary:' Notes on *Union Maids and Harlan Country USA*," *Screen*, Vol. 22, No. 2 (1981), 7–18.

Kolaja, J. and A. W. Foster. "*Berlin: The Symphony of a City* as a Theme of Visual Rhythm," *Journal of Aesthetics and Art Criticism*, Vol. 23, No. 3 (1965), 353–358.

Kolker, Robert P. "Circumstantial Evidence: An Interview with David and Albert Maysles," *Sight and Sound*, Vol. 40, No. 4 (1971), p. 183–186.

Kopple, Barbara. 1977. "Interview," *Cineaste*, Vol. 8, No. 1, 22–25.

———. 1977. "Interview," *Jump Cut*, No. 13 (March), 4–6.

Lansell, Ross and Peter Beilby, eds. *The Documentary Film in Australia* (Australia: Cinema Papers in Association with Film Victoria, 1982).

Lansing, Stephen J. "The Decolonization of Ethnographic Film," *Society for Visual Anthropology Review*, Vol. 6, No. 1 (1990), 13–15, 81.

Leacock, Richard. 1961. "For an Uncontrolled Cinema," *Film Culture*, No. 22/23, 23–25.

———. 1974. "Interview," *Sight and Sound*, Vol. 43, No. 4, 104–107.

Leahy, James. "Notes on the Navajo Films," *Film Form*, Vol. 1, No. 2 (1977), 76–100.

Legg, Stuart. "Shell Film Unit—Twenty-One Years," *Sight and Sound*, Vol. 23, No. 4 (1954), 209–211.

Lekatsas, Barbara. "Encounters: The Film Odyssey of Camille Billops," *Black American Literature Forum*, Vol. 25 (Summer 1991), 395–408.

Leong, Russell, ed. *Moving the Image: Independent Asian Pacific American Media Arts*

(Los Angeles: UCLA Asian American Studies Center and Visual Communications, 1991).

Lesage, Julia. "Political Aesthetics of Feminist Documentary Films," *Quarterly Review of Film Studies*, Vol. 3, No. 4 (1978), 507–524.

Levin, Roy G. *Documentary Explorations: 15 Interviews with Film Makers* (New York: Doubleday, 1971).

Levine, George. *The Realist Imagination* (Chicago: Chicago University Press, 1981).

Leyda, Jay. 1964. *Films Beget Films: A Study of the Compilation Film* (New York: Hill and Wang).

———. 1974. "Vision is my Dwelling Place (On Sidney Meyers)" *Film Culture*, No. 58/59/60, 1–36.

———. 1983. *Kino: A History of the Russian and Soviet Film* (New York: Macmillan Co.; London: Unwin and Allen, 1960).

Linton, James. "The Moral Dimension in Documentary," *Journal of the University Film Association*, Vol. 28, No. 2 (1976), 17–22.

Living Films: A Catalog of Documentary Films and Their Makers (New York: Association of Documentary Film Producers, 1940), Mimeographed.

Lloyd, Peter. "Objectivity as Irony: Herzog's *Fata Morgana*," *Monogram*, No. 5 (1974), 8–9.

Lovell, Alan. "The Unknown Cinema of Britain," *Cinema Journal*, Vol. 11, No. 2 (1972), 1–8.

Lovell, Alan and Jim Hillier. *Studies in Documentary* (New York: Viking, 1972).

Lovell, Alan et al. "Interview: Alberto Cavalcanti," *Screen*, Vol. 13, No. 2 (1972), 33–53.

Low, Rachel. 1979. *The History of the British Film 1929–39: Documentary and Educational Films of the 1930s* (London: George Allen and Unwin Ltd).

———. 1979. *The History of the British Film 1929–39: Films of Comment and Persuasion of the 1930s* (London: George Allen and Unwin Ltd).

Lyle, Valda, Tom Politis, and Ross Stell. *Stanley Hawes: Documentary Filmmaker* (Sydney: WEA Film Study Group, 1980).

MacBean, James Roy. 1975. "*La Hora de los Hornos:* Let Them See Nothing But Flames," *Film and Revolution* (Bloomington: Indiana University Press, 1975).

———. 1983. "*Two Laws* from Australia: One White and One Black," *Film Quarterly*, Vol. 36, No. 3, 30–43.

MacCann, Richard Dyer. 1973. *The People's Films: A Political History of US Government Motion Pictures* (New York: Hastings House).

———. 1977. "Subsidy for the Screen: Grierson and Group 3," *Sight and Sound*, Vol. 46, No. 3, 168–173.

MacDonald, Scott. "Southern Exposure: An Interview with Ross McElwee," *Film Quarterly*, Vol. 41 (Summer 1988), 13–23.

MacDougall, David. 1970. "Prospects of Ethnographic Film," *Film Quarterly*, Vol. 23, No. 2, 16.

———. 1978. "Ethnographic Film: Failure and Promise," *Annual Review of Anthropology*, Vol. 7, 405–26.

MacPherson, Don, and Paul Willemen, eds. *Traditions of Independence: British Cinema in the Thirties* (London: British Film Institute, 1980).

Mamber, Stephen. 1973. "*Cinéma Vérité* and Social Concerns," *Film Comment*, No. 9 (Nov.–Dec.), 8–15.

———. 1974. *Cinema Verite in America: Studies in Uncontrolled Documentary* (Cambridge: MIT Press).

Marcorelles, Louis. 1963. "Nothing But the Truth," *Sight and Sound*, Vol. 32, No. 3 (Summer), 114–117.

———. 1973. *Living Cinema* (London: George Allen and Unwin Ltd. (Routledge, Kegan, Paul).

———. 1986. "The Leacock Experiment," *Cahiers du Cinema in English*, Vol. 2 (RKP).

Marcus, George E. "The Modernist Sensibility in Recent Ethnographic Writing and the Cinematic Metaphor of Montage," *Society for Visual Anthropology Review*, Vol. 6, No. 1 (1990), 2–12.

Marie, Michel. "Direct," *On Film*, No. 8 (Spring 1978), No. 19–25.

Martinez, Wilton. "Critical Studies and Visual Anthropology: Aberrant vs. Anticipated Readings of Ethnographic Film," *Commission on Visual Anthropology Review* (Spring 1990), 34–47.

Matthews, John. " . . . And after? A Response to Solanas and Getino," *Afterimage*, No. 3 (Summer 1971), 36–39.

Mayne, Judith. "Kino-Truth and Kino-Praxis: Vertov's *Man With a Movie Camera*," *Ciné-Tracts*, Vol. 1, No. 2 (1977), 81–91.

Maysles, Albert and David Maysles. "A Conversation with the Maysles," *Journal of the University Film Association*, Vol. 28, No. 2 (1976), 9–16.

Maysles, Albert and David Maysles with Charlotte Zwerin. *Salesman* (Transcript) (New York: New American Library, 1969).

"Maysles Brothers," *Film Culture*, No. 42 (Fall 1966), 114.

McGarry, Eileen. "Documentary Realism and Women's Cinema," *Women and Film*, Vol. 2, No. 7 (1975), 50–59.

McWilliams, Donald E. "Frederick Wiseman," *Film Quarterly*, Vol. 24, No. 1 (1970), 17–26.

Mead, Margaret. "Anthropology and the Camera," *Encyclopedia of Photography*, ed. W. D. Morgan (New York: National Educational Alliance, 1963).

Mehta, Ved. *The Photographs of Chachaji: The Making of a Documentary Film* (New York: Oxford University Press, 1980).

Mellencamp, Patricia. "Excursions in Catastrophe: Power and Contradiction in the Philippines," *Afterimage*, Vol. 17, No. 9 (1990), 8–11.

Michelson, Annette. "*The Man with the Movie Camera*: From Magician to Epistemologist," *Artforum*, Vol. 10, No. 7 (1972), 60–72.

Michelson, Annette, ed. *The Writings of Dziga Vertov* (Berkeley: University of California Press, 1984).

Millar, Daniel. "Fires Were Started," *Sight and Sound*, Vol. 38, No. 2 (1969), 100–104.

Minh-ha, Trinh T. 1984. "Mechanical Eye, Electronic Ear, and the Lure of Authenticity," *Wide Angle*, Vol. 6, No. 2, 58–63.

———. 1989. *Woman, Native, Other* (Bloomington: Indiana University Press).

———. 1990. "Documentary Is/Not a Name," *October*, No. 52 (Spring), 76–98.

———. 1991. *When the Moon Waxes Red—Representation, Gender and Cultural Politics* (New York: Routledge).

Mullen, Pat. *Man of Aran* (New York: Dutton, 1935; Cambridge, MA: MIT Press, 1970).

Murphy, William T. 1972. "The Method of *Why We Fight*," *Journal of Popular Film*, Vol. 1, No. 3, 185–196.

———. 1978. *Robert Flaherty: A Guide to References and Resources* (Boston: G. K. Hall & Co).

Murrow, Edward R. and Fred W. Friendly. *See It Now* (New York: Simon and Schuster, Inc., 1955).

Naficy, Hamid. "Jean Rouch: A Personal Perspective," *Quarterly Review of Film Studies*, Vol. 4, No. 3 (1979), 339–362.

National Film Archive Catalogue, Part II: Silent Non-Fiction Films 1895–1934 (London: BFI, 1960).

Neale, Steve. 1977. "Propaganda," *Screen*, Vol. 18, No. 3, 9–40.

———. 1979. *"Triumph of the Will:* Notes on Documentary Spectacle," *Screen*, Vol. 20, No. 1, 63–86.

Neergaard, Ebbe. *Documentary in Denmark: One Hundred Films of Fact in War, Occupation, Liberation, Peace 1940–1948* (Copenhagen: Statens Filmcentral, 1948).

Nichols, Bill. 1972–73. "The American Photo League," *Screen*, Vol. 13, No. 4, 108–115.

———. 1976–77. "Documentary Theory and Practice," *Screen*, Vol. 17 (Winter), 34–48.

———. 1980. *"Newsreel": Documentary Filmmaking on the American Left* (Salem, NH: Ayer Co. Publishers, Inc.).

———. 1981. *Ideology and the Image* (Bloomington, Indiana: Indiana University Press).

———. 1983. "The Voice of Documentary," *Film Quarterly*, Vol. 36, No. 3, 17–30.

———. 1987. "History, Myth, and Narrative in Documentary," *Film Quarterly*, Vol. 41 (Fall), 9–20.

———. 1991. *Representing Reality* (Bloomington, Indiana: Indiana University Press).

O'Connor, John E., ed. *American History/American Television* (New York: Ungar, 1983).

Ophuls, Marcel. 1972. "Interview," *Film Notes*, No. 2 (December), 18.

———. 1972. "Interview," *Film Critic*, Vol. 1, No. 2, 54.

———. 1972. *The Sorrow and the Pity.* (Filmscript translated by Mireille Johnston.) (New York: Outerbridge and Lazard-Duton).

———. 1973. "Interview," *Arts in Society*, Vol. 10, No. 2, 226–233.

———. 1973. "Interview," *The Velvet Light Trap*, No. 9 (Summer), 40–45.

———. 1974–75. "Interview," *Sight and Sound*, Vol. 43, No. 1, 20–22.

Orbanz, Eva. *Journey to a Legend and Back: The British Realistic Film* (Berlin: Verlag Volker Spiess, 1977).

Orodea, Miguel. 1980. "Alvarez and Vertov," *BFI Dossier #2: Santiago Alvarez* (London: BFI).

Penley, Constance and Andrew Ross. "Interview with Trinh T. Minh-ha," *Camera Obscura,* No. 13/14 (1985), 86–111.

Percheron, Daniel. "Sound in Cinema and Its Relationship to Image and Diegesis," *Yale French Studies,* No. 60 (1981), 16–23.

Perkins, Daniel James. *The Problems and Prospects of Documentary Film and History* (Ann Arbor, MI: UMI Research Press, 1977).

Petric, Vlada. 1978. "Dziga Vertov as Theorist," *Cinema Journal,* Vol. 18, No. 1, 29–44.

———. 1987. *Constructivism in Film*—The Man with the Movie Camera: *A Cinematic Analysis* (Cambridge: Cambridge University Press).

Pick, Zuzana M., "Special Section on Chilean Cinema," *Ciné-Tracts,* Vol. 3, No. 1 (1980), 17–55.

Plantinga, Carl. "The Mirror Framed: A Case for Expression in Documentary," *Wide Angle,* Vol. 13, No. 2 (1991), 40–55.

Potamkin, Harry Alan. *The Eyes of the Movie* (New York: International Pamphlets, 1934).

Powell, Rachel. "Types and Variations of News Photographs," *Working Papers in Cultural Studies,* No. 3 (Autumn 1972), 47.

Pryluck, Calvin. "Ethics of Documentary Filming," *Journal of the University Film Association,* Vol. 28, No. 1 (1976), 21–29.

Pulliam, Rebecca. "Newsreel," *The Velvet Light Trap,* No. 4 (Spring 1972), 8–9.

Quarterly Review of Film Studies. ("Special Issue on Documentary"), Vol. 7, No. 1 (1982).

Rafferty, Terrence. "Marker Changes Trains," *Sight and Sound* vol. 53, no. 4 (Autumn 1984).

Renov, Michael. 1986. "Re-Thinking Documentary: Towards a Taxonomy of Mediation," *Wide Angle,* Vol. 8, No. 3/4, 71–77.

———. 1987. "Early Newsreel: The Construction of a Political Imaginary for the New Left," *Afterimage,* Vol. 14, No. 7, 12–15.

———. 1987. "Newsreel: Old and New—Towards an Historical Profile," *Film Quarterly,* Vol. 41, No. 1, 20–33.

———. 1989. "The Subject in History: The New Autobiography in Film and Video," *Afterimage,* Vol. 17, No. 1, 4–7.

———. 1990. "Imaging the Other: Representations of Vietnam in Sixties Political Documentary," *From Hanoi to Hollywood: The Vietnam War in American Film,* eds. Linda Dittmar and Gene Michaud (New Brunswick, NJ: Rutgers University Press).

Rodakiewicz, Henwar. "Documentary: A Personal Perspective," *Film Library Quarterly,* Vol. 2, No. 3 (1969), 33–41.

Rodney, James C. "John Grierson: England, Canada, the World," *Journal of the University Film Association,* Vol. 24, No. 3 (1972), 52–55.

Rogosin, Lionel. "Interpreting Reality," *Film Culture,* No. 21 (1960), 20–28.

Rollet, Ronald T., guest editor. Special Issue on "The Documentary Films of Louis Malle," *Film Library Quarterly,* Vol. 9, No. 4 (1977).

Rollins, Peter C. "Ideology and Film Rhetoric: Three Documentaries of the New Deal Era," *Journal of Popular Film,* Vol. 5, No. 2 (1976), 126–145.

Rollwagen, Jack R., ed. *Anthropological Filmmaking* (Chur, Switzerland: Harwood Academic Publishers, 1988).

Roney, Lisa C., ed. *Films and Video: The Visualization of Anthropology* (University Park, PA: Penn State Audio-Visual Services, n.d.).

Rosenstone, Robert A. "History in Images/History in Words," *The American Historical Review*, Vol. 93 (December 1988), 173–227.

Rosenthal, Alan. 1971. *The New Documentary in Action: A Casebook in Film Making* (Berkeley: University of California Press).

———. 1978. "Emile De Antonio—An Interview," *Film Quarterly*, Vol. 32, No. 1, 4–16.

———. 1980. *The Documentary Conscience: A Casebook in Film Making* (Berkeley: University of California Press).

———. 1982. "Jon Else," *Sightlines*, Vol. 15, No. 3, 13–7.

———. 1988. *New Challenges for Documentary* (Berkeley: University of California Press).

Rosenzweig, Roy. "Working Class Struggle in the Great Depression: The Film Record," *Film Library Quarterly*, Vol. 13, No. 1 (1980).

Rotha, Paul, et al. 1952. *Documentary Film: The Use of the Film Medium to Interpret Creatively and in Social Terms the Life of the People as It Exists in Reality* (London: Faber and Faber Ltd).

———. 1954. "On Documentary," *Films* (December), 12–16.

———. 1958. *Rotha on Film* (London: Faber and Faber Ltd.)

———. 1962. *The Cinema in Africa: Present Position and Current Trends* (Paris: UNESCO). Mimeographed.

———. 1973. *Documentary Diary: An Informal History of the British Documentary Film, 1928–1939* (New York: Hill and Wang).

———. 1983. *Robert J. Flaherty: A Biography*, ed. Jay Ruby (Philadelphia: University of Pennsylvania Press).

Roud, Richard, "SLON," *Sight and Sound*, Vol. 42, No. 2 (1973), 82–83.

Rubinstein, E. "Visit to a Familiar Planet: Buñuel Among the Hurdanos," *Cinema Journal*, Vol. 22, No. 4 (1983).

Ruby, Jay. 1969. "Visual Anthropology: Film as Means of Presenting Man," *Journal of the University Film Association*, Vol. 21, No. 3, 68–71.

———. 1976. "Anthropology and Film," *Quarterly Review of Film Studies*, Vol. 1, No. 4, 436–445.

Russell, Catherine. "The Politics of Putting Art on Film: Derek May and the National Film Board of Canada," *Journal of Canadian Studies*, Vol. 21 (1986), 104–115.

Ryan, Michael. "Militant Documentary: *Mai-68 Par Lui-Meme*," *Ciné-Tracts*, No. 2 (Summer/Fall 1979), 1–20.

Sadoul, Georges. "A Flaherty Mystery," Trans. Robert Steele, *Cahiers du Cinéma in English*, No. 11 (September 1967), 46–51.

Sammis, Edward. "Flaherty at Abbeville," *Sight and Sound*, Vol. 21, No. 2 (1951), 68–70. (Part of a special tribute to Robert Flaherty.)

Schoonmaker, Mary Ellen. "Memories of Overdevelopment: In Love and Anger, Tony

Buba Documents a Dying Pennsylvania Steel Town," *American Film*, Vol. 11 (October 1985), 47–47.

Schwartz, David. "Documentary Meets the Avant-Garde," *Independent America: New Films 1978–1988* (Astoria: American Museum of the Moving Image, 1988), 24–29.

Screen. (Special Issue on Soviet film of fact of the 1920's), Vol. 12, No. 4 (1971).

———. (Special Issue on Brecht), Vol. 15, No. 2 (1975).

Sekula, Allan. "Dismantling Modernism, Reinventing Documentary (Notes on the Politics of Representation)," *Massachusetts Review*, Vol. 19, (1978), 859–883.

Selzer, Leo. "Documenting the Depression of the 30s," *Film Library Quarterly*, Vol. 13, No. 1 (1980), 15–22.

Shale, Richard. *Donald Duck Joins Up: The Disney Studio During World War Two* (Ann Arbor, MI: UMI Research Press, 1982).

Shephard, Leslie. "What Happened to Documentary?" *Film and Television Technician* (December 1963). Vol. 29, No. 227. pp. 311–312.

Shivas, Mark et. al. "Cinema Verite," *Movie*, No. 8 (April 1963), pp. 12–26.

Short, K. R. M., ed. *Film and Radio Propaganda in World War II* (Knoxville: University of Tennessee Press, 1983).

Shue, Vivienne. "The Long Bow Film Trilogy: A Review Article," *The Journal of Asian Studies*, Vol. 46 (November 1987), 843–848.

Silet, Charles L. P. *Lindsay Anderson: A Guide to References and Resources* (Boston: G. K. Hall & Co., 1978).

Silverstone, Roger. "The Right to Speak: On a Poetics for Television Documentary," *Media, Culture, and Society*, Vol. 5, No. 2 (1983).

Sitton, Bob. "An Interview with Albert and David Maysles," *Film Library Quarterly*, Vol. 2, No. 3 (1969), 13–18.

Sklar, Robert, "Joris Ivens: The China Close Up," *American Film*, Vol. 3, No. 8 (1978), 59–65.

Sloan, William. 1964/65. "The Documentary Film and the Negro: The Evolution of the Integration Film," *Journal of the Society of Cinematologists* (*Cinema Journal*), Vol. 4/5, 66–69.

———. 1967. "Two Sides of the Civil Rights Coin: *Troublemakers* and *A Time for Burning*," *Film Comment*, Vol. 4, No. 2/3, 54–56.

Snyder, Robert L. *Pare Lorentz and the Documentary Film* (Norman, OK: Oklahoma University Press, 1968).

Sobchack, Vivian. 1980–81. "Synthetic Vision: The Dialectical Imperative of *Las Hurdes*," *Millenium*, No. 7/8/9 (Fall/Winter) 140–150.

———. 1984. "Inscribing Ethical Space: Ten Propositions on Death, Representation, and Documentary," *Quarterly Review of Film Studies*, Vol. 9, No. 4 (Fall), 283–300.

Sontag, Susan. "Fascinating Fascism," *The New York Review of Books*, Vol. 22, No. 1 (1975).

Squiers, Carol, ed. *The Critical Image: Essays on Contemporary Photography* (Seattle, WA: Bay Press, 1990).

Stam, Robert, "*Hour of the Furnaces* and the Two Avant Gardes," *Millenium Film Journal*, No. 7/8/9 (Fall/Winter 1980–81), 151–164.

Stebbins, R. and J. Leyda. "Joris Ivens: Artist in Documentary," *Magazine of Art*, No. 31 (July 1938), 392.

Stoller, Paul. *The Cinematic Griot: The Ethnography of Jean Rouch* (Chicago: University of Chicago Press, 1992).

Stoney, George. 1971/72. "The Mirror Machine," *Sight and Sound*, Vol. 41, No. 1, 9–11.

———. 1977. "Man of Aran Revisited," *Journal of British Academy of Film and Television Arts*, Vol. 2, No. 2 (1977).

———. 1978. "Must a Filmmaker Leave His Mark?" Personal Paper, March 13.

Stott, William. *Documentary Representation and Thirties America* (New York: Oxford University Press, 1973).

Strand, Paul. "Realism: A Personal View," *Sight and Sound*, Vol. 19 (January 1950), 23–26.

Sufrin, Mark. "Filming a Skid Row," *Sight and Sound* (Winter 1955/56), 113–139.

Sullivan, Patrick J. "What's All the Cryin' About? The Films of Frederick Wiseman," *Massachusetts Review*, Vol. 13, No. 3 (1972), 452–468.

Sussex, Elizabeth. 1970. *Lindsay Anderson* (New York: A. Praeger).

———. 1972. "The Golden Years of Grierson," *Sight and Sound*, Vol. 11, No. 3, 149–153.

———. 1972. "Grierson on Documentary—The Last Interview," *Film Quarterly*, Vol. 26, No. 1, 24–30.

———. 1975. "Cavalcanti in England," *Sight and Sound*, Vol. 44, No. 4, 205–211.

———. 1975. *The Rise and Fall of the British Documentary: The Story of the Film Movement Founded by John Grierson* (Berkeley: University of California Press).

Swallow, Norman. *Factual Television* (New York: Hastings House, Publishers, 1966).

Swann, Paul. *The British Documentary Film Movement, 1926–1946* (Cambridge: Cambridge University Press, 1989).

Sweet, Fred, Eugene Rosow, and Alan Frankovich. "Pioneers: An Interview with Tom Brandon," *Film Quarterly*, Vol. 26, No. 5 (1973), 12–24.

Tagg, John. *The Burden Of Representation* (Amherst: The University of Massachusetts Press, 1988).

Tallents, Sir Stephen. "Birth of the British Documentary," *Journal of the University Film Association*, Vol. 20, No. 1 (1968), 15–21; Vol. 20, No. 2 (1968), 27–33; Vol. 20, No. 3 (1968), 61–66.

Thorpe, Frances and Nicholas Pronay. *British Official Films in the Second World War: A Descriptive Catalogue* (London: Imperial War Museum, Inter-University Film Consortium, and University of Leeds, 1979).

Utterback, Ann. "Voices of the Documentarist," *Journal of the University Film Association*, Vol. 29, No. 3 (1977), 31–35.

Van Dyke, Willard. 1946. "The Interpretive Camera in Documentary Films," *Hollywood Quarterly*, Vol. 1, No. 4, 405–409.

———. 1973. "Documentaries of the Thirties," *Journal of the University Film Association*, Vol. 25, No. 3, 45–46.

———. 1975. "Letters from The River," *Film Comment*, Vol. 33, No. 2, 38–60.

Vas, Robert. "Sorcerors or Apprentices: Some Aspects of Propaganda Films," *Sight and Sound*, Vol. 32, No. 4 (1963), 199–204.

Vaughan, Dai. 1976. *Television Documentary Usage* (London: BFI).

———. 1979. "Arms and the Absent," *Sight and Sound*, Vol. 48, No. 3, 182–187.

———. 1983. *Portrait of an Invisible Man: The Working Life of Stewart McAllister* (London: British Film Institute).

Vertov, Dziga. 1935. "On Film Technique," *Filmfront*, Vol. 1, No. 3, 7–9.

———. 1935. "On Kino-Eye," *Filmfront*, Vol. 1, No. 3, 6–8.

———. 1962. "The Writings of Dziga Vertov," *Film Culture*, No. 25 (Summer), 50–60.

———. 1971–72. "Film Directors: A Revolution," *Screen*, Vol. 12, No. 4, 52–58.

———. 1972. "From the Notebooks of Dziga Vertov," *Artforum*, Vol. 10, No. 7, 73–82.

———. 1972. "The Vertov Papers," *Film Comment*, Vol. 8, No. 1, 46–51.

Waldron, Gloria. *The Information Film* (New York: Columbia University Press, 1949).

———. 1978. "Factory of Facts and Other Writings," *October*, No. 7, 109–128.

Waley, H. D. "British Documentaries and the War Effort," *Public Opinion Quarterly*, Vol. 6, No. 4 (1942), 604–609.

Waller, Gregory A. *"The Great Ecstasy of the Woodsculptor Steiner:* The Stylized Documentary," *Film Criticism*, Vol. 5, No. 1 (1980), 26–35.

Walsh, Martin. *"Introduction to Arnold Schoenberg's 'Accompaniment for a Cinematographic Scene'," The Brechtian Aspect of Radical Cinema.* (London: BFI, 1981), 78–90.

Watkins, Peter. "Media Repression: A Personal Statement," *Ciné-Tracts*, Vol. 3, No. 1 (1980), 1–7.

Watt, Harry. *Don't Look at the Camera* (London: Paul Elek, Ltd., 1974).

Waugh, Thomas. 1976. "Beyond *Vérité:* Emile de Antonio and the New Documentary of the Seventies," *Jump Cut*, No. 10/11, 33–38.

———. 1982. "Men Cannot Act in Front of the Camera in the Presence of Death: Joris Ivens' *The Spanish Earth*," *Cineaste*, Vol. 12, No. 2, 30–33.

———. 1984. *"Show Us Life": Towards a History and Aesthetic of the Committed Documentary* (Mettuchen, NJ: The Scarecrow Press, 1984).

Wegg-Prosser, Victoria. "The Archive of the Film and Photo League," *Sight and Sound*, Vol. 46, No. 4 (1977), 245–257.

Welsh, James M. 1982. "Banned in Britain: *The War Game*," *American Film* Vol. 8, No. 1 (October 1982), 64, 69–71.

———. 1982. "The Dystopian Cinema of Peter Watkins," *Film Criticism*, Vol. 6, No. 1, 26–36.

———. 1986. *Peter Watkins: A Guide to References and Resources* (Boston: G.K. Hall).

White, Hayden. 1973. *Metahistory: The Historical Imagination in Nineteenth-Century Europe* (Baltimore, MD: John Hopkins University Press).

———. 1978. *Tropics of Discourse* (Baltimore, MD: Johns Hopkins University Press).

————. 1987. *The Content of the Form* (Baltimore, MD: The Johns Hopkins University Press).

White, Mimi. "Rehearsing Feminism: Women/History in *The Life and Times of Rosie the Riveter* and *Swing Shift*," *Wide Angle*, Vol. 7, No. 3 (1985).

Williams, Alan. "The Camera-Eye and the Film: Notes on Vertov's 'Formalism'," *Wide Angle*, Vol. 3, No. 3 (1979), 12–17.

Williams, Donald. "Frederick Wiseman," *Film Quarterly*, Vol. 24, No. 1 (1970), 17–26.

Williams, Christopher, ed. *Realism and the Cinema* (London, BFI, 1978; London: Routledge, 1980).

Williams, Raymond. 1975. *Television: Technology and Cultural Form* (New York: Schocken Books).

————. 1977. "A Lecture on Realism," *Screen*, Vol. 18, No. 1, 61–74.

————. 1977/78. "Realism, Naturalism, and Their Alternatives," *Ciné-Tracts*, Vol. 1, No. 3, 1–6.

Willis, Jack. "TV and the Social Documentary," *Film Library Quarterly*, Vol. 1, No. 1 (1967–1968), 50–54.

Winston, Brian. 1981. "Reconsidering *Triumph of the Will*: Was Hitler There?" *Sight and Sound*, Vol. 50, No. 2, 102–107.

————. 1983. "Direct Cinema: The Third Decade," *Sight and Sound*, No. 52 (Autumn), 238–244.

————. 1983. "The Most Perfect Contrivance—Interviewing as an Unnatural Act," *The Independent*, Vol. 6, No. 3, 11–112.

————. 1988. "Before Flaherty, Before Grierson: The Documentary Film in 1914," *Sight and Sound*, Vol. 57, No. 4, 277–279.

Wiseman, Frederick. "Interview," *Filmmakers Newsletter*, Vol. 7, No. 4 (1974), 19–25.

Wolfe, Charles. "Modes of Discourse in Thirties Social Documentary: The Shifting 'I' of *Native Land*," *Journal of Film and Video*, Vol. 36, No. 4 (1984), 13–20.

Wood, Robin. "Terrible Buildings: The World of Georges Franju," *Film Comment*, Vol. 9, No. 6 (1973), 43–47.

Worth, Sol and J. Adair. 1970. "Navajo Filmmakers," *American Anthropologist*, Vol. 72, No. 1, 9–34.

————. 1972. *Through Navajo Eyes: An Exploration in Film Communication and Anthropology* (Bloomington: Indiana University Press).

Wright, Basil. 1948. *The Uses of Film* (London: John Lane).

————. 1950. "Documentary: Flesh, Fowl, or . . .?" *Sight and Sound*, Vol. 19, No. 1, 43–48.

————. 1956. "The Documentary Dilemma," *Hollywood Quarterly*, Vol. 5, No. 4, 321–325.

Yakir, Dan. "*Ciné-transe:* The Cinema of Jean Rouch—An Interview," *Film Quarterly*, Vol. 31, No. 3 (1978), 2–11.

Youdelman, Jeffrey. "Narration, Invention and History: A Documentary Dilemma," *Cineaste*, Vol. 12, No. 2 (1982), 8–15.

Zheutlin, Barbara. "The Art and Politics of the Documentary: A Symposium," *Cineaste*, Vol. 11, No. 3 (1981), 12–21.

Zuker, Joel Stewart. *Ralph Steiner, Filmmaker and Still Photographer* (New York: Arno Press, 1978).

Filmography

Compiled by Harry M. Benshoff

If the ebb and flow of documentary scholarship has been difficult to track, it has been even more challenging to stay abreast of independent documentary production. In the interest of facilitating the best use of this book, we offer the following listing of all the films and tapes mentioned in these pages, including maker, year of release, and distribution source. It is a distressing fact of life for the documentary community that a number of these works remain unavailable in the United States, including almost all of the films from Latin America.

[Editor]

The AIDS Show (Peter Adair and Rob Epstein, 1986, Direct Cinema)
African Pop (1989, Presently Unavailable in the United States)
America (Joao Moreira Salles, 1989, Presently Unavailable in the United States)
An American Family (A. and S. Raymond, 1973, Video Verité)
And So They Live (Ferno and Roffman, 1940 MOMA)
A Propos de Nice (Jean Vigo, 1930, Budget Films)
Atomic Café (Rafferty, Loader, and Rafferty, 1982, New Yorker Films)

Battle of Culloden (Peter Watkins, 1969, UCLA)
Berlin: Symphony of a Great City (Walter Ruttmann, 1927, Budget Films)
The Bridge (Joris Ivens, 1928, Budget Films)
Bright Eyes (Stuart Marshall, 1986, Video Data Bank)

Chronicle of a Summer (Jean Rouch and Edgar Morin, 1961, Corinth Films)
The City (Steiner and Van Dyke, 1939, Budget Films)
The Civil War (Ken Burns, 1990, Direct Cinema)
The Closet Case Show (Rick X, 1985–87)

Daisy: The Story of a Facelift (Michael Rubbo, 1983, NFBC)
Daughter Rite (Michelle Citron, 1978, Women Make Movies)
David Holzman's Diary (McBride and Carson, 1968, Direct Cinema)
Demon Lover Diary (Joel DeMott, 1980, Order Directly from Joel DeMott)
Don't Look Back (D. A. Pennebaker, 1966, Kino)
Driving Me Crazy (Nick Broomfield, 1990, First Run/Icarus)

Electronic Diary (Lynn Hershman, 1989, Order Directly from Lynn Hershman)
The Endless Summer (Bruce Brown, 1966, Budget Films)
Ethnic Notions (Marlon Riggs, 1987, CA Newsreel)

A Face of War (Eugene Jones, 1968, Budget Films)
Far From Poland (Jill Godmilow, 1984, Women Make Movies)

Hal Banks: Canada's Sweetheart (Donald Britain, 1985, NFBC)
HARVEST OF SHAME (CBS News, 1961, UCLA)
Hearts and Minds (Peter Davis, 1974, UCLA—only in California)
High School (Frederick Wiseman, 1968, Zipporah)
Housing Problems (Anstey and Elton, 1935, Kit Parker Films)

Introduction to "An Accompaniment for a Cinematographic Scene" (Jean-Marie Straub
   and Danielle Huillet, 1972, New Yorker Films)

Jane (Drew Associates, 1962, Direct Cinema)
JFK: A Time Remembered (Mark Oberhaus, 1988)
JFK: YEARS OF LIGHTNING, DAYS OF DRUMS (Bruce Herschensohn, 1964)

Kon Tiki (Thor Heyerdahl, 1947, Budget Films)

Law and Order (Frederick Wiseman, 1969, Zipporah)
Letter from Siberia (Chris Marker, 1958, New Yorker Films)
The Life and Times of Rosie the Riveter (Connie Field, 1980, Direct Cinema)
Lightning Over Braddock (Tony Buba, 1988, Zeitgeist Films)
Lightning Over Water (Wim Wenders, 1980, Check Video Stores)
Line to Tschierva Hut (Alberto Cavalcanti, 1937, MOMA archive—no rental)

Man Who Dances: Edward Villella (Drew Associates, 1970, Direct Cinema)
Man With a Movie Camera (Dziga Vertov, 1929, Kit Parker Films)
Meet Marlon Brando (Drew Associates, 1965, Maysles Films)
Moana (Robert Flaherty, 1926, MOMA)
Monterey Pop (D. A. Pennebaker, 1967, Kit Parker Films)
Moscow Does not Believe in Queers (John Greyson, 1986, Video Data Bank)
Mrs. Ryan's Drama Class (Michael Rubbo, 1969, NFBC)
The Murder of Fred Hampton (Michael Gray and Howard Alk, 1971, Canyon Cinema)

Naked Spaces—Living is Round (Trinh T. Minh-ha, 1985, Women Make Movies)
Nanook of the North (Robert Flaherty, 1922, Budget Films)
Nehru (Drew Associates, 1962, Direct Cinema)
Night and Fog (Alain Resnais, 1955, Budget Films)
Night Mail (Watt and Wright, 1936, Kit Parker Films)
No Lies (Mithcell Block, 1973, Direct Cinema)
Now! (Santiago Alvarez, 1965, Presently Unavailable in the United States)

Of Great Events and Ordinary People (Raul Ruiz, 1979, Presently Unavailable in the
   United States)
Our Marilyn (Brenda Longfellow, 1988, Full Frame Film & Video)

Paris is Burning (Jennie Livingston, 1990, Films, Inc.)
Pittsburgh Trilogy [*eyes, The Act of Seeing with One's Own Eyes, Deus Ex*] (Stan Brakhage, 1971, Canyon Cinema)
The Plow That Broke the Plains (Pare Lorentz, 1936, Budget Films)
Portrait of Jason (Shirley Clarke, 1967, Mystic Fire Video)
Power and the Land (Joris Ivens, 1940, Budget Films)
Primary (Drew Associates, 1960, Direct Cinema)

Rain (Joris Ivens, 1929, Budget Films)
Red Light Bandit (Rogerio Sganzerla, 1968, Presently Unavailable in the United States)
The River (Pare Lorentz, 1937, Budget Films)
Roger and Me (Michael Moore, 1989, Swank)
Rush to Judgment (Emile de Antonio, 1967, MOMA)

Sad Song of Yellow Skin (Michael Rubbo, 1970, NFBC)
Salesman (Maysles Brothers and Charlotte Zwerin, 1969, Maysles Films)
Sans Soleil (Chris Marker, 1982, New Yorker Films)
79 Springtimes of Ho Chi Minh (Santiago Alvarez, 1967, Third World Newsreel)
Sherman's March (Ross McElwee, 1986, First Run/Icarus)
Showman (Albert and David Maysles, 1962, Maysles Films)
Solzhenitsyn's Children . . . Are making a lot of noise in Paris (Michael Rubbo, 1978, NFBC)
Some Aspects of a Shared Lifestyle (Gregg Bordowitz, 1986, Video Data Bank)
Some of These Stories Are True (Peter Adair, 1982, Order Directly from Peter Adair)
Special Bulletin (Ed Zwick, 1983, TV-Movie: Check Video Stores)
Stations of the Elevated (Manny Karchheimer, 1981, First Run/Icarus)
Stop the Church (Robert Hilferty, 1990, Frameline)
Surname Viet Given Name Nam (Trinh T. Minh-ha, 1989, Women Make Movies)

The Thin Blue Line (Errol Morris, 1990, Films, Inc.)
Titicut Follies (Frederick Wiseman, 1967, Zipporah)
Tongues Untied (Marlon Riggs, 1989, Frameline)
Torre Bella (Thomas Harlan, 1977, Presently Unavailable in the United States)
Triste Tropico (Artur Omar, 1974, Presently Unavailable in the United States)
Triumph of the Will (Leni Riefenstahl, 1935, Budget Films)
Truth or Dare (Alex Keshishian, 1991, Films, Inc.)
Twenty Years Later (Eduardo Coutinho, 1984, The Cinema Guild)

Unfinished Diary (Marilu Mallet, 1983, Women Make Movies)
Union Maids (Klein, Mogulescu, and Reichert, 1977, New Day Films)
Unsere Afrikareise (Peter Kubelka, 1967, Canyon Cinema)

Waiting for Fidel (Michael Rubbo, 1974, NFBC)
The War Game (Peter Watkins, 1966, Budget Films)
Warrendale (Allan King, 1967, Grove Press Films)
Wet Earth and Warm People (Michael Rubbo, 1971, NFBC)
With Babies and Banners (Gray, Goldfarb, and Bohlen, 1977, New Day Films)
Word is Out (Mariposa Film Group, 1977, New Yorker Films)

Budget Films
4590 Santa Monica Blvd.
Los Angeles, CA 90029
tel: (213) 660–0187
fax: (213) 660–5571

California Newsreel
149 Ninth Street
Suite 420
San Francisco, CA 94103
tel: (415) 621–6196

Canyon Cinema, Inc.
2325 3rd Street
Suite 338
San Francisco, CA 94107
tel: (415) 626–2255

Cinema Guild
1697 Broadway
New York, NY 10019
tel: (212) 246–5522
fax: (212) 246–5525

Corinth Films
34 Gansevoort Street
New York, NY 10014
tel: (800) 221–4720

DeMott and Kreines Films
90 Kennedy Lane
Coosada, AL 36020
tel: (205) 285–6179
fax: (205) 285–6040

Direct Cinema, Ltd.
22D Hollywood Avenue
Ho-Ho-Kus, NJ 07423
tel: (800) FILMS 4-U
fax: (201) 652–1973

Films, Inc.
5547 North Ravenswood Ave.
Chicago, IL 60640–1199
tel: (800) 323–4222, ext. 42

First Run/Icarus Films
153 Waverly Place
6th Floor
New York, NY 10014
tel: (800) 876–1710

Frameline
P.O. Box 14792
San Francisco, CA 94114
tel: (415) 861–5245
fax: (415) 861–1404

Full Frame Film and Video
394 Euclid Avenue
Toronto Ontario, Canada M6G2S9
tel: (416) 925–9338
fax: (416) 324–3268

Grove Press Films
196 West Houston Street
New York, NY 10014
tel: (212) 242–4900

Lynn Hershman
1935 Filbert Street
San Francisco, CA 94123

Kit Parker Films
1245 10th Street
Monterey, CA 93040–3692
tel: (800) 538–5838

Maysles Films, Inc.
250 West 54th Street
New York, NY 10019
tel: (212) 582–6050

MOMA
Circulating Film Library
11 West 53rd Street
New York, NY 10019
tel: (212) 708–9530

Mystic Fire Video, Inc.
P.O. Box 1202
Montauk, NY 11954

National Film Board of Canada
1251 Avenue of the Americas
New York, NY 10020
tel: (212) 586–5131
fax: (212) 246–7404

New Day Films
121 West 27th Street
Room 902
New York, NY 10001

New Yorker Films
16 West 61st Street
New York, NY 10023
tel: (212) 247–6110

Swank (New York)
201 S. Jefferson Ave.
St. Louis, Missouri 63103
tel: (800) 876–3344
fax: (516) 434–1574

Third World Newsreel
335 West 38th Street
5th Floor
New York, NY 10018
tel: (212) 947–9277

UCLA
Instructional Media Library
Powell Library, Room 46
UCLA
Los Angeles, CA 90024
tel: (310) 825–0755

Video Data Bank
37 South Wabash Ave.
Chicago, IL 60603
tel: (312) 899–5172
fax: (312) 263–0141

Video Verité
927 Madison Avenue
New York, NY 10021
tel: (212) 249–7356

Women Make Movies
225 Lafayette Street
Suite 206
New York, NY 10012
tel: (212) 925–0606
fax: (212) 925–2052

Zeitgeist Films
247 Centre Street
Second Floor
New York, NY 10013
tel: (212) 274–1989
fax: (212) 274–1644

Zipporah Films
1 Richdale Ave.
Unit #4
Cambridge, MA 02140
tel: (617) 576–3604
fax: (617) 864–8006

Index

Abraham, David, 210–11n.9
Academy of Motion Picture Arts and Sciences, 5
Actuality, documentary and, 72–77
Adair, Peter, 168, 178
AIDS, 164–73, 222n.10–11
Alter, Jonathan, 196–97n.24
Alvarez, Santiago, 29
America (1989), 152–63
An American Family (1973), 84–87
American Film Institute, 1987 Video Festival, 168
Analysis, as function of documentary, 30–32
Anderson, Lindsay, 92
Anthropology, 22, 51, 102–104, 223–24n.7
Anti-documentaries, 218n.58
Arago, M. François, 37, 38–40, 57
Architecture, 34
Archival footage, 176, 177–78
Aristotle, 12, 23
Aronowitz, Stanley, 155–56
Art
    documentary as original form of, 94
    independently produced, state-supported, 21
    realism and truth in the documentary, 97–98

science and, 37–42, 200–201n.38
Arthur, Paul, 4
Audubon, John James, 39
Auerbach, Erich, 121
Austin, J. L., 139, 219n.7
Authenticity
    archival footage and, 177–78
    performative and constative aspects of language, 140
    photographic image and authority, 141–42
    reenactments and recounting of historical events, 177
    technology and the documentary, 94–95
Authority, documentaries and problem of, 118–26, 126–34, 141–42
Avant-garde, 34–35

Bach, Walter, 204n.19
Bacon, Francis, 40
Bandido da Luz Vermelha (Red Light Bandit, 1968), 160
Barthes, Roland
    historical discourse, 27
    meaning and power relations, 107
    nature and bourgeois ideology, 55
    on photography, 25, 136, 141
    poetics and science, 14, 15, 198n.11

253

realistic effect in literature, 121
structuralism and, 199n.28
Baudrillard, Jean, 82–89, 154, 159, 162
Bazin, André, 4, 22–23
Bell, Marilyn, 185, 186
Benjamin, Walter, 79, 87
Bettetini, Gianfranco, 125–26
Bhabha, Homi K., 151–52
Blanchot, Maurice, 105
Bloch corporation, 155
Blumenthal, Lyn, 168
Body
  female identity and, 185–86
  perspectives of in documentaries, 184–85
  psychoanalytic approaches to documentary, 6
  as reminder of specificity, 176
  representation of experience in documentaries, 175
Bordowitz, Gregg, 168
Bordwell, David, 15–16
Brakhage, Stan, 34
Brazil, 152–63, 220n.4–8
Brecht, Bertolt, 5, 31
Breitrose, Henry, 53
Brennan, Timothy, 158
Brittain, Donald, 178
Buba, Tony, 131–32
Burns, Ken, 177

Cabra Marcada Para Morrer (Twenty Years Later, 1984), 158
Capitalism, 117
Capra, Frank, 30
Carnival, Brazilian, 160
Carroll, Noël, 47, 53–54, 120
Chronique d'Une Éte (Chronicle of a Summer, 1961) 51–53
Cinema-Verité, 50–57, 140, 152
The City (1939), 110–17
The Civil War (1990), 177
Class, 96–97. See also Middle class
Clifford, James, 18–19
Closure, 146
Coleridge, Samuel Taylor, 14
Colonialism, 78–79

Comolli, Jean-Louis, 126
Conservatism, political, 21, 116, 171
Constable, John, 38
Coulanges, Fustel de, 67–68
Coutant, André, 204–205n.19
Coutinho, Eduardo, 158
Crowdus, Gary, 128
Culture
  Brazilian and carnival, 160
  documentary and historicity in contemporary, 78–89
  images of Third World, 184
  popular and postmodernism, 156
  preservation as function of documentary, 22

Daisy: The Story of a Facelift (1983), 182
Danto, Arthur, 69–71, 211n.10
Darsham, Indian concept of, 125
Daughter Rite (1978), 178
David Holzman's Diary (1968), 178
Dayan, Daniel, 143
Death, 146–48, 149–50
Deep Dish TV, 168
Del Rio, Delores, 185
Demon Lover Diary (1980), 127
DeMott, Joel, 124
Derrida, Jacques
  on death and mastery, 147
  Freudian concept of bahnung, 196n.22
  genre designations, 28
  Lacanian psychoanalysis, 6–7, 192n.2
  memory and forgetfulness in writing, 201–202n.45
  performative and constative aspects of language, 145
  science and poetics, 13
  structuralism, 18
  truth and fiction, 10
Desire, 9–10, 22–35
Devereaux, Leslie, 174–75
Diary, electronic or filmed, 25–26
Direct Cinema
  aesthetic philosophy of, 118–26, 200n.35
  audience reception of films, 207n.67

commercial success and impact, 214–15n.2
criticism of Cinéma-Vérité, 52
current documentaries compared to, 133–34
resistance to lure of celebrity, 217n.40
Rouch's positions compared to, 208n.78
science and development of documentary, 42–50
use of images in *America*, 156–57
Discourse, 144
Doležel, Lubomír, 12, 197n.5
Don't Look Back (1966), 122, 123
Drew, Robert
  aesthetic philosophy of Direct Cinema, 119, 121
  insistence on Direct Cinema techniques, 45
  science and the documentary, 43
  subjectivity and Direct Cinema, 47
Drew Associates, 122, 200n.35
Driving Me Crazy (1990), 127
Dylan, Bob, 123

Editing, film, 44, 95
Eisenstein, Elizabeth, 37–38, 40
Elites, cultural and political, 88
Empire Marketing board (EMB), 29, 78–79
Epstein, Rob, 168
Ethnic Notions (1987), 178, 188
Ethnography, 18, 51, 102–103. *See also* Anthropology
Experience, representation of, 175
Expository cinema, 140
Expressivity, as function of documentary, 32–35

Far From Poland (1984), 178
Father, 147–48
FCC, Fairness Doctrine, 120
Felman, Shoshana, 139
Feminism, film practices and, 170
Fiction, documentary and, 2–3, 10–11, 193n.6, 197n.27

Field, Connie, 177, 178
Film history, 4–5, 72–77, 77–82, 194n.11
Filmmaker, 142, 176, 180–81, 224n.9
Film theory, 9, 92–93, 199n.28
Flaherty, Robert, 25, 32–33, 173
Flashdance (1983), 186
Foucault, Michel, 16–17, 19, 199n.25
Franju, Georges, 97, 98, 99
Freud, Sigmund, 26, 196n.22

Galassi, Peter, 38
Gallery Association of New York State, 168
Gay Men's Health Crisis, 168
Geertz, Clifford, 30, 223–24n.7
Gender, 18, 186
Genres, 28–29, 169–70
Giroux, Henry, 155–56
Globo television network, 155, 220n.8
Godard, Jean-Luc, 46
Godmilow, Jill, 178
Gokhale, Shanta, 104
Goldmann, Lucien, 53
Grand Canyon (1991), 190
Of Great Events and Ordinary People
  (*De Grands Evénements et des gens ordinaire*, 1979), 24, 183–84, 224n.9
Greimas, A. J., 16
Greyson, John, 168, 169–70
Griaule, Marcel, 51
Grierson, John
  actuality films, 74
  art and realism in documentary, 97–98, 113
  definition of documentary, 66
  documentary as dramatization of reality, 76
  functions of documentary, 77–82, 94
  higher form of documentary, 64–65, 88
  observation and documentary, 44
  persuasion and promotion in documentaries of, 29
Gunning, Tom, 194n.10
Guynn, William, 195n.17

Habermas, Jurgen, 55
Hal Banks: Canada's Sweetheart (circa 1985), 178
Hall, Stuart, 54–55, 167
Happy Mother's Day, 44
Harlan, Thomas, 158
Harvest of Shame, 30
Hearts and Minds (1974), 30, 126
Hegel, Georg, 148
Hershman, Lynn, 26, 195n.18
High School (1968), 122
His Girl Friday, 65
Historiography, 58–65, 210n.6
History
  America and analysis of, 161
  concept of document and documentary, 65–71
  David Abraham controversy, 210–11n.9
  documentary and authenticity, 23
  knowledge of reality, 176
  oral history films as preservation, 27
  revisionist films, 26
Horrigan, Bill, 4, 168
Horsefield, Kate, 168
Hudson, Rock, 166
Huillet, Danielle, 32

Ideology, 116, 119–20, 200n.35
Independent Television Service, 21
Inscriptions, scientific, 41
Intellectuals, 80–81
International Society for AIDS Education, 166
Interrogation, as function of documentary, 30–32
Introduction to "An Accompaniment for a Cinematographic Scene" (1972), 32
I, Rigoberta Menchu: An Indian Woman in Guatemala (1984), 183
Ivens, Joris, 33

Jaffe, Pat, 44
Jakobsen, Roman, 18, 172–73
Jameson, Fredric, 138, 155, 157–58, 162

Jencks, Charles, 155
JFK: A Time Remembered (1988), 63–65, 88, 133
Johnson, Magic, 165
Johnston, Claire, 101, 105, 107
Journal Inachevé (*Unfinished Diary*, 1983), 181–82, 183, 224n.9
Journalism, Direct Cinema and, 44–45
Jury, Rodney King case, 9–10

Kael, Pauline, 50
Karchheimer, Manny, 35
Kazin, Alfred, 113
Kennedy, John F., coverage of assassination, 58–65, 88, 89
King, Rodney G., videotape of, 8–10, 188–91, 196–97n.24
Kluge, Alexander, 98, 100, 164
Knowledge, documentary and representation, 138, 139–40, 175, 176
Kon Tiki, 23
Kreines, Jeff, 124
Kristeva, Julia, 9
Kubelka, Peter, 34
Kuhn, Annette, 140, 141–42

Lacan, Jacques, 7
Laclau, Ernesto, 97
Language
  constative and performative aspects of, 139–50, 219n.7
  Direct Cinema and voice-over narration, 119
  film theory and concept of, 93
  semiotic film theory and film as, 195–96n.19
Las Vegas, 159–60
Latour, Bruno, 40–41, 54
Lauretis, Teresa de, 186, 188
Lavie, Smadar, 19, 20
Leacock, Richard
  aesthetic philosophy of Direct Cinema, 123, 124, 125
  criticism of Cinéma-Vérité, 52
  observational claims of Direct Cinema, 44, 47, 48

technology and Direct Cinema, 42–43
Letter From Siberia (1958), 32
Levin, Kim, 218n.56
The Life and Times of Rosie the Riveter (1980), 177, 178
Lightning Over Braddock (1988), 127, 131–32
Lightning Over Water (1979), 135–50
Lima, Luiz Costa, 158
The Line to the Tschierva Hut (1937), 215–16n.15
Lippmann, Walter, 78
Literature, science and study of, 15
Longfellow, Brenda, 185–86, 224n.9
López, Ana M., 2, 3–4
Los Angeles, 8–10
Loving in the War Years (1983), 183

McElwee, Ross, 129, 223n.6
Madonna, 195n.16
Mallet, Marilu, 181–82, 183, 224n.9
Mamber, Stephen, 44, 118, 124
Manchete television network, 155, 220n.8
Mannheim, Karl, 80
Man Who Dances: Edward Villella (1970), 124
Man With a Movie Camera (1929), 29, 31
Marcorelles, Louis, 43, 95, 102
Marcuse, Herbert, 114–15
Marker, Chris, 32, 195n.18
Marshall, Stuart, 168
Maysles, Al, 43, 45, 48, 119
Maysles, David, 124
Meaning, documentary and, 92, 103, 107, 149
Meet Marlon Brando (1965), 122
Mckas, Jonas, 25–26
Menchu, Rigoberta, 183
Merman, Ethel, 185
Metz, Christian, 2, 199n.28
Mexico, 159
Middle class, 38–39
Miller, Jacques-Alain, 143
Miramax Films, 5
Monroe, Marilyn, 185

Montaigne, Michel de, 26
Moore, Michael, 129–31, 218n.54
Moraga, Cherrie, 183
Morin, Edgar, 52
Morris, Errol, 127, 178–80, 187
MTV, 8, 196n.23, 222n.10
The Murder of Fred Hampton (1971), 126
Murphy, Charles, 61, 62
Murrow, Edward R., 30
Musser, Charles, 75
Mveng, E., 103

Nanook of the North (1922), 33, 74
Narration, voice-over, 119, 153, 157
Narrativity, 2
National Endowment of the Arts, 21, 201n.40
Nation-state, 151–52
Neale, Steve, 212–13n.22
Nehru (1962), 124–25
New Deal, documentaries
analysis of structures and visual patterns, 110–17
current documentaries compared to, 127, 128, 133–34
Direct Cinema compared to, 120–21, 122
persuasion as function of, 29
News, television. *See also* Television
coverage of Kennedy assassination, 58–65
development of network departments, 209n.1
reporting on AIDS, 165–66, 171
technology and mise-en-scène of contemporary, 71
Newsreels, 113, 215n.12
Nichols, Bill
Aristotelian proofs and the documentary, 30
body and representation, 6
on Direct Cinema, 118
fiction-based and virtual performance, 193n.5
filmmaker/camera/spectator as observer, 142

historical sequentiation, 210n.6
history and meaning in documentary,
140
magic of documentary form, 136
organizational strategy of Wiseman's
films, 24
postmodern voice in text, 159
relations between documentaries and
fictions, 193n.6
Night and Fog, 30, 32
No Lies (1973), 178

O'Brien, Larry, 63
Observation, 40, 44, 120
October (journal), 168
Olander, William, 168
Omar, Artur, 160
Oral history, 27, 177
Oudart, Jean-Pierre, 143
Our Marilyn (1988), 185–86, 224n.9

Peixoto, Nelson Brissac, 152, 154, 162
Pennebaker, Donn, 43, 119, 124
Performance
aesthetic philosophy of Direct Cinema,
118–26
fiction-based and virtual, 193n.5,
223n.2
and reflexivity in *Lightning Over Water*, 136–50
relation between fiction and nonfiction,
2
Perrault, Pierre, 96
Personal Best (1982), 185–86
Persuasion, as function of documentary,
28–30
Peterson, Ivars, 200–201n.38
Photography
camera as scientific instrument, 37–42,
193–94n.8
epistemological and ontological credibility of documentary, 141
expressivity in documentary tradition,
33–34
and narration in *America*, 157
"Pittsburgh Trilogy" (1970s), 34

Plato, 12
Poetics
fundamental tendencies of documentary, 21–22
history of, 12–18
model of, 35–36
politics and, 18–21
science and interpretation, 198n.9–15
Polan, Dana, 155
Politics
Brazilian and television, 220n.4
Direct Cinema and, 200n.35
Griersonian concept of documentary,
78
of location in documentaries by exiles,
181, 183, 184
mainstream media and AIDS, 171
MTV and Presidential campaign,
196n.23
New Deal and social documentaries,
110–17
poetics and, 18–21
technology and power, 133–34
Postmodernism, 53–57, 81–89, 154–63
"P.O.V." (television series), 5
Power, 17, 19, 116, 199n.25
Power and the Land (1940), 114, 116
Preservation, as function of documentary,
25–28
Promotion, as function of documentary,
28–30
Psychoanalytic criticism, 6, 192n.2,
195n.17

Ranke, Leopold von, 68, 210n.6
Ray, Nicholas, 135–50
Realism, 42–46, 97–98
Reality, 98–101, 107, 134
Recording, as function of documentary,
25–28
Reenactments, historical events, 176–77,
179–80, 202n.55
Reflexivity, 101, 104–105, 136–50,
203n.63
Renov, Michael, 55, 144
Representation
anthropology and meaning, 223–24n.7

Baudrillard's view of, 83
evocation and conventions of historical, 187
knowledge and documentary form, 138
photographic referent and, 141–42
process of in documentary, 175–76
textuality and politics in practice of,
100–101
Resnais, Alain, 30
Revelation, as function of documentary,
25–28
Rich, B. Ruby, 168–69
Richter, Hans, 22, 24–25
Riefenstahl, Leni, 30
Riggs, Marion, 178, 186–88, 224n.9
The River (1939), 111, 114, 116, 122
Roger and Me (1989)
authenticity and aesthetic approach,
129–31, 133
authenticity and reenactments, 202n.55
characteristics of current documenta-
ries, 127, 128
classical conventions and, 218n.54
Rosen, Philip, 3–4, 192n.4
Rouch, Jean, 51–53, 95, 128, 208n.78
Rubbo, Michael, 182, 223n.5
Ruiz, Raoul, 24, 183–84, 187, 188,
224n.9
Russell, Ethan, 56
Ryan, Bill, 62, 63, 89

Said, Edward, 223n.4
Salesman (1969), 123
Salles, João Moeira, 152, 220n.7
Sax, Gail, 168
Scheibler, Susan, 3–4
Science
art and, 37–42, 200–201n.38
camera as instrument of, 193–94n.8
Cinéma-Vérité and, 53
development of documentary film, 42–
57
Foucault on power, 199n.25
history of poetics and, 13–18
observation and Direct Cinema, 120
poetics and interpretation, 198n.9–15

postmodernism and documentary film,
53–57
Scitex, 56
Semiotics, 2, 16, 195–96n.19
Sequenciation, historical, 74, 86, 210n.6
Sganzerla, Rogerio, 160
Sherman's March (1987), 127, 128–29,
223n.6
Shuker, Greg, 124, 125
Silverman, Kaja, 142–43
Smith, Roger, 130
Social engineering, 112, 114–15
Sociology, 120
Some of These Stories Are True (1982),
178
Soviet cinema, 114
Special Bulletin (1983), 202n.55
Spivak, Gayatri, 146
Stam, Robert, 160
Staten, Henry, 136
Stations of the Elevated, 35
Stieglitz, Alfred, 33
Stott, William, 96
Strand, Paul, 33–34
Straub, Jean-Marie, 32
Structuralism, 18, 199n.28
Subjectivity, Direct Cinema and, 47–48
Suleiman, Susan Robin, 18–19
Surname Viet Given Name Nam (1989),
175, 178, 180, 224n.9
Suture, cinematic, 142–43, 144

Tagg, John, 27–28, 29
Taylor, Frederick, 115
Technology
authenticity and documentary film, 94–
95
coverage of Kennedy assassination,
59–61
development of cameras and recorders
for documentary use, 204–
205n.19
digital retouching of photographic images, 56
Griersonian Realist filmmakers and, 42
New Deal, Direct Cinema, and current
documentaries compared, 133–34

New Deal documentaries and politics of social change, 114–17
preservational utility of mechanical and broadcast, 192–93n.4
videotape and documentary film, 197–98n.7
Television. *See also* News
Brazilian documentary series *America* (1989), 152–63, 220n.8
earthquake coverage and camera as scientific instrument, 193–94n.8
growth and development of documentary, 20–21
popular interest in nonfiction cinema, 126–27
proliferation of nonfiction forms, 194n.12
role in capitalist developing societies, 220n.4
Text, 135–36, 144–45, 159
The Thin Blue Line (1990), 127, 178–80, 202n.55, 218n.55
Titicut Follies (1967), 48–49, 122, 123
Todorov, Tzvetan, 13, 14–15, 17–18, 198n.9
Tongues Untied (1989), 186–88, 224n.9
Torre Bella (1977), 158
Trinh T. Minh-ha
anthropology and representation, 224n.7
authority and nonfiction epistemology, 132–33
body and representation of experience, 175
documentary and truth, 7, 11
position of filmmaker, 224n.9
reworking of archival footage, 178, 180
Riggs compared to, 187
Triste Tropico (1974), 160
Triumph of the Will, 30
Truth
art and realism in the documentary, 97–98

and meaning in film theory, 90, 92, 93
relation between documentary and fiction, 6–7, 10–11
Truth or Dare, 195n.16
Turner, Frederick Jackson, 68–69
Tyler, Stephen, 187, 224–25n.11

Union Maids (1976), 126
United States, 152–63
Unsere Afrikareise, 34
Urban planning, 113

Valéry, Paul, 13
Vendler, Helen, 16
Vertov, Dziga, 29, 114
Veyne, Paul, 102
Video Against AIDS, 168
Videotapes, 197–98n.7
Vietnam, 175

The War Game (1966), 202n.55
Watkins, Peter, 195n.18, 202n.55
Waugh, Thomas, 118
We Can't Go Home Again, 137, 147
Wenders, Wim, 135–50
White, Hayden, 7, 10, 67, 201n.41, 210n.6
Why We Fight (circa 1940–1945), 30
Willemen, Paul, 77, 81
Williams, Raymond, 24
Winston, Brian, 4, 109, 152
Wiseman, Frederick
aesthetic philosophy of Direct Cinema, 119–20, 123
observational claims of Direct Cinema, 48–50, 119
organizational strategy of films, 24
postmodernism and objectivity, 55
With Babies and Banners (1977), 126
Word Is Out (1977), 177

Zwick, Ed, 202n.55

List of Contributors

PAUL ARTHUR is Assistant Professor of English at the Montclair State College.

BILL HORRIGAN is Curator of Media Arts at the Wexner Center for the Arts, Columbus, Ohio.

ANA M. LÓPEZ is Associate Professor of Communications at Tulane University.

BILL NICHOLS is Professor of Cinema at San Francisco State University.

MICHAEL RENOV is Associate Professor and Chair of Critical Studies in the School of Cinema-Television at the University of Southern California.

PHILIP ROSEN is Associate Professor in the Center for Modern Culture and Media at Brown University.

SUSAN SCHEIBLER is Lecturer in Communications at Loyola-Marymount University in Los Angeles, California.

TRINH T. MINH-HA is Associate Professor of Cinema at San Francisco State University.

BRIAN WINSTON is Director of the Center for Journalism Studies at the University of Wales, College of Cardiff.